# STERN
# JUSTICE

Adam Wakeling was born in Brisbane in 1986 and grew up in Logan City, Queensland. He studied law at Griffith University and now works as a risk and a compliance professional in Victoria. He writes for, peer-reviews and edits publications for the Law Institute of Victoria, and is a volunteer in the Victorian State Emergency Service.

ALSO BY ADAM WAKELING

*The Last Fifty Miles*

# ADAM WAKELING

# STERN JUSTICE

VIKING
*an imprint of*
PENGUIN BOOKS

VIKING

UK | USA | Canada | Ireland | Australia
India | New Zealand | South Africa | China

Penguin Books is part of the Penguin Random House group of companies
whose addresses can be found at global.penguinrandomhouse.com.

Penguin
Random House
Australia

First published by Penguin Random House Australia Pty Ltd 2018

Cover design by Louisa Maggio © Penguin Random House Australia Pty Ltd
Cover photograph courtesy Australian War Memorial
Map by Guy Holt
Typeset in Adobe Garamond by Midland Typesetters, Australia
Printed and bound in Australia by Griffin Press, an accredited ISO AS/NZS 14001
Environmental Management Systems printer.

A catalogue record for this
book is available from the
National Library of Australia

ISBN 978 0 14379 333 5

penguin.com.au

# CONTENTS

*'We do not intend that the Japanese shall be enslaved as a race or destroyed as a nation, but stern justice shall be meted out to all war criminals, including those who have visited cruelties upon our prisoners.'*

From the Potsdam Declaration, issued by the Allies to the government of Japan, 26 July 1945

# PROLOGUE

# TOMIYOSHI'S LAST SUNRISE

As the sun rose swiftly over the tropical island of Morotai on the morning of 6 March 1946, Okada Tomiyoshi was counting down the final minutes of his life. Six weeks previously he had been convicted of the murder of two captured Australian airmen in the final days of the Second World War and sentenced to death.[1] His avenues for appeal exhausted, he and three other convicted war criminals were to face an Australian Army firing squad at 7.30 am, with nine others to follow later that morning.

In the crowded huts of the war criminals' compound – the cage, as it was sometimes called – it was still dark. Some of the prisoners had complained that the lack of light made it difficult to read and write the documents they needed to prepare their defence. It was also hot and humid, even by tropical standards; Morotai is only two degrees north of the equator. Most of the island was jungle and the Australians had occupied only a peninsula on the south-west. Even with the ocean on three sides, the Australian officers working in the court still went through two uniforms a day to keep presentable.

In the war criminals' compound, behind gates guarded by two Australian military police armed with Owen guns, the heat never really dissipated. The sea breezes could work their way through the coconut palms and the wire fence, but the huts had not been built with ventilation in mind. Or for permanence; the time was fast approaching when the Australians would leave and return the island to the Dutch. Whether the Dutch would be able to retain control was another matter. Already, large areas of their former colony in the East Indies were under the control of Indonesian independence fighters. In January 1946, shortly before Okada's trial began, guerrilla fighters loyal to Indonesian independence leader Sukarno had attacked Dutch forces in nearby Makassar, killing one officer and capturing two. The short-lived Australian military court at Ambon, 400 miles (643 kilometres) to the south, had already been abandoned in the face of mounting civil unrest.

Okada and his three fellow convicts were the first people to be executed by the Australian Army. Despite this dubious honour, not much is known about him. At the time of his conviction he was twenty-eight and unmarried. He had completed high school and then worked as a clerk in a drapery store before joining the Imperial Japanese Army in 1939. He served in the brutal and seemingly endless war in China and was awarded the China Service Medal. At some point he joined the *Kempeitai*, Japan's feared army special police. Recognisable by their white armbands bearing the kanji characters for 'law' and 'soldier' in red ink, they were symbols of terror to ordinary Japanese, civilians in Japanese-occupied territories and Allied prisoners of war alike. Okada's performance of his duties was clearly satisfactory to his superiors. At the time of his crime he was a corporal; soon after he was promoted to sergeant.

The journalist for the Adelaide *Advertiser* described his offence as 'one of the most horrible crimes in the Pacific'.[2] This probably overstated its magnitude, but it was undeniably a chilling one. On 27 July 1945, less than a month before the end of the war, an RAAF bomber crashed near Tomohon in Japanese-occupied North Sulawesi. The day before, the Allies had issued the Potsdam Declaration, promising Japan 'prompt and utter destruction' if it did not surrender. Three crew members survived the crash, and were captured and imprisoned at the *Kempeitai* headquarters at Kaaten. At some point one was either killed or escaped – none of the Japanese at Kaaten knew what became of him.

The two men responsible for the *Kempeitai* detachment at Kaaten, Captain Saito and Sergeant Major Morimoto, had been discussing what was to be done with the prisoners. Finally, one evening in early August, Morimoto woke the men of the detachment at midnight and told them the prisoners were to be executed. Sentries were posted on the roads around the HQ to make sure no local Indonesians stumbled onto the scene, and two graves were dug under the garage. Morimoto ordered the first prisoner to be bound and carried from his cell. He was chloroformed and, when he stopped struggling, buried alive. The second was also chloroformed, but when this failed to completely subdue him he was strangled with a rope. The *Kempeitai* then went into their mess, ate a meal of fish and wine, and returned to their quarters. According to the survivors of the detachment, they never spoke of the incident among themselves.

Why did Morimoto choose such a brutal method of execution over shooting the prisoners or bayoneting them? Preserving ammunition was always a consideration in the thrifty Japanese Army, particularly operating on islands cut off from supplies. But two bullets would have hardly mattered, and even if they could not be spared, the *Kempeitai* still had their bayonets. Morimoto's preparations suggest that he wanted the men to be killed silently, with no trace left of their deaths. But as Morimoto himself was dead by the time of the trial – how and when was not mentioned in the proceedings – his reasoning remains unknown. Therefore it was Okada and the sergeant, Hondo Kazuma, who were placed on trial for the murders.

The story of the executions may have first come from a Japanese Army deserter who was being held prisoner in the cells near the two airmen, but several privates in the *Kempeitai* detachment were also willing to give evidence for the prosecution. Why they chose to turn against their sergeants was speculated on but never revealed.

The trial began on 21 January 1946 in a hut built by Japanese prisoners, not far from the beach and surrounded by coconut trees. It was a strangely informal setting for men to be tried for their lives, even with the two Australian flags and the picture of King George VI displayed behind the bench to give it a more official air. The prosecution and defence both agreed that Morimoto was chiefly responsible for the two deaths. Witnesses testified that he was a hard man and a disciplinarian, and some admitted to being frightened of him, although he does not appear to have been particularly brutal by Japanese Army standards.

All of the former *Kempeitai* who testified, witnesses and defendants alike, claimed they had acted only as sentries or gravediggers. None admitted to actually taking part in holding the men down or chloroforming them. They also claimed that it was too dark to clearly distinguish one man from another. Nonetheless, all the prosecution witnesses agreed that it was Okada who took the chloroform-soaked cloth from Morimoto and held it over both prisoners' faces. Several also told the court that it was Okada who strangled the second prisoner. The evidence against Hondo was less compelling – two of the privates testified he was one of the men who held the prisoners down.

In his own testimony, Okada maintained that he was only a sentry and was not involved in the execution, and the witnesses for the prosecution were mistaken. Asked why they all gave the same evidence, he suggested that someone had accused him, after which the prosecution put the question 'Was it Okada?' to all of them, in turn, often enough to persuade them he was guilty. A few times the prosecutor's questions were more general, and some of Okada's answers are particularly interesting:

> Q: It's a very dreadful thing to say that a man has strangled a man with a piece of rope, isn't it?
> A: As it was during the war, I don't think a soldier would consider it a very bad thing, to say that about. It's right in law for an enemy

airman if he bombs non-military installations or local civilians'
homes to be executed.
Q: And do you know that these airmen had done that?
A: They did.
Q: Do you think it was quite a proper thing to kill them?
A: Without orders from above I can't judge whether it was right or
not, but as it is an order from above, I think it's natural.[3]

Nor did Okada seem to have much faith in the judicial process to
which he was being subjected:

Q: They are very dreadful things these men have said about you
don't you think?
A: Whatever people say about it, the fact is that Japan has lost
the war and you people can do as you like and call me guilty or
innocent.[4]

In those few lines, Okada went through many of the objections raised by Japanese defendants in war crimes trials, from the
Tokyo Tribunal down. First, he claimed that executing the airmen
was lawful as they had committed war crimes of their own. The
Allied bombing of Japanese cities, which killed between 300,000
and 500,000 civilians and left millions homeless, was raised by
both defendants and opponents of the war crimes trials process
as an example of an Allied war crime that had gone unpunished.
Given where the RAAF bomber had crashed, it would have been
striking military targets in the East Indies rather than civilian targets in Japan, but the objection was a common one. Second, Okada
maintained that as a soldier it was for him to follow orders, and for
his superiors to determine their legality or illegality. Or, to go even
further, their morality or immorality. Third, he implied the whole
process was a sham and the court would come to whatever decision
it wanted, regardless of the evidence.

In response to this last comment, the prosecution put it to him that the damning evidence came from his own countrymen, but Okada insisted the evidence was conflicting. In his testimony, Okada comes across as cold and inflexible, qualities that perhaps explain both his rise in the *Kempeitai* and the willingness of his subordinates to turn on him.

Hondo, Okada's co-accused, made a better impression on the court.[5] For a start, the evidence against him was weaker. And while we only have his word to go on, it seems he gave more thought to the lawfulness and morality of killing the two airmen. He testified that he had asked Morimoto why the prisoners were to be killed without first being tried by a court martial, because to do so, he thought, was improper.

Morimoto responded, 'I've got my orders from above and I don't know the details either.'

Hondo said he felt sorry for the prisoners and didn't want to see them killed, but he was afraid of Morimoto and raised no further objections. Whereas Okada claimed the witnesses who accused him were mistaken, Hondo directly accused them of lying out of fear. An ordinary Japanese private, he said, faced by a court of Allied officers, would say whatever he thought his captors would want to hear. Given the brutal discipline of the Imperial Japanese Army, Hondo's argument is believable.

The court convicted Okada and acquitted Hondo. It accepted that one of the murdered men was Flight Sergeant A.A. Lockyer, based on a captured Japanese document that referred to one of the prisoners as 'Rockyard'. Okada was therefore convicted of the murders of Lockyer and an unidentified member of the RAAF, and on 23 January he was sentenced to death by shooting.

Courts martial are not required to give reasons for their verdicts and sentences, so we do not know why the three Australian officers making up the court found Hondo more persuasive than Okada, or why they decided that Okada warranted the supreme penalty and not a prison sentence. We also don't know why they opted for death by shooting rather than hanging, either penalty being permitted by the *War Crimes Act* – it may have simply been because there were no gallows at Morotai and any man sentenced to hang would need to be sent to Rabaul in New Britain.

Okada, through his defence counsel, appealed both his conviction and his sentence. In a two-page document dated 27 January 1945, he argued that his conviction was unsound because the witnesses had acknowledged it was too dark to clearly see who was present and what they were doing. He further argued that, while he denied having anything to do with the death of the airmen, his sentence was excessive, given that 'nothing was done by the free will of the persons concerned, but was done in accordance with that unquestioning obedience to the command of a superior officer which is inculcated into every Japanese soldier from the day he enters the Army'.[6]

Under the *War Crimes Act 1945*, all sentences of death had to be confirmed by the commander-in-chief of the Australian Army. This requirement was the product of an unusual political compromise. Originally, all sentences of death handed down by Australian military courts needed to be confirmed by the federal cabinet. The *War Crimes Act* had been passed by the Chifley Labor government, and the Australian Labor Party was at that time moving against the death penalty. However, community pressure to execute war criminals was overwhelming, including among Labor Party members. To Australians, the Japanese war crimes were personal – 8,031 of 22,376 Australian servicemen and servicewomen captured by the Japanese had died in captivity, representing a staggering 46 per cent of all Australian deaths in the Pacific War.[7] With the horrors of the Burma Railway and the Bangka Island massacre of twenty-two Australian nurses fresh in the public mind, there was little tolerance for leniency. So the government passed an Act allowing courts martial to impose the death penalty on Japanese war criminals, and then gave the responsibility of either confirming or commuting them to the

commander-in-chief of the army, then Lieutenant General Vernon
Sturdee. That way it could satisfy community demands without putting blood on its own hands.

The transcripts of Okada's trial and his appeal were sent to
Sturdee's office in Melbourne. Sturdee, a veteran of Gallipoli and
the Western Front, was a quiet and conscientious man who took his
responsibilities seriously. He was not a lawyer, but was advised by the
Judge Advocate General, John Bowie Wilson. While the trials had
begun on Morotai on 29 November 1945 and the first death sentence
was handed down a few days later, as of March 1946 there had been
no executions. Between November and January, Sturdee had commuted the death sentences of twenty-eight Japanese war criminals to
life imprisonment, based on concerns about the soundness of the conviction or the severity of the sentence.

The commuting of the death sentences of Japanese war criminals was not well received in the Australian community, particularly
among those who had lost loved ones or friends in Japanese prison
camps. Some people felt that the Chifley government was putting
pressure on Sturdee to commute sentences. Captain Athol Moffit,
a prosecutor at the war crimes trials at Labuan, wrote in his diary on
1 February 1946 of his frustration: 'The court on the spot thought
death was fitting and somebody in Melbourne sitting at a polished
desk says otherwise . . . [T]he Government is still too burdened with
its no capital punishment and is too weak-kneed to come out into the
open.'[8]

In an article entitled 'Soldiers Want Guilty Japs to Die' in the
*Daily Telegraph* on 22 February 1946, the president of the New South
Wales RSL was reported as saying:

> If the Japanese had been found guilty shortly after the war finished
> they would most likely have been shot, but now it's the old story
> of letting bygones be bygones. Our own boys suffered at the hands
> of these jungle apes, yet our own military leader is exercising the

power to reprieve them. There should only be one sentence for them – death. Then this would be too swift for them. There is no shortage of executioners, if that is what is holding the Government or the Army up. I know of plenty of ex-prisoners of war who would willingly do the job free.[9]

The Labor rank-and-file were also not pleased. On 12 March the Paddington branch of the party passed a resolution protesting the commuting of sentences and sent it to Eddie Ward, Labor Member for East Sydney and Minister for External Territories. Ward, who went on to become one of the strongest voices in the parliament on taking a tough line on Japanese war criminals, sent the petition to the Department of the Army with his endorsement.

Wilson reviewed Okada's appeal on 18 February, writing to Sturdee that, in his view, the court had acted properly. Sturdee accepted Wilson's advice, and wrote the word 'dismissed' across the second page of Okada's letter, followed by the date and his signature. On 26 February, Sturdee confirmed Okada's sentence. Shortly afterwards, the death warrants of Okada and another twelve Japanese war criminals convicted at various trials were on their way to Morotai.

The Australian Army had never carried out an execution before. Australian soldiers were subject to the death penalty for mutiny and desertion, but every death sentence handed down by Australian courts martial in both world wars had been commuted to a term of imprisonment. Special instructions for the execution of Japanese war criminals were therefore issued on 25 February 1946, with execution by firing squad to follow the British Army procedure.[10] This was the procedure used for the execution of 306 British Empire soldiers in the First World War for crimes such as desertion and cowardice, the leaders of the 1916 Easter Rising in Ireland, and the German spies executed at the Tower of London during both world wars. And, ironically, it was the same procedure used for the execution of Australian Lieutenants Harry 'Breaker' Morant and Peter Handcock for war crimes during the Boer War in 1902, an event perhaps contributing to the Australian Army's unease with the death penalty.

The British Army procedure was designed for a fast, private and humane execution. Some of its requirements seem almost quaint – the place of execution was to be as near as possible to the prisoner's place of confinement, so he would not face a long walk to his death; the commands were to be given in a low voice or using hand signals so as to not panic him; and the stretcher for carrying the body away was to be kept out of sight until the execution was complete. Executions by firing squad were to be held shortly after sunrise – hence the term 'shot at dawn'.

A secluded place among the coconut palms was selected on Morotai. Men with combat experience were preferred for the firing squad, and each was given the choice to opt out for conscientious reasons. It's not known how many of the men first tapped on the shoulder for the job did so. The procedure called for ten per condemned prisoner, but there were only enough for five – twenty men for four prisoners. Aside from the firing squad, a medical officer was needed to certify death and a provost marshal to manage the execution.

The provost marshal was Lieutenant Colonel Joseph Courtney, who had been a policeman in civilian life. He had also been responsible for bringing the prisoners in and out during the trial, so he could act as the official witness confirming their identities. In the event of the fusillade failing to kill one of the men, Courtney would have to shoot him in the head at point-blank range with his pistol.

In the meantime, Okada and the others were left to count the days in the compound. Was he mistreated by his captors? It seems there was some violence against suspected war criminals at Morotai in the early days, while former Australian prisoners of war were recovering in the hospital there, but discipline was restored fairly quickly. The Japanese themselves left mixed accounts. Army Lieutenant Yamamoto Shōichi, who was sentenced to die for his involvement in the death march of several hundred prisoners of war from Sandakan to Ranau, wrote that he was 'subject to all manner of persecutions' in Australian custody at both Labuan and Morotai, and that he 'continued to endure all manner of punishments from the Australian soldiers and wished every day for them to quickly carry out my execution'.[11] In contrast, Army Captain Yabe Tokuhiro, who faced the firing squad on Morotai fifty minutes after Okada, wrote that the Australians 'treated us like gentlemen, the guards were especially cordial and spoke to us with kindness, to which we were deeply moved'.[12] Perhaps the guards simply found some of their prisoners more likeable than others.

On the night before their execution, the condemned men wrote letters, played music, and sang songs. Those with a classical inclination wrote *waka* poems in the style of a samurai death poem, reflecting on the shortness of life. They often drew on Zen Buddhist teachings that the material world was transient and impermanent, symbolised by the decay of the cherry blossom. Some wrote thank-you letters to the Australian Army officers who defended them in court. They also wrote to their families, bidding them goodbye, making requests for the care of their children, and expressing regret they could not return home to play a part in rebuilding their war-ravaged country. Yabe, who described his captors as gentlemen, wrote to his uncle, asking him to look after two men who had lost their families.[13]

Unusually for the occasion, there was an air of merriment. Captain Iwasa Tokio played a lively tune on his shakuhachi, a bamboo flute, and several women from the Australian Women's Army Service got up and danced the jitterbug. Some of the war criminals drew a cartoon showing Iwasa playing for a firing squad made up of AWAS women armed with Owen guns. 'Don't forget the shooting!' he calls out in English. Okada, for his part, wrote a letter to his parents: 'I hope you will certainly pardon me as my life is extinguished just as a drop of dew vanishes on the execution place. However, I believe our faith will continue forever and our country will be built again. I am worrying that when you receive this letter, you may lose your health. If it should happen thus, I should consider myself a bad son, my fears are only in this.'[14]

The next morning, while Okada waited in his hut, Courtney assembled the firing squad. There were also journalists present – the government had wavered on whether to permit them to watch, but allowed them on the condition that they did not report gory details to the public.

The squad loaded their rifles, rested them against a rack, and were then called away by a non-commissioned officer. He told them that the best thing they could do for the prisoners was to shoot straight and kill them quickly. In the meantime, Courtney had the task of unloading two of the rifles and reloading them with blank rounds, the idea being that no member of the firing squad could then know if he had killed a man. This had worked in the days of the musket; however, a skilled marksman firing a modern rifle would probably be able to feel the difference in recoil between a blank and a live round. But it gave them plausible deniability.

Shortly before 7.30, Okada and the other three men in the first batch were taken from their huts by military police for the short walk through the coconut trees to the execution ground. The medical officer, Captain Noel Fowler, commented on the condemned men's 'most extraordinary dignity, composure and fortitude, which commanded nothing but respect from those of us who were present'.[15] The procedure allowed for the prisoners to either be strapped to a post or tied in a chair, and four chairs had been prepared. The journalists were lined up along the side. According to them, the Japanese were relaxed, talking and singing. As they were led to the chairs, each condemned man saluted, said goodbye, and thanked the Australian officers. 'I wish to convey friendly relations between Australia and Japan,' said one of the men, Lieutenant Tanaka. 'We are ready to die. For your kindness we thank you very much.'[16]

The Japanese were tied into the chairs so tightly they wouldn't be able to overturn them. None of them struggled. Courtney brought out four black hoods. The Japanese protested at this, but Courtney explained that the hoods would ease the consciences of the men who had to shoot them. At this they relented. The men of the firing squad took up their rifles and lined up between 10 to 12 yards (9–11 metres) from the prisoners. Fowler attached a white disc over each man's heart as a target.

When Fowler walked away from the last prisoner Courtney signalled for the men to ready their rifles. One of the Japanese yelled, '*Tennō Heika!*' to which they all responded with three cries of '*Banzai!*': 'Long live the Emperor!', the Japanese battle cry. It was a hollow gesture and they would have known it. In Tokyo, Emperor Hirohito was openly co-operating with the Americans, and they were returning the favour by not prosecuting him as a war criminal. But the prisoners had been trained to call on the Emperor at the moment of death, and their training held to the end.

In a quiet, firm voice, Courtney gave the order to fire. According to the *Sydney Morning Herald* journalist, the prisoners 'chatted, laughed, and sang until the bullets silenced them'.[17]

Fowler held his stethoscope to the chest of each prisoner. One was still alive, but only just – Fowler told Courtney he would be dead in thirty seconds. Nonetheless, Courtney did not want the man to suffer, however briefly, and he levelled his pistol at the man's temple and fired. Even as a soldier, it is unlikely he had ever been called upon to shoot a wounded man at point-blank range in cold blood before. The bodies were handed over to a Japanese burial party, the members of which bowed reverently to each corpse before removing it from the chair.

Fowler later wrote to David Sissons, a 21-year-old Australian who had acted as a translator at the trial: 'It was a proceeding which was carried out with dignity and was controlled by a man who was compassionate and who found the whole thing a distasteful necessity.'[18]

Sissons kept the letter and many others, and spent the rest of his life collecting research on the trials. 'Japs Pay Penalty' ran a headline on the front page of Brisbane's *Courier-Mail* on 8 March.[19] The death warrant was returned to Australia bearing Courtney and Fowler's signatures, confirming Okada Tomiyoshi had been duly executed.

# INTRODUCTION

# THE FORGOTTEN TRIALS

In the wake of the Second World War, the Allies established a program of trials to prosecute Axis war crimes and crimes against humanity. It was ambitious: there was no precedent for holding individual men criminally responsible for starting a war, and very little precedent for trying leaders for crimes against humanity. And while war crimes trials had been held after the First World War for soldiers and officers accused of conventional war crimes, they were widely considered to have been a failure. However, the Allies took the view that the aggression of the Axis powers and the gargantuan scale of their atrocities in the countries they conquered demanded formal trials, to prevent the horrors of the Second World War from being repeated.

The Holocaust in Europe provided the central justification for the war crimes trials program. But the attempt by the Japanese armed forces to create the Greater East Asia Co-Prosperity Sphere (*Dai Tōa Kyōeiken*) was also brutal. The Burma Railway, the Rape of Nanking, the comfort women system of sexual slavery, and the Bataan Death March remain symbols of this brutality throughout the world. It is now accepted everywhere outside a clique of nationalist writers and politicians in Japan that Japan was responsible for massive war crimes against Allied prisoners of war and civilians throughout Asia and the Pacific. For example, 27 per cent of western Allied prisoners died in Japanese captivity, compared to 4 per cent of those held by the Germans and Italians. Aside from outright execution through shooting, bayoneting or beheading, thousands died from starvation, forced labour, beating, torture, and exposure to the elements.

The centrepieces of the Allies' program were two international tribunals. One which sat at Nuremberg in 1946 known as the International Military Tribunal (IMT), and one which sat in Tokyo between 1946 and 1948 known as the International Military Tribunal for the Far East (IMTFE); it was less important to the major Allies. The United States, the United Kingdom, France and the Soviet Union were on both tribunals, and the Tokyo Tribunal also included Australia, Canada, New Zealand, Nationalist China, the Netherlands, India and the Philippines. These courts tried the surviving leaders of Germany and Japan for starting wars in violation of international treaties (classified as class-A war crimes, although the term was mostly used only in the East); for conventional war crimes, or crimes committed during a war (class-B war crimes); and for crimes against humanity (class-C war crimes).

At the same time, individual countries conducted war crimes trials throughout Europe and the Asia-Pacific, trying ordinary German and Japanese soldiers. Around 5,000 Germans were convicted by the Western Allies in the Subsequent Nuremberg Trials and other tribunals, and over 50,000 Germans and other Axis personnel were prosecuted in Eastern Europe. A further 18,000 were prosecuted by the domestic courts of East and West Germany, a process that has continued since the war.[1] At the time of writing, the most recent trial was in 2016, of Reinhold Hanning, a 94-year-old former member of the SS, convicted of being an accessory to murder at Auschwitz.[2]

In the Pacific, seven Allied governments – Australia, the United Kingdom, Nationalist China, France, the Netherlands, the Philippines and the United States – tried at least 5,677 suspects in fifty locations for class-B and -C war crimes. The majority were convicted, with 984 condemned to death, 475 to life sentences, and 2,944 to other prison terms.[3] Most of the defendants were Japanese, but they included some 300 Koreans and Taiwanese serving in the Japanese armed forces. Communist China and the Soviet Union did not participate in the class-A/B/C system, but held similar trials of their own.

Australia played an active role in the war crimes trials program in the Asia-Pacific at both levels: as a member of the IMTFE, where Queensland judge Sir William Flood Webb served as the tribunal's president; and by conducting 295 trials of 814 officers and men of the Imperial Japanese Army and the Imperial Japanese Navy accused of class-B and -C war crimes. These trials were held in the territories of what are now Malaysia, Singapore, Hong Kong, Indonesia, Papua New Guinea, and Australia itself. Of the defendants, 280 were acquitted and 644 were convicted (some individuals were defendants at multiple trials, hence the total of 924). A hundred and thirty-eight were executed – 114 by hanging, 24 by shooting – and 498 were given prison sentences of varying lengths.[4]

This was the first time Australia had taken an independent role in the enforcement of international law. The Australian government committed itself deeply to the task, guided by Herbert Vere Evatt, a lawyer and historian who served both as Minister for External Affairs (Foreign Minister) and Attorney-General from 1941 to 1949. Evatt's later career was troubled by mental illness, but throughout the 1940s he was one of the world's major proponents of international law, serving as President of the United Nations General Assembly from 1948 to 1949, and acting as one of the drafters of the Universal Declaration of Human Rights.

Evatt's most visible influence on the war crimes trials process lay perhaps in Australia being regarded as the most legalistic of the Allies. This can be seen in four characteristics. First, Australia was one of the first of the Allies to begin investigating and documenting Japanese war crimes and pushing for trials in the Far East. The Australian

Army commissioned the Allen Inquiry into war crimes in Papua New Guinea in May 1942, while the Japanese were still on the offensive. Queensland judge Sir William Webb led three inquiries between 1943 and 1945 before presenting his evidence to the United Nations War Crimes Commission in London and then joining the Tokyo court. The Webb Reports, commissioned by Evatt, were an important and very detailed record of Japanese war crimes for the Allies.

Second, the Australian government was one of the strongest advocates among the Allies for prosecuting Emperor Hirohito as a war criminal, despite the strong practical reasons for not doing so. He had agreed to co-operate with the American authorities, and leaving him in power facilitated a smoother transition in Japan from totalitarianism to democracy. However, the Australian government maintained that it would be unjust to execute Japanese soldiers for war crimes and fail to prosecute the Emperor, who was the notional leader of the Japanese state and armed forces. Australia insisted that the trials be based on actual responsibility for crimes rather than political considerations.

Third, Australia was determined to follow a rigorous process in its own prosecution of war criminals, shown by the high acquittal rates of Australian courts: 29 per cent. By comparison, American courts acquitted 13 per cent of defendants, and British courts 11 per cent. Just 5 per cent of defendants before Dutch courts were acquitted, although the Dutch prosecutors generally only brought cases to trial if they had a high chance of success. Only the Nationalist Chinese courts, which acquitted 30 per cent, had a higher rate than Australia.[5]

Finally, when it came to the trials, Australia was the most tenacious of the Allies. It was the last country to try Japanese war criminals, in 1951, even though this involved holding suspects for years without trial (one of the most controversial aspects of the Australian trials), and resisting pressure from the US to end the trials. Australia was the last of the Allies to execute Japanese war criminals (also in 1951), the last of the Allies within the formal class-A/B/C system to hold convicted Japanese war criminals in prison outside Japan, and one of the last to consent to have them paroled and released.

The Australian government's position was always, in its own words, justice rather than revenge. Speaking in London shortly after the end of the war, Evatt summarised his approach by saying that 'in its demand that all Japanese war criminals be brought to trial, the Australian Government is actuated by no spirit of revenge, but by profound feelings of justice'.[6] Others took a similar view, including some high-profile former prisoners of the Japanese. Sergeant Adair Blain, Independent Member of the House of Representatives for the Northern Territory from 1934 to 1949, remains the only sitting Australian member of parliament to be held as a prisoner of war. On his release from Changi he commented: 'While we must see that stark justice is meted out to their responsible leaders, and that the memory of the consequences of the acts are never forgotten by them, we must also apply the principles of justice in the detached, inexorable spirit ever associated with British rule. We must teach them that it is possible for them to live in peace with us, to greater advantage than they can live in enmity.'[7]

The *Tweed Daily* ran Blain's remarks under the headline 'Blain Urges: Treat Japs Like Bad Children', suggesting the paper's subeditors were unconvinced. Indeed, the trials took place against a backdrop of violent anti-Japanese feeling in Australia and among its Allies. Public opinion ran strongly against anything resembling leniency, and many voices in the popular media were quite keen on revenge.

American historian and journalist Allan Nevins wrote that 'probably in all history, no foe has been so detested as were the Japanese'.[8] Allied propaganda portrayed the Japanese as a unique enemy, different from and worse than the Germans, Italians, or others which had been fought before. It compared the Japanese to termites, implying that soldiers were so fanatically loyal to their country and Emperor they had virtually ceased to be individuals. There was understandable horror at the brutality of the Japanese Army and Navy. And their practice

of pretending to surrender before opening fire or booby-trapping the
dead and wounded made it easy for soldiers at the front lines to conclude that 'the only good Jap was a dead Jap', a view that spread to
civilians as well.

General Thomas Blamey had told Australian soldiers going into
battle that the Japanese were 'a subhuman beast' and 'a curious race –
a cross between the human being and the ape'.[9] Officers observed
that the Japanese brought out a killer instinct in otherwise mellow
Australian soldiers.[10]

Ironically, this raised something of a conundrum. If the Japanese
were brutal, subhuman, and incapable of deciding right from wrong,
what was the use of placing them on trial at all? As an opinion column
in the *Riverine Herald* in April 1945 argued: 'They [the Japanese] have
placed themselves in a position where mercy would be wasted upon
them. They chose to act like savage beasts of the jungle, and as such
they should be treated. They have forfeited all right to human consideration and must be driven back to the lair whence they should never
again be allowed to emerge as a military power.'[11]

The Allies, however, had goals beyond the enforcement of international law. They wanted the war crimes trials to also facilitate
Japan's transition to democracy, by establishing that its wartime
leaders were criminals. But while individual Japanese in the government and the armed forces could be held responsible for the brutality,
the general public and the Emperor they revered would be absolved.
In this the Allies generally succeeded, and Japan became a peaceful
democracy, although the role of the trials in this process was disputed.
Additionally, the European colonial powers, who had been discredited in the eyes of their Asian subjects by the rapid Japanese victories
of 1941–42, could show that their rule represented justice. In this they
failed, and the war crimes trials ended up becoming entwined with
East Asia's often-troubled transition from colonialism to self-rule.

*

Inevitably, with so many legal and political aims, the war crimes trials in the Far East were subject to criticism. The entire Allied program of trials, in both theatres, was criticised on broad and particular grounds. Broadly, critics argued that some of the 'laws' being enforced by the trials had been invented out of thin air, and although they deplored the atrocities of the Germans and Japanese, there was no basis for convicting an individual of a war crime. And while there was a precedent for prosecuting soldiers for war crimes, there was no basis for prosecuting someone for waging an aggressive war or committing a crime against humanity.[12]

To the critics, the trials violated the ancient legal principle of 'no crime and no penalty without a law'. As Harlan Fiske Stone, Chief Justice of the US Supreme Court, wrote in a letter to a friend of the Chief American Prosecutor in Nuremberg: 'Jackson is away conducting his high-grade lynching party in Nuremberg. I don't mind what he does to the Nazis, but I hate to see the pretense that he is running a court and proceeding according to common law. This is a little too sanctimonious a fraud to meet my old-fashioned ideas.'[13]

Furthermore, some of the defendants, in both courts, argued that the Allies were guilty of war crimes themselves. The brutality of the Soviet Union and the indiscriminate bombing of German and Japanese cities were highlighted.

Specific criticisms of the Tokyo Trial included the claim that the entire thing was a charade to protect the Emperor, that there was too much focus on conspiracy rather than the responsibility of the individual defendants, and that major crimes against Asians were sidelined in favour of the attack on the British Empire and the United States in December 1941. While sexual slavery was among the crimes against humanity prosecuted, the Allies did not go so far as to expose the organised, empire-wide system of comfort women, nor did they make any mention of the Japanese Army's Unit 731, which performed chemical and biological experiments on thousands of Chinese. Additionally, the tribunal in Tokyo suffered from translation issues

and a series of procedural difficulties that saw it drag on for nearly
two years. While Nuremberg remains celebrated in spite of its flaws,
Tokyo has not fared so well. Kirsten Sellars, for example, described
it as 'deeply flawed' and 'the very blackest of courtroom dramas',
particularly compared with its European equivalent.[14]

In some ways, the class-B and -C trials conducted by the individual Allies look better in history's judgement than Tokyo. They dealt
with conventional war crimes, which were established in international
law and could be brought home, albeit with some difficulty, to individual perpetrators. They too, however, have come under criticism.
Translation was again a big problem, as few Westerners could speak
Japanese well enough to translate legal proceedings; nor could many
Japanese speak Western languages at a sufficient level. The Western
Allies accepted evidence to a lower standard of proof than they did
in their domestic courts. As with Tokyo, the trials were accused of
prioritising crimes against European victims over non-European
ones, although the Australian trials also dealt with many offences
committed against Chinese prisoners of war, Malays and Papuans.
Additionally, there were specific criticisms of the Australian approach,
which Sandra Wilson summarised in her research on the trials as 'the
patchy application of the death sentence, the relaxation of the rules
of evidence, the incomplete defence of "superior orders", controversy
over command responsibility and inconsistency in sentencing'.[15]

As trials throughout the Asia-Pacific continued, some commentators began to fear that they were not having the desired effect. The
differences between Western and contemporary Japanese concepts of
law, justice and individual responsibility made for an unbridgeable
chasm. George Caiger, an Australian intelligence officer attached to
General Douglas MacArthur's staff who had spent ten years teaching
English in Japan, wrote in the *Sydney Morning Herald* in February 1946:

> About one Japanese in a million realises that these trials are
> establishing a new precedent in human affairs – the very idea of

a precedent in law is totally strange to them. The Japanese can understand victors shooting the conquered. They feel that the elaborate legal processes being followed merely witness the weakness of the Allied cases. Unless the full significance of the trials is patiently and clearly explained to the Japanese through their Press, radio, and cinema, they will either scorn us for being sadists as we now scorn them, or be flattered by the attention (as when no less than five American generals look part in [General] Yamashita's trial), or brood over it with plans for ultimate revenge . . . A few Japanese now admit that atrocities were committed. They want their perpetrators punished for bringing shame on Japan, not because they were crimes against humanity. The majority of Japanese merely accept these trials as examples of the curious behaviour of Western conquerors. To them it seems a rather cumbersome and expensive way of revenge.

'Revenge' became the word most commonly associated with criticism of the war crimes trials. Many individual Japanese soldiers struggled to understand why they were being charged for simply following the orders of their superiors with the unquestioning obedience that had been expected of them. Naval Paymaster Gōto Daisaku, convicted by an Australian court and executed by firing squad at Rabaul on 17 August 1946, wrote a statement condemning the Allies for their own war crimes, including the use of atomic bombs on Japanese cities. His conclusion was: 'War crimes laws were written by the victors for their own purposes. It was an act of revenge under the guise of law.'[16]

As the trials in the Far East continued, for months and then years, criticism mounted on all sides. Nuremberg was wrapped up and the death sentences carried out in 1946, but Tokyo staggered on until 1948. As the United States pushed for rapprochement with Japan and its rehabilitation as a Cold War ally, Australia was still trying Japanese war criminals or, worse, holding them without trial. The Australian trials went on until 1951 – some Japanese suspects did not face a court for six years – and by then they had become unpopular. As Labor MP Tom Burke of Perth told the House of Representatives during a debate in 1953:

> The system of war trials which we have adopted brings us down
> to the inhuman level of those whom we propose to bring to trial
> for atrocities committed under the strain and stress of war . . .
> Was the purpose of those trials to wreak revenge on those who had
> broken the legal or moral laws of civilized nations? Have those trials
> succeeded in deterring others from breaking the legal or moral laws
> of civilized nations? Was the purpose of the trials to attempt to
> prevent future wars, and if so, has that objective been achieved? I do
> not believe that the future peace of the world is any more assured
> because of them. Indeed, I believe that the whole basis on which the
> war trials were initiated has been falsified by the results that have
> been achieved.[17]

Australia had in the late 1940s looked on with unease at the shift in American attitudes from seeing Japan as a threat to seeing it as a potential bulwark against communism in the Far East. But by 1953 the Australian government was coming to the same view. And, of course, keeping the war criminals imprisoned (then on Manus Island) was expensive and troublesome. Between discomfort over the trial process itself and the desire to improve relations with Japan, the Australian government did not make a great deal of effort to uphold the judgements. By the end of 1953 all the class-B and -C war criminals held by the Allies had been returned to Japan. By the end of 1958 all of them, including those sentenced to life imprisonment, had been quietly released.[18]

Once they ended, the Pacific trials faded quickly from the public consciousness, particularly in the prosecuting nations, but even to some extent in Japan. Nuremberg remains the great beacon of international law and justice; Tokyo is in the shadows. People may have a dim awareness of the class-B and -C war crimes in Europe, such as the Dachau Trials, but the class-B and -C war crimes in the Pacific are almost unknown. Few Australians are aware of the Australian program of trials, despite its scale and importance to Australia's role in the international community.

David C.S. Sissons (1925–2006), an interpreter at Morotai in 1946, was for his entire life the leading expert on the Australian trials. He accumulated a vast amount of information which later researchers have found invaluable, but published little himself. American Philip R. Piccigallo's 1979 book *The Japanese on Trial* remains a good source for the class-B and -C trials generally, but until recent years the Australian trials had only a handful of articles and book chapters devoted to them. In the last few years, work by Georgina Fitzpatrick, Sandra Wilson, Emmi Okada, Yuma Totani, Robert Cribb, Beatrice Trefalt and Dean Aszkielowicz has gone a long way to correcting this, particularly with the 2016 publication of *Australia's War Crimes Trials, 1945–51*. But there is still little knowledge of or interest in the subject on the part of the general public.

This book is therefore an attempt to bring back to the attention of the public Australia's program of war crimes trials, and to revive the debates that accompanied them. Were the trials fair? Were their goals realistic? Were they justice, as was claimed at the time, or revenge? That final question deserves more than a one-word answer, but the historical consensus is that, despite their flaws, they cannot be dismissed out of hand as victors' justice. There is a lot to be learned from them, both from their successes and their failures, and they should not remain forgotten or ignored.

# PART ONE

# EMPEROR

The Australian plan to prosecute Hirohito as a war criminal

# I

# THE PREROGATIVES
# OF HIS MAJESTY

Sometime over the course of Thursday, 9 August 1945, the Emperor of Japan made the single most significant decision of his career. Hirohito, the Shōwa Emperor, was then forty-four years old and had occupied the Chrysanthemum Throne for just short of two decades. Two tumultuous decades, during which the policies of his governments had swung wildly. It is difficult to know what he thought of his governments' jarring shifts or of the momentous events that had come to overshadow his reign and threaten his dynasty's 2000-year hold on the throne. It is difficult to judge what he personally thought about anything. He was by nature a quiet, shy, reserved man, characteristics which were enhanced by the training for his high and distant office. He was as much a religious leader as a temporal one, Japan's connection with its divine past. But now, due to American air raids, the descendant of the sun-goddess Amaterasu was living underground like a burrowing animal. Outside the walls of the Imperial Palace, Tokyo lay in ruin, burned out by fire bombs.

Most likely, Hirohito made his decision at a meeting in the middle of the afternoon with Marquis Kido Kōichi, Lord Keeper of the Privy Seal. Kido had been the Emperor's confidant through all those troubled years, but could he be described as the Emperor's friend? He was certainly one of the few people close to the Emperor, meeting with him regularly and looking out for his welfare. As later events would show, he was willing to go to extreme lengths to protect his sovereign. But it is difficult to determine whether or not Hirohito had any friends outside the Imperial family. His interactions with others were tightly controlled, he rarely had what might be called a normal conversation with another human being, and he could confide his private thoughts to no-one. None except the Empress were permitted to touch him; even his doctors wore gloves. His tailors were required to guess his measurements, and as a result his clothes never fitted particularly well.

Perhaps this isolation is why he kept a diary since childhood. The Imperial Palace in Tokyo still holds it, although without a significant change in policy its contents will never be made public. He may have second-guessed himself in its pages, but he demonstrated no self-doubt in public, and indeed, little self-awareness in his words to others. Had he needed charisma or personal popularity to retain his throne, he would surely have lost it. But the institution supported him, just as he supported it.

The Lord Keeper of the Privy Seal traditionally controlled access to the Emperor, and in his five years in the office Kido had made himself one of the most powerful men in Japan. Historians have come to view him as something of a Machiavellian figure, working behind the scenes to protect the throne. Hirohito was not a fool, but he was not as clever or as cunning as Kido. Kido's schemes, however, had failed to prevent militarists from taking over the government and throwing Japan into an unwinnable war. When Kido's friend and ally Prince Konoe Fumimaro resigned as prime minister in October 1941, Kido had backed the appointment of extremist Tōjō Hideki on the principle of 'fight poison with poison', an old Japanese proverb.[1] But it is difficult to see what he was trying to achieve, and six weeks after Tōjō took office, Japan was at war with the United States, the United Kingdom, the Netherlands, Australia, Canada and New Zealand.

The situation for Japan had been uniformly bad for over a year, but never before had Kido come to the Emperor in circumstances quite as serious as these. On the morning of Monday, 6 August 1945, a clear and warm summer's day across much of the country, communications had suddenly been lost between Tokyo and military and civilian authorities in the southern city of Hiroshima. Confused reports of a massive explosion began to trickle in, but they made no sense – while Hiroshima had a significant army presence, there was no great stockpile of explosives, and the seven American B-29 bombers seen passing over the city could not possibly have carried enough firepower. A pilot was sent to investigate, and confirmed on his return that the city had apparently been engulfed in a fireball, leaving tens of thousands dead. It looked like the Americans had developed a super-weapon capable of destroying cities with ease.

The next day, in a radio broadcast shortly after midday, US President Harry S. Truman confirmed that Hiroshima had been destroyed by an American bomb. An atomic bomb, harnessing the basic forces of the universe and unleashing their destructive power. Alarmingly, the speech contained a grim threat directed at Tokyo:

> We are now prepared to obliterate more rapidly and completely every productive enterprise the Japanese have above ground in any city. We shall destroy their docks, their factories, and their communications. Let there be no mistake; we shall completely destroy Japan's power to make war. It was to spare the Japanese people from utter destruction that the ultimatum of July 26 was issued at Potsdam. Their leaders promptly rejected that ultimatum. If they do not now accept our terms they may expect a rain of ruin from the air, the like of which has never been seen on this earth. Behind this air attack will follow sea and land forces in such numbers and power as they have not yet seen and with the fighting skill of which they are already well aware.[2]

The ultimatum of 26 July was the Potsdam Declaration, a demand for Japan's unconditional surrender issued jointly by the governments of the United States, the United Kingdom and China. Japan would need to disarm its military, abandon its overseas empire, and allow the Allies to try its leaders and soldiers for war crimes. It would also need to submit to military occupation until the terms had been met and its government had been reformed along democratic lines.

'We do not intend that the Japanese shall be enslaved as a race or destroyed as a nation, but stern justice shall be meted out to all war criminals, including those who have visited cruelties upon our prisoners,' the Allies had said in the declaration, before finishing with 'the alternative for Japan is prompt and utter destruction'.[3] The Supreme Council for the Direction of the War, a body of six men which effectively ran Japan, had not accepted the terms of the Potsdam Declaration when it was issued. It was now clear what prompt and utter destruction would look like.

Through the dark months of 1945, as Japan's cities were destroyed by fire-bombing and Iwo Jima and Okinawa fell, the Japanese government's hopes rested on using the Soviet Union as an intermediary to negotiate peace with the Allies. This hope had now been crushed. On the night of Wednesday, 8 August, Soviet Foreign Minister Vyacheslav Molotov had informed Japanese ambassador Satō Naotake that the Soviet Union would consider itself at war with Japan from midnight, Far Eastern time. Soon after, units of the Kwantung Army guarding the border between the Japanese puppet state of Manchukuo (Manchuria) and the Soviet Union reported they had come under attack by the Red Army. These attacks quickly developed into a full-scale invasion, with 1.5 million Soviet troops pouring into Manchukuo from every direction.

The Japanese government scrambled to find out how many atomic bombs the Americans had, and when and where they intended to use them. Lieutenant Marcus McDilda, a P-51 Mustang pilot captured two days after the Hiroshima bombing, told his interrogators under torture that America had a hundred atomic bombs and would use one on Tokyo in the next few days. McDilda actually knew nothing about the bombs and was bluffing, but his warning was taken seriously by the members of the Supreme Council.

The Supreme Council had met on Thursday morning, 9 August, but after two hours of discussion remained undecided on how to respond to the Potsdam Declaration. During the meeting, shortly after 11 am, they received the news that another atomic bomb had destroyed Nagasaki. After two hours, the Supreme Council had still not made a decision. Prime Minister Suzuki Kantarō had called a meeting of the full cabinet, and it was now in session. While the cabinet was shut away in another part of the complex, Kido, who was a member of neither the Supreme Council nor the cabinet, went to see the Emperor.

Hirohito was meticulous, and under pressure his attention to detail became obsessive. It seems his mind was not then on atomic bombs or the relentless advance of the Red Army into Manchuria, but on where the Americans would land when they launched their inevitable invasion of the Japanese mainland. The army had assured him that fortifications at Kujūkuri Beach to the east of Tokyo Bay would be complete by August, but they were nowhere near done. And if the Americans landed at Ise Bay to the south of Tokyo, there was a risk they could capture the Shinto shrines holding the imperial regalia. These were a sword, a mirror and a jewel, meant to be of divine origin, which were the symbols of the legitimacy of the Imperial house. No-one except for the Emperor and the very highest Shinto priests were even permitted to see them.

Hirohito suggested to Kido that the regalia was under threat, and their loss would be a serious blow to the Chrysanthemum Throne. 'If the enemy landed near Ise Bay, both Ise and Atsuta Shrines would immediately come under their control,' Hirohito said in *Shōwa Tennō Dokuhakuroku*, a monologue dictated in 1946 and made public in 1990 after his death. 'There would be no time to transfer the sacred treasures of the imperial family and no time to protect them. Under these circumstances, protection of the *kokutai* would be difficult.'[4] Kido agreed with him.

*Kokutai* is a difficult-to-translate word describing Japan's national polity or national identity, and above all, rule by an emperor from an unbroken line stretching back into mythological times. Kido was also concerned about the *kokutai*, but he saw a bigger picture than the imperial regalia. As unthinkable as it was, the public might be turning against the Emperor.

After the devastating fire-bombing raid of 9–10 March, the Emperor was driven out in a car to see what remained of Tokyo. The city, painstakingly rebuilt from its near complete ruin in the Great Kantō Earthquake of 1923, had been consumed by fire. Three hundred and thirty-four American bombers had dropped 1,665 tons (1,510 tonnes) of incendiary bombs, creating a firestorm so powerful it boiled water in the canals, melted glass, and destroyed some of the bombers flying overhead. Somewhere between 80,000 and 125,000 people had burned to death, and a million were left homeless. The survivors were living in makeshift shelters made from anything they could find, while hundreds of thousands had fled into the countryside, surviving by eating weeds and insects. Rice, the staple of the Japanese diet, had become scarce. People turned to barley and potatoes, but by mid-1945 these were running out as well. Millions were now threatened with starvation. Absenteeism at some factories had reached 40 per cent, simply because the workers were too malnourished to come to work.[5]

A witness in a car following the Emperor's described exhausted survivors 'digging through the rubble with empty expressions on their faces that became reproachful as the imperial motorcade went by'.[6] For Japanese people to look reproachfully at the Emperor was troubling. The royal houses of Russia, Germany and Austria had not survived the First World War. Kido saw no reason to assume Japan's must survive the Second.

What, then, did Kido say to the Emperor in response to his concerns about the preservation of the regalia and the *kokutai*? Neither Kido's diary nor Hirohito's monologue record this exactly. Given what happened over the following hours, though, it seems likely Kido finally persuaded the Emperor that Japan must accept the terms of the Potsdam Declaration and surrender to the Allies.

Legally, it was not immediately clear what this meant. The position of the Emperor in the Japanese government was ambiguous, and this ambiguity remains one of the reasons for the ongoing debate about Hirohito's personal responsibility for the war and Japanese war crimes. As part of their modernisation project, Japan's leaders had given it the Meiji Constitution in 1889.[7] Based on the constitutions of the United Kingdom and the German states, it combined Western political institutions with the *kokutai*. The joining of the two was far from seamless: some of the provisions of the Meiji Constitution seemed to assume that the Emperor was an absolute monarch, and some that he was a constitutional monarch. For example, Article 3 described the Emperor as 'sacred and inviolable', Article 11 gave him supreme command of the army and navy, and Article 13 gave him the power to declare war, make peace, and conclude treaties. However, Article 5 stated the Emperor could only exercise his powers in accordance with the constitution. In practice, this left a great deal to the people occupying the high offices of state, including the Emperor.

A strong-willed emperor could, perhaps, have controlled the government, but Hirohito was not a particularly independent or decisive man. Many times he was content to be made the tool of other men, if he saw it as being in his own interests and the interests of the survival of the Japanese monarchy. Throughout his career he did not show a great deal of courage or initiative, and except on a few occasions he blew with the prevailing wind. But at the same time, he was an active participant in the government of Japan. As his biographer Herbert Bix wrote: 'For more than twenty years Hirohito exercised, within a complex system of mutual restraints, real power and authority independent of government and the bureaucracy. Well informed of the war and diplomatic situations, knowledgeable about political and military affairs, he participated in the making of national policy and issued the orders of the imperial headquarters to field commanders and admirals.'[8]

Formally, the interaction between the government and the Emperor was carried out in a *Gozen Kaigi*, an imperial conference. Typically, the government would put an agreed policy before the Emperor for his approval. But when the meeting of the full cabinet broke up at 8 pm on 9 August with no decision made, Prime Minister Suzuki decided to call an imperial conference that night and put two proposals before the Emperor for his decision. It was unusual, but then, the circumstances were unprecedented.

The conference began late at night, in the final minutes of Thursday, 9 August. Present were the six members of the Supreme Council for the Direction of the War, the president of the Privy Council, and five aides. The Supreme Council consisted of the prime minister, the foreign minister, and the ministers and the chiefs of staff for both the army and navy. Informally, they were called the Big Six. Four of the six were army and navy officers appointed by those services, showing the effective control the military had over the country. But unlike Nazi Germany, Japan did not have continuity of leadership throughout the war (the Emperor being a notable exception). These were not the men responsible for the ill-advised decision to attack the British Empire and the United States in December 1941, and most had only been appointed when their predecessors were dismissed or resigned following defeat after defeat during 1944 and early 1945.

The Emperor entered the room; everyone rose and bowed. When they resumed their seats, Prime Minister Suzuki was the first to speak. Suzuki, a 77-year-old retired admiral, had been brought out of retirement to take over as prime minister in April 1945, once it became clear that Japan was going to lose the Battle of Okinawa. He had served as grand chamberlain from 1929 to 1936, where he became a target of the militarists for his moderate views and opposition to war against Britain and the United States. In the February 26 Incident of 1936, an attempt by radical officers of the *Kōdōha* (Imperial Way Faction) to take control of the government, he was listed as a target. The rebels burst into his house and shot him twice. As their captain drew his sword to deliver the killing blow, Suzuki's wife begged him to let her do it herself. Believing Suzuki was mortally wounded, the captain bowed and replied, 'I am particularly sorry about this, but our views differ from His Excellency, so it had to come to this.'[9] This was an accurate summary of the attitude the militarists had towards those who disagreed with them.

The rebels left and Suzuki survived, although one of the bullets stayed in his body for the rest of his life. Unsurprisingly, he played little further role in politics until his recall to office. And even as prime minister, he maintained a placid facade and rarely expressed an opinion, preferring Taoist philosophy to political debate. The Emperor trusted him implicitly.

Suzuki explained that the Big Six were deadlocked three–three on whether they should accept the Potsdam Declaration subject to one condition or four conditions. Three of the Big Six – Suzuki, Foreign Minister Tōgō Shigenori, and Navy Minister Admiral Yonai Mitsumasa – favoured accepting the declaration subject to one condition, the preservation of the *kokutai*. This proposal lay on the table before everyone. In practice, this meant surrendering on the understanding that the Emperor would stay on the throne, and new institutions of government would be built around him to ensure continuity and to guarantee the country's survival as a distinctly Japanese nation. Like Suzuki, Tōgō and Yonai had opposed going to war with the United States and Britain, and had been sidelined by the militarists until the war turned decisively against Japan.

Army Minister[10] General Anami Korechika, Chief of the Army General Staff General Umezu Yoshijirō, and Chief of the Navy

General Staff Admiral Toyoda Soemu were willing to accept the declaration but only on three more conditions: Japan must control its own disarmament; there must be no occupation of the Japanese homeland by foreign troops and the Japanese government must have control of any war crimes trials. The last had historical precedent. The Treaty of Versailles, imposed on defeated Germany by the Allies of the First World War in 1919, contained clauses for the trials of German war criminals. But they never happened. The plan to try Germany's deposed Kaiser fell apart when the Netherlands refused to extradite him, and to prevent further political instability in Germany the Allies allowed the German government to conduct its own trials, which ended in a farce. Anami and Umezu were militarists, closely associated with former prime minister Tōjō Hideki. Toyoda had opposed the war, but now believed it must be fought to the death if favourable conditions for Japan could not be obtained.

Suzuki, Tōgō, Yonai, Anami and Umezu all spoke in turn, explaining their position to the Emperor. He listened to each of them, then turned to Baron Hiranuma Kiichirō, President of the Privy Council and chair of the meeting. Hiranuma was a hardliner, a reactionary lawyer with a deep fear of public disorder. As justice minister in the 1920s he had drafted a law that made it illegal to start or join an organisation dedicated to overthrowing the *kokutai*, and used it to imprison the leaders of the Japanese Communist Party. They were still in gaol. But he was also a realist. When he spoke at the conference, he raised the shortage of food and the domestic unrest. He gave a long and legalistic speech, going into the exact wording of the proposal, finally coming to the conclusion that Japan must end the war but probing the Allies for additional terms could not hurt. The subtle Hiranuma had committed himself to nothing, but the Emperor concluded that he was with Suzuki.

Nonetheless, his willingness to accept the proposal lying on the table had limits. 'Even if the entire nation is sacrificed to the war, we must preserve both the *kokutai* and the security of the Imperial house,'

Hiranuma said.[11] He agreed with Suzuki that the final decision must rest with the Emperor. 'In accordance with the legacy of your Imperial forefathers, Your Imperial Majesty is also responsible for preventing unrest in the nation,' the Baron added. 'I should like to ask Your Imperial Majesty to make your decision with this point in mind.'[12]

After Toyoda spoke, supporting Anami and Umezu, Suzuki rose and faced the Emperor. 'Your Imperial Majesty's decision is requested as to which proposal should be adopted – the one stated by the Foreign Minister [with the one condition] or the one containing the four conditions.'[13]

The Emperor did not hesitate; his mind was clearly made up. He rose swiftly from his seat, and the councillors all rose around him. With visible emotion, he began to speak before the imperial conference. It was then the early hours of Friday 10 August. Nobody recorded exactly what he said, but the official transcript of his speech runs as follows: 'I have given serious thought to the situation prevailing at home and abroad and have concluded that continuing the war can only mean destruction for the nation and prolongation of bloodshed and cruelty in the world. I cannot bear to see my innocent people suffer any longer . . .'[14]

He spoke about the failure of the army to ready fortifications at Kujūkuri Beach, a controversial statement as it implied criticism of the military. From this he concluded that any plan to defend Japan may not work. 'There are those who say the key to national survival lies in a decisive battle in the homeland,' he said, referring to the militarists and their desire for a cataclysmic battle in Japan where the people would die 'like shattered jewels' and the Allies would be defeated by sheer numbers. 'The experiences of the past, however, show that there has always been a discrepancy between plans and performance.'

He then spoke of the disarmament and war crimes conditions: 'It goes without saying that it is unbearable for me to see the brave and loyal fighting men of Japan disarmed. It is equally unbearable that others who have rendered me devoted service should now be punished as instigators of the war. Nevertheless, the time has come to bear the unbearable . . . I swallow my tears and give my sanction to the proposal to accept the Allied proclamation on the basis outlined by the Foreign Minister.'

Baron Hiranuma alone answered him. 'Your Majesty, you also bear responsibility for this defeat. What apology are you going to make to the heroic spirits of the imperial founder of your house and your other imperial ancestors?'[15]

It is not recorded whether Hirohito answered this unusually direct question. He left the conference room, having made his decision.

'His Majesty's decision should be made the decision of the Conference,' said Suzuki, breaking the silence. They argued about it for a few hours more, but sometime between 3 and 4 am, the Big Six formally adopted it. In the last hour before dawn, Foreign Ministry officials were put to work preparing the documents to go to the Allies via the governments of neutral Switzerland and Sweden. A communication was drafted, sent by cable to Bern and Stockholm, and then broadcast over Radio Tokyo at midnight on 10–11 August. It worded the acceptance of the Potsdam Declaration subject to the preservation of the *kokutai* like this:

> In obedience to the gracious command of his Majesty the Emperor
> who, ever anxious to enhance the cause of world peace, desires
> earnestly to bring about a speedy termination of hostilities with
> a view to saving mankind from the calamities to be imposed
> upon them by further continuation of the war . . . The Japanese
> Government are ready to accept the terms enumerated in the joint
> declaration which was issued at Potsdam on July 26, 1945, by the
> heads of the Governments of the United States, Great Britain,
> and China, and later subscribed by the Soviet Government with
> the understanding that the said declaration does not comprise
> any demand which prejudices the prerogatives of His Majesty as
> a Sovereign Ruler.[16]

There was nothing for it then but to wait for a response, and hope the military would not overthrow the government when it learned of the Emperor's decision.

The communication was received in London, Washington, D.C., Moscow, and the Nationalist Chinese capital of Chungking over the course of 10 August. At 7.33 am Washington time, the first report reached President Truman at the White House. He immediately called a conference for 9 am with Secretary of State James Byrnes, Secretary of War Henry Stimson, Secretary of the Navy James Forrestal, and Chief of Staff Admiral William Leahy. The question on Truman's mind, and on the minds of the other Allied leaders, was this: what did the Japanese government mean by accepting the Potsdam Declaration with the understanding that it did not 'comprise any demand which prejudiced the prerogatives of His Majesty as a Sovereign Ruler'?

At the meeting, Leahy and Stimson were both in favour of accepting the offer, keeping the Emperor in place, and using him to control defeated Japan and speed the demobilisation of its forces. Byrnes, however, was opposed to anything less than unequivocal surrender. In his view, it was not Japan's place to impose terms on the Allies. Forrestal proposed a compromise – accept the offer in such a way that the Potsdam Declaration was still accomplished. Truman gave some thought to this, then asked Byrnes to draft a reply.[17] The Secretary of State returned to the White House at midday with his draft, had lunch with the President, then went into a meeting of the cabinet at 2 pm. The cabinet approved the draft and sent it to London, Moscow and Chungking for comment.

The draft stated that the position of the Allies was, from the moment of surrender, that the authority of the Emperor and the Japanese government would be subject to the Supreme Commander of the Allied powers. The Emperor and Japanese high command would be required to sign the document of surrender and issue orders

to all armed forces to surrender. In accordance with the Potsdam
Declaration, Japan's government would be made democratic and
Japan would be occupied by the Allies until the terms were achieved.

In London, the newly elected Labour government of Clement
Attlee had already considered the Japanese declaration. The cabinet
was 'inclined to accept the continuation of the emperor' but acknowledged a 'more precise definition of the reservation was necessary in
light of the Potsdam Declaration'.[18] On receiving Byrnes' draft on
the night of 10 August, the British agreed with it in principle, but
recommended the Emperor be required to simply authorise the signing of the Instrument of Surrender rather than signing it himself.
Additionally, they recommended that the Emperor personally order
all Japanese forces throughout the Asia-Pacific to lay down their arms
and accept the orders of the Allies. 'This, we believe, also will secure
the immediate surrender of the Japanese in all outlying areas and
thereby save American, British and Allied lives.'

Like Leahy and Stimson, the Attlee cabinet believed they should
keep the Emperor and use him to their advantage. Winston Churchill,
then Leader of the Opposition, approved of Attlee's approach. Lord
Addison, Secretary of State for the Dominions, then sent the proposed reply to Ottawa, Canberra, Wellington and Pretoria asking for
the views of the Dominion governments.[19]

The Australian government was at that point in a state of deep
discontent. Of the four Dominions, it had contributed the most to
the Pacific War, yet it felt marginalised and excluded by London and
Washington. For a start, Australia had been powerless to challenge
Churchill and Roosevelt's Europe-first strategy. Australian forces had
originally been the largest part of General MacArthur's command in
the South-West Pacific Area, and had been responsible for a number
of early victories over the Japanese in Papua New Guinea. But as the
war continued and the American presence in the Pacific increased,
Australian forces grew much less important. By 1945 the Australian
Army was mostly fighting sideline campaigns in bypassed areas such

as Papua New Guinea and Borneo. Furthermore, the Australian government first heard of the Potsdam Declaration in the press, and unlike the governments of the United Kingdom and Canada, received no advance knowledge of the atomic bomb.

Prime Minister John Curtin was gravely ill from October 1944 until his death on 5 July 1945, and in that time his eventual successor Ben Chifley, Army Minister Frank Forde, and Foreign Minister and Attorney-General Herbert Vere Evatt were responsible for Australia's conduct of the war. Chifley and Evatt pushed for Australia to play a greater role in order to win influence in the peace settlement, just as Australian victories on the Western Front in 1918 had secured Australia a place at Versailles. But that was not to happen this time. Knowing MacArthur must have been planning an invasion of Japan, Chifley wrote to him to offer Australian assistance. He was rebuffed. MacArthur wrote back on 20 May advising, 'There are no specific plans so far as I know for employment of Australian troops after the Borneo campaign,' and any further Australian involvement in the Pacific War would need to be decided between Australia and Britain.[20]

For Evatt, having to learn of the Potsdam Declaration from the newspapers was the final straw. Speaking on 28 July, he criticised the declaration for failing to demand the removal of Japan's government and Emperor. He said it was: 'published without prior reference to, still less the concurrence of, the Australian Government . . . All that need be said about the actual terms of peace foreshadowed in the ultimatum is that they appear to treat Japan more leniently than Germany, in spite of the fact that the slightest sign of any tenderness towards Japanese imperialism is entirely misplaced, having regard to the outrageous cruelties and barbarities systematically practiced by the imperialist regime.'[21]

When the Churchill Conservative government was suddenly and decisively defeated in the July 1945 general election, Evatt had hopes that the new Attlee government would pay more attention to

Dominion rights. He sent a series of cables to London, observing that the government of David Lloyd George had given the Dominions far more say in the peace talks at the end of the First World War than the current British government was doing, and insisting Australia be included in the Council of Foreign Ministers then being formed.[22] 'The inclusion of China in the Council in respect of European affairs and the non-inclusion of the Dominions seems to me to be absolutely unjust and almost irrational,' Evatt wrote to Lord Addison.

Atlee and Addison were understanding but maintained that consulting with the Dominions on every major detail was impractical.

Evatt also wrote to the other Dominion governments to gather support. New Zealand Prime Minister Peter Fraser was also sympathetic, but Jan Smuts of South Africa took a more prosaic view: 'Under the circumstances I am afraid we shall have to be satisfied with putting our individual Government's views clearly and strongly before the United Kingdom Government for their guidance in negotiations with their other colleagues,' he wrote. 'If we press for Dominion representation, Russia will at once press for the Ukraine, Poland and the rest to participate also, and soon there will be a major San Francisco Conference.'[23]

It was only with difficulty that the US and UK had been able to prevent Soviet leader Josef Stalin from flooding the proposed council with his newly established puppet governments in Eastern Europe. Permitting the Dominions to join would make it much harder to make the case against their inclusion.

Something of Evatt's character and political views, both of which were complex, can be read from his telegrams. Biographer John Murphy described him as 'an enigma, full of puzzling contradictions'.[24] Evatt was without a doubt an exceptional lawyer and a skilled historian, with a real commitment to international justice and the enforcement of international law in respect of perpetrators of atrocities. But he was also an irascible eccentric with questionable people skills, and spent his career haunted by fears that others were secretly working against him. In later life, this paranoia developed into delusion. He was afraid of flying – always an impediment for a foreign minister – wore newspapers under his clothes in cold weather, and couldn't understand why his colleagues resented being phoned at 3 am.

When Labor returned to government in 1941, Evatt was the inevitable choice for both Attorney-General and Minister for External Affairs, but he remained forever an outsider in the Labor Party. In both law and politics he built his reputation as a liberal and a civil libertarian, and he remained far more interested in fighting for justice against tyranny than in industrial relations, nationalisation of industry, and the other mainstream concerns of 1940s Labor.

Born in 1894, Evatt was found unsuitable for service in the First World War because of his poor eyesight. Two of his brothers were able to enlist and were killed. His academic career at the University of Sydney was brilliant – bachelor of arts with first-class honours and the university medal in 1915, master of arts in 1917 bachelor of laws with first-class honours and the university medal in 1918, and doctorate of laws in 1924. The final degree gave him his nickname, Doc Evatt. He found the time to play cricket and rugby league, and remained an enthusiast for both sports throughout his life. He worked as a barrister, and was elected to the New South Wales Legislative Assembly under the Labor banner in 1925. He became a fierce critic of Labor leader Jack Lang, and was refused Labor endorsement in the 1927 election. He won re-election anyway as an independent Labor candidate. In 1930 the federal Labor government of Jim Scullin appointed Evatt to the High Court. There his 'secretive and disputatious working habits and his frequent dissenting judgements' attracted criticism, but he was praised by civil libertarians for his judgements in favour of communist journalist Hal Devanny (facing conviction under a First World War-era law banning unlawful associations) and Czech communist Egon Kisch (facing deportation from Australia).[25] With the outbreak of the Second World War Evatt concluded that parliament, rather than the court, was the place for him to achieve the most good, and he ran for and won the federal seat of Barton in 1940.

The Australian government's reply to Addison's message reflected Evatt's concerns.[26] It insisted on the Emperor personally signing the Instrument of Surrender, as in the original American draft, but acknowledged the British proposal to have the Emperor personally issue detailed orders to surrender was an obvious improvement. The main concern, however, was with the status of the Emperor.

'Neither the United States draft nor your own comment on it meets point of prime importance implicit in the Japanese message, namely whether the prerogative of the Emperor includes immunity from charge and possibility of conviction arising out of Emperor's responsibility for commencement of war of aggression and for atrocious methods used in the conduct of the war by Japan,' the Australian government wrote. 'Reply to Japanese message must therefore make it clear that every person to whom war crimes can be justly imputed shall be liable to punishment and that under the Potsdam principles no exception to this general rule is admissible.'

Finally, the Australian government, fearing London was not giving credit to its views, said it would from now on consult directly with the United States, the Soviet Union and China.

In response to this belligerent telegram, Atlee wrote personally to Ben Chifley, perhaps desiring to bypass the excitable Evatt: 'You may be sure that at all times we desire to act in closest co-operation with you and to afford the utmost opportunity for consultation but events move fast and we are deeply concerned lest delay should lead to the unnecessary sacrifice of the lives of Australian, other British and Allied fighting men. Hours are of importance. We have therefore at times to take rapid action particularly in matters where as in this case the initiative lies with the United States of America.'[27]

He also responded to Australia's concerns about the guarantees given to the Emperor: 'to have delayed the reply in order to obtain special reference to the culpability of the Emperor would in my view have been unjustifiable especially if it jeopardised obtaining an all-round surrender'.

This does not seem to have satisfied Evatt, and the Australian government continued to send cablegrams to London over 11 and 12 August, complaining that its views were not being taken into account, insisting on nothing less than Japan's unconditional surrender, and calling for the Emperor's removal from the throne and his prosecution as a war criminal. Evatt referred to the huge collection of evidence of Japanese war crimes which the Australian government had been diligently collecting since 1942.

Finally, on 20 August, Addison wrote: 'We are sorry to read in your telegram that you feel that Australia's effort has not been sufficiently recognised in the armistice arrangements. We have for our part as you know done our best to secure the greatest possible recognition of Australia's special position and her maximum participation in these arrangements. But the matter is not entirely or even primarily one for us alone and it is impossible for us to go beyond what we can persuade our American and other major Allies to accept.'[28]

Meanwhile, Truman was having as much trouble with Stalin as Attlee was with Evatt. The Soviet Union assumed it would play a role in occupying Japan as it did in Germany, possibly with a joint commander. As Stalin was then cheerfully establishing totalitarian communist states in the territories controlled by the Red Army, Truman was not minded to allow this. 'I did not want divided control or separate zones,' he wrote in his memoir. 'I did not want to give the Russians any opportunity to behave as they had in Germany and Austria. I wanted the country administered in such a manner that it could be restored to its place in the society of nations.'[29] Even at this early stage, the divisions leading to the Cold War were readily apparent among the Allies.

Eventually the Soviet government agreed (although the Red Army showed no signs of slowing its advance into Manchuria and Korea), and Truman received replies from London and Chungking. Having made the amendments suggested by the British, the American government sent a communication to neutral Switzerland and Sweden for forwarding to Tokyo:

> With regard to the Japanese Government's message accepting the terms of the Potsdam Proclamation, but containing the Statement – 'with the understanding that the said declaration does not comprise any demand which prejudices the prerogatives of His Majesty as a Sovereign Ruler' – our position is as follows:
>
> From the moment of surrender the authority of the Emperor and the Japanese Government to rule the State shall be subject to the Supreme Commander of the Allied Powers who will take such steps as he deems proper to effectuate the Surrender Terms.
>
> The Emperor will be required to authorise and ensure the signature by the Government of Japan and the Japanese Imperial General Headquarters of the Surrender Terms necessary to carry out the provisions of the Potsdam Declaration, and shall issue his commands to all the Japanese Military, Naval and Air authorities and to all the forces under their control, wherever located, to cease active operations, surrender their arms, and to issue such other orders as the Supreme Commander may require to give effect to the Surrender Terms.[30]

The Allies then waited for a response. But none was immediately forthcoming.

# II

# ENDURING THE UNENDURABLE

Tension lay on the Imperial Palace over 10 and 11 August. Nobody knew whether the Allies would accept Japan's counter-offer, and, if they did so, whether the military would abide by the decision to surrender. In the period of 'Government by assassination' during the 1930s, young officers from ultra-nationalist sects freely killed politicians who opposed the militarist agenda, and there was no reason to think they would not do so again.

General Anami announced the outcome of the conference at the Imperial Army headquarters on the morning of 10 August. Understandably, the officers were 'greatly shocked', particularly because the Emperor's comments about the failure to prepare fortifications and his pessimism about the 'final victory' suggested a loss of faith in the army. Nonetheless, Anami stood by the Emperor and the decision of the Big Six. He made it clear to the officers that anyone who wished to act contrary to the Emperor's decision would have to do so 'over my dead body'.[1]

On the afternoon of 10 August, Hirohito consulted with his former prime ministers on his decision. There was no shortage of them – in the twenty years of his reign, Japan had managed to run through fifteen prime ministers. Five were dead, two by assassination at the hands of ultra-nationalists, but seven were in Tokyo and available to meet with the Emperor.

Of the former prime ministers, none was more influential than Prince Konoe Fumimaro.[2] He had held the office from 1937 to 1939, and again from 1940 to 1941. Even outside of the cabinet, he remained one of the most powerful men in the country due to his personal popularity and connections within the government. Coming from the ancient and powerful Fujiwara clan, Konoe's position entitled him to a seat in the House of Peers, the upper house of the Japanese parliament, or Diet. As a politician he had been independent, affiliated with neither the militaristic nor liberal democratic factions but acceptable to both. He had praised US President Franklin Roosevelt's New Deal in the 1930s and pushed democratic reforms, such as the expansion of the electoral franchise. He had staunchly opposed war against the Western powers and sought desperately to negotiate with Roosevelt, finally resigning in October 1941 when he saw that the militarists had taken control of the government and war was inevitable. But he had also accepted the Japanese invasion of China, approved the abolition of political parties and their forcible incorporation into the Imperial Rule Assistance Association, and coined the slogan *Hakkō ichiu* – 'the whole world under one roof' – used to justify Japanese aggression.

Following his resignation Konoe watched events from the sidelines. Despite the censorship of the Japanese press, it was apparent to him by mid-1943 that Japan was going to lose the war, and that this loss could jeopardise not only the *kokutai* but the survival of the Chrysanthemum Throne itself. The fall of the royal houses of Russia, Germany and Austria-Hungary in the wake of defeat in 1917 and 1918 weighed on his mind. Konoe became the centre of a group of politicians – his friend Kido Koichi was among them – pushing to negotiate peace with the Allies. They succeeded in bringing down the government of hardliner Tōjō Hideki following the disastrous Japanese defeat at Saipan in July 1944, but the militarists, with their nihilistic fantasies of an apocalyptic battle to the death, kept the government in a vice. 'When I think of the madmen leading the present situation, I can't help but feel weary of life,' Konoe remarked to his secretary the day before American troops landed on Okinawa.[3]

Konoe had previously urged the Emperor to seek terms with the Allies at a private meeting in February. He had arrived at the Imperial Palace at 1 pm on 9 August, and had managed to persuade Kido that Japan must accept the Potsdam Declaration. Kido, in turn, had gone to the Emperor.

Most of the former prime ministers Hirohito now consulted agreed with Konoe and supported the Emperor's decision to accept the declaration. Two, however, had reservations.

One was Tōjō Hideki, who had led Japan into the war against the Western powers, and held office until the fall of Saipan. Even by the standards of the militarists, he was a zealot. An unimaginative, humourless man, Tōjō was the first to admit he owed his success to reliability and a capacity for hard work rather than innate brilliance. He boasted that he had no hobbies outside of his job. He was a life-long anti-American, the experience of a single train journey across the United States having persuaded him that Americans were 'soft' people. The 1924 US law banning Asian immigration hardened his attitudes. He was a fierce critic of Western influence in Japan, from democratic ideas to young couples holding hands in public. Originally a member of the 'strike north' school, which favoured expansion at the expense of the Soviet Union, by the late 1930s he had changed his views in favour of forming an alliance with Nazi Germany (which he admired) and striking south. He became known as the enforcer of the *Tōseiha* (Control Faction), purging the Kwantung Army of officers of the rival *Kōdōha* (Imperial Way Faction) following the February 26 Incident. In doing so, he earned himself the nickname *Kamisori* – The Razor.

Tōjō became the face of Japanese militarism in the English-speaking world during the Second World War, although he was not a leader by temperament. His country's military disasters lessened his influence, but he nonetheless remained a powerful figure, and he now advised the Emperor against accepting disarmament. Japan, he said, was like a shellfish. The military was its shell, and without it the organism inside would die.[4] He was joined in this view by General Koiso Kuniaki, his successor. Like Tōjō and Chief of Staff General Umezu, Koiso was a militarist from the *Tōseiha* faction.

Hirohito listened to all the advice he received, but made no further decision.

In the early hours of the morning on 12 August, the answer finally arrived from Washington in the form of Byrnes' note, which was also broadcast on American radio at 12.45 am Tokyo time. It was not the response the Japanese government had hoped for. It contained no guarantee of the Emperor's position, and worse, stated that his authority would be subject to the Allies' supreme commander. The Japanese translators were so rattled they deliberately mistranslated 'subject to' to a term more like 'circumscribed by' to make it more palatable.[5] Even so, a number of junior officers were enraged by it.

At a meeting of the full cabinet, Suzuki vacillated. Based on the content of Byrnes' note, he now favoured rejecting the Potsdam Declaration. For this he was castigated by Tōgō Shigenori, and later by Kido. Not only would millions more die, Kido pointed out, but Suzuki was going against the express will of the Emperor. They succeeded, and Suzuki returned to the fold. Admiral Yonai, for his part, argued it would be much better to surrender in response to the atomic bombs and the Soviet entry into the war than to surrender due to civil unrest. And civil unrest could not be avoided indefinitely, particularly now that American bombers were dropping leaflets over Japan outlining the negotiations.

So throughout 13 and 14 August, there was once more deadlock in Tokyo. Posters began to appear in the city bearing the message 'Kill Lord Keeper of the Privy Seal Kido!'. They were probably the work of fanatical officers who (correctly) guessed Kido was persuading the Emperor to accept the declaration. In the circumstances, Kido moved into the Imperial Palace. The Big Six had a series of fruitless meetings. At one, on the night of 14 August, they got an indication of just how far some of Japan's military leaders were willing to go. Admiral Ōnishi Takijirō, the 'father of Kamikaze', burst into the room and called on them to form a plan to continue the war and take it to the Emperor for his approval. 'If we are prepared to sacrifice 20,000,000 Japanese lives in a special attack [Kamikaze] effort, victory will be ours!' he assured them.[6] The US began doubting that Japan would surrender and resumed bombing raids.

But the Emperor himself did not waver. If the Allied response amounted to an acceptance of his offer to surrender subject to the *kokutai* being preserved, then he was willing to take it. He advised his family of his decision, but also assured them he would continue the war if this condition could not be met.[7]

A second and final imperial conference to discuss the Byrnes note was held at 11 am on 14 August, Tokyo time, at the same location as the earlier one. Umezu, Toyoda and Anami urged the Emperor to reject the note and continue the war. But he was resigned: 'I have listened carefully to each of the arguments presented in opposition to the view that Japan should accept the Allied reply as it stands and without further clarification or modification, but my own thoughts have not undergone any change . . . In order that the people may know my decision, I request you to prepare at once an imperial rescript so that I may broadcast to the nation. Finally, I call upon each and every one of you to exert himself to the utmost so that we may meet the trying days which lie ahead.'[8]

It was an emotional meeting. 'Tears flowed unceasingly,' recalled one witness. But it was a final decision. At 2.49 am on 14 August, the first confirmation of the Japanese surrender reached Washington, D.C.


Anami briefly considered taking some sort of extreme action to prevent the reply being sent to Washington, bailing up Umezu in the toilets to sound him out on a plan. But Umezu would not support him. At 3 pm Anami reported the Emperor's decision to the officers at the Imperial Army headquarters. After some tense discussion, the senior officers coerced each other into signing an agreement not to act contrary to the Emperor's direction.

But it was far from clear if officers further down the chain of command would also comply, not to mention the millions of soldiers still deployed overseas. Hence the Emperor's decision to make his broadcast, a plan created by Kido and the Palace household staff. Sometime during 14 August employees from the Japan Broadcasting Corporation attended the Palace and Hirohito delivered the speech into a phonograph.

Kido's concerns about the military rejecting the surrender were far from unjustified. As soon as Japan's offer became public on 10 August, a group of fanatical junior officers from the Army General Staff and the Imperial Guards Division began plotting against the government. Coming to the conclusion that loyalty to the Imperial house trumped loyalty to the Emperor, they decided the people of Japan were better off dead than surrendered. On 14 August, they created their final plan. They would overthrow the government, destroy the phonograph of the Emperor's speech, kill Suzuki, Kido and Hiranuma, and create a new regime to continue the war.

That evening, they went to Anami's residence to persuade him to join them. They found him writing his will, clearly preparing to commit suicide. He refused to go along with them, but did not take any action to prevent the impending coup. Later that night, he cut open his belly and then his throat, leaving the following cryptic message in his suicide note: 'Believing firmly that our sacred land shall never perish, I – with my death – humbly apologise to the Emperor for the great crime.'

The rebels managed to win over some other officers and soldiers by claiming they were acting on Anami's and Umezu's orders. When two senior officers, Lieutenant General Mori Takeshi and Lieutenant

Colonel Shiraishi Michinori, refused to join the rebels they were cut down with swords. Shortly after midnight, the rebels surrounded the Imperial Palace and cut the telephone wires leading to it.

The sources conflict on whether Hirohito was awake and aware of what was happening. He wrote in *Shōwa Tennō Dokuhakuroku* that he was watching events unfold through the shutters of his window. If so, the scene must have reminded him of the snowy night in February 1936 when officers of the *Kōdōha* faction attempted to seize control of the government. Bearing banners reading 'Revere the Emperor – Destroy the Traitors', the *Kōdōha* officers had drawn up a hit list of senior public figures whose views were unacceptably liberal and pro-Western. They managed to take control of the Army Ministry and police headquarters, and assassinated the Lord Keeper of the Privy Seal, the Finance Minister, and the Inspector-General of Military Education. But they failed to secure the Imperial Palace, and most of their intended targets (including Suzuki) escaped. The army did not move against the rebels, and a stalemate ensued.

Back then, Hirohito had acted decisively, threatening to personally lead the Imperial Guard against the rebels if the army did not stop them. Leaflets were dropped over the rebel-held positions calling on them to surrender. The ordinary soldiers, who had blindly followed the orders of the rebel officers without question, deserted back to the government. The rebellion collapsed and the officers either committed suicide or were captured and executed.

Now, Hirohito had acted decisively again, although as in February 1936, it had taken him some time to come to his decision.

The rebels moved into the Palace and began searching for Kido and the phonograph. They found neither – Kido was hiding in a basement, and the phonograph was subsequently smuggled out of the Palace and back to the offices of the Japanese Broadcasting Corporation in a basket of laundry. In the labyrinthine Palace, the rebels became lost and confused. In the meantime, other groups went to the homes of Suzuki and Hiranuma, intending to kill them. Both were warned and escaped, although the rebels burned down their houses, which had managed to survive American air raids.

Early in the morning of 15 August, hearing that the Eastern District Army was quickly moving against them, the rebels gave up. They took to the streets, trying to broadcast their views, and by midmorning the leaders had committed suicide. By then the news that Japan had surrendered had been broadcast around the world. The Second World War was over.

Hirohito's speech was broadcast on radio throughout Japan at midday on 15 August, just a few hours after the collapse of the uprising (which came to be known as the Kyūjō incident). It was then picked up, translated, and spread throughout the world. The 'Jewel Voice Broadcast', as it is called, might not have had the effect it was intended to. It was written in the classical, literary form of the Japanese language, which most Japanese speakers struggled to understand, and it was made vague on purpose.

'To our good and loyal subjects,' the Emperor began, before offering a euphemistic, self-justifying, and at times comically understated explanation of Japan's situation. As the official English translation of the speech ran:

> We have ordered Our Government to communicate to the
> Governments of the United States, Great Britain, China and the
> Soviet Union that Our Empire accepts the provisions of their Joint
> Declaration. To strive for the common prosperity and happiness
> of all nations as well as the security and well-being of Our subjects
> is the solemn obligation which has been handed down by Our
> Imperial Ancestors and which lies close to Our heart. Indeed,
> We declared war on America and Britain out of Our sincere
> desire to ensure Japan's self-preservation and the stabilization of
> East Asia, it being far from Our thought either to infringe upon

the sovereignty of other nations or to embark upon territorial aggrandizement. But now the war has lasted for nearly four years. Despite the best that has been done by everyone – the gallant fighting of the military and naval forces, the diligence and assiduity of Our servants of the State, and the devoted service of Our one hundred million people – the war situation has developed not necessarily to Japan's advantage, while the general trends of the world have all turned against her interest.[9]

It was necessary to avoid the words 'defeat' and 'surrender', as to imply that the army and navy had failed was unacceptable. Saying outright that Hirohito's governments had thrown Japan into an unwinnable war with an alliance of much stronger powers was like-wise impossible, as the Emperor identified himself as the one who had declared war on the United States and Britain in the first place. Once the official narrative changed to place the blame on Tōjō and the other militarists for starting the war against the Emperor's wishes, the ulti-mate futility of the war was readily accepted in Japan. The reference to the war developing 'not necessarily to Japan's advantage', which comes across as laughable to English speakers, probably had two causes – the heavy editing of the original document and the difficulties of translating classical Japanese into English. Some sources suggest the original line was closer to 'the war situation gets worse and worse every day' but that this was edited for being too blunt. The Japanese translators, not being native English speakers, probably missed how absurd the line sounded. Even with the heavy censorship in wartime Japan, ordinary people would have been aware the situation was much worse than 'not necessarily to Japan's advantage'. John W. Dower gives the line as the war 'did not turn in Japan's favour, and trends of the world were not advantageous to us'.[10]

One of those trends was the 'new and most cruel bomb' threaten-ing the 'total extinction of human civilisation'. Hirohito reiterated Japan's justification for war, by expressing his 'deepest sense of regret to Our Allied nations of East Asia, who have consistently cooperated with the Empire towards the emancipation of East Asia'. He assured his subjects that he had been able to protect and safeguard the *kokutai*, and warned them against emotional outbursts and causing strife (perhaps with that morning's rebellion in mind). He finished by confirming that his thoughts were with the bereaved families of Japan's war dead, the wounded, and those who had lost their homes, and he called for unity in the face of hardship.

For Hirohito, the broadcast was the beginning of the revision of his image, both in Japan and overseas. He painted himself as a humanist and a pacifist, who had made the difficult decision to end the war in order to spare the world the horror of further destruction from nuclear weapons. Kido may have had a hand in this; certainly he was one of the authors of the broadcast.

In Japan, the broadcast was received initially with confusion, then with shock and disbelief. When it was announced that the Emperor would be speaking to the nation, many people assumed he would quash the rumours of surrender and make a final appeal to the people to fight to the death. This was what 28-year-old Aihara Yū, a farmer's wife in a small rural village in Shizuoka prefecture, expected when she was called back from the fields to hear the broadcast. The villagers gathered around the village's sole radio to listen to the single, state-run radio station.[11]

Like most of the people listening, she struggled to understand the message. There was a lot of static, the Emperor's voice was oddly high-pitched and his delivery halting, and he used a great many unfamiliar words and phrases. The villagers looked at each other for any sign of comprehension. Finally, an educated man from Tokyo, having sought refuge in the village from the bombing raids, said simply, 'This means that Japan has lost.'

Aihara's first thought was for her husband, who had been conscripted into the army and sent to Manchuria. All night, she prayed that he would not commit suicide but would instead return to her.

But it was very difficult to get any news from Soviet-occupied areas, and she heard nothing for three years. Then she learned that he had been killed in battle with the Red Army five days before the surrender.

For people who had been told to die 'like shattered jewels', the news of surrender was difficult to understand. Army propaganda emphasised the brutality of the Allied soldiers and insisted again and again that the people of Japan would be better off dead than falling alive into their hands. During the Battle of Okinawa some 150,000 of the island's 300,000 civilians had died, used as human shields by the Japanese Army or pressured to commit suicide. In extreme cases, parents killed their children, or children killed their parents. At Tokashiki Island near Okinawa, Kinjō Shigeaki recalled how he and his brother, both teenagers, acted when they knew the fall of the island was imminent:

> The first one we killed was the person who had given us life, our own mother. It was chaos so I don't remember the details. But I do remember using a cord . . . we tried to strangle her and . . . we tried many things but finally we killed her with a rock by hitting her in the head. We did a really brutal thing . . . I was 16, an age at which one is most impressionable. For the first time in my life I cried out loud, overwhelmed by grief. For the rest of my life, I will never cry like that again. Then we killed our younger siblings before we were to die. That's what the war made us do. We were manipulated.[12]

Across Japan, people who had been prepared to take similar steps now had to accept the reality of defeat. An abhorrence of war and an appreciation of the folly of taking on the United States and the British Empire began to take hold. In the space of a few weeks, one of the most militaristic societies in the world changed to one of the most pacifistic.

*

Japan had already been driven from some of its conquered territories by the Allies, but at the time of surrender the Japanese Empire
still ruled hundreds of millions of people in Japanese-occupied China,
Manchukuo, Korea, Burma, South-East Asia (modern Malaysia, Laos,
Vietnam, Thailand and Cambodia), and the East Indies (modern
Indonesia). In their rapid advance through the region in December
1941 and early 1942, the Japanese had captured some 140,000
Western prisoners and interned 130,000 Western civilians.[13] A complete unpreparedness to provide for so many captives, a profoundly
hostile attitude towards the surrender and Westerners generally,
and the collapse of communication and supply lines throughout
the Empire in the face of Allied attacks meant that most of the captives had been appallingly treated. As at August 1945, the Japanese
were holding throughout the Asia-Pacific 37,583 prisoners from the
United Kingdom, Commonwealth and Dominions, 28,500 from
the Netherlands and 14,473 from the United States.[14] Around a quarter
to a third of the total Japanese prisoners of war and civilian internees
had died in captivity.

Australia had lost 22,376 men and women captured in the
Pacific War, of whom 8,031 died through overwork, starvation, disease, mistreatment, or outright execution.[15] Many thousands of
Indians and Chinese were also being used for forced labour, but the
Japanese government refused to recognise them as prisoners of war.
Additionally, hundreds of thousands more Asian civilians, men and
women, were being held either as forced labourers, called *rōmusha*, or
as sex slaves in army and navy brothels through the comfort women
system.

At the time of the surrender, 12,000 British, Dutch and Australian
prisoners of war were being held in Changi Prison in Singapore.
Having built a pirate radio, at night they were able to listen to the
news and get some idea of what was going on with the war. One young
prisoner recalled the first rumours of surrender spreading among the
emaciated and starving men during the night of 10 August:

. . . shortly after midnight, the official and pirate radio operators had their greatest moment. Crouched in the darkness beside their faintly-glowing machines they heard from London the breath-taking news . . . the penalty for wireless operating was death. The only safeguard was secrecy. Yet who could rest all night with this stupendous fact bursting within him?

Out of the cells they came, dark shadows slipping along the corridors. 'Wake up'. Sleepers felt themselves shaken as the words were hissed in their ears.

'What's up?' Another party to unload rice, perhaps, or another move.

'The news – it's all over son, Japan is out. Down at home they are going mad and God-knows-everything.'

'Who says so?' a voice is heard drawling sarcastically. Everyone had been caught by rumours.

'It's right, I tell you. I heard it myself. The Nips are going for the Parker [i.e. reaching for a pen to sign the Instrument of Surrender]. You are free, digger. Think of it; free.'

In their excitement and desire to convince the doubters, the newsbringers were half-choking.[16]

The news was broken officially to the prisoners on 17 August. It took longer to reach remote work parties in Burma and Thailand, but spread quickly nonetheless. The reactions of guards and prisoners alike varied a great deal from place to place. At a camp on Mergui Road in Burma, the Japanese soldiers suddenly became friendly and distributed their stockpiles of food to the prisoners. At a large camp in Thailand, the news first came unofficially on 15 August from a Thai with a radio, then the prisoners were given the rest of the day off work. On 17 August, a prisoner from Australia's 2/2nd Pioneer Battalion recalled the exact moment of the official announcement:

At 11 a.m. the bugle sounded. It was not the lugubrious Japanese
call which for so long had been the summons to parade. It was the
old familiar 'Fall in A, Fall in B, Fall in every Company!' There
was a tremendous din of chatter as 2,500 British, Australians and
Americans took their places on the parade ground.

The senior prisoner in the camp, a British warrant-officer,
climbed on to a box in front of the parade. The noise subsided, and
the silence was complete as he spoke.

'Gentlemen!' he said, 'this is the happiest moment of my life.
The Japanese commandant has asked me to inform you that the war
has ended!'

For perhaps ten seconds there was not a sound. The unbelievable
had happened, and it first had to be believed. Then the air was
rent with sound as 2,500 men yelled and shouted as they had never
done before.[17]

At his headquarters in Manila, General MacArthur learned that
President Truman had appointed him Supreme Commander for
the Allied Powers and placed him in charge of the impending Allied
occupation of Japan. 'It was a notable day for me, too – I was made
Supreme Commander for the Allied Powers,' he wrote in his memoir,
*Reminiscences*. 'The felicitations, the congratulatory messages, and the
honours that were now heaped upon me were too numerous to count.
They gave me far too much credit.'[18] He then quoted them at length
for the rest of that page and most of the next. Indeed, *Reminiscences*
contains many such passages where MacArthur lists his own achievements and quotes the praise given him by others. Modesty was not
one of his attributes.

Douglas MacArthur was the son of an army captain. His father,
Arthur MacArthur, raised the Union Flag over Missionary Ridge
above Chattanooga, Tennessee, in November 1863. The army was
Douglas's life; he was born in an army hospital and he died in one. In
the interim he graduated first in his class at West Point and saw action

in the Philippines, the Veracruz Expedition, the First World War, and then, as Supreme Commander, in the Second World War in the Pacific. He had fought in battle with his own pistol, been decorated, and had never felt shy about wading into politics. Perhaps his most controversial moment was when he led the army against the Bonus Army, unemployed veterans who marched on Washington, D.C. in 1932, and cleared their camp out with tear gas. As Chief of Staff, he criticised pacifism, isolationism, and cuts to military spending. 'When we lost the next war, and an American boy, lying in the mud with an enemy bayonet through his belly and an enemy foot on his dying throat, spat out his last curse, I wanted the name not to be MacArthur, but Roosevelt!' MacArthur shouted at the new president when he proposed to cut military spending during the Depression.[19]

MacArthur captured the public imagination, in no small part due to his own self-promotion. Biographer Arthur Herman wrote that he was 'arguably the last American public figure to be worshipped unreservedly as a national hero', although that adoration mostly followed his victory in the Second World War.[20] He did not shy away from publicity. 'Arthur MacArthur was the most flamboyantly egotistical man I had ever seen, until I met his son,' recalled the elder MacArthur's aide.[21] After leaving the Philippines, General MacArthur famously announced, 'I shall return,' in a speech given from Australia. The US government asked him to amend it to: 'We shall return.' He refused.

In April 1942 MacArthur was appointed Supreme Allied Commander in the South-West Pacific Area. At the time, most of his troops were Australian. MacArthur found them unimpressive. Not appreciating either the difficulties of jungle fighting or the strength of the Japanese in Papua New Guinea, he did not understand why the Australian Army there was carrying out a fighting retreat rather than advancing.[22] Then, when American troops arrived in New Guinea in force, he didn't understand why they were struggling to make progress as well. He was an attacker, not a defender. But now he would take on a new role, as the effective leader of a defeated nation. He advised

Tokyo to send emissaries to him in Manila and to place a radio station at his disposal, and then began preparations to move his HQ.

In Australia, newspapers on 16 August carried the headlines 'Japan Surrenders' and 'Japanese War Minister Commits Hara-Kiri'. The rest of the day and the entirety of the next was given over to thanksgiving services and public celebrations.[23] After a mass prayer service in the Domain gardens, half a million people gathered in Sydney to watch the victory parade. In Melbourne, the city centre was closed to traffic, a hundred-gun salute was fired from Alexandra Gardens, and crowds gathered outside the Shrine of Remembrance. The editorial of the *Sydney Morning Herald* captured the feelings of surprise, relief and elation:

> Japan's defeat closes the most terrible and far-flung war in history. From the flame lit by the Nazis in 1939 their Asiatic confederates kindled the torch that set this half of the world ablaze. Few dared hope that the fire could be extinguished so quickly after Europe's deliverance. Not only have the Pacific nations been spared the prolongation of their sacrifices and sufferings – not only does heroic China see the end of her long agony – but the peoples of Europe will take fresh heart from the termination of the world war. Help which might have had to wait many months for Japan's collapse can now be given them, at a most crucial time, through the early liberation of shipping and supplies. This is not the least of the consequences of the resounding victory which the Allies have won. Everywhere the tasks of salvage and reconstruction can go forward; the whole world emerges, dazedly but thankfully, into the dawn of peace.[24]

In Canberra, there was little to be done. Parliament was not sitting, and no cabinet meeting was scheduled until 26 August. Prime Minister Ben Chifley had a bad cold. Public servants in the Treasury were occupied rewriting the recently released 1945–46 budget.[25]

Evatt, however, had his mind on other things. As early as 17 August, he spoke to the press to make two key points. First, he insisted that Australia should have a voice at the upcoming peace conference. He was thinking of the Paris Peace Conference that followed the First World War, although as it turned out, no such conference happened. The almost immediate falling-out between the Western Allies and the Soviet Union was probably a significant reason. Evatt's second point concerned the prosecution of war criminals, his personal war aim: 'Just as those men responsible for the atrocities in Europe are being hunted down, so will be those Japanese responsible for the atrocities and barbaric treatment of men and women in the Pacific area. These men are going to get their deserts, and Australia will see that they do.'[26]

To Evatt, 'these men' included the Emperor, and the cabinet was with him unanimously.[27]

# III

# RESPONSIBILITY

The Emperor's surrender broadcast was followed by bitter recriminations in Japan, particularly in the military, and unrest throughout the Japanese Empire. There were suicides, although nowhere near as many as expected. Probably no more, proportionally, than there had been in Germany after its defeat. Order broke down in the Japanese Army and Navy as soldiers and sailors turned on those responsible for enforcing the system of brutality against them. When a report appeared in the *Asahi Shimbun* newspaper about an abusive officer being lynched by his men, sixteen of the eighteen letters to the editor received by the paper supported the men.[1]

Australian Associated Press reported a case of Japanese soldiers holding their own war crimes trial on the transport back to Japan from Bangkok, finding thirty-three officers guilty of beating and punishing their subordinates unnecessarily and making excessive use of their authority.[2] The officers' baggage was thrown overboard and they were beaten so severely that thirty needed to be hospitalised. Army and navy stores were freely plundered. Kamikaze pilots who had been ready to fly suicide missions only a week before joined in the looting. Veterans found themselves stigmatised, particularly when reports of Japanese atrocities were published for the first time. The military, the nation's pride, had become its shame. It had not only lost the war but had dishonoured itself in doing so.

Preparations began immediately for the impending Allied occupation. There were fears Allied troops in Japan would kill, rape and plunder on a huge scale, just as the Japanese had done in China – fears perhaps most obviously held by veterans of the China campaigns. On 18 August, the Home Ministry sent secret orders to regional police chiefs to prepare 'comfort facilities' for Allied troops, based on the infamous Japanese military brothels.[3] These, however, would need to be staffed by volunteers. The forward-thinking Prince Konoe became involved in the project but the government did not manage it directly. Instead, senior ministers met with 'entrepreneurs' able to find women to staff the brothels and gave them 50 million yen. The entrepreneurs, delighted to be of service, gathered outside the Imperial Palace and gave three shouts of *Tennō Heika Banzai!* Not, perhaps, the discreet outcome the government had hoped for. Ultimately, enough young women were found to staff the brothels based on two inducements. One was the same patriotic message of self-sacrifice which had inspired Japanese men to sacrifice their lives in battle, the other was the simple promise of food and shelter.

Outside Japan, some 6.5 million Japanese soldiers and civilians had to be repatriated from the erstwhile Japanese Empire. This was probably the largest ever movement of people by sea, and possibly largest ever co-ordinated movement of people in history.[4] Even defeated, Japan's soldiers were still scattered from Korea to Papua New Guinea, often on remote islands or deep in the jungle. Many of them refused to accept the reality of surrender and held out; some kept the promise of the Greater East Asia Co-Prosperity Sphere alive by joining Indonesian, Malayan and Vietnamese independence movements, and others could simply not be found. Furthermore, Japan had not been able to keep its troops supplied with food and medicine, and many soldiers, prisoners of war and civilians were near starvation or badly sick from tropical diseases.

The Allies knew the condition of the prisoners and civilian internees was generally poor, but otherwise they had little information about them. On 28 August, Allied aircraft dropped leaflets on the known camps. On one side was an English message to the prisoners: 'To all Allied prisoners of war – the Japanese forces have surrendered unconditionally and the War is over.' It advised them to wait at their camps for relief to reach them. And if they were starved or underfed, it told them not eat to large quantities of solid food.[5]

Over the next several weeks, Allied soldiers reached the POW and internment camps, including those in Manchukuo and Japan itself. The prisoners were given bread – many had not tasted it for three years. The Australian government knew the prisoners and internees would have essential information about Japanese war crimes, and issued questionnaires to them. Evatt also decided to send his war crimes investigator, Justice Sir William Flood Webb of the Queensland Supreme Court, to gather information.

Born in 1887, Webb was the son of a storekeeper who went to school first in Brisbane, then Warwick.[6] His teachers recognised his ability and coached him to a job in the Queensland public service. He studied law to advance his career and was called to the bar. He was favoured by the Labor governments of T.J. Ryan and Ted Theodore, appointed Solicitor-General of Queensland, and then a justice of the Queensland Supreme Court. He was appointed Chief Justice in 1940, and then Chairman of the Australian Industrial Relations Council by the federal Labor government in 1942.

The Allies had formed the United Nations War Crimes Commission (UNWCC) in London in October 1942 with the goal of investigating war crimes and gathering evidence. On 7 October 1942, President Roosevelt confirmed that these investigations and trials would be an Allied war aim. As 1942 turned to 1943, the war shifted decisively in favour of the Allies, making it look increasingly likely that they would prevail and be able to bring their plans for the prosecution of war crimes to reality.

Eager to play an important role in the process, Australia applied to join the UNWCC on 8 December 1942 as an original member. Over April to July 1942, an Australian Army inquiry headed by Brigadier A.R. Allen had already investigated and produced a report on the massacre of surrendered Australian soldiers at Tol Plantation in New Britain in January 1942. On 30 January 1943 the army began issuing orders for evidence of war crimes to be collected. On 31 March, Minister for the Army Frank Forde wrote to Prime Minister Curtin requesting 'the appointment of a judicial authority who would take the evidence and submit a full report on this matter'.[7] The Prime Minister, in turn, referred this task to Evatt as Minister for External Affairs. Evatt selected Webb, and on 23 June 1943 commissioned him to investigate Japanese war crimes against civilians and prisoners of war in Papua New Guinea.

Australian troops had contained the Japanese advance at Milne Bay and along the Kokoda Track by September 1942, and as Australian and American units advanced into Japanese-occupied territory over the next few months they found ample evidence of Japanese atrocities against captured Allied soldiers and Papua New Guineans. Particularly at Milne Bay, where special Japanese naval parties had been sent ashore to ruthlessly suppress resistance through terror. There Allied units found thirty-six dead Australian soldiers and fifty-nine dead Papuan villagers, many horribly mutilated. Women had been raped, tied down, slashed open with bayonets, or impaled. One woman had seventy used condoms scattered around her. Australian prisoners were bound to trees and used for bayonet practice, or bound and tied to leashes and used as running targets. None had died quickly. Paul Ham wrote in *Kokoda* that 'the prolonged torture and apparent pleasure with which they dispatched their victims suggests that the Australians were fighting, not soldiers, but a criminally insane mob of serial murderers and rapists.'[8] At the battle, the Australians had taken six or seven prisoners. The Japanese had killed all theirs.

Webb interviewed Australian and American servicemen and civilians throughout North Queensland and Papua New Guinea, and gathered captured Japanese documents and reports of the interrogation of Japanese prisoners. In March 1944 he issued a 450-page report, along with affidavits from 471 witnesses. The report included accounts of the massacres of surrendered Australian soldiers at Tol and Waitavalo plantations in New Britain, the torture and killing of captured soldiers and Papua New Guineans at Milne Bay, the execution of eleven missionaries at Buna, Popondetta and Guadalcanal in August 1942, the practice of using live Australian and American prisoners for bayonet practice in the Owen Stanley Range, mutilation of the dead and cannibalism, and the execution of Australian bomber pilot Flight Lieutenant W.E. Newton VC at Salamaua on 29 March 1943.

The Australian government, concerned about the families of servicemen in Japanese captivity, did not release the report to the public. In November 1944, Evatt made a statement to the House of Representatives summarising the inquiry and its findings and confirming the government had grounds for prosecuting Japanese war criminals based on: 'evidence of massacre, torture and maltreatment of Australians, both military personnel and civilians, and of the New Guinea natives, as well as evidence of numerous lesser breaches of the rules of warfare. These rules, had been solemnly laid down in the Geneva Conventions of 1906 and 1926 and the Hague Convention of 1907, all of which Japan signed and ratified, and the Prisoners of War Convention 1929, which Japan signed and which it publicly undertook shortly after the war broke out to observe on a basis of reciprocity.'[9]

Evatt decided to commission Webb to produce another report, this time with a mandate to investigate any war crimes committed by Japanese forces against Australians regardless of location. Webb accepted the commission on 24 February 1944, conducted hearings with 112 witnesses between 14 August and 20 October, and delivered a 104-page report on 31 October. While the hearings were being held

American submarines rescued twelve Australian prisoners of war who had been on the transport *Rakuyō Maru*, torpedoed and sunk off Hainan on 12 September. They gave evidence of widespread killing and mistreatment of prisoners of war on the Burma–Siam Railway. Other witnesses reported the torpedoing of the hospital ship *Centaur* by a Japanese submarine off Brisbane on 14 May 1943, as well as further crimes in Papua New Guinea.

The Second Webb Report was forwarded to the UNWCC, and Webb himself was sent to London shortly afterwards to address the UNWCC directly. Over January and February 1945, he presented specific cases to the UNWCC's Facts and Evidence Committee, after which the committee listed for arrest seventy-three individuals and all the members of ten units, and listed for further investigation an additional eighteen individuals or units yet to be identified. Webb also conferred with the British government on appropriate trial procedures, and advised that he favoured relaxing the rules of evidence to allow hearsay and documents. The British agreed, confirming that the royal warrant being prepared reflected this. Webb returned to Australia and his regular duties with the Queensland Supreme Court until summoned again by Evatt.

The Australian government issued the terms of reference for the third Webb inquiry on 3 September 1945. It also appointed Justice Alan Mansfield of the Queensland Supreme Court and Judge Richard C. Kirby of the New South Wales District Court to assist Webb. The terms were similar to those for the second inquiry, but were expanded to include war crimes against not only Australians, but also any citizen of an Allied nation, and three further war crimes were added to the thirty-two already defined. Two of them, cannibalism and mutilation of the dead, fitted within the other class-B and -C war crimes. But the third gave Webb and his co-inquirers the power to investigate class-A war crimes, specifically the 'planning, preparation, initiation or waging of a war of aggression or a war in violation of international treaties, agreements or assurances, or participation in a common plan or conspiracy for the accomplishment of any of the foregoing'.[10] This represented a significant broadening of Webb's role.

The three commissioners were then dispatched to former Japanese-occupied areas in the Philippines, the Netherlands East Indies and British Borneo by air. They found that most of the prisoners had been released and returned home, but were nonetheless able to take statements from 248 witnesses, including Australian and Indian prisoners of war and Dutch and British civilian internees. Additionally, 12,000 of the questionnaires issued to released Australian prisoners of war and civilian internees were filled out and returned.

As many as 25,000 Japanese Army and Navy personnel were arrested on suspicion of war crimes, but fewer than 6,000 were charged.[11] There were so many suspects only a minority could be brought to trial. As the Chairman of the UNWCC, Lord Wright of Durley, put it, 'the majority of war criminals will find safety in their numbers'.[12]


Amid all this, the Emperor showed little sign of feeling any personal responsibility, either for the war or Japan's ignominious defeat. On 9 September, he wrote a letter to his eldest son, who had been sent away from Tokyo because of the air raids. He explained to the twelve-year-old Crown Prince Akihito why, in his view, Japan had lost and he had been forced to surrender. The letter was long on self-justification and short on self-reflection. Unlike his grandfather, the Meiji Emperor, Hirohito wrote, he had not been blessed with great generals and admirals. And those generals he did have had failed to appreciate the technological advantages enjoyed by the British and Americans. In the end, he had had no choice but to accept the Potsdam Declaration in order to protect the sacred regalia of the Imperial house. Moreover, he wrote, had the war continued, most of his subjects would have died.[13] Hirohito's mention of the sacred regalia before the potential deaths of millions seems to reflect his obsession with them.

The Japanese government took a similar line. From the start, it held a seemingly contradictory position whereby the Emperor had the power to end the war, yet otherwise bore no responsibility for it. Seven hours after the surrender broadcast, on the evening of 15 August, Prime Minister Suzuki gave a radio address where he told the people of Japan, 'His Majesty gave the sacred decision to end the War in order to save the people and contribute to welfare and peace of mankind.'[14] He praised the Emperor's benevolence and assured him of the nation's sincere apologies. It was not clear what the people were meant to be apologising for.

This address was one of Suzuki's final acts as prime minister. On 17 August, he resigned. In an unusual move, Hirohito appointed his uncle-in-law, Prince Higashikuni Naruhiko, to replace him. Never before had a member of the Imperial family served as prime minister; it had always been considered unwise to tie the monarchy too closely to government policy. Now, however, the situation was exceptional. Higashikuni took the same line as his predecessor. On 28 August, he announced that 'repentance of a hundred million' was the key to rebuilding Japan. Speaking of the Emperor, he said that 'we deeply regret to have caused him so much anxiety'.[15]

It was a truly extraordinary pronouncement. People who had lost their sons, fathers, husbands, brothers and uncles in a war fought in the Emperor's name, who had had their homes and possessions burned in bombing raids, and who were now reduced to eating a starvation diet of pancakes and dumplings made of barley flour bulked up with husks and sawdust, were expected to apologise to the Emperor for upsetting him. It was a remarkable request, but the Japanese government, then busying itself with destroying incriminating documents, did not seem to think it unreasonable.

While Hirohito mused on defeat, the US prepared to occupy Japan. Its two main goals were to ensure that Japan posed no further threat to America and its allies and to transform it into a democracy. These were, of course, interlinked. MacArthur arrived in Tokyo on

30 August. He had been warned against coming before his army, as there were three Japanese divisions in and around the city and nobody knew exactly how they would react. But as usual, he could not be dissuaded. As they approached the airfield, MacArthur's aides went to strap on their side-arms. He told them not to: if the Japanese were going to attack them then handguns would be useless. As MacArthur strode down the plane's steps smoking his foot-long corncob pipe and wearing his aviator sunglasses, he looked every inch the Hollywood American general. When he and his aides were driven into the city, they were met with an alarming sight – the roads were lined with thousands of Japanese soldiers with fixed bayonets. They stood calmly with their backs to the road as MacArthur's car drove past; it wasn't clear whether this was a snub or a guard of honour.

MacArthur was a well-informed choice for his new role (as he assured the readers of his memoir), being both familiar with the Orient and no stranger to military occupation. He had served as a junior officer in the engineers in the Philippines between 1903 and 1904, and as a brigadier general he spent the winter of 1918–19 as part of the American force occupying the Rhineland following the end of the First World War. He was critical of both these efforts and was determined to do better in Japan. Part of his plan was to rely on the government and the Emperor to administer the country. When Germany had surrendered in May, the Allies abolished the German government and divided the country into occupation zones. In Japan, the government was to be kept in place. But it would answer to MacArthur. 'Your authority is supreme,' President Truman had told him.[16]

MacArthur established himself in the imposing grey Dai-ichi Life Insurance Building, one of the few large structures in central Tokyo left undamaged by bombing. Arguably no American had ever held more power, but he settled easily into his new position. Officially he was the Supreme Commander for the Allied Powers, or SCAP, and over time SCAP became the name for the American administration in Tokyo. From there, the term became adopted more widely. For example, the broken English used by the Japanese to talk to American troops became known as 'SCAPanese'. To the Japanese MacArthur was the *Gaijin Shōgun*, or Foreign Shogun, and his appointment marked a reversion to the pre-1868 system of government where the Shogun was the effective ruler of Japan and the Emperor was cloistered away in Kyoto.

Japan had never been ruled by a foreigner before, so the situation was potentially volatile. But MacArthur and the Japanese quickly took to each other. He was, in many ways, well suited to Japan, and the Japanese were well suited to him. MacArthur was so caught up in his own destiny he was practically incorruptible, and so self-assured that he felt no need to pander to anyone, either in Tokyo or Washington. He had no malice towards the Japanese and he sought no revenge. He was a distant, aloof figure who showed little emotion and rarely left his Tokyo bubble or mixed with ordinary Japanese. But this was just the type of leader the Japanese had come to expect. MacArthur's age (he was in his late sixties during the occupation) and his string of military victories also lent him authority. And, not unimportantly, he looked the part.

While the American occupation forces in Japan (and later those of Australia, Britain and other Commonwealth nations) were responsible for outbreaks of robbery, murder and rape, it was on a far smaller scale than the Japanese had feared, and MacArthur personally took a hard line against the mistreatment of Japanese civilians. Immediately upon arrival, he ordered in thousands of tonnes of food. To ordinary Japanese he was therefore a magnanimous figure, triumphant in battle and gentle in victory, a perfect embodiment of the warrior spirit of *Bushidō*. And the Emperor had told them to do what he said.

The general had two immediate tasks: the organisation of the formal surrender ceremony scheduled for 2 September and the arrest of the main political and military leaders suspected of war crimes. By 14 August, the US government had already drafted a surrender instrument and communicated to the UK, China and the Soviet Union its plans to have a formal ceremony where representatives from their governments would sign it. The British accepted the plan, nominated Admiral Sir Bruce Fraser, and communicated this to the Dominions.

This triggered another minor dispute between Evatt and the American and British governments. The Australian government argued for separate representation of the Dominions in their own right at the ceremony. This was, on the face of it, not unreasonable. Australia and New Zealand had been in the war against Japan for far longer than the Soviet Union, and Australia had been America's principal ally in the South-West Pacific. Without waiting for a British response to their proposal, the Australian government nominated General Thomas Blamey as its representative on 14 August, and communicated the decision to London. New Zealand, naturally, agreed, and nominated Air Vice Marshal Leonard Monk Isitt as its own representative. There was a brief squabble, upon which Australia escalated its request (or demand) directly to the American Secretary of State and MacArthur. MacArthur assented and went further, also accepting the inclusion of delegates from Canada, France and the Netherlands.

Understandably, finding delegates on the Japanese side was even harder. Sending the Emperor was out of the question. Likewise Prime Minister Higashikuni, being a member of the Imperial family, was also out. Prince Konoe, minister without portfolio in the Higashikuni cabinet, was powerful enough to decline. So Shigemitsu Mamoru, the foreign minister, ended up representing the government. He had taken over the office from Tōgō Shigenori on 17 August, having been an opponent of the militarists and a member of the Konoe–Kido group pushing for the end of the war. Shigemitsu had lost a leg in a bomb attack by a Korean independence activist in Shanghai in 1932, and so walked on a wooden one with the aid of a cane.

Finding a delegate from the Japanese Army was harder still. In the end, it fell to an unwilling Umezu, who threatened to commit *seppuku* in protest. Only the personal intervention of the Emperor compelled him. Shigemitsu and Umezu were joined by nine other delegates – three each from the army, navy and foreign ministry.

The ceremony took place in Tokyo Bay on the deck of the battleship USS *Missouri*. One of the US Navy's largest and most modern battleships, it made for a formidable display of American military power. And in a symbolic touch, it was named after President Truman's home state. The Allies made a further show of force by filling the bay with their warships and having aircraft fly in formation overhead, impressing on the Japanese the futility of further resistance.

The Japanese delegates left Tokyo at 5 am, travelling under the utmost secrecy in case militarist rebels should attempt to disrupt their mission. On either side of the road, Tokyo and Yokohama lay in ruins. 'The ghastly sight of death and desolation was enough to freeze my heart,' wrote Kase Toshikazu, a Japanese Foreign Ministry delegate. He reflected on just how closely Japan had come to annihilation: 'The waste of war and the ignominy of surrender were put on my mental loom and produced a strange fabric of grief and sorrow.'[17] As they approached the port where they would board a boat to take them to the *Missouri*, they passed soldiers of the US Eighth Army disembarking to begin the occupation of Japan.

There is a well-known photograph of the Japanese delegates grouped together on the deck of the *Missouri*. At the front is Shigemitsu, leaning heavily on his cane, having struggled to climb the stairs with his wooden leg. Next to him is Umezu, looking as unreadable as always (the Allies called him 'Stoneman'). The others were standing behind.

Kase looked around and saw journalists clustered 'monkey-like' on scaffolding and against railings. Under their intense and hostile gaze he felt like a guilty schoolboy awaiting the headmaster. He saw rising sun flags painted on the wall with tally marks next to them, and realised with a shock that they were a record of destroyed Japanese ships and planes.

MacArthur was waiting for them. 'I had received no instructions as to what to say or what to do,' he recalled. 'I was on my own, standing on the quarterdeck with only God and my conscience to guide me.'[18] He had brought with him British General Arthur Percival and American General Jonathan Wainwright. Percival had surrendered the British forces at Singapore in February 1942, and Wainwright had surrendered American forces in the Philippines a few months later. Both men looked gaunt and haggard from three years in Japanese captivity.

Shigemitsu sat down at the table, took up the pen, and hesitated, unsure where to sign. An aide directed him. He signed the Instrument of Surrender at 9.04 am; Umezu signed next, then MacArthur, who gave one of his pens to Percival and one to Wainwright. The representatives of the nine allies followed, led by Admiral Chester Nimitz for the United States. The process went smoothly save for one hitch – Colonel Lawrence Moore Cosgrave of Canada, blinded in one eye by a First World War injury, signed on the wrong line of the Japanese version.

MacArthur then gave a lengthy speech on the importance of peace. Kase was impressed, describing MacArthur as 'a shining obelisk in the desert of human endeavour that marks a timeless march onward toward an enduring peace'.[19] Naturally, MacArthur quoted Kase in his memoir.

Following the principal ceremony at Tokyo Bay, others were held throughout the Pacific. From Tokyo, Blamey flew to Morotai to receive the surrender of Lieutenant General Teshima Fusataro of the Japanese 2nd Army on 9 September. After receiving Teshima's sword and signing the instrument, he gave a speech that left his listeners in no doubt of his position towards the Japanese:

> In receiving your surrender I do not recognise you as an honourable and gallant foe, but you will be treated with due but severe courtesy in all matters. I recall the treacherous attack upon our ally, China, in 1938 [sic; he meant 1937]. I recall the treacherous attack made

upon the British Empire and upon the United States of America in December 1941, at a time when your authorities were making the pretence of ensuring peace. I recall the atrocities inflicted upon the persons of our nationals as prisoners of war and internees, designed to reduce them by punishment and starvation to slavery. In the light of these evils, I will enforce most rigorously all orders issued to you, so let there be no delay or hesitation in their fulfilment at your peril.[20]

In Japan, the new occupation authorities moved quickly to arrest major war criminals. On 11 September, SCAP announced that it had ordered the arrest of thirty-nine suspects, including everyone who had been a member of the Tōjō cabinet at the time of the Pearl Harbor attack. This included the recently replaced Foreign Minister Tōgō Shigenori, who had opposed the war even though it was his signature on the declaration, along with Tōjō himself.

The former prime minister had been living quietly in his house in suburban Tokyo since his fall from power in July 1944. But as soon as the news that his arrest had been ordered was out it was immediately mobbed by American and Japanese journalists. A little past four in the afternoon, American soldiers surrounded it. Tōjō appeared at the window, yelled something in Japanese, slammed the window shut and disappeared. Shortly afterwards there was a gunshot. The soldiers broke down the door and found Tōjō in his study, where he had shot himself in the chest. Ironically, he had used an American handgun, perhaps taken from a downed airman. A suicide note lay on the table.

But the bullet had missed his heart, and he was alive and conscious enough to give a rambling statement to the Japanese reporters. Different papers reported different words, but the sentiment was the same. One account ran: 'I am sorry for the peoples of Greater East Asia. I shoulder the whole responsibility. I hope they will not go amiss in dealing with the situation. The Greater East Asia war was a just war. With all our strength gone, we finally fell. I did not want to stand before the victor to be tried as the vanquished. This is my own case. I wanted to kill myself at one stroke. I first thought of using my sword to kill myself, but instead I used a revolver, for fear I might fail and revive.'[21]

As it turned out, he did fail and revive. Taken away promptly in an ambulance, he was saved by MacArthur's personal doctor with a transfusion of blood from an American soldier. He recovered enough the next day to thank his captors for their care.

In the whole episode, Tōjō had done himself no favours. Many people had expected him to kill himself when the war ended, as Anami and others had done. After all, it was Tōjō who published the Field Service Code which drummed the doctrine of 'death before capture' into every Japanese soldier. When he didn't commit suicide, they assumed he was going to take some role in defending Japan in whatever court or tribunal the Allies would foist on them. His suicide attempt shortly before his arrest made him look like a coward, a man who was willing to live with defeat provided he didn't have to bear the consequences of it, and his failure to kill himself properly was met with scorn. Writer Takami Jun wrote in his diary: 'Cowardly living on, and then using a pistol like a foreigner. Why did General Tōjō not die right away as Minister for War Anami did? Why did General Tōjō not use a Japanese sword as Minister for War Anami did?'[22]

Most Japanese people had little sympathy for their wartime leaders. Throughout September and October, editorials and letters to the editors of newspapers (now subject to American rather than Japanese censorship) freely called for their arrest and prosecution. The Higashikuni cabinet even briefly considered holding its own trials, but MacArthur vetoed the idea. It was possibly a lost opportunity.

MacArthur was not only thinking of the trial of Japan's leaders in Tokyo. Shortly after the arrests of Tōjō and the others, he ordered the arrest of two of the most infamous (to the Allies) Japanese commanders, General Yamashita Tomoyuki and Lieutenant General Homma Masaharu. Yamashita, the 'Tiger of Malaya', had inflicted on the British Empire what was possibly its worst ever military defeat at Singapore. Homma, the 'Beast of Bataan', had done likewise to the Americans in the Philippines. Homma had been the overall commander of the troops responsible for the Bataan Death March in April 1942, where some 5,000 to 18,000 American and Filipino prisoners of war were shot or bayoneted. After Malaya, Yamashita had been placed in command of Japanese forces in the Philippines when, between February and March 1945, thousands of Japanese Army and Navy troops sacked and burned the city of Manila, raping thousands of women and girls and massacring as many as 100,000 Filipino civilians.

For MacArthur, the Bataan Death March and the Sack of Manila were personal. He had lived in the Philippines on and off for many years, he had been a field marshal in the Philippine Army, and he knew and loved the city of Manila and its people. Bataan was his defeat, and the men who suffered in the march, Filipino and American alike, were his men. Furthermore, he had a very traditional view of the role of the soldier, based on chivalry. To him, soldiers who mistreated and killed civilians and prisoners brought the entire profession of soldiering into disrepute. His profession.

However, neither Homma nor Yamashita made for a particularly satisfactory villain. Homma's American defence lawyers found him to be a cultured, erudite, mild-mannered man with a distaste for violence. He had travelled extensively in Europe and America, spoke fluent English, held pro-Western views, and had opposed going to war against Britain and the United States. He had even served with the British Army on the Western Front in the First World War and been awarded the Military Cross. In his defence, he maintained he had consistently issued orders for the good treatment of prisoners and civilians and had had no knowledge of the atrocities at Bataan. Additionally, he'd had no power to transfer or dismiss his subordinates, who were appointed directly by Tokyo. Yamashita, for his part, pointed out that he had only been given command in the Philippines once Japanese forces were dispersed throughout the country and therefore outside his control, and throughout his career he had consistently given orders for the humane treatment of both civilians and prisoners.

The Allies had originally been working on the assumption that the prosecution of war criminals would be co-ordinated centrally by the UNWCC. To this end, Evatt and Webb had spent two years busily presenting hundreds of pages of evidence to the committee. On 3 October, however, MacArthur announced that Yamashita would be brought to trial immediately before an American military court in Manila.[23] On 6 October, Lord Wright advised Evatt that it would not be necessary for the UNWCC to list suspects before the Allies could try them.[24] The original plan had allowed for suspects to be sent to the country where their alleged crimes were committed so they could be tried there in accordance with the Moscow Declaration. But it had become apparent that this was impractical, and so the Allies began holding ad hoc class-B and -C trials in the areas where their armies were.

On 18 June 1945, the British government had issued a royal warrant (a type of executive order) allowing for the trial of war criminals in both the European and Pacific theatres of war, wherever British forces were operating.[25] On 17 September, the British commenced trials of the staff of the Belsen concentration camp in Germany. America indicted Yamashita on 25 September. The Australian *War Crimes Act 1945*, allowing for the Australian trials to commence, was pushed quickly through parliament in October and the first trials commenced in November.

Yamashita's trial began on 29 October 1945, Homma's on 3 January 1946. Both were charged with being responsible for the atrocities carried out by the officers and men under their command, based on the doctrine of command responsibility. Both resolutely maintained their innocence, and both were robustly defended by their American lawyers. One member of Homma's defence team criticised MacArthur's influence over the trial, saying 'no man should be placed in the position of being in essence accuser, prosecutor, defense counsel, judge, jury, court of review, and court of final appeal. He should particularly not be placed in this position where he is a military commander who was defeated by the accused in a campaign out of which the charges arose.'[26] The court threw out the argument, but Homma's lawyers were undaunted. Another criticised the relaxation of the rules of evidence and the admission of hearsay, saying it would be 'shocking to anyone trained in Anglo-American law to see a man sentenced to death after trial by affidavit and deposition'.[27]

At Yamashita's trial, his defence argued that 'the Accused is not charged with having done something or having failed to do something, but solely with having been something'. On the idea of holding a commander responsible for the actions of their troops, they went on to say, 'American jurisprudence recognizes no such principle so far as its own military personnel are concerned . . . No one would even suggest that the Commanding General of an American occupational force becomes a criminal every time an American soldier violates the law . . . [O]ne man is not held to answer for the crime of another.'[28]

In spite of their lawyers' best efforts, Homma and Yamashita were both convicted and sentenced to death, Yamashita by hanging, and Homma, perhaps as a concession to the arguments made in his defence or in response to an appeal by his wife, by shooting. MacArthur reviewed both their sentences and approved them. Admitting it was not easy to pass judgement on a defeated foe, he wrote he could find no mitigating circumstances in Yamashita's case. He reiterated the responsibility of all soldiers to protect the weak and unarmed and uphold the reputation of the military profession, and wrote that he intended to follow through with his pledge to hold those responsible for atrocities to account. 'No new or retroactive principles of law, either national or international, are involved,' he wrote. 'The case is founded upon basic fundamentals as immutable and as standardized as the most natural and irrefragable of social codes.'[29]

With regards to Homma, MacArthur again wrote of the 'repugnant duty of passing final judgement on a former adversary'.[30] However, 'no trial could have been fairer than this one, no accused was ever given a more complete opportunity of defense, no judicial process was ever freer from prejudice . . . [I]f this defendant does not deserve his judicial fate, none in jurisdictional history ever did.'

Yamashita was hanged on 23 February 1946, Homma shot on 3 April.

Their trials established the principle of command responsibility, and for this reason are the only class-B and -C trials in the Pacific to be considered significant today. They raised an interesting question – how far up the chain of command did command responsibility go?

'Soldiers of an army invariably reflect the attitude of their general,' wrote MacArthur in respect of Homma, bringing the atrocities of the Bataan Death March home to him.[31] Did this mean that subjects of an empire could also be said to reflect the attitudes of their emperor?

# IV

# THE EMPEROR
# IN THE DOCK?

From the moment it received confirmation of the Japanese surrender offer, the Australian government was determined to see the Emperor prosecuted for the atrocities carried out by his armies. Evatt remained at the lead of the Australian push, and the rest of the cabinet agreed with him. 'The deliberate view of senior members of the Cabinet is that the Emperor cannot be regarded as a mere puppet, a suggestion that has been put forward in some quarters,' reported *The Argus* on 14 August. 'Emperor Hirohito, it was pointed out, had brought Japan into the war and had waged war without mercy.'[1] The Australian community was also broadly supportive. An August 1945 poll found that 50 per cent of Australians favoured indictment of the Emperor for war crimes.[2]

Nor was Evatt alone internationally. Lord Wright of Durley, who represented Australia on the UNWCC in London, backed him. And luckily, Wright had been appointed chairman of the commission in 1945. Webb and Mansfield had also come to the conclusion that the atrocities they had investigated were so widespread that responsibility for them must go to the very top. Webb was tasked by Evatt with preparing an initial list of suspects for Australia to recommend prosecuting in the upcoming class-A trial in Tokyo. On 19 September,

Lord Wright cabled Evatt, advising him to get Webb to submit this list without delay. 'Presumably Chief Justice Webb will consider including Hirohito as Head of the Army, and as a knowing participant in systematic and barbaric practices in actual warfare,' he added.[3] Webb agreed. On 26 September, he wrote to Evatt supporting the Emperor's indictment on these grounds. His reasons can be summarised as:

1. As far as he was aware international law did not give immunity to sovereigns or their advisers who abet or connive at breaches of the laws of war by their soldiers and people.

2. The atrocities were so widespread and terrible the Emperor must have been aware of them.

3. Having taken no steps to prevent them, he must have abetted or at least approved of them.

4. Having been able to end the war in August 1945, he would have presumably been able to end it sooner.

5. Perhaps most forcefully, Webb wrote, 'it would be a travesty of justice, seriously reflecting on the United Nations, to hang or shoot the common Japanese soldier or Korean guard while granting immunity to his sovereign perhaps even more guilty than he.'

In its quest to indict Hirohito, Australia quickly found it had little support from its allies. There were calls for the Emperor's indictment in Wellington, but these never became official New Zealand government policy. New Zealand opted not to submit its own list of war criminals, and when press reports claimed that both Australia and New Zealand had listed Hirohito as 'war criminal number one' this was denied by the New Zealand government.[4]

The British government was strongly in favour of keeping the Emperor in power. On 11 August, the Australian government cabled London, appealing to Lord Addison to 'resist any claim of the

Emperor or on his behalf to immunity from punishment, to support us in bringing him to justice and to deprive him of any authority to rule from the moment of surrender. We submit that any other course will effectually prevent the emergence of a democratic and peace-loving regime in Japan.'[5]

In his response on 17 August, Lord Addison described indicting the Emperor as a 'capital error': 'We desire to limit commitment in manpower and other resources by using the Imperial throne as an instrument for the control of the Japanese people and indictment of the present occupant would, in our view, be most unwise.'[6]

The American government sent secret instructions to MacArthur asking him to begin investigating the Emperor as a suspect, but this never went further.[7] Only the Soviet Union came around to Australia's view, and it did so much later, long after the opportunity to prosecute the Emperor had passed. But even without support, Australia decided to push ahead. At the very least, the *New York Times*, the Japanese Communist Party, and a number of political figures throughout the world had supported prosecuting the Emperor.

Hirohito was not particularly active in his own defence. Kido and Higashikuni both discussed abdication with him, and he briefly considered leaving the Chrysanthemum Throne to pursue a career in marine biology. Studying and classifying sea life no doubt appealed to his quiet and meticulous character. The Emperor's supporters, however, strongly opposed his abdication and sprang to work keeping him as Japan's head of state. Foreign Minister Shigemitsu Mamoru, who had signed the Instrument of Surrender on Japan's behalf, took the lead. He assured the Emperor that the military had hijacked Japan's 'essentially democratic' spirit, and that democracy would unify the Emperor's thoughts with his subjects' wishes.[8]

Hirohito uncritically accepted this argument, even though it completely contradicted the core position held by his governments for the better part of a decade. As John W. Dower wrote: 'Had Shigemitsu been so foolhardy as to openly declare that the national polity [*kokutai*] had been compatible with Western-style democracy one month earlier, in all likelihood he would have been jailed (or committed to a mental institution); and in all likelihood the Emperor would have observed his disappearance in silence, just as he had the repression of other critics of the policies and orthodoxies proclaimed in his name.'[9]

Having thoroughly prepared the Emperor, Shigemitsu then went to the Americans. In an audience with MacArthur on 3 September, he argued that Japan's emperors had always been pacifists. Hirohito had opposed the war from the start, he completely understood the Potsdam Declaration, and he enjoyed the continued admiration of his subjects. In short, it was better to leave him in power and govern the country through him. It was the conclusion that MacArthur had already arrived at. Shigemitsu was able to go back to the Emperor with the good news that SCAP would be receptive to his co-operation. Under Soviet pressure, SCAP would later indict Shigemitsu as a class-A war criminal.

MacArthur did not go to the Imperial Palace, but waited at his headquarters for the Emperor to come to him. And, a little over three weeks after Shigemitsu's visit, the Emperor came. At 10 am on 27 September, a convoy of cars and motorcycles pulled up outside the Dai-ichi Life Insurance Building. Wearing a morning coat and top hat, an uncomfortable-looking Hirohito stepped out of a Daimler limousine. MacArthur did not meet him at the car.

Coming into the building, the Emperor and his entourage were met by MacArthur aides Bonner F. Fellers and the 'exuberant Kabuki lover' Faubion Bowers.[10] Fellers had loved Japan since he first visited the country in 1922 – an unusual attitude for an American officer to hold through the Second World War – and was fiercely hostile to the idea of prosecuting the Emperor. 'To the masses will come the realization that the gangster militarists have betrayed their sacred Emperor,' he wrote to MacArthur. 'Hanging of the Emperor to them would be comparable to the crucifixion of Christ for us.'[11]

Hirohito and the two Americans bowed to each other and then shook hands. Bowers took the Emperor's hat, a gesture he no doubt intended to be hospitable, but Hirohito looked slightly alarmed. He was probably a little apprehensive about having his possessions taken from him by Americans.

MacArthur then entered the room. In contrast to the Emperor, he was dressed casually in a summer khaki uniform with no coat or tie. He greeted his visitor warmly, saying, 'You are very, very welcome, sir!' as he approached him. Bowers was surprised; he had never heard MacArthur address anyone as 'sir' before. The general and the Emperor both bowed and shook hands, the Emperor bowing so deeply that the handshake took place above his head. MacArthur then whisked the Emperor off to a separate room with his interpreter, Okamura Katsuzō, leaving Fellers and Bowers to make awkward conversation with Hirohito's retainers. Bowers had probably never witnessed a kabuki performance quite like this one.

MacArthur gave his guest a cup of coffee and a cigarette. As he took the cigarette, the Emperor's hand shook slightly. 'He was nervous and the stress of the past months showed plainly,' MacArthur recalled.[12]

Perhaps Hirohito wrote an account of the meeting in his diary, but if he did, it has never been released. Okamura wrote one, although it did not surface for three decades. Therefore it was MacArthur's version of events that was for a long time the only public record of the meeting. His version, which he released to the press and recorded in his memoir, claims Hirohito began the meeting by saying, 'I come to you, General MacArthur, to submit myself to the judgement of the powers you represent as the one to bear sole responsibility for every political and military move taken by my people in the conduct of the War.'[13] MacArthur noted that the Emperor had stopped short of admitting the war was unjustified, but nonetheless he was moved by Hirohito's courage. After speaking with him for a few minutes, he concluded that the Emperor had a 'more thorough grasp of the democratic concept' than most Japanese and would make a good partner for the democratisation and demilitarisation of Japan.

Okamura's account of the meeting, while broadly similar, differed in a few key respects.[14] According to him, the Emperor never accepted responsibility for the actions of his people or government, but said he had wanted to avoid war and regretted its outbreak. MacArthur seized on this comment and praised the Emperor for it, and then did most of the talking for the rest of the meeting. The men left the room after about forty minutes – the Emperor had left his coffee untouched but was visibly more relaxed. They then posed for a photo before MacArthur took the Emperor back to his car.

The photo, when it was published, caused a minor scandal in Japan. MacArthur was standing with his hands on his hips, much taller than the Emperor, older, and more confident. The Emperor stood with arms to his sides, not as nervous as when he arrived but still looking far from comfortable. The Japanese press had been subject to strict rules about how and when the Emperor could be photographed, and these had now been thrown out the window. For the first time, the Japanese people saw the Emperor as an ordinary, middle-aged man. And now, a man subservient to a more powerful one.

Nonetheless, both sides left the meeting satisfied, and MacArthur and the Japanese Home Ministry both later issued positive statements about it. Relieved, Hirohito told Kido about MacArthur's compliments. Kido, too, was happy. The Emperor and Empress began sending gifts to the MacArthurs, and they would meet again several times. From that point on, SCAP was resolutely opposed to prosecuting the Emperor.

SCAP pushed ahead with the political reforms. The Civil Liberties Directive of 4 October 1945 lifted restrictions on freedom of speech and association, and removed 4,000 people associated with militarism from positions of power.[15] When they learned the members of the Communist Party were to be freed from prison, all the members of the Higashikuni cabinet resigned in protest. But they could do nothing to prevent it, and the new government of liberal pro-American aristocrat Baron Shidehara Kijūrō released 3,000 political prisoners. Japan's communist leaders walked free after eighteen years in Sugamo Prison, and some joined the calls to indict the Emperor for war crimes.

MacArthur then threw himself into the task of turning Imperial Japan into a democracy. Democratic ideas were not completely foreign to the Japanese. During the reign of Hirohito's father, the Taishō Emperor (1912–26), Japan went through a period called the Taishō Democracy. The electoral franchise was broadened and the Diet and civilian politicians grew more powerful. True, this was because the Emperor was physically and mentally disabled and lived a life of isolation, and it did not outlive him, but SCAP nonetheless had a base to work on.

On 4 October, MacArthur met with Konoe to discuss a new constitution for Japan. Konoe went away and began working on one. In the meantime, SCAP undertook further reforms. In December, Shinto was disestablished as the national religion and trade unionism legalised. The Imperial Rule Assistance Association (IRAA), the single official political party that had held power throughout the war, was disbanded and multi-party politics restored. Japan had held an election in April 1942 but no political parties other than the IRAA were permitted to contest it. MacArthur now worked towards a new election in April 1946, in which all parties could participate and women could vote for the first time.

This raised the possibility of the newly legalised Communist Party winning power. To discourage this, MacArthur introduced land reforms, having the government buy large landholdings and distribute them to the farmers. It was a radical policy, particularly coming from the conservative Republican MacArthur, but he argued it was necessary to remove the appeal of communism in Japan. The great *zaibatsu* corporate conglomerates began to be broken up.

MacArthur quickly became popular in Japan. He began to receive dozens of letters every day, most thanking him for his benevolence. He was sent hundreds of gifts, from prints to bonsai trees. He was praised for his Buddha-like compassion and Confucian wisdom. People confessed their past support of militarism and promised to work now towards a peaceful and democratic Japan. Some of the reactions seemed absurdly over the top. A cultural association in Kobe sent MacArthur a picture of Jesus delivering the Sermon on the Mount, with a letter suggesting that his introduction of democracy to Japan was a similar event. There was a report of an old man putting up a picture of MacArthur in his house next to his picture of the Emperor and worshipping it, apparently accepting the new democratic regime but failing to appreciate he was no longer required to worship its leader.[16] What all of this must have done for the Supreme Commander's already over-inflated ego can only be imagined. But in all his endeavours, he enjoyed the support of the Emperor.

The Australian government was also determined to play a role in the democratisation and demilitarisation of Japan. An agreement between the American, British and Australian governments saw a British Commonwealth Occupation Force take responsibility for several prefectures in southern Honshu and Shikoku. BCOF included an Australian brigade group, three RAF squadrons and three RAAF squadrons; a New Zealand brigade group and a RNZAF squadron; a British brigade; a British-Indian brigade, and a Royal Indian Air Force squadron.[17] All the land forces were to be under Australian command and all the naval forces under British command, and the Australian government appointed Lieutenant General John Northcott as BCOF's commander. The force began its deployment on 21 February 1946 and at its maximum strength, on 31 December 1946, it comprised 37,021 personnel, including 11,918 Australians. It was responsible for 49,000 square kilometres of land and 9 million of Japan's 77 million people.[18] But to Australia, democratisation also meant removing the militarist, totalitarian Emperor.

From 24 September to 22 October, the Australian Department of External Affairs assembled a list of sixty-four suspected class-A war criminals, including the Emperor. Webb endorsed it for pragmatic reasons but he now expressed reservations about prosecuting the Emperor. 'As regards the Emperor, my attitude is as stated in my cable of 26th September, but if it be within my province I suggest . . . need for Hirohito's case being decided at the highest political and diplomatic levels'. He elaborated:

> Out of deference to the British view-point, as indicated to me, but by no means pressed . . . I respectfully suggest that we omit the Emperor from this tentative list. Of course, the Emperor's immense power, as shown by the prompt way he ended the war, carried a commensurate responsibility to prevent the war, or, if he could not do that, to see that it was conducted in a civilised way. The defence that he was head of a State is negatived by the Four Power Pact of 8 August last [i.e., the Charter of the Nuremberg Tribunal], which also negatived the defence that he was a puppet, which is only the defence of superior orders. Further, any defence of ignorance must fail unless he shows he discharged his duty to inquire. But, even if he is guilty, there is a way out if one is desired on the ground of expediency, which does not concern us – a pardon for informing on his associates in war crimes. Fifty years ago in Queensland a doctor, who headed a blackbirding expedition and personally committed murders, escaped by turning King's evidence while his minions went to gaol or to the scaffold . . .[19]

But the acting Head of External Affairs, J.W. Burton, disagreed. 'The question of taking action for bringing to trial any person on our list will require inter-governmental decision on high level,' he wrote. 'But this is not necessary for listing of any person by Commission for further investigation and position of Emperor on list is in keeping with declared Australian Government policy.'[20]

On 26 October, the complete Australian list was sent to the UNWCC. Hirohito's name appeared at the top. On 8 December, Mansfield boarded a plane to London to speak in support of the list. On arrival, he lodged a seventeen-page document with the commission. In support of indicting the Emperor, he argued that:

1. The Emperor gave his approval to the invasion of Manchuria and the advance on Chinchow in 1931, the crossing of the Great Wall in 1935, the invasion of China in 1937, and the attacks on the Western powers in 1941.
2. As the Meiji Constitution gave the Emperor the power to declare war, he must have approved of the war.
3. He was under no duress and could have refused to go along with the militarists, supporting his protests 'by abdication or hari-kari [sic]'.[21]

The UNWCC reviewed the documents but made no decision. In the meantime, the next round of additions to the list of suspected class-A war criminals was announced in Tokyo on 19 November. There were eleven, including General Koiso Kuniaki, prime minister from 1944 to 1945; General Matsui Iwane, commander of the Japanese armies at the Nanking Massacre; Matsuoka Yōsuke, the Foreign Minister who signed the Tripartite Pact with Germany and Italy; and General Araki Sadao, one of the early advocates of militarism. One defendant, General Honjō Shigeru, committed suicide before his arrest.[22]

As with the first round of arrests, there was not much public sympathy for the suspects. George Atcheson, representative of the US State Department in Tokyo, wrote to the department in mid-December saying that 'the general mood of the Japanese people is strongly in the mood of fixing war responsibility on the major suspects. Bitterness on account of Japan's defeat and an apparently growing realisation that Japan should not have undertaken aggressive warfare has created a strong resentment against the Japanese leaders.'[23]

In general, these leaders were willing to play along with the SCAP scheme to protect the Emperor. One, however, was not. In October Prince Konoe made a public statement declaring the Emperor had responsibility for the war and should abdicate. Konoe's lack of team spirit and flamboyant self-promotion was of little liking to the American authorities. An American general who interviewed him several times described him as 'a rat' who was willing to sacrifice his Emperor to save himself.[24]

It was quickly becoming clear there was not room in Japan for both Konoe and MacArthur. On 1 November, SCAP publicly disassociated itself from Konoe's constitution project, as liberal and democratic as his ideas were, and began writing a constitution of its own. Konoe did not back down but instead went further, claiming credit in an interview for the drive to democratise Japan. This was unacceptable to SCAP, which was seeking to get the approval of the Japanese public for democratisation by promoting the idea that it was coming from the Emperor directly. On 6 December the work of the prosecution began in earnest when the newly appointed chief prosecutor Joseph B. Keenan arrived in Tokyo with forty aides. The same day, a new list of eight suspects was released by SCAP. It included both Konoe and Kido, now cast as being among the militarists who had misled the Emperor.[25]

Konoe had no intention of being put on trial. On 16 December, shortly before he knew he was to be arrested, he committed suicide. Unlike many of his contemporaries, he opted for the speed and surety of a cyanide pill. An American journalist found copies of Edward Gibbon's *Decline and Fall of the Roman Empire* and Oscar Wilde's *De Profundis* and *Ballad of Reading Gaol* on his veranda, where he had apparently been reading shortly before his death. The following passage in *De Profundis* was underlined: 'Society as we have constituted it will have no place for me: but nature, whose sweet rains fall on the unjust and just alike, will have clefts in the rocks where I may hide and secret valleys in whose silence I may weep undisturbed.'[26]

Keenan responded by saying that anyone who killed themselves 'did so as a result of an unsound mind or an unsound and unwarranted estimate of American justice'.[27] Australian intelligence officer George Caiger criticised him for this, arguing he had misunderstood the Japanese in general and Konoe in particular:

> Christians give the excuse of 'unsound mind' for suicide, but it
> needs no excuse in Japan. Suicide is 'right' not 'wrong' to the
> Japanese. Far from condemning suicide as a crime, the Japanese
> think it is the correct action to take in certain circumstances . . .
> Can you expect a man with [Konoe's] background, three times
> Prime Minister, to submit to being baited in a dock, subjected to
> the tender mercies of news films and newspapers? As it was, one
> account of his death, as it appeared in Australia, played up his
> private life. Surely his sex life was not the most important feature of
> his career. In any case, why should a non-Christian be pilloried for
> not observing Christian rules?[28]

Even after his death, Konoe was a virtual defendant at Tokyo, named repeatedly by the prosecution as a senior member of the militarist conspiracy.

Kido did not commit suicide like his friend, but instead resolved to go willingly to the dock to defend the Emperor. At their final, emotional meeting on 10 December, Kido urged the Emperor to abdicate once the time was right – presumably meaning once the occupation had ended. The Emperor listened intently but did not take the former Lord Keeper of the Privy Seal's advice. By then, he had other advisors.

Nevertheless, Kido was willing to go to great lengths to protect the Emperor. He even discussed with a close friend the idea of pleading guilty and taking full responsibility for the war on himself – responsibility for a war he had opposed at the start and played a key role in ending. His friend talked him out of it, saying that Kido's close association with the Emperor would make the Emperor also look guilty. Instead, between 24 December and 23 January, Kido handed over his valuable diary to the prosecution. With a little bit of light editing, perhaps, it gave the impression that the Emperor was blameless. The prosecution took it up eagerly and it became their bible.

The various countries making up the International Military Tribunal for the Far East (IMTFE) were then busily appointing judges and prosecutors to the court. Webb was offered the position of Australian judge, and accepted on 13 December. He therefore withdrew from his third inquiry, noting he had not yet made any findings against a major war criminal. But the fact that he had been investigating war crimes was controversial in itself. Justice Brennan of the Supreme Court of Queensland held the view that it was therefore inappropriate to appoint Webb as a judge: 'What will foreign nations think of such a state of affairs? Could British justice allow a detective who had investigated crimes and made findings against a class preside as judicial officer to try other offenders of the same class? The issue will surely be raised, and Sir William Webb may be placed in a false and invidious position and Australia made to look stupid.'[29]

Brennan was satisfied personally as to Webb's impartiality, but was concerned about the perceptions of British justice overseas. He suggested there were other 'excellent and brilliant jurists' who could be appointed. Evatt hit back in defence of his decision, pointing out that Webb had not been investigating the particular crimes he was now trying. Specifically, he had been investigating minor war crimes in the South-West Pacific; now he would be trying major ones.[30] But Brennan would not be the last person to question Webb's eligibility.

On 10 January, Mansfield was appointed as the Australian prosecutor, leaving Kirby to finish the Third Webb Report. Published on 31 January, it gave further evidence of Japanese war crimes but made

no findings or recommendations in relation to responsibility for starting or waging the war.

As 1945 turned to 1946 the issue of the Emperor's responsibility was
still unresolved. The Australian government was still pushing for his
indictment while SCAP was working equally hard to integrate him
into a Japanese democracy. In his New Year's Day address, Hirohito
formally renounced his divinity. Sort of. The English translation of
the speech had him saying that the ancient connection between the
Japanese people and the Chrysanthemum Throne was not based on
the 'false conception that the Emperor is divine'.[31] It was implied,
although not said outright, that this false conception had been spread
by the militarists in their propaganda. The Japanese wording was
vaguer still, with even educated readers often failing to recognise the
obscure kanji characters the drafters had used for 'divine'. While it
was enough to satisfy both SCAP and the Japanese government,
others were a little more cynical. According to a popular joke among
the occupying troops, the Emperor stopped pretending to be a god
when he discovered that MacArthur actually was one.

The Supreme Commander, for his part, was making no claims
to divinity but was steadily advancing the plan to bring Japan's wartime leaders to trial, less the Emperor. On 1 January 1946 he issued the
charter of the IMTFE, allowing the court to be formed and indict-
ments to be issued. Around the same time, he wrote to his superiors
in Washington, D.C. warning them of the negative consequences of
prosecuting the Emperor. 'It is quite possible that a minimum of a
million troops would be required which would have to be maintained
for an indefinite number of years,' he advised them.[32]

In a surprising move, MacArthur appointed Webb as president
of the tribunal. His motives for this are unknown, but he may have
been influenced by Webb's existing experience and the desire to
placate what had been a troublesome ally. Unsurprisingly, Webb's

appointment went down very well in Australia. *Argus* correspondent Crayton Burns wrote approvingly of Australia's new leadership for
the Commonwealth in East Asia, a fulfilment of the British government's commitment to Dominion equality and autonomy contained
in the 1926 Balfour Declaration and the 1931 Statute of Westminster.
He wrote: 'Lieutenant-General Northcott is leader of all the British
Occupation Forces in Japan; Mr Macmahon Ball is representative on the Allied Council not only of Australia but of the United
Kingdom, India, and New Zealand as well; and Sir William Webb,
Australia's War Crimes Commissioner, is president of the Allied
tribunal for the trial at Tokyo of Japanese major war criminals. For
the first time Australia speaks, not for herself alone, but for the whole
British Commonwealth.'[33]

But MacArthur was showing no sign of moving towards Australia's
point of view regarding the Emperor, and SCAP continued to find
Hirohito amenable to their plans. Having established he wasn't a god,
they now intended to present the Emperor to the Japanese people as a
constitutional monarch. He was furnished with a picture book on the
British royal family and a plain civilian suit, overcoat and homburg
hat, and sent on tours of the country to see his subjects up close. On
19 February 1946, he went on his first public outing, to Yokohama,
touring a factory and a black market. He found the black market
'interesting'.[34]

These tours were, particularly at the start, excruciatingly awkward. Hirohito's subjects were extremely nervous about meeting him,
and he had little ability to put them at ease. Commonly he would ask
people where they were from. They would answer, 'Yokohama, Your
Majesty,' or 'Hokkaido, Your Majesty,' and he would nod and respond
with '*Ah, so*' ('Oh, is that so?'). There would then be an uncomfortable
moment of silence when neither could think of anything more to say
to the other, before the Emperor moved on to the next person. Soon
even the Japanese press was making jokes about 'Emperor Ah-So'.
Political cartoonists, for their part, depicted him as a broom, alluding

to the fact that everywhere he visited was invariably cleaned up, no matter how war-ravaged it had been.

Hirohito's tours, while they wouldn't have given him an accurate picture of how his subjects lived, achieved their effect. Photos of the Emperor freely meeting his subjects were published in the newspapers (always taken from an angle to conceal the large guard of American soldiers with fixed bayonets accompanying him everywhere), and his shyness and awkwardness even raised sympathy and compassion among observers.

These tours briefly halted in March when the Emperor was laid down with a bad cold. Propped up in bed on a stack of pillows and wearing white silk pyjamas, he took the opportunity to dictate a series of monologues to assembled aides. In them he claimed that 'as a constitutional monarch under a constitutional government, I could not avoid approving the decision of the Tōjō Cabinet at the time of the opening of hostilities', and also 'I was virtually a prisoner and powerless'.[35] Only in suppressing the rebellion in 1936 and ending the war in 1945 did he exercise authority. After they were finished in April, these monologues were given to MacArthur's aide. It was unnecessary, as MacArthur had already resolved to defend the Emperor, but after the Emperor's death they were released as *Shōwa Tennō Dokuhakuroku* and provided a valuable, if hardly impartial, insight into the Emperor's experience of the war.

While Hirohito dictated his memoirs, MacArthur's aides worked in the Emperor's favour. In March 1946, Fellers had a meeting with Admiral Yonai. Yonai had not been indicted, but he was working closely with the defendants. According to an interpreter, Fellers told him: 'It would be most convenient if the Japanese side could prove to us that the Emperor is completely blameless. I think the forthcoming trials should be the best opportunity to do that. Tōjō, in particular, should be made to bear responsibility at his trial. In other words, I want you to have Tōjō say as follows: "At the Imperial Conference prior to the start of the war, I had already decided to push for war even if His Majesty the Emperor was against going to war with the United States.'"[36]

They were painting a different picture to the one Hirohito himself had inked out with his comment in the Jewel Voice Broadcast: 'We declared war on America and Britain out of Our sincere desire to ensure Japan's self-preservation and the stabilization of East Asia . . .'

The Australian government was now practically alone in doggedly continuing to push for the Emperor's indictment. When the UNWCC resumed after its Christmas break on 9 January 1946, the American and British delegates kept putting off a vote on the Australian list.

An 18 January report from Associated Press noted that the Australian scheme to indict the Emperor was 'causing some embarrassment' at SCAP.[37] With the UNWCC unable to come to a decision on the Australian list, Lord Wright decided to pass the question on to the IMTFE prosecution. Accordingly, on 13 February, the UNWCC resolved that the question of who should and should not be prosecuted be referred to Tokyo, and washed its hands of the matter.[38]

The Australians were not yet willing to give up. When Mansfield went to Tokyo to take up his position on the IMTFE prosecution, he took the list with him. On 6 April, he cabled Evatt from Tokyo: 'The inclusion of the Emperor as defendant is now being discussed. There is at least a prima facie case of guilt which can be proved. This is not contested by the Allied prosecutors. When the final decision is taken, political considerations will probably prevent votes in favour of inclusion. I am pressing strongly for inclusion . . .'[39]

On 9 April, Evatt responded, confirming his instructions: 'As previously advised to you, if you are satisfied that there is a case, it is left entirely to you to act upon considered view. At same time you should avoid any public protest if decision is against indictment or if MacArthur vetoes proposal. You are familiar with the facts and it has always been our view that if the facts warranted indictment,

Hirohito is no more entitled to special immunity than the common soldier who inflicted such cruel barbarities against Allied soldiers and civilians.'[40]

By then, however, it was too late. The previous day Mansfield had moved a motion to prosecute the Emperor. Keenan opposed it, and none of the other prosecutors were willing to back Mansfield. The minutes recorded the decision:

> Suggestions were invited as to any additions to the List. Mr Justice Mansfield proposed that the Emperor be included. A discussion ensued, after which it was agreed that owing to various considerations outside the Prosecution, it would be an error to indict the Emperor.
>
> AGREED not to include the Emperor.
>
> AGREED To prepare the Indictment of the 26 Defendants whose names had been decided upon.[41]

At a meeting of the Far Eastern Commission in Washington, D.C. on 3 April 1946, New Zealand representative Sir Carl Berendsen confirmed that he believed the Emperor was a 'war criminal of the deepest dye', but said he felt the decision to prosecute him should be made at the highest levels.[42] The commission agreed, and sent instructions to MacArthur a few weeks later advising him not to indict the Emperor without specific instructions.[43]

When the Australian list and the Far Eastern Commission's instructions ended up on MacArthur's desk in mid-April, he had already decided against prosecuting the Emperor. Writing of the 'tragic consequences' which would follow the 'unjust action' of indicting the Emperor, including the need to impose military government on Japan and deploy a million troops to fight a guerrilla insurgency, he filed the list.[44] In his memoir, he took credit for talking Washington out of prosecuting the Emperor himself, but it doesn't appear that the American government was ever committed to the idea.

On 18 June, Keenan formally announced that there were no grounds to indict the Emperor. In their cells in Sugamo, his loyal supporters were overjoyed. Shigemitsu composed a poem in celebration. Kido could finally breathe easily. 'With this, my mission is complete,' he wrote.[45]

# PART TWO

# MINISTERS

The class-A war crimes trial in Tokyo

# V

# TOKYO VIA NUREMBERG

The International Military Tribunal for the Far East opened on 3 May 1946 in the auditorium of the Imperial Army Officers' School at Ichigaya in central Tokyo. The symbolism of holding the trial in an Army Ministry building was not lost on SCAP, and besides, few other large buildings had survived the Allied air raids. The structure had been renovated at a cost of almost 100 million yen, stripped of the coating of black paint given to protect it during the war, and fitted with central heating and air-conditioning. 'Much care had gone into fitting the courtroom with dark, walnut-toned panelling, imposing daises, and convenient perches for the press and motion-picture cam-eramen,' wrote the *Time* magazine correspondent. 'The klieg lights suggested a Hollywood premiere.'[1]

Bert Röling, the Dutch judge, had a similar impression. He described the scene as 'Hollywoodesque', like a 'huge-scale theatrical production'.[2] Richard Hughes, writing for the *Courier-Mail*, called it 'a glittering, impressive, and distinctive show, staged with a star cast and absolutely no regard for expense'. Even so, he snidely remarked that the defendants 'could be livelier, more animated or more ruthless-looking', and with the exception of Webb, the black-robed judges were 'disappointing'.[3]

The court was open to the public, and many Japanese journal-ists and ordinary residents of Tokyo came to watch. 'Packing the dress circle are goggle-eyed Japanese onlookers, for whose enlightenment and entertainment this colossal, stupendous production of Western justice has been specially staged,' Hughes wrote.[4] As they entered, they were searched for weapons by military police.

The nine judges sat at a bench at the head of the court, beneath the flags of the constituent countries. Webb, as president, was in the centre. Aside from Australia and the United States, MacArthur had invited appointments from New Zealand, the United Kingdom, Canada, China, the Netherlands and France. New Zealand appointed Justice Erima Harvey Northcroft of the Supreme Court of New Zealand, a First World War artillery officer and military lawyer in the New Zealand Army. Northcroft arrived in Japan with Webb, and the two men initially got on well, playing golf together. However, the relationship soured once the trial began.

The United Kingdom sent a Scottish judge, Lord Patrick. An air ace in the First World War, he had been shot down and captured by the Germans, and remained troubled by the wounds to his legs for the rest of his life. The Canadian appointee was Edward Stuart McDougall, Justice on the Court of King's Bench of Quebec. A First World War veteran like Northcroft and Patrick, he was briefly a politician in a government of the Liberal Party of Quebec.

China appointed Mei Ju-ao, who had studied law in the US and had a Juris Doctor from the University of Chicago. His familiarity with the English language and Anglo-American law was a significant advantage, and he worked well with the other English-speaking judges.

The appointments of the French and Dutch governments reflected their colonial concerns in Asia, although both men would prove to be interesting additions to the court. The French judge was Henri Bernard, who had acted in various legal appointments throughout France's African colonies. He had been either a magistrate or prosecutor in Conakry (Guinea), Dakar (Senegal) and Bangui (Central African Republic). At one point, he was nearly unseated for upholding the rights of Africans against French settlers.[5] He had been involved in European war crimes trials in France prior to his appointment. Bernard could speak English conversationally but not fluently, and so struggled a little to follow the proceedings and to interact with his fellow judges. Röling, the Dutch judge, was Professor of Law at the University of Utrecht. He had an extensive background in criminal law and criminology but no experience of international law, and his appointment seems to have been based entirely on a brief stint as a professor of Indonesian law. He proved to be a close and keen observer of the entire process, and much of what we know about the inner workings of the Tokyo Trials comes from his writings.

The Soviet Union sent Major General Ivan Michyevich Zaryanov, a member of the Military Collegium of the Supreme Court of the Soviet Union, the body that conducted Stalin's show trials in the 1930s. Zaryanov could speak no English (except, apparently, 'Bottoms up!') and so relied on a translator. His devoted loyalty to Stalin seems to have been a significant factor in his appointment. In contrast to the black robes of the other judges he wore the uniform of a Red Army general.

The American judge was originally John Patrick Higgins of the Massachusetts Superior Court. He resigned in July 1946 to return to the US and was replaced by Major General Myron C. Cramer, Judge Advocate General of the US Army. Cramer had experience in planning the war crimes trials in Europe.

There were only four judges at Nuremberg, one from each of the United States, the United Kingdom, the Soviet Union and France (plus an alternative for each primary judge). Additionally, it was obvious from their choices that the major powers placed less importance on Tokyo than on Nuremberg. For example, the US sent Attorney-General Francis Biddle and a federal judge, John J. Parker, to Nuremberg, and a state judge to Tokyo. Many more countries would have a say at Tokyo, and this would present challenges.

Once the court had been formed, it was decided to add two more judges – from the Philippines (newly independent) and India (moving towards independence). This was an important acknowledgement of the right of post-colonial nations to play a role in trying Japanese war crimes committed against Asians. But both specific appointments proved controversial.

The Philippines sent Delfín J. Jaranilla, who was eminently qualified for the role. He had studied law in the United States, was a former attorney-general of the Philippines, and had been Judge Advocate General in the Philippine Army during the war. Röling described him as 'totally Americanised', which in the circumstances could have been either an advantage or a disadvantage.[6] The issue with his appointment was one of impartiality – he had been a prisoner of war of the Japanese and forced to endure the Bataan Death March, and had seen his comrades shot or bayoneted by Japanese soldiers. In an ordinary criminal court the victim of a crime would not be permitted to act as a judge of it, and there was a good argument that this principle should apply to an international war crimes tribunal. As it turned out, Jaranilla took the hardest line when it came to sentencing.

Indian judge Radhabinod Pal posed a completely different, more complicated, and perhaps more serious problem. On the surface the Bengali jurist was an excellent choice to represent India. A judge of the High Court of Calcutta and president of the University of Calcutta, he was well versed in British law and had written extensively on Hindu law. He had never written a dissenting opinion, and seemed sound in every way. However, the Indian government failed to realise he was an Axis sympathiser. He was a strong supporter of Indian independence, a pan-Asianist, and a fierce anti-communist – in short, the very sort of person to whom Japan's pitch for a Greater East-Asia Co-Prosperity Sphere had been made. It is not known whether he had any personal connection with Subhas Chandra Bose and his Japanese-backed Provisional Government of Free India. But he practised law alongside Subhas' brother, Sarat Chandra Bose, in Bengal, a known hotbed of anti-colonial sentiment. Röling concluded that Pal had made up his mind against the prosecution from the start.[7] Pal and Jaranilla – one believing the defendants were innocent and the other calling for them to be hanged – represented two extremes of Asian views of Japanese imperialism.

Before Pal and Jaranilla arrived, the judges had already decided to accept a majority judgement. This would, however, prove impossible, even without taking Pal's and Jaranilla's views into account.

Webb opened the tribunal, speaking, according to the AAP correspondent, 'in clear, measured tones'.[8] He said that 'there has been no more important criminal trial in all history', that the court 'should consider the cases without fear or favour', and the high rank of the defendants would 'entitle them to no more consideration than if they had been privates'. MacArthur had asked to make an opening statement in the courtroom, but Webb, rightly fearful of the perception of political interference, refused.

The twenty-eight defendants sat across from the judges in two rows, listening to Webb's address via Japanese translators through headphones. Translation would prove to be a huge problem at Tokyo, not only between Japanese and English, the court's two official languages, but also between those languages and others spoken by the witnesses, such as Chinese and Mongolian. At Nuremberg, the court had managed to run on simultaneous translation, where statements were translated immediately so everyone in the courtroom could hear what everyone else was saying in real time. This was, however, between related languages like English, French and German, and the close historical and cultural associations between the European countries meant many translators were available. Japanese and English are totally unalike, and few people could speak both well enough to translate complex legal arguments. As a result, initial experiments in simultaneous translation failed at Tokyo, and everything had to be translated sentence by sentence, with a red light flashing before witnesses to tell them to slow down when the translator fell behind.

Needless to say, the proceedings at Tokyo went far more slowly than those at Nuremberg.

There had originally been twenty-six defendants, but the Soviet Union had pushed for the inclusion of Foreign Minister Shigemitsu Mamoru and General Umezu Yoshijirō, perhaps because of their well-known anti-Soviet views.[9] There were fifteen Japanese Army officers, three navy officers, nine bureaucrats and one author. The last was Ōkawa Shūmei, accused of being 'the Japanese Goebbels' and distributing anti-Western and pro-militarist propaganda. Drawing direct comparisons between the wartime Japanese and German governments was fraught with peril, and this analogy overstated Ōkawa's importance. Nonetheless his bestselling 1926 book, *Japan and the Way of the Japanese* (*Nihon oyobi Nihonjin no michi*), had laid out a path for Japan to reject Western ideas, make itself the leading power in Asia, and take on the United States and Britain. 'Before a new world appears there must be a deadly fight between the powers of the west and the east,' he wrote in 1925.[10] So he found himself in the second row of defendants, immediately behind Tōjō.

Regardless of his culpability, Ōkawa had no intention of seeing the proceedings out to the end. While the arraignments were being read, he leaned forward and slapped Tōjō in the back of the head, prayed loudly while making wild gestures, unbuttoned his shirt, and shouted gibberish (or a combination of several languages – he was an erudite and multi-lingual man). Tōjō simply grinned. Later on, after Ōkawa slapped Tōjō in the head a second time, he was dragged from the court, shouting more gibberish behind him.[11] US Army psychologists ruled that he was unfit to stand trial, and so the twenty-eight defendants became twenty-seven. Quite likely, Ōkawa was feigning madness to show his contempt for the trial, and his antics did little for the gravity of the proceedings.[12] According to the *Time* magazine correspondent, while Nuremberg had an air of Wagner, Tokyo was more reminiscent of Gilbert and Sullivan: 'Prosecutor Keenan (who looks like [American comic actor] W.C. Fields) had to deal with the opéra

bouffe element which the West so often finds in the Japanese character. The chief Jap defendant, Hideki Tōjō . . . flirted with an American
stenographer. Hiroshi Ōshima, wartime ambassador to Germany,
affected the dandy . . . Shumei Ōkawa, onetime Manchurian Railway
official, carried comic indifference into broad buffoonery.'

It was, he concluded, 'a third-string road company of the
Nuremberg show'.[13]

The Palace of Justice at Nuremberg cast a long shadow. The IMTFE
was based in most respects on the International Military Tribunal
(IMT), the court at Nuremberg which had been set up to try the military and political leaders of defeated Germany, and the Tokyo Trial
would naturally be compared at every stage to its older sibling.

Both tribunals were only conceived of quite late. The Potsdam
Declaration promised 'stern justice' for Japanese war criminals, but
did not specify what form such justice would take. Even as close
to the end of the war as July 1945, the Allies were not entirely sure
themselves. The idea of an international war crimes tribunal holding
individuals responsible was then novel, and it was not certain that it
would be practical.

There were certainly grounds for arguing the atrocities carried out by the German and Japanese armies were unlawful, not just
immoral. Over the late nineteenth and early twentieth centuries,
most of the world's nations had entered into binding multilateral
treaties regulating the conduct of militaries in wartime. The first was
the 1856 Paris Declaration Respecting Maritime War, followed by the
1864 Geneva Convention for the Amelioration of the Wounded in
Time of War, and most importantly, the Hague Conventions of 1899
and 1907. These last two were a series of treaties and declarations,
which were adopted piecemeal but nonetheless enjoyed wide acceptance. The most significant of them were the 1899 Convention for the
Pacific Settlement of International Disputes, regulating 'just cause'

for warfare, and the 1899 and 1907 Conventions Respecting the Laws and Customs of War on Land, regulating the conduct of combatants in warfare. These conventions established rules regarding surrender and prisoners, prohibited denying quarter, and rejected the justification of military necessity as an excuse for breaches of the laws of war. However, the Hague Conventions did not address punishment for breaches of the laws of war, leaving this to individual states. It would become apparent quickly that this was a weakness.

The victorious Allies had attempted to establish a program of war crimes trials following the First World War. They acknowledged there was no precedent for prosecuting a head of state for war crimes, but took the view that not acting against Kaiser Wilhelm II of Germany would allow the generals and admirals to plead the defence of superior orders, all the way up to the Kaiser himself. The committee therefore recommended that he be prosecuted before an international tribunal for provoking an unjust war and then waging that war illegally through unrestricted submarine warfare and the shooting of hostages. Most infamously, German armies had sacked the Belgian city of Dinant and summarily executed 674 of its inhabitants, including women and children. They also sacked Leuven, killed 248 residents, and burned its university library and priceless collection of medieval and Renaissance manuscripts.

The plan to try the deposed Kaiser, then in exile in the Netherlands, was supported by France but produced a sharp division between the Allies. The United States sought legal advice, and then rejected the proposal on the grounds that no law in 1914 prohibited aggressive war or unrestrictive submarine warfare, and no basis existed for holding a sovereign criminally responsible for a breach of the Hague Conventions on 'the laws of humanity'. The Americans held to the principle in American law that sovereigns were immune from the jurisdiction of other sovereigns.

The two sides finally reached a compromise, written into Articles 227 to 230 of the Treaty of Versailles, which included a request to the government of the Netherlands to extradite the Kaiser so he could be tried by an international tribunal, not for a crime, but for a 'supreme offence against international morality and the sanctity of treaties'. The tribunal would consist of judges from the United States, the United Kingdom, France, Italy and Japan.

The treaty also provided for the trial of individual Germans for breaches of laws of war by a tribunal from the affected nation. Germany would need to agree to supply the suspects and the evidence.

This proposal for the victors to try the vanquished in court was completely new, and the Germans rejected it, instead proposing that all war crimes committed on both sides be tried by courts appointed by neutral countries. The Allies, however, were not inclined to compromise. They threatened to immediately resume their invasion of Germany if Germany did not sign the treaty. The German government caved.

The Allies' bold plans came to little. The government of the Netherlands refused to extradite the Kaiser if he was to be tried only by Allied judges; nor did it agree to a compromise of exiling him to Java in the Netherlands East Indies. So the Allies worked on the other trials, presenting a list of 896 accused, including Field Marshal Paul von Hindenburg and General Eric Ludendorff, to the German government on 3 February 1920. The next month Germany was rocked by the Kapp Putsch, proving how fragile the political situation was. Fearing that severe measures against the country would lead to either a bolshevik or nationalist revolution, the Allies scaled back their demands. On 7 May 1920, they presented a new list of only forty-five suspects. The trials were held at Leipzig in 1921 by a German court and were not a success. Only twelve defendants were placed on trial and only six of those were convicted, all of whom were reported to have escaped custody shortly afterwards.

While Germany was the main focus of the Allies, they were also concerned with the Ottoman Empire. Believing Christian minorities to be conspiring with the Allies, the Ottoman government had commenced a program of repression, deportation, and finally outright massacre, considered by most modern historians an act of genocide. The Armenians were most affected, and somewhere between 500,000 and 1.5 million of them perished. Greeks and Assyrians were also targeted. On 24 May 1915 Britain, France and Russia made a joint declaration on the Armenians, making the first known reference to 'crimes against humanity': 'In view of these new crimes of Ottoman Empire against humanity and civilization, the Allied Governments announce publicly to the Sublime Porte [the Ottoman government] that they will hold personally responsible for these crimes all members of the Ottoman Government, as well as those of their agents who are implicated in such massacres.'[14]

After the Ottoman Empire surrendered to the Allies, the British pressed the Ottoman government to take action. Sultan Mehmed IV agreed to carry out trials of officers implicated in the atrocities, and these took place over 1919–20. They were even less successful than the German ones. Senior officers were allowed to flee the country and then sentenced to death in absentia. A number of junior officers were sentenced to death or hard labour. The Treaty of Sèvres (1920) contained provisions requiring the Turks to deliver war criminals to the Allies, but this never happened. After the Ottoman Empire collapsed, the new Turkish government of Mustafa Kemal Atatürk rejected the treaty, and any chance of further trials with it.

In short, the First World War had made the laws of war seem hollow. Political considerations would inevitably trump judicial ones, actually pinning responsibility for breaches would be extremely difficult, and on the whole the chance of the guilty on either side being held to account was slim. Michael Bryant, in his history of war crimes, described the First World War as the 'failure of the law of war'.[15] The lessons of these failed trials were on the minds of the Allied leaders as they considered bringing the German leadership to trial once accounts of Nazi atrocities began to reach them during the Second World War.

The advocates for trials won out. In the Moscow Declaration of 30 October 1943, the major Allied governments formally outlined their plans for German war criminals to be dealt with either by national or international tribunals:

> At the time of granting of any armistice to any government which may be set up in Germany, those German officers and men and members of the Nazi party who have been responsible for or have taken a consenting part in the above atrocities, massacres and executions will be sent back to the countries in which their abominable deeds were done in order that they may be judged and punished according to the laws of these liberated countries and of free governments which will be erected therein . . . Thus, Germans who take part in [atrocities] will know they will be brought back to the scene of their crimes and judged on the spot by the peoples whom they have outraged.[16]

Those whose crimes had no specific geographical location would be dealt with by joint tribunals, and lists of suspects were to be compiled by all the Allies. As Allied policies on Japan tended to match those on Germany, it followed there would be trials in the Far East as well, although no specific comments were made on this point. On 1 December 1943 the governments of the US, the UK and China issued the Cairo Declaration, promising to fight Japan to the point of unconditional surrender and force it to give up its overseas empire, without making the same commitment to war crimes trials.[17] But they were clearly thinking along these lines. In February 1944, US Secretary of State Cordell Hull warned the Japanese government that the Bataan Death March contravened the laws of war.[18]

The concept of international tribunals in both theatres solidified during conferences at Potsdam and Yalta in 1945. From 26 June to 8 August 1945, the Nuremberg Charter was drafted by the representatives of the US, the UK, the Soviet Union and France in London.[19]

It established that individuals, including government leaders, could be prosecuted for breaches of the laws of war. And it also distinguished and established the distinction between three different types of offences: starting wars of aggression, or crimes against peace (class-A), conventional war crimes (class-B), and crimes against humanity (class-C). The distinction between class-A and class-B was based on a traditional distinction in the Western legal tradition between the ideas of *jus ad bellum* and *jus in bello*. In order to be just, a war needed to be started for a just cause *(jus ad bellum)* and fought in accordance with principles of natural and divine law *(jus in bello)*. This was discussed, for example, by Dutch jurist and philosopher Hugo Grotius in his highly influential 1625 work *De Jure Belli ac Pacis (On the Law of War and Peace)*. Crimes against humanity (class-C) were distinguished from conventional war crimes (class-B) as they did not actually need to be connected to a war. In this, the drafters of the Nuremberg Charter were thinking chiefly of the Holocaust. This was a novel idea, as it had not been established that it was actually illegal (and not just immoral) for a government to kill its own citizens. The class-A crimes were also novel, because no court or tribunal had ever convicted someone for a crime against peace.

The charter of the IMTFE had the advantage of drawing its authority from Japan's acceptance of the Potsdam Declaration which gave the Allies the right to try its leaders for war crimes. The initial priority of the US government, however, was only the Japanese attack on Pearl Harbor. MacArthur favoured holding a tribunal for this offence alone, hence SCAP's quick move to have the members of the December 1941 Tōjō cabinet arrested as soon as the occupation commenced. In November 1945, the same month the Nuremberg Trials began, the US Congress began a formal investigation into the attack on Pearl Harbor. Some Republicans used the opportunity to criticise the Roosevelt administration for provoking Japan and then getting taken by surprise when it attacked, and so establishing that the attack was a crime was a priority for Washington. Other Allied governments were also concerned that prosecuting the Japanese for class-B and -C war crimes would open up to unwelcome scrutiny the conduct of their own armed forces.[20] In contrast, the IMT having been set up with the Holocaust in mind, prosecuting crimes against humanity was a priority at Nuremberg. But in the end, consistency won out, and the charter for the Tokyo Tribunal which MacArthur issued on 1 January 1946 was very similar to Nuremberg's.

The prosecution at Tokyo was led by Joseph B. Keenan, an American appointed directly by President Truman. Working for the US State Department, Keenan had prosecuted major gangs during the Depression. He arrived in Tokyo in December 1945, and the other teams followed. At its height, the International Prosecution Section (as it was called) was 500 strong, including members from all of the original nine judging nations and advisors from Burma and Indonesia.

The prosecution was troubled from the start, the first of its problems being the poor drafting of the indictment. At Nuremberg, the prosecution used a simple system whereby each defendant was indicted on one or more of four counts. The first two related to class-A war crimes – one for participating in a common plan or conspiracy to commit a crime against peace, and a second for planning or waging wars of aggression – and the third and fourth for class-B and -C war crimes respectively.

At Tokyo, the prosecution wrote a long and confusing indictment with fifty-five separate counts. These included participating in a conspiracy to commit murder by causing Japanese forces to attack various countries, committing war crimes at specific places (such as Nanking), and planning and waging aggressive war against various individual countries in violation of international treaties. The convoluted indictment was the result of squabbling between the different teams. For example, when lead British prosecutor Arthur Strettell Comyns Carr

KC arrived in Tokyo in February 1946 he was dismayed by Keenan's lack of progress on his massive indictment, and decided to take more of the drafting on himself. The final indictment, lodged with the tribunal on 29 April, was 'monstrous' according to one member of the defence team.[21]

In its judgement, the court held that most of the counts were vague, overlapping, or inconsistent with the tribunal's charter, so it made substantiative decisions on only ten – count 1 (conspiracy to wage aggressive war), counts 27, 29, 31, 32, 33, 35 and 36 (waging aggressive war), and 54 and 55 (war crimes and crimes against humanity).[22] Keenan had said he wanted to have leaders who waged aggressive war 'stripped of the glamour of national heroes and revealed for what they were – plain, ordinary murderers'.[23] It was a noble sentiment, but the charter gave the court no jurisdiction to try conspiracy to murder, so it made no finding on these charges. It was an elementary mistake to make at such a high-profile trial.

The defence was originally provided by Japanese lawyers. In the view of one witness, they gave up before the trial even began, satisfying themselves with 'putting flowers gracefully upon the graves of their client'.[24] At their request, the defendants were provided with American lawyers as well (except for militarist ideologue Hashimoto Kingoro, whose anti-Western views apparently trumped his instincts for self-preservation). Complaining, not unreasonably, that they had been given no time to prepare, half the American lawyers quit before the substantiative proceedings began on 4 June. Those who remained put up quite a fight. They had the advantage of familiarity with both the English language and the common law system.

There are two broad legal systems in use in the Western world, English common law and continental European civil law. The former is used in the UK and other English-speaking countries, including Australia, New Zealand, Canada and the United States (although the Canadian province of Quebec and the American state of Louisiana retain the French civil law system). The system of civil law is based on Roman law, and was developed and codified in France and Germany in modern times, and spread from there. Japan adopted a form of the civil law system as part of its modernisation in the late nineteenth century.

The two systems have many similarities, but there are some significant differences. The civil law system is sometimes referred to as an inquisitorial system, as the judge questions witnesses and plays a very active role in the trial. Common law is described as adversarial, as the proceedings are conducted by the prosecution and the defence, with the judge acting only as an arbiter. The IMTFE was conducted according to common law principles, to which the Japanese defence lawyers and some of the judges found it difficult to adapt. According to Röling, Bernard was frustrated by his inability to question the witnesses directly, as he would in a French court, and felt the IMTFE was not doing all it could to arrive at the truth.[25]

There were other cultural factors at play. Japanese courts had, and still have, extremely high conviction rates. Even today, conviction rates for contested criminal trials exceed 98 per cent.[26] This means that Japanese defence lawyers often start a trial on the assumption their client will be convicted, and so place their focus on winning the lowest possible sentence. The American defence lawyers started with no such assumption at Tokyo, and they proved remarkably energetic, challenging the court and the prosecution at every turn. Their efforts were particularly impressive given how many fewer resources they had compared with the prosecution, and how little time they'd had to prepare.

The defence's first strike came almost immediately. On 6 May, as soon as the preliminaries had been carried out, it challenged Webb's presidency, on the basis he had investigated Japanese war crimes and so was potentially biased. After a judicial huddle, Northcroft, on behalf of the bench, overruled the challenge. Then, over 13 and 14 May, the defence challenged the jurisdiction of the court – the authority of the tribunal to convict and sentence the defendants – on several grounds.

They argued that aggressive war was not a crime under international law, and that in accepting the Potsdam Declaration, the Japanese government had only acceded to the right of the Allies to hold trials for conventional war crimes. Webb dismissed their motions, promising to give reasons later.

Even at this early stage, the other judges were having doubts about Webb (Pal and Jaranilla had not yet arrived). As president, only Webb could speak before the tribunal, and the others did not always approve of his approach to managing the court. Northcroft, who initially liked Webb, said he was 'brusque to the point of rudeness. He does not control the court with dignity, he is peremptory and ungracious in his treatment of counsel and witnesses, and instead of giving shortly the legal justification which in most cases exists for his decisions, he leaves everyone in the court with the impression his rulings are dictated by petulance or impatience and an impression, which may easily develop in the future, of prejudice.'[27]

Presiding over a court such as the IMTFE would have taken an extraordinary jurist, one extremely well versed in international law, keenly aware of political and cultural considerations, able to work well with the international bench of judges, and confident and respectful in his approach. Webb was probably out his depth, and his handling of the challenge to the tribunal's jurisdiction was an early indicator of this.

Webb waited until the IMT at Nuremberg handed down its judgement in October 1946, where it ruled that the treaties entered into before the war made waging aggressive war a crime. Then, with the aid of two research assistants and an academic, he drafted a statement of reasons explaining why the IMTFE's charter was valid. It was a long and rambling essay, full of quotations from philosophers ranging from the ancient Greeks to the neo-Kantians.[28] The other judges were not impressed. Patrick called it 'an extraordinary document' while Northcroft said it was 'like a student's not very good essay on international law'.[29]

Webb, stung by the criticism, began a second draft. By the time he invited comment on this one, however, the judges themselves could not agree on the basic principles behind it. Röling, who also had doubts about the charter, said, 'The victor in a war, even a world war, is not entitled to brand as an international crime everything he dislikes and wants to prosecute for.'[30] Bernard agreed, arguing that the court should refuse to apply sections of the charter that its authors did not have the authority to make. It soon became clear to everyone that Pal had no intention of being bound by it. Patrick, by contrast, thought it dishonest for a man to accept appointment as a judge under a charter and then refuse to accept its validity.[31]

Webb was not able to smooth these differences over. Like Northcroft, Röling did not like Webb's approach, describing him as a 'very arrogant and dictatorial man', a loner who didn't socialise with the other judges and never shared their dinner table.[32] As a result, the effective leadership of the bench shifted to a clique consisting of the other Commonwealth judges except Pal – Patrick of the United Kingdom, Northcroft of New Zealand, and MacDougall of Canada. The three men were similar and had similar motives. Having fought in the First World War and lived through the Second, all were determined there should never be a third. To achieve this aim, they needed an unchallengeable conviction of Japan's leaders for the crime of waging aggressive war.

The problems with Webb, as troubling as they could be, were dwarfed by the problems with Keenan. He was disorganised, he did not make enough effort to secure documents, he absented himself without notice for long periods, and made off-the-cuff remarks to the press during the trial. The other prosecutors quickly lost confidence in him. As Brigadier Ronald Henry Quilliam of New Zealand wrote: 'owning [sic] to the lack of any prosecution scheme (for which Mr Keenan must be held responsible), I have found that valuable evidence has been allowed to be sent back to the [S]tates and that essential witnesses have been demobilised and sent home'.[33] Röling concluded that Keenan was not up to the task and that Arthur Comyns Carr of the United Kingdom was far more competent.[34]

There were persistent rumours that Keenan was an alcoholic and his drinking was affecting his job.[35] It appears that at one point his fellow prosecutors compelled him to swear off liquor. Claims that he was drunk in court were almost certainly unfounded, but having them made was not great publicity for the IMTFE. Unsurprisingly, unofficial leadership of the prosecution section shifted to Comyns Carr, Quilliam, Mansfield, and the second American prosecutor Frank S. Tavenner, Jr. This domination by the Commonwealth was little to Keenan's liking: 'We cannot permit ourselves ever to be in a situation where we have one vote and the British Commonwealth five,' he wrote to Washington in late 1947. 'Although they have differences among themselves from time to time and perhaps rather bitter ones, when the time comes, they all gather together under one roof and the vote is five to one, and they know it and take full advantage of it . . . It is simply impossible to get the idea out of their minds that this is not a British trial to be held according to British rules and practices.'[36] But his problem was one of his own making.

The prosecution presented its case from 4 June 1946 to 24 January 1947, then the defence followed from 27 January 1947 to 9 September 1947. Each prosecuting country presented its own case against the defendants (with the Commonwealth putting forward a collective case), and each day the defendants were bussed 3 miles (4.8 kilometres) to and from Sugamo Prison to hear them. Rather than break the trial down by country, or by prosecution and defence, I will break it down into the three main types of offences: conspiracy (count 1), waging aggressive war or crimes against peace (counts 27 to 36), and conventional war crimes and crimes against humanity (counts 54 and 55).

# VI

# THE CONSPIRACY

The first, and most controversial, count in the IMTFE indictment accused all twenty-eight defendants with entering into a conspiracy among themselves and with the leaders of Germany and Italy. According to the prosecution, 'the main object of this conspiracy was to secure the domination and exploitation by the aggressive States of the rest of the world, and to this end to commit, or encourage the commission of crimes against peace, war crimes, and crimes against humanity as defined in the Charter of this Tribunal, thus threatening and injuring the basic principles of liberty and respect for the human personality'.[1]

This was an adaptation of the ordinary concept of criminal conspiracy to international law. A group of people who plan to commit an offence together can traditionally be charged with a conspiracy to commit the offence, although the law itself in the countries where this is recognised has been modified over the years. But significantly, conspiracy is only a crime in the common law system, so Bernard, Röling, Zaryanov, and the Japanese lawyers were all unfamiliar with the idea.

Forming an unlawful conspiracy had also been the first count at Nuremberg, which was how it made its way into the Tokyo indictment. However, the prosecution at Tokyo came to rely on the charge far more than did the prosecution at Nuremberg. Which was ironic, as the defendants at Nuremberg had formed a far more close-knit group than the defendants at Tokyo. The defendants at Nuremberg were all members of the Nazi government, senior members of Nazi organisations such as the SS, or senior members of the German military who had worked together throughout the war. In contrast, the Tokyo defendants were an eclectic mix, some of whom didn't know each other, had only held power at different times, or had even been bitter enemies with different objectives. As Comyns Carr wrote, 'the whole Japanese situation is infinitely more complicated than the German for the purposes of a prosecution, as all the politicians, soldiers and sailors were all squabbling and double-crossing one another all the time, and it is by no means easy to pick the right defendants'.[2]

It is counterintuitive, but possible, for people to be convicted of criminal conspiracy under common law even if they have never met. For example, if a bank robber comes to an agreement with someone to act as getaway driver, and another to launder the proceeds of the crime, then the driver and money-launderer can be held to be in a common conspiracy to rob the bank even if one didn't know the other existed. But there would still need to be the common goal – robbing the bank. At Tokyo, the prosecution was making the extremely broad claim that all the defendants were in on a common plot for world domination. Not for the last time, it had set itself a very difficult task through poor drafting of the indictment.

The defence was fiercely critical of the whole thing. The American lawyer John Brannon called it 'a saving device for their [the prosecution's] failure to elicit positive evidence of guilt of the individual accused'.[3] This was broadly correct – the prosecution did put the charge in the indictment so they could tie all the defendants to the attack on China in 1937 and on the Western powers in 1941, even those who held no political power at the time or who, like the author Ōkawa, never held political power at all. Furthermore, Brannon pointed out, the prosecution had not decided if the conspiracy was a crime in itself (as the indictment seemed to say) or a means of finding individual defendants guilty of other specific crimes. 'The prosecution seeks to use the doctrine of conspiracy as a double-barrelled weapon to accomplish a dual purpose,' he said. 'Firstly, conspiracy is used as a *separate crime*, and secondly, a *method of proof* of a crime alleged to have been committed.'[4]

To Keenan, these were mere technicalities compared with the ultimate goal of discrediting Japanese militarism. He later wrote that an 'actual miscarriage of justice' didn't matter in the big picture. 'The situation of the defendants is comparable to that of American soldiers about to take a beach-head: That is, the lives of morally and legally innocent men may be sacrificed in the achievement of the ultimate purpose, but the common good requires the taking of the beach-head.'[5] It was a factually correct summary of the Allies' position on the purpose of the IMTFE, but still an extraordinary argument for a prosecutor to make in what was meant to be a court of law.

The charge of conspiracy served another purpose: creating a record of how the militarists came to take power in Japan.

Early in the 1957 film *The Bridge on the River Kwai* there is a tragicomic scene illustrating the clash between Western and contemporary Japanese attitudes to international law. Colonel Saito, the uncompromising commander of a prison camp on the Burma Railway, orders a battalion of British prisoners of war to work on the eponymous bridge regardless of their rank. Lieutenant Colonel Nicholson, the senior British officer with a near-religious faith in rules and regulations, points out that the Geneva Conventions exempted officers from manual labour. He produces a crumpled copy of the regulations from his pocket and hands them to Saito. Saito takes the folded paper, slaps him across the face with it, and repeats the order. The implication is clear – the Japanese had no regard for international law and Nicholson was a fool for expecting anything else.

But many British officers serving in the Far East and familiar with the Japanese Army actually did expect the Japanese to respect international law.[6] In its last two wars with a European power, the

Russo-Japanese War of 1904–05 and the First World War, Japan had adhered very closely to both the 1899 and 1907 Hague Conventions, which it had both signed and ratified. Some writers have attempted to explain the brutality and fanaticism of the Japanese armies through history and culture, with concepts of collective responsibility, shame and isolationism, and particularly the *Bushidō* code of the samurai warriors (which was, in reality, unknown to the samurai and invented by modern writers between 1890 and 1914).[7] But these explanations cannot account for the fact that, from the Meiji Restoration in 1868 until the 1920s, Japan strove to incorporate itself into the international community, follow international law, and build a reputation as a civilised country. From 1902 to 1922, Japan was a close ally of Great Britain. A Japanese warship escorted the Anzacs to Egypt in 1914, and Japanese officers served with the British Army and Navy in the First World War. When Hirohito ascended the Chrysanthemum Throne in 1926, he took the reigning name Shōwa, meaning 'enlightened peace'. 'I have visited the battlefields of the Great War in France,' he wrote in the enthronement address read to his subjects on his behalf. 'In the presence of such devastation, I understand the blessing of peace and the necessity of concord among nations.'[8]

Then, from the 1920s until 1945, Japan's leaders threw the country headlong into a moral abyss that led to the deaths of more than 20 million people in the Asia-Pacific, including 3 million Japanese, and which left its armed forces with a reputation for barbarism and created an enmity throughout Asia that has diplomatic ramifications to this day. It left Japan's industries destroyed, its merchant ships sunk, its cities bombed into devastation and its people reduced to starvation. The prosecution at the IMTFE set out to explain how the twenty-seven men in the dock were collectively responsible for this downfall.

While the militarists who began to rise to prominence in Japan in the 1920s bore many similarities to German and Italian fascists, there was also much about them that was uniquely Japanese. They were fiercely anti-communist, fearing the Japanese monarchy could fall in revolution as had the Russian, German and Austro-Hungarian, but they were also critical of the West, liberalism, individualism, and the perceived excesses of capitalism, which in their view made men weak and accustomed to luxury. Like the fascists of Europe they promised a third way, an alternative to the failed systems of liberal capitalism and revolutionary socialism, but theirs was a path only Japan could take.

The militarists fed on anti-Japanese racism in the West and the social pressures of the Great Depression. Japan's delegation to the 1919 Paris Peace Conference was led by Prince Saionji Kinmochi and Count Makino Nobuaki, both leading liberals. Initially everything appeared to be going well – Japan was recognised as a great power, granted a permanent seat in the newly formed League of Nations, and given Germany's Pacific Islands north of the equator as a mandate. But when Makino moved a motion that the Covenant of the League of Nations have a clause affirming racial equality, it was defeated. The strongest opposition came from the United States, where racial segregation was a crucial policy of President Woodrow Wilson's Democratic Party in the southern states, and from Australia, which viewed the White Australia policy as vital to its security and prosperity.

The defeat of the motion was a hard blow. Even as a modern great power, a participant in the international system and a Western ally, the Japanese had never been recognised by Europeans as equals. Furthermore, Japan had been rebuffed by a British dominion (Australia) in spite of its alliance with the United Kingdom. Once again, Japan felt isolated. Japanese journalist K.K. Kawakami wrote in 1919 with ominous foreboding:

> It cannot be denied that in the past the nations of the West have
> applied to Asiatic peoples standards of justice and equity quite
> different from those applied to themselves . . . It is highly doubtful
> that this anomalous relationship between the Orient and Occident
> will be appreciably altered by the organization of the League of

Nations which refuses to accept the obviously just principle that
no race in the league shall be discriminated against in any of the
countries bound by its covenant. As far as Asia is concerned, the
League is not likely to be a harbinger of glad tidings.[9]

Prince Konoe had been with the Japanese delegation at Versailles
and afterwards he wrote an article called 'Reject the Anglo-American-
Centered Peace'. However, he praised President Wilson and his
Fourteen Points on the principles of peace. It was one of his many
contradictions.

Then Japan's political institutions were given a shock by the Great
Depression. The country had few raw materials and was completely
dependent on international trade, leaving it vulnerable to a global
economic shock. The price of silk, one of Japan's major exports, fell
by more than half from 1929 to 1930. The price of rice, the other, fell
to one-third of its pre-crash value.[10] Farmers were reduced to eating
bark and weeds, selling their daughters into prostitution, or committing suicide. Japan's young industries, which had grown on First
World War-era demand, were crippled by global tariffs. In two years,
it seemed that decades of progress had ended. 'A pall of gloom has
been cast about the people,' wrote K.K. Kawakami.[11]

The first serious clash between the militarists and the government came in 1930, in negotiations over the London Naval Treaty.
Following the end of the First World War the great powers entered
into a series of treaties intended to limit military spending and the
growth of armed forces. One of these, the Washington Naval Treaty of
1922, permitted Japan the world's third-largest navy but limited it to
three-fifths of the size of the British and American fleets.

When the London Naval Conference proposed further limits on
the size of navies, the Hamaguchi government in Japan intended to
agree to them. Not only did this appear to be good diplomacy, but
there was no money to spend on warships anyway, and the budgets of
the army and navy had been cut. But this approach was criticised by

the navy, and by extension, the militarists and their ultra-nationalist societies. The navy's argument was based on Articles 11 and 12 of the Meiji Constitution, which stated that the armed forces answered directly to the Emperor. Traditionally this had been interpreted to mean the armed forces had some independence in their strategy and tactics in wartime. Now the navy argued that the government should not be able to control its size or spending. Prime Minister Hamaguchi Osachi, however, did not budge, and the treaty was signed.

At Tokyo station in November 1930, Hamaguchi was shot in the stomach by Sagoya Tomeo, a member of the ultra-nationalist *Aikokusha*, or Society of Patriots. The 'Old Lion' of the Taishō Democracy survived the assassination attempt but died of his wounds in August 1931. Sagoya was initially sentenced to death, but successive governments more sympathetic to militarism commuted his sentence and then released him. It was the first in what became a familiar cycle: a political leader opposed to the militarists would be shot by a junior member of an ultra-nationalist organisation, the assassin would be dealt with leniently by courts or military courts martial, and their example would inspire others.

To the militarists, the Japanese were the leading race in Asia, and so Japan was Asia's natural leader. This idea was not based on the racist pseudoscience used to justify European domination of non-European peoples. Rather, it came from the premise that the Japanese were exceptional, being led by an Imperial house of divine origin and enjoying the protection of heaven. Alone of the peoples of Asia, the Japanese had been able to resist European colonisation, and their swift victories over China in 1894–95 and Russia in 1904–05 were evidence of Japanese fighting spirit and divine intervention. The Japanese had made themselves the equals of the Europeans in wealth and power without falling into their corrupt habits. The European colonists had made themselves rich on exploiting Asians, and so it naturally fell to the Japanese to drive them out. Anti-white racism was a significant component of Japanese militarist ideology, but it sat uneasily with a natural admiration of the wealth and power of Western civilisation and, more practically, with Japan's wartime alliance with Germany and Italy. Was Japan going into Asia to liberate and unite its people, or was it establishing itself as a colonial power in its own right? While the militarists preached the former, they could never quite decide what position they held in reality. In a classic example of Orwellian double-think, they often seemed to believe both ideas at once.

Several of the defendants at Tokyo were included mostly for their involvement in the rise of militarism in Japan. One was the charismatic General Araki Sadao, who combined a spartan military lifestyle with a flamboyant public persona. Araki came from a poor family and began his working life in a pickle factory, but soon found that the army offered far more opportunity than cabbages and cucumbers. Graduating from the Army Staff College at the head of his class, he rose quickly through the ranks until he became responsible for training new officers in 1928. Perhaps because of his decidedly un-samurai background he eagerly promoted his own version of the samurai ethos, including reviving the wearing of swords. Immediately upon becoming head of the Army War College he revised the *General Principles of Strategic Command* to remove problematic terms like 'surrender', 'retreat' and 'defence'.[12] His 1930 *Moral Training for Soldiers* began with a fabricated history of *bushidō* in which the samurai warlords who had fought for control of the country were actually motivated by loyalty to the Emperor.[13]

Araki's experiences in Russia during the civil war left him with a deep dislike of bolshevism, but he also rejected Western decadence, going so far as to argue that earthquakes were good for the Japanese people as they taught them fortitude. He described his views on foreign affairs in the early 1930s: 'We cannot let things drift any longer. We are the leading Asiatic power and we should now take matters into our own hands. We must be active, ever-expending the last portion of our national strength. We must be prepared to wage a desperate struggle. The whites have made the countries of Asia mere objects of oppression and imperial Japan should no longer let their impudence go unpunished.'[14]

Araki was one of the founders of the *Kōdōha* (Imperial Way Faction), which also included his fellow defendant Colonel Hashimoto Kingoro. Kingoro was an Army Staff College officer who believed modernisation had led to a corrupt and bureaucratic political system where drunken Diet members took bribes from *zaibatsu* capitalists while ignoring the plight of people in the countryside. He wrote a newspaper article calling for the end of democracy and founded an organisation called the *Sakurakai* (Cherry Blossom Society), which attracted idealistic young officers desiring the purification of Japan's debased political institutions. Unsurprisingly, he was backed by Ōkawa, the writer, who shared his disdain for the foreign and amoral ideas of capitalism, liberalism and communism.

The militarists had gained power over the government indirectly, in a period of 'government by assassination'. Hamaguchi was one victim, Prime Minister Inukai Tsuyoshi, also a leader of the Constitutional Democratic Party, was another. In May 1932 Inukai delivered a speech in which he extolled democracy and condemned fascism. In response, nine young officers from the army and navy travelled in taxis to the Yasukuni Shrine, paid their respects to Japan's war dead, then drove on to Inukai's official residence. 'Let us talk,' he said to them when they confronted him. 'Dialogue is pointless,' they replied, and cut him down in a hail of bullets. When the assassins were court-martialled, the court received a petition containing hundreds of thousands of signatures in favour of their release, some signed in blood. Araki, despite being a minister in Inukai's government, publicly praised the killers' patriotism and sincerity. They were given light sentences and soon released.

This encouraged the officers of the *Kōdōha* faction, but in the end they went too far with the attempted coup of 26 February 1936. The army did not support them, the Emperor turned against them, and the principal officers either committed suicide or were court-martialled and shot. But this was a military rather than a civilian decision, as by then civilian control over the military had effectively ended.

The story of the rise of Japanese militarism was an interesting one, but not in the way the prosecution presented it. Writing at the end of the trial's second month, an AAP correspondent said it had become a 'second-rate show' and the attitude was 'general apathy'. 'Tokyo newspapers have voiced disgust with the prisoners' shabbiness and listless attitude, and have concluded that the defendants have already decided that they have lost their case,' he wrote. 'The trial has been dominated by legal wrangling and the monotonous introduction of un-revealing documents and affidavits.'[15]

By the time the trial ended, 4,335 exhibits had been admitted in evidence, 419 witnesses had testified in person and 779 had provided written statements, and the transcript of the proceedings occupied 48,412 pages. As the months dragged on, it seemed like the prosecution had decided to punish Japan's wartime leaders by boring them to death.

Interest picked up again with the cross-examination of the major defendants in late 1947. By then the trial had been going on for over fifteen months, and Nuremberg had ended almost a year before.

In December 1946, Keenan left on one of his unexplained absences and did not return to Tokyo for seven months. During that time, the prosecutors worked out a plan among themselves, but even though he had been away for so long, Keenan did not intend to follow it.

In October 1947, the cross-examination of Kido Kōichi began. He was no longer Lord Kido, the Japanese aristocracy having been abolished. The prosecution knew he would be a formidable witness, and so Comyns Carr made a lengthy study of him and prepared carefully. When the day came, though, Keenan insisted on doing the cross-examination himself without preparation.[16] The results were less than impressive. In his lengthy statement, Kido maintained he had been an opponent of the militarists from beginning to end, he had been

brought into the cabinet by Konoe to work towards an end of the
China Incident, he had opposed and never given any support to the
Pacific War, and he had taken action to end it. Keenan failed to elicit
any new information from him, and worse (from the perspective of
the prosecution), began to press him on the Emperor's knowledge of
the Pearl Harbor attack. 'Mr Chief of Counsel, we are not trying the
Emperor,' Webb warned him.[17]

But keeping the Emperor out of the trial proved difficult, particularly when Tōjō took the witness stand on 27 December, bringing a
crowd to the courtroom for the first time in a year and a half. 'Tōjō's
shaven pate shone under the glare of arc lights as he walked across the
courtroom with his 245-page affidavit, to the whirr of newsreel cam-
eras,' wrote one journalist. 'His plain khaki military-type jacket and
trousers were carefully pressed.'[18]

Tōjō's defence counsel, George Blewett, read out his 50,000-
word statement to the court. Tōjō took full responsibility for Japan's
actions, but maintained that Japan had fought a war of self-defence
forced on it by the Western powers. He attacked the US for its anti-
Asian immigration law of 1924 and Australia for the White Australia
policy, and spoke at length of the support he had received from the
leaders of Japanese collaborationist regimes in Asia. 'The China incident [Second Sino-Japanese War] broke out as the result of the spread
of Communism in Asia and the anti-Japanese policy of China,' he
said.[19] He was careful to keep emphasising the Emperor's 'peace-
loving spirit', but on 31 December, when being examined by Kido's
defence attorney, William Logan, he slipped. Tōjō said in response to
a question that 'there is no Japanese subject who would go against the
will of His Majesty: More, particularly, among the high officials of the
Japanese Government.'[20]

'You know the implications from that reply,' said Webb. The
courtroom became hushed, and Logan quickly said he had no further
questions. The prosecution arranged to have Tōjō coached on how
to reword his statement, and when he returned to the witness stand

he corrected it, making it clear to the court that his government had pushed ahead with the attack on Pearl Harbor without the Emperor's support.

To cross-examine the former prime minister, the prosecution had called on John Fihelly, an American war crimes trials investigator and 'Tōjō expert'. Keenan brought him in especially from the US, intending to share the cross-examination with him. However, the court insisted on only one examination per defendant. Keenan therefore took on the task of cross-examining Tōjō himself. Fihelly left, saying, according to one witness, 'Keenan, you fool!'[21]

'I will not call you General, as there is no Japanese Army any more,' Keenan said to Tōjō at the start of his questioning. Tōjō ignored this slight but throughout his questioning responded to Keenan and Webb using the mode of the Japanese language normally reserved for social inferiors and servants.[22] This was lost in translation, but it might have amused the Japanese listeners present.

Keenan failed utterly to discredit Tōjō's claims. Unfamiliar with the facts, he asked vague questions. In response, Tōjō asked for clarification, eventually compelling Keenan to agree to some statement or another. When arguments arose, Keenan frequently appeared to lose. After a while, it began to look like Tōjō was cross-examining Keenan. 'Tōjō came off best,' concluded Quilliam. Associated Press correspondent Frank L. White went further, saying the incident turned the entire trial into 'one of the most expensive propaganda failures ever charged to American taxpayers'.[23] Tōjō's able defence became celebrated by Japanese nationalists, and his stocks rose with the Japanese public. It was, according to historian Yuma Totani, the low point of the entire prosecution at Tokyo.[24]

# VII

# THE PACIFIC WAR
# ON TRIAL

Counts 27 to 36 of the indictment accused the defendants of waging a war of aggression against China, the Philippines, the British Commonwealth, the Netherlands, Thailand, France, the Soviet Union and Mongolia. The IMTFE Charter defined class-A war crimes as 'Crimes against Peace: Namely, the planning, preparation, initiation or waging of a declared or undeclared war of aggression, or a war in violation of international law, treaties, agreements or assurances, or participation in a common plan or conspiracy for the accomplishment of any of the foregoing'.

This definition was slightly longer than that in the Nuremberg charter, with its inclusion of 'declared or undeclared' and 'international law'. While not diminishing the importance of the charges concerned with atrocities, the prosecution considered the crimes against peace to be the most important. According to Quilliam, the tribunal's priority must be 'the conviction and punishment of the persons responsible for the policy of waging wars of aggression and expansion'.[1]

To win its case on these counts, the prosecution had to prove two things; first, that aggressive war was a crime, and second, that individual leaders could be held responsible for it. In order to establish the first, the prosecution at Tokyo (as at Nuremberg) relied chiefly on the 1928 Kellogg–Briand Pact, also called the Pact of Paris, which had been signed and ratified by Japan. Under Articles I and II:

I. The High Contracting Parties solemnly declare in the names of their respective peoples that they condemn recourse to war for the solution of international controversies, and renounce it, as an instrument of national policy in their relations with one another.

II. The High Contracting Parties agree that the settlement or solution of all disputes or conflicts of whatever nature or of whatever origin they may be, which may arise among them, shall never be sought except by pacific means.

The prosecution contended that this pact made aggressive war illegal, and cited several specific cases where it alleged one or more of the defendants had initiated it – the attack on China and the conquest of Manchuria in 1931, the attack on Shanghai in 1932, the invasion of China in 1937, the border war with the Soviet Union and Mongolia in 1939, the occupation of French Indochina following the fall of France in 1940, and the attack on the United States, Philippines, the British Commonwealth and the Netherlands East Indies in 1941.

The Mukden Incident of 1931 was the first time Japan's militarists had looked overseas. Following its victory over Russia in 1905, Japan had won the Kwantung Leased Territory, a small but strategically important piece of land in southern Manchuria. Its importance came from Port Arthur and the Kwantung Railway, and the Kwantung Army had been formed to hold it.

Free from the influence of Tokyo and domestic politics, the Kwantung Army was a breeding ground for ultra-nationalism. Many of its officers were members of secret organisations like the Cherry Blossom Society, and had developed a colonial mindset towards the local Manchurians and Chinese and a firm belief in Japan's imperial destiny in Asia. Furthermore, the Kwantung Army was large and well trained, yet had nothing to do except guard a port and a railway. The militarists found it a perfect tool for their purposes – in particular a young, ambitious, exceedingly clever staff lieutenant colonel, Ishiwara Kanji.

Araki admired Ishiwara, observing that he had 'lightning intellect' and was not afraid to show it.[2] He was fiery and insubordinate, but also charismatic enough to win over others, including his superiors. He had converted to a narrow sect of Nichiren Buddhism which taught there would be an apocalyptic battle between the forces of good, represented by the Japanese monarchy, and the forces of evil. Ishiwara was also familiar with the world at large, having toured Europe, and was convinced it was Japan's role to unite Asia and liberate it from Western colonialism. He came to view cold, windswept Manchuria as the granary that would feed Japan's armies, and he drew up a plan to seize it from the weak and divided Chinese government.

On 18 September 1931 a small parcel of explosives was detonated under the South Manchurian Railway near the city of Mukden (modern Shenyang). The bomb was not powerful enough to damage the railway itself, but Ishiwara immediately blamed the Chinese Army for the sabotage and ordered his troops to seize control of Mukden. The commanders of the Kwantung Army in Port Arthur had no chance to react, much less the government in Tokyo. From Mukden, the Kwantung Army swiftly launched a full-scale invasion of Manchuria.

The operation was presented to the Imperial General Headquarters as a *fait accompli*. But the government and Army HQ nonetheless played along, creating the Japanese puppet state of Manchukuo once the Kwantung Army had completed its conquest in February 1932, against lacklustre Chinese resistance. The conflict became known as the 'Mukden Incident' or 'Manchurian Incident', with the Japanese Army and government beginning their habit of using the neutral term 'incident' (*jiken*) to describe acts of military aggression against Japan's neighbours.

On 24 February 1933, the League of Nations voted forty-two to one to refuse to recognise the state of Manchukuo, and hence the legitimacy of the conquest of Manchuria (Japan's vote being the only negative). Rather than withdraw its troops, Japan withdrew from the League. It was a turning point: an explicit rejection by the Japanese government of the Western international order and of international law. Japan would now go its own way and present an alternative order for East Asia to the world.

Ishiwara Kanji was not a defendant at Tokyo. A fierce critic of Tōjō, whom he thought a fool, he had been sidelined following the latter's rise to power. He did, however, make an appearance for the defence, as swaggering as he ever was. General Itagaki Seishirō, a former senior officer in the Kwantung Army, was accused of taking part in planning the incident, as was Hashimoto, indirectly.

The Ishiwara–Tōjō rivalry was not just personal – the two men came from two different militarist factions, Ishiwara from the *Kōdōha* (Imperial Way Faction) and Tōjō from the *Tōseiha* (Control Faction). The *Kōdōha*, which was formed first, drew on a mystical interpretation of Japan's past, was anti-modern, saw communism as the principal threat to Japan, and so favoured a 'strike north' policy in foreign affairs. From Manchuria, *Kōdōha* officers in the Kwantung Army would be able to launch an attack on the Soviet Union.

Tōjō belonged to the *Tōseiha*, which was formed in response to the *Kōdōha*. The name 'Control Faction' was given to it by its enemies within the military. The *Tōseiha* had a more twentieth-century mindset, supporting industrialisation and the modernisation of the military; it was far more influenced by and friendlier towards German and Italian fascism, and favoured a 'strike south' foreign policy directed against China and the East Indies. The *Tōseiha* officers were therefore willing to go to war against the Western powers for control of the Asia-Pacific.

The two factions waged a bitter struggle through the 1930s, culminating in the assassination of *Tōseiha* leader General Nagata Tetsuzan by a *Kōdōha* officer, Lieutenant Colonel Aizawa Saburō. Aizawa burst into Nagata's office, accused him of prostituting the army to *zaibatsu* capitalists, and cut him down with a sword. The army showed less tolerance towards the assassination of generals than that of civilian politicians, and Aizawa was court-martialled and shot. Then, following the failure of the attempted military coup in the February 26 Incident, the *Tōseiha* became ascendant and the *Kōdōha* was purged from the army.

Both factions sought to gain political power and solve Japan's internal problems with military aggression. But as they squabbled, the direction of this aggression swung one way and then the other. China was an obvious target, being next to Japan and suffering deep internal divisions. Large parts of the country remained under the effective control of warlords, whose armies were little more than mercenaries paid in plunder. Since 1927, the Nationalist Chinese government of Chiang Kai-shek had been engaged in a civil war against the communists led by Mao Tse-tung. Both sides were responsible for political repression and outright massacre. Japan had (unsuccessfully) used the parlous political situation in China as an excuse for the annexation of Manchuria, claiming it could bring peace and stability where the Chinese could not.

The Japanese nationalists had a complex relationship with China. They could not fail to acknowledge Japan's cultural debt to the country – the kanji writing system, Confucianism, and dozens of other things integral to Japanese civilisation had come from China. But China was then in a continuing state of disarray, making a feeling of cultural superiority easier. Members of the 'strike north' group, like Ishiwara, correctly thought an invasion of China would be too ambitious. But over time, the 'strike south' school won out. While Manchuria was being conquered in early 1932, the Japanese attacked Shanghai (in the 'January 28 Incident', or 'Shanghai Incident'), then the Kwantung Army conquered the northern Chinese province of Jehol in 1933.

The inevitable full-scale Japanese invasion of China finally came
with the Marco Polo Bridge Incident of July 1937, shortly after Prince
Konoe became prime minister for the first time. After Japanese and
Chinese soldiers exchanged fire across the bridge, the Japanese Army
launched an attack on Beijing and Tianjin, and rapidly escalated its
commitment, sending hundreds of thousands of troops into China.
Even so, the Japanese government stubbornly maintained that there
was no war in China and kept referring to the 'China Incident', to the
point where one German diplomat joked about his participation in
the 'World Incident' of 1914–18.[3]

At the same time, the Japanese government imposed austerity
measures, moving the economy steadily towards a total war footing.
More and more ordinary Japanese were called upon to make sacrifices for a war they were told wasn't even happening. 'Like Stalin's
Russia, Konoe's Japan seemed intent on starving itself great,' wrote
historian Piers Brendon.[4] As the militarists gained more power, critics
like Hirota Kōki and Kido Kōichi were sidelined. Weary of having his
government's policy controlled by the militarists, Konoe resigned in
January 1939.

In May 1939, believing the Red Army would be critically weakened from Stalin's purges, the Kwantung Army provoked a border
war with the Soviet Union, with the Battles of Khalkhin Gol. The
results were less than satisfactory. By September, Japanese forces had
been compelled to execute a 'lateral advance' back into Manchuria
(the Japanese Army could not retreat).[5] The 'Nomonhan Incident'
(as the Japanese government called it, admitting to neither invading
the Soviet Union nor being defeated) was Japan's first military reversal
since Toyotomi Hideyoshi's samurai were forced from Korea in 1598.
It discredited the 'strike north' school of thought, and Japan increasingly looked to the south and east.

The spectacular German victories in Europe in May and June 1940
made a formal alliance with Germany against the Western powers look
more attractive. They also left France defeated and prostrate, allowing

the Japanese to swiftly occupy French Indochina without resistance in September 1940. On 26 September, Japan signed the Tripartite Pact with Germany and Italy, formally establishing the Rome–Berlin–Tokyo Axis. The Axis powers resolved to break the Anglo-American world order established by the Treaty of Versailles, contain communism in the Soviet Union, and establish themselves as the dominant powers in their respective regions of the globe. For Japan, this was an irrevocable step towards war with the West; US Secretary of State Cordell Hull described the Tripartite Pact as the 'joining of the bandit nations'.

Konoe returned to power in October 1940, but events had moved beyond his control. Over the summer and autumn of 1941, relations between Japan and the West deteriorated sharply. Britain and the United States imposed economic sanctions on Japan and demanded Japanese withdrawal from China and Indochina, and Japan in turn demanded non-interference within its sphere of influence in East Asia. While Konoe unsuccessfully sought an audience with President Roosevelt, Chief of General Staff Field Marshal Sugiyama Hajime presented the Emperor with plans for an attack on British, Dutch and American territories in the East. Hirohito was not convinced Sugiyama could deliver the quick victory he was promising, and pointed out that the 'China Incident' was far from resolved, even though Sugiyama had assured him it would take only three months. But over time, the Emperor came around to the view of Sugiyama and Army Minister Tōjō. Sugiyama committed suicide shortly after the surrender and so was not a defendant at Tokyo.

Recognising that he could not prevent war, Konoe resigned for the second and final time, on 16 October 1941. He proposed Prince Higashikuni Naruhiko, uncle to the Empress, as his replacement. Prince Higashikuni was popular with the army and navy, and Konoe believed he also maintained sufficient independence to prevent a complete militarist takeover of the government. The Emperor, however, did not want to risk tying a member of the Imperial family to political decision-making, and made a different choice. Tōjō took office, and seven weeks later, his government informed the Japanese public they were now engaged in a holy war against the Western powers for the liberation of Asia.

The prosecution argued that these incidents were all crimes against peace, carried out by the defendants in order to bring about Japanese domination of the Asia-Pacific.

There were two basic premises to the defence's case. The first was that aggressive war was not a crime under international law. In an April 1946 article on the Nuremberg Trials, American jurist Charles E. Wyzanski had questioned whether there was any legal basis for the idea of crimes against peace. 'If prevention, deterrence, retribution, nay even vengeance, are ever adequate motives for punitive action, then punitive action is justified against a substantial number of Germans,' he wrote. 'But the question is: Upon what theory may that action properly be taken?'[6] In his view, to interpret the Kellogg–Briand Pact as simply allowing individuals to be prosecuted in a criminal court for waging aggressive war would violate the legal maxim of *nullum crimen et nulla poena sine lege* – 'there can be no crime and therefore no punishment without an existing law'. This phrase would be used again and again by critics of the idea of crimes against peace.

The defence's second premise was that Japan's wars had been fought in self-defence. Owen Cunningham, counsel for General Ōshima Hiroshi, argued: 'It is our contention that the growth of communism in China and its spread was a matter of vital concern to the Japanese nation and to the other nations of East Asia and was rightfully the subject of fear on behalf of the Japanese' and 'the existence of a Communist army in China actually threatened the very existence of Japan and justified a defensive agreement [i.e. the Tripartite Pact] to prevent its spread'.[7]

This was a clever argument, as it was not anti-Western. During 1947 and 1948, the Cold War was deepening and concerns about the spread of communism were growing in many of the prosecuting nations. On 12 March 1947, President Truman delivered a speech to Congress warning of the dangers of communism and calling for aid to Greece and Turkey. On 22 April, George Lazarus, counsel for Field Marshal Hata Shunroku, submitted the statement for the defence at the Tokyo Trial, saying it supported the Japanese people's 'reasonable fear' of communism.[8]

'As American counsel, do not take advantage of the great tolerance displayed by this Allied court to indulge in what might be termed enemy propaganda,' Webb warned him.

'We never expected that evidence of the remarks by the President of the United States to the Congress of the United States would be called enemy propaganda,' Lazarus shot back.[9] Eventually Webb put a stop to these arguments by ruling that the spread of communism in Asia was irrelevant to the guilt or innocence of the defendants.[10]

Next, the defence argued that the economic restrictions imposed on Japan by the Western powers amounted to an act of aggression. Japan, surrounded as it was by hostile nations in 1941, had no choice but to attack and break the stranglehold. Kido's counsel, William Logan, argued 'as the A-B-C-D [American–British–Chinese–Dutch] powers had made the encirclement both military and economic complete, we submit that the first blow was not struck at Pearl Harbor; it was struck when the economic war started long before then'.[11] In support, the defence advanced comments made by Secretary of State Frank Kellogg, one of the architects of the Kellogg–Briand Pact, in the US Senate's Committee on Foreign Relations. There, he confirmed that an economic blockade was 'an act of war absolutely', and so an attack made in response would hardly be an act of aggressive war in violation of the treaty.[12]

Webb was not persuaded, and told the defence that economic aggression was not a crime. In response, the defence pointed out that one of the charges in the indictment was 'economic aggression in China and Greater East Asia'. Webb clarified his position, saying economic aggression was not a crime unless it was associated with an aggressive war. The defence criticised him for allowing the widest possible interpretation of self-defence for Western actions and the narrowest for Japan's; America's freezing of Japanese assets in response to Japan's attack on China, for example, was accepted as an act of self-defence. The defence felt that Webb and the prosecution were constantly moving the goalposts.

Tōjō's able handling of Keenan's cross-examination in December 1947 made the defence's case look even stronger, and by early 1948 some observers thought the prosecution was in trouble on the charge of crimes against peace. On 29 January 1948, Quilliam wrote to Wellington warning the New Zealand government that exoneration for aggressive war was possible, which would imply that the Allies were partially responsible for the Pacific War.[13] His fears were not entirely groundless, as American judges in the Subsequent Nuremberg Trials (the lesser trials following the IMT) were proving very reluctant to convict second-tier German leaders and industrialists for crimes against peace. Of the sixty-six so charged, only three were convicted.[14] The IMT had convicted Germany's Nazi leaders for crimes against peace, but Nuremberg was receding quickly into the past.

# VIII

# ATROCITIES IN ASIA

Counts 54 and 55 of the indictment related to conventional war crimes and crimes against humanity. The Allies had the greatest reservations about prosecuting them, but with conventional war crimes they were on the firmest ground, as there was no doubt these had a legal precedent. Conventional, or class-B, war crimes were defined in the IMTFE charter as 'violations of the laws or customs of war'.

Here the Tokyo charter was much shorter than Nuremberg's, which added to the definition: 'Such violations shall include, but not be limited to, murder, ill-treatment or deportation to slave labor or for any other purpose of civilian population of or in occupied territory, murder or ill-treatment of prisoners of war or persons on the seas, killing of hostages, plunder of public or private property, wanton destruction of cities, towns or villages, or devastation not justified by military necessity.'

Both charters stated that acting under superior orders was not a defence, but could mitigate the punishment. 'This is hard doctrine, but the law cannot recognize as an absolute excuse for a killing that the killer was acting under compulsion,' wrote Charles E. Wyzanski. 'For such a recognition not only would leave the structure of society at the mercy of criminals of sufficient ruthlessness, but also would place the cornerstone of justice on the quicksand of self-interest.'[1]

The idea of laws regulating the conduct of states and armies in
wartime was ancient, but the concept of a war crime was much newer.
Lassa Oppenheim may have coined the term in his treatise on international law in 1906.[2] A 1944 memorandum for the US judge advocate
general wrote that the term had 'no well-established meaning in military or international jurisprudence' but would include 'acts which
outrage common justice or involve moral turpitude'. The memorandum provides a list, including 'killing or cruel treatment of prisoners
of war', torture, rape and wanton devastation.[3]

The final offence tried at Tokyo, crimes against humanity, class-C
crimes, was defined as 'murder, extermination, enslavement, deportation, and other inhumane acts committed against any civilian
population, before or during the war, or persecutions on political or
racial grounds in execution of or in connection with any crime within
the jurisdiction of the Tribunal, whether or not in violation of the
domestic law of the country where perpetrated. Leaders, organizers,
instigators and accomplices participating in the formulation or execution of a common plan or conspiracy to commit any or the foregoing
crimes are responsible for all acts performed by any person in execution of such a plan.' The definition of crimes against humanity in the
Tokyo charter was longer than Nuremberg's.

At Nuremberg, crimes against humanity were written into
the indictment to allow for the prosecution of perpetrators of the
Holocaust. As many of the Jews and members of other targeted groups
who were killed were citizens of Germany and Austria, their murders
could not be prosecuted as a war crime. The charge was morally irre-
proachable but still legally controversial. As Charles E. Wyzanski wrote,
'there is no citation of any particular international convention which
in explicit words forbids a state or its inhabitants to murder its own
citizens, in time either of war or of peace'.[4] In the Pacific, these distinc-
tions did not matter so much. While the wartime Japanese government
was oppressive and totalitarian, it did not kill large numbers of people within Japan; the mass killings and atrocities were committed in

external territories and so could be considered to be conventional war crimes. In all the Pacific trials, therefore, no real distinction was drawn between conventional war crimes and crimes against humanity, hence the lesser trials were referred to a class-B and -C trials collectively.[5]

The Tokyo prosecution had to first prove that the atrocities happened, and then that the men in the dock were responsible for them. On the first, they came in very well prepared, with each prosecution section presenting its own case. The Chinese prosecutors presented on the Rape of Nanking, war crimes committed in other parts of China, and Japan's involvement in the opium trade. The Philippines and the United States jointly presented evidence on the Rape of Manila and atrocities committed against prisoners of war. The Commonwealth case included numerous examples of war crimes against both civilians and prisoners of war throughout the Asia-Pacific. The French prosecution team made a shorter presentation, on atrocities in Indochina. The principal charge made by the Dutch related to the mistreatment and killing of Dutch civilian internees in the Netherlands East Indies, but they also included evidence of atrocities committed by the *Kempeitai* and *Tokkeitai* (the army and navy special police respectively), the conscription of Indonesians as *rōmusha* (forced labourers), and sexual slavery.

The prosecution at Tokyo has sometimes been criticised for failing to fully pursue charges relating to the comfort women scheme, the systemic sexual slavery of 100,000 to 300,000 women in army and navy brothels throughout the Japanese Empire. While it did present evidence of women being forced into military brothels, it stopped short of alleging there was a single planned scheme orchestrated at the highest levels of government.

To show how the prosecution made its case, and how it sought to establish command responsibility, I will look at two examples in detail: the Rape of Nanking, prosecuted by China, and the use of prisoners of war as forced labour on the Burma Railway, prosecuted by the Commonwealth.

*

The Second Sino-Japanese War became very large and very brutal very quickly after the Marco Polo Bridge Incident in July 1937. Up until then, Japan had been accustomed to fast and decisive victories. But while Japanese armies swiftly conquered Beijing and Tianjin, it took them over three months and tens of thousands of casualties to conquer Shanghai. China was vast, and once Nationalist forces withdrew into the interior, Japan did not have enough men to do more than hold the major towns and railways. The conflict became bogged down, with all the worst characteristics of guerrilla and anti-guerrilla fighting of the Chinese civil war.

Japan maintained it was not fighting a war in China but was enforcing order, and therefore the laws of war did not apply. On 5 August 1937, Hirohito approved a proposal by the army to cease treating captured Chinese soldiers in accordance with international law. On top of this, articles 11 and 12 of the Meiji Constitution were interpreted as giving the military virtual autonomy in the areas they controlled. Occupied China was thus under the rule of the Japanese Army rather than the Japanese government, although this distinction would matter less as the war progressed.

In occupied China, the army promoted steadily more radical measures. General Okamura Yasuji divided north China into pacified, semi-pacified and unpacified areas, and issued increasingly extreme orders for the pacification of semi-pacified and unpacified areas. The Japanese Army adopted an approach called *Sankō Sakusen*, the 'burn to ash strategy', which the Nationalist Chinese referred to as the 'Three Alls Policy' – kill all, burn all, loot all. Chinese civilian deaths ran into the millions. Japan established a puppet regime in the occupied areas under collaborator Wang Jingwei and insisted it was the legitimate government of China. Unsurprisingly it received very little support.

Brutal measures became widespread in China and then throughout the Pacific theatre. One such was the use of captured soldiers or civilians for bayonet practice in order to harden the Japanese troops. As the diary of Private Tajima recorded:

One day Second Lieutenant Ono said to us 'you have never killed anyone yet, so today we shall have some killing practice. You must not consider the Chinese as a human being, but only something of rather less value than a dog or cat. Be brave! Now, those who wish to volunteer for killing practice, step forward.'

No-one moved. The Lieutenant lost his temper.

'You cowards!' he shouted. 'Not one of you is fit to call himself a Japanese soldier. So no-one will volunteer? Well then, I'll order you.' And he began to call out names 'Otani – Furukawa – Ueno – Tajima!' (My God, me too!)

I raised my bayoneted gun with trembling hands, and – directed by the lieutenant's almost hysterical cursing – I walked slowly towards the terror-stricken Chinese standing beside the pit – the grave he had helped to dig. In my heart I begged his pardon, and – with my eyes shut and the lieutenant's curses in my ears – I plunged the bayonet into the petrified Chinese. When I opened my eyes again, he had slumped down into the pit. 'Murderer! Criminal!' I called myself.[6]

Tajima's description of atrocities was confirmed by veterans interviewed by the BBC for a 2005 documentary on Hirohito.[7] 'If something were for the sake of the Emperor, we had to do it. So I actively took part in the killing,' said Enomoto Masayo, who was in the Japanese Army from 1939 to 1945. 'For the Emperor there was nothing we couldn't do. So we raped, gang-raped women and did everything.'

Kondo Hajime, another member of the Japanese Army, from 1940 to 1945, said, 'We'd flush out hiding villagers and ask them where they'd hid their arms. When we finished questioning them we killed them straight away. Our commander told us that of course we used our gun in combat but in other cases the gun entrusted by the Emperor was too good to kill Chinese, rocks were all they deserved.'

The change in the attitude of the Japanese military was made shockingly apparent to the world when the Nationalist Chinese capital of Nanking (modern Nanjing) was captured in December 1937. General Matsui Iwane issued orders forbidding plundering but made no orders regarding Chinese captives. When Matsui became bedridden with malaria, Hirohito's uncle by marriage, Prince Asaka Yasuhiko, was placed in command of the army. An order to 'kill all captives' was issued bearing his seal – there is still debate over whether the order came from Asaka himself or an ultra-nationalist officer on his staff, Lieutenant Colonel Chō Isamu.

When they entered Nanking, the Japanese soldiers disregarded Matsui's orders and eagerly followed those issued under Asaka's name. Prisoners were killed en masse with machine guns, then anyone suspected of being a Chinese soldier, then civilians at random. They then sacked the city and carried out what may be the largest mass rape in history. The killings became even more depraved: civilians were buried alive or impaled. The exact number of Chinese killed in and around Nanking in December 1937 is unknown, but almost certainly over 100,000 and possibly as high as 300,000 (the latter is the official Chinese figure).[8]

The Rape of Nanking, as it is now known, was not hidden but was carried out in full view of the world. Horrified Japanese war correspondents wrote of piles of bodies, some still struggling, being pushed into the Yangtze River. These accounts were censored in Japan, or dismissed as communist propaganda. Western journalists witnessed the event as well, and soon reports were appearing in newspapers around the globe. American journalist Frank Tillman Durdin wrote in the *New York Times* on 9 January 1938: 'In taking over Nanking the Japanese indulged in slaughters, looting and raping exceeding in barbarity any atrocities committed up to that time in the course of the Sino-Japanese hostilities. The unrestrained cruelties of the Japanese are to be compared only with the vandalism in the Dark Ages in Europe or the brutalities of medieval Asiatic conquerors.'[9]

There was a decisive shift in feeling against the Japanese throughout the Western world. To make matters worse, the Japanese Army
had sunk the American gunboat *Panay* on the Yangtze River and killed
three sailors, although Japan did subsequently pay compensation.

General Matsui formally entered Nanking on 17 December. The
next day, after reviewing the devastation, he wrote, 'I now realise
that we have wrought a most grievous effect on this city . . . I offer
my sympathy, with deep emotion, to a million innocent people.'[10]
He called his officers together and rebuked them for the conduct of
their soldiers. In Tokyo, Foreign Minister Hirota was furious when
he heard the news, and apologised to the Western powers for the
damage to their property (including the *Panay*).[11] Ironically, Matsui
and Hirota were the ones in the dock at Tokyo. Asaka was granted
immunity as a member of the Imperial family, and Lieutenant
Colonel Chō, who had been later sent to Okinawa, committed
suicide after the defeat there in June 1945.

Konoe's government went into damage control, its actions
suggesting it had taken leave not just of international law but of
reality itself. It denied any massacre had taken place, and insisted
Japan's armies were engaged in bringing order to lawless China.
On 22 January 1938, Konoe issued a statement maintaining that
'Japan's immutable national policy aims at building the edifice of
permanent peace for East Asia on the unshakable foundation of
close cooperation between Japan, Manchukuo and China, and
to contribute thereby to the cause of world peace'.[12] A man of his
intellect could not have possibly believed it. Nonetheless, throughout the Japanese Empire, the media took the same line. *Shin Shun
Pao*, a Chinese-language newspaper in Shanghai published by
the Japanese government, reported on 8 January 1938: 'Men and
women, old and young, bent down to kneel in salutation to the
Imperial army, expressing their respectful intention . . . Soldiers
and the Chinese children are happy together, playing joyfully on
the sides. Nanking is now the best place for all countries to watch,

for here one breathes the atmosphere of peaceful residence and happy work.'[13]

Nanking was at the centre of the Chinese case against the defendants at Tokyo, and the Chinese prosecutors presented numerous affidavits, witness statements and reports, and called about a dozen witnesses. This was a large number by the standards of the IMTFE, where most of the evidence was documentary, but having witnesses appear in person was extremely effective. Shang Teh-Yi, a 32-year-old retailer, described what happened when he, his brothers and his neighbours were arrested on 16 December at about 11 am:

> Each two of us were bound together by a rope fastening our hands, and sent to 70 Shikawen, on the bank of the Yangtze River. More than 1,000 male civilians were there and all were ordered to sit down, facing more than ten machine-guns about forty or fifty yards in front of us. We sat there for more than an hour. At about 4 o'clock, a Japanese Army officer came by motor car, and he ordered the Japanese soldiers to start machine-gunning us. We were ordered to stand up before they did the shooting. I slumped to the ground just before firing started, and immediately I was covered with corpses and fainted. After approximately 9 p.m., I climbed out from the piles of corpses and managed to escape and go back to my house.[14]

Dr Hsu Chuan-Ying, a 62-year-old academic, recounted what happened when Japanese soldiers reached a house at number 7 Sin Kai Road, South Gate:

> When the [Japanese] soldiers came to the door the grandfather, an old man, answered the knock on the door. He was shot on the spot and killed. His wife, over 70 years of age, came out to see what was the trouble and she was shot and killed a few steps from her husband. Their daughter with a baby at her bosom

came and the soldiers killed both the mother and the child. There were two unmarried daughters in the family, ages 14 and 17 respectively, both of them were raped by the soldiers and then killed. One was left in a pool of blood on the table with a stick stuck in her vagina and the other was left in blood on the bed with a perfume bottle stuck in her vagina. Five other women were killed at this home, that is, all the persons found there by the Japanese.[15]

The defence did little to contest this evidence and did not cross-examine the witnesses. Unlike some revisionist Japanese historians, they made no attempt to deny that the massacre actually took place. They called three witnesses of their own and made some effort to suggest the executed Chinese men were bandits or guerrillas, or that the atrocities were committed by the Nationalist Chinese army. On the whole, though, they were confronted by the evidence in a way they hadn't been when defending the charges of conspiracy or crimes against peace. Defence lawyer Sugawara Yutaka claimed that 80 or 90 per cent of the prosecution's evidence was 'false or exaggerated'. However, 'we were compelled to accept, to our regret, that 20 per cent of it did actually take place'.[16] Another defence lawyer, Takigawa Masajirō, said that 'while their testimony has some exaggeration, it is an indisputable fact that the outrages the Japanese Army committed against the citizens of Nanking after the capture of the city were dreadful'.[17]

Having established the scale of the atrocities, the prosecution contended that Matsui, Hirota and one of Matsui's subordinates, Mutō Akira, were responsible for them. Counts 54 and 55 both dealt with conventional war crimes and crimes against humanity, but the former accused the defendants of having 'ordered, authorized and permitted' war crimes and crimes against humanity, while the latter accused them of having 'deliberately and recklessly disregarded their legal duty' to prevent such atrocities and rectify breaches. The prosecution argued that international law placed an obligation on both senior commanders and government ministers to prevent war crimes:

> . . . it is the Government as a whole which is primarily responsible for prevention of breaches of these laws of war. This casts in the first place a duty upon every member of the cabinet and their advisors, and every high officer in the chain of command directly concerned with these matters to satisfy himself that the laws are being obeyed. Ordinarily no doubt this duty could be discharged by satisfying himself that proper machinery had been established for the purpose. But when information reaches him which raises a doubt as to whether they are being flagrantly disregarded, or shows plainly that they are, then a much higher duty devolves upon him.[18]

This higher duty was to properly investigate the breaches and then take active steps to rectify them. This was broadly in line with the decisions made in Yamashita's and Homma's cases, but the prosecution at Tokyo took it further by finding the civilian government responsible as well.

The three men certainly knew of the crimes at Nanking. During the pre-trial investigation, Mutō had been asked whether the atrocities troubled him. He replied, 'After the atrocities in Nanking and Manila, and being a member of the general staff during both incidents, I felt that something was lacking in Japanese military education.'[19] However, the defence contended that holding him and the others responsible would be to take the doctrine of command responsibility too far. They argued that there were no grounds for holding Hirota, a civilian politician who wasn't even in China, responsible for war crimes committed there. They did not deny Matsui's overall command of the Japanese Army, but as he was in bed in Soochow, 140 miles (225 kilometres) away, he could not have known about the atrocities, and even if he did, he could not have prevented them.

Under cross-examination Matsui was not a particularly good witness. He was forced to acknowledge that his divisional commanders reported to him regularly, and that he knew the atrocities had occurred. He contradicted himself by denying knowledge of them and then speaking of action he took to prevent them.

The rest of China's case at Tokyo did not match the impact of Nanking, although it raised public consciousness of the massacre. Japan's stated war aim in the Pacific War was to liberate East Asia from Western colonialism and establish the Greater East Asia Co-Prosperity Sphere (*Dai Tōa Kyōeiken*). The brutality of Japanese soldiers towards civilians throughout East Asia undermined their claim. Ba Maw, the Burmese independence leader who was the head of the Japanese collaborationist government in Burma, wrote: 'The militarists saw everything only in a Japanese perspective and, even worse, they insisted that all others dealing with them should do the same. For them there was only one way to do a thing, the Japanese way; only one goal and interest, the Japanese interest; only one destiny for the East Asian countries, to become so many Manchukuos or Koreas tied forever to Japan. These racial impositions . . . made any real understanding between the Japanese militarists and the people of our region virtually impossible.'[20]

Many people throughout East Asia came to the same conclusion.

Just as Nanking has come to stand for Japanese war crimes in China, so has the Burma Railway come to stand for crimes against Commonwealth prisoners of war. The Japanese attitude towards surrender in the Second World War has become notorious, and its notoriety has come to overshadow the strange fact that, up until the 1930s, the Japanese military was in fact known for its good treatment of civilians and prisoners. In the First Sino-Japanese War of 1894–95, Japan wanted to show the world that it was both more powerful and more civilised than China, and hence win the respect and support of

Western countries. Japanese forces were directed to follow the laws of war. General Ōyama Iwao, for example, gave this message to the Japanese Second Army in October 1894:

> Our forces act according to what is right and we fight in accordance with civilisation. Our enemy is China's army, not individual Chinese. Those who surrender, who are captured, wounded, or offer us no resistance, must be treated gently. The utmost care must be used towards the ordinary Chinese people so that they are made to feel safe with us. No matter how slight, they must in no way be mistreated, but rather made to recognise our virtue. Each divisional commander must bear this in mind and must caution those below him so that the majesty of our Emperor and the chivalry of our Army are demonstrated to the world.[21]

These directions were generally followed, albeit imperfectly. Not a great deal is known about Japanese treatment of surrendering or wounded Chinese soldiers, but those who were brought into prisoner-of-war camps seem to have been treated fairly. However, it is worth noting that the total number of Chinese prisoners taken by Japan in that war is low: 1,790. Given that hundreds of thousands of troops were engaged over the course of six months, the figure suggests that orders to refrain from killing Chinese soldiers who ceased to resist were not always followed.[22] And while Korean and Manchurian civilians generally had more to fear from the retreating Chinese than from the advancing Japanese, the Japanese Army did massacre the Chinese population of the city of Lüshun (Port Arthur) in November 1894, perhaps in response to finding the mutilated bodies of Japanese soldiers.

During the Russo-Japanese War of 1904–05, however, there were no such blemishes on Japan's record. The British were impressed by the 'discipline and warrior spirit' showed by their new Japanese allies.[23] As British lawyers N.W. Sibley and F.E. Smith wrote at the time, 'the

Japanese observe the recommendations of the Hague Convention at least as scrupulously as the Russians . . . the Russians have learned to respect the gallantry of the Japanese'.[24]

The Japanese Army and Navy captured 79,367 Russian prisoners in that war.[25] Japan played up its adherence to the laws of war for a Western audience in a way that was at times almost comical. Russian prisoners reported their Japanese captors being friendly and giving them cigarettes. They were then sent to prisoner-of-war camps in Japan, a number of which were opened up to Western observers. Ethel McCaul, a British Red Cross nurse, wrote, 'I had witnessed a treatment of their enemies which would reflect the greatest credit on any nation. The Russians were being treated as guests of the country, not mere prisoners of war.'[26] A special, Russian-language newspaper was printed for them, albeit one full of Japanese propaganda. The wounded were given expensive medical care, and any who died were buried with full military honours and flowers placed on their graves. The Japanese government reported at the end of the war that the prisoners had been treated so well that some did not want to go home. This claim should obviously be treated with caution, but given the abject poverty in many parts of the Russian Empire at the time it is not entirely implausible.

While both sides were implicated in looting and the summary execution of civilians, it seems that the Russians did so far more commonly than the Japanese. The Cossacks quickly developed a reputation for treating Manchurian and Chinese civilians with brutality, a reputation which would only be reinforced during the First and Second World Wars.

In the end, the diligence of the Japanese military and the public relations campaign of the government paid off. Western correspondents were impressed with both the fighting skill of the Japanese and their humanity. Theirs seemed to be a perfect army, the 'Knights of *Bushidō*': disciplined, fearless in battle, and magnanimous in victory. Many observers emphasised their similarity to Europeans. As Nurse

McCaul wrote, 'What a brave, cheery man the [Japanese] transport soldier is . . . The nearly naked Chinaman, also assisting with his quaint, squeaking wheel-barrow . . . lent the one Oriental touch to this moving mass, for in the distance the men looked European in their trim uniform.'[27]

On the other side, 1,626 Japanese were captured by the Russians, including twenty-six officers. The Japanese government admitted that prisoners had been taken (it never made any such acknowledgements in the Second World War), made inquiries via neutral countries about their welfare, and sent them packages of food and other goods. A number of officers evaded capture by committing ritual suicide in the manner of the samurai, cutting open their stomachs in the act of *hara kiri*, or *seppuku*, which has fascinated Western audiences since Christian missionaries first arrived in Japan in the sixteenth century. Some commentators approved of the officers' actions, while others condemned it as archaic and wasteful, saying that captured soldiers could learn about the enemy while in captivity and then return to fight for Japan.[28] Upon release, all the Japanese prisoners of the Russians were interrogated but almost all were set free. Some were even decorated when they returned to Japan. However, seven officers were court-martialled and stripped of rank and decoration.[29]

By the outbreak of the Second Sino-Japanese War in 1937, the Japanese Army had ceased to accept surrender from its own troops and had begun maintaining that captured Chinese soldiers were not entitled to the protections of the Geneva Convention. Once war with the Western powers became likely, the Japanese government intensified its anti-Western propaganda campaign directed at both soldiers and civilians. As with China, the Japanese militarists did not have completely simple views on the West. The militarists could not fail to recognise the strength of Western civilisation and its scientific and technological achievements. And, of course, Germany and Italy were now notionally Japan's allies, although the Tripartite Pact had been signed in bad faith on all sides.

But European colonialism in Asia gave Japan a moral justification for war. Having become rich from exploiting Asians, Westerners had grown shallow and materialistic. Hollywood films depicted their obsession with wealth, sex and glamour. Unlike the Japanese, they had no self-restraint, they were spiritually dead and did not honour their ancestors. They were described in Japanese propaganda in terms like *nanbanjin* ('barbarian'), *kedamono* ('brute') and *yajū* ('wild beast').[30] The Allies were depicted as hypocrites, preaching democracy while oppressing their colonial subjects in Asia. Once the war started there was something of a feedback loop, where anti-Japanese racism in Allied propaganda was used by Japanese propagandists to show that all Western soldiers were brainwashed to 'kill every Jap' and whites could not accept Asians as human.

On 8 January 1941 the pocket-sized *Senjinkun* Field Service Code was published by then Army Minister Tōjō and issued to all soldiers. It began: 'The battlefield is where the Imperial Army, acting under imperial command, displays its true character, conquering wherever it attacks, winning whenever it engages in combat, in order to spread the Imperial Way far and wide so that the enemy may look up in awe to the august virtues of His Majesty.'[31] It also included Tōjō's infamous command to every Japanese soldier: 'never live to experience shame as a prisoner'.[32] This was used to highlight another critical difference between Japan and its enemies – the British and Americans were cowardly and self-centred and would surrender to save their lives; the Japanese would take pride in dying for their comrades and Emperor. 'To give in when beaten is the spirit of the Americans and the British, not that of the Japanese, who will fight all the harder when defeat stares them in the face,' wrote one soldier.[33]

This ideology was made official. From March 1941, the army began imposing criminal penalties on Japanese soldiers who surrendered in China. Under this practice, which continued into the Second World War, any surrendered officer who was recaptured was forced to commit suicide, and other ranks were sent to labour battalions.

Furthermore, the military promoted the idea that if a man surrendered, his family would be disgraced, his father would lose his job, and his sisters would never find husbands. It was probably this threat, more than any innate fanaticism, through which the Japanese Army finally succeeded in forcing its men to fight to the death in so many losing battles from 1942 onwards. And as a final incentive, the soldiers were also told that Westerners tortured and killed their prisoners.

Civilians were not forgotten, and in August they received a book called *Shinmin no Michi* (*The Way of the Subject*).[34] This short publication was intended to illuminate the evils of European and American thought, educate Japanese people about the *kokutai*, and lead a return to the virtues of pre-modern Japan. It held most foreign ideas to be suspect. Communism was condemned for being materialistic and promoting class conflict. As for Western liberal democracy: 'The thoughts that have formed the foundation of Western civilization since the early period of the modern age are individualism, liberalism, materialism, and so on. These thoughts . . . regard the strong preying on the weak as reasonable, unstintedly promote the pursuit of luxury and pleasure, encourage materialism, and stimulate competition for acquiring colonies and securing trade, thereby leading the world to a veritable hell of fighting and bloodshed.'

Italian fascism and German Nazism, however, were praised for 'destroying the world domination of the Anglo-Saxon race'.

One of the book's conclusions read: 'Viewed from the standpoint of world history, the China Affair is a step toward the construction of a world of moral principles by Japan.' Another read: 'Japan has come to be keenly conscious of the fact that the stabilization of East Asia is her mission, and that the emancipation of East Asian nations rests solely on her efforts.'

This final thought led to another book, *Kore Dake Yomeba Ware Wa Kateru* (*Read this and the war is won*), issued to Japanese soldiers shortly before the attack on the United States and the British Empire in December 1941. It asked its readers to attempt to reconcile

Western liberal and democratic ideas with the slave trade, the dispossession of Native Americans, racial segregation in the southern United States, and the conquest of colonial empires in Asia. In short, war was unavoidable due to the 'selfish desire for world conquest' of the Western powers.[35]

These two attitudes – racial hatred of Westerners and contempt for surrender – informed Japanese treatment of prisoners of war. They were compounded by practical difficulties. By mid-1942, the Japanese government was struggling to decide what to do with all the people, prisoners and civilians alike, who had fallen under its power. In July Tōjō addressed an assembly of new prisoner-of-war camp commanders in Tokyo, where he gave the sort of mixed message that characterised his government's approach to international law. On one hand he told them to 'adhere to the laws and regulations and apply them fairly and properly so it will enhance and exhibit the prestige of our Empire'.[36] This was consistent with Japan's pledge to the Allies via Switzerland in December 1941 to adhere to the principles of the Geneva Conventions (even though the Japanese government maintained it was not binding as Japan had not ratified it), and the promulgation of directions regarding prisoners dating from the Russo-Japanese War.

But Tōjō also reminded the attendees that 'our country has a different conception of prisoners of war and consequently has different methods of treatment compared with those of American and European nations'. He told them to use the labour of POWs for the war effort, supervise them rigidly, and not leave them idle for a single day. While prisoners of the Japanese had wildly differing experiences depending on who the local commander was, commanders seem to have followed Tōjō's harsh directions far more than his lenient ones.

Then there was the simple fact that the Japanese Army was also struggling to feed its own soldiers, let alone its prisoners. Not having expected to capture so much territory so quickly, Japan found maintaining supply lines throughout its huge empire of ocean and jungle extremely difficult. This was exacerbated when the Allies regained

control of the sea and air in much of the theatre. As the Pacific War
stagnated over 1943, starvation became a reality for many Japanese
soldiers in distant parts of their empire.

On 11 September 1943 the Emperor said to Field Marshal Sugiyama
Hajime, Chief of General Staff, 'I understand you're committing most
of the seventeenth division to Rabaul. Just how do you intend to keep
them supplied? I'm not going to tolerate another "our men fought
bravely, then died of starvation".'[37]

As it turned out, there would be many more examples of 'our
men fought bravely, then died of starvation'. In September 1943, the
Japanese High Command established an 'absolute defence line', and
if it was not seen as practical to evacuate the men beyond it they were
abandoned. In a decision of breathtaking callousness, 140,000 men
who had fought bravely for the Japanese Empire in some of the toughest campaigns of the Pacific War were left to starve in the jungles of
Papua New Guinea. An army that showed such disregard for the lives
of its own men naturally placed little priority on getting food and
medicine to prisoners of war. Tōjō coldly observed after the war that
'it was unfortunate that standards which a Japanese soldier would not
find unbearable had apparently proved to be inadequate for western
prisoners'.[38] His comment reflected his view that Westerners were
soft, but it was also a view common among Japanese soldiers guarding
prisoners of war.

Nonetheless, on 3 March 1944 the Army Ministry was finally
forced to admit that 'the average POW's health condition is hardly
satisfactory', and the high death rate was bad both for achieving labour
targets and Japan's international reputation.[39] But little changed.

The Burma–Siam Railway is the best-known example of the
fatal consequences of Japan's use of prisoners of war as forced
labour. Between mid-1942 and late 1943, the Japanese Army drove
a 415-kilometre railway through brutally rugged country to link
Bangkok in Siam (Thailand) and Rangoon (Yangon) in Burma
(Myanmar). Built with the labour of tens of thousands of mostly

British, Dutch and Australian prisoners of war and hundreds of thousands of Asian *rōmusha*, it was designed to supply Japan's armies in Burma. Through disease, starvation and outright killing, some 12,300 of the 61,800 Allied prisoners of war and 42,000 to 74,000 of the 200,000 *rōmusha* labourers perished.[40]

The Tokyo prosecution held a number of the defendants responsible for the mistreatment of prisoners of war, including Tōjō and Shigemitsu. It was contended that command responsibility, up to the level of the cabinet, applied to systemic crimes against prisoners of war in the same way it applied to the Nanking Massacre. The prosecution argued that the similarity of the crimes committed against prisoners of war throughout the Japanese Empire was evidence of a single policy orchestrated at the highest levels.

Speaking before the tribunal, Tōjō accepted administrative responsibility for the treatment of prisoners, but denied using their labour to build the Burma Railway was a war crime. His defence was not particularly strong, as, like Matsui, he appeared to give contradictory information. At one point, he admitted that he knew conditions on the railway were poor and had sent medical staff to address them, then he later insisted that local commanders were responsible for caring for the prisoners. The unprepared Keenan was not able to take advantage of these inconsistencies in cross-examination.

Even so, the prosecution's case on conventional war crimes and crimes against humanity remained powerful and compelling.

# IX

# JUDGEMENT
# AND DISUNITY

Nuremberg was wrapped up in six months, but the trial at Tokyo dragged on for two and a half years. Two of the defendants, Admiral Nagano Osami and former Foreign Minister Matsuoka Yōsuke, died of natural causes during the process. And while the four powers at Nuremberg managed to overcome their differences and deliver a joint judgement (albeit with the Soviet judges dissenting on some of the sentences for being too lenient) it became apparent fairly early that this was not going to happen at Tokyo. On 30 January 1947, Bernard informed Webb that he would dissent from the majority judgement.[1] Röling noted Bernard was something of a loner on the bench, his social contact constrained by his limited English.[2] Then, in late March 1947, Northcroft, Patrick and MacDougall all threatened to resign. Their governments stopped them. Patrick was afraid the tribunal would fail to convict the defendants, which would acquit Japanese militarism in the eyes of the world and make Western justice a laughing-stock in Asia. He blamed Webb for the way things were developing and wanted him replaced, preferably with Northcroft.

Then, in a decision that seems bizarrely parochial in the circumstances, the Australian government called Webb home to sit on the High Court for the Bank Nationalisation Case. MacArthur called the decision 'deplorable', particularly as the Australian government had pushed so hard to play a leading role in the postwar settlement.[3] The other judges were likewise incensed. Patrick now wanted Northcroft appointed as acting president, but MacArthur felt New Zealand was not a significant enough country to warrant the presidency. Instead he appointed Patrick to the role. He did not tell him in advance, and Patrick only learned of his promotion in the press release.

Embarrassingly for MacArthur, Patrick declined on the grounds of ill health. MacArthur, who never assumed Patrick would refuse, was once again furious. MacArthur believed risking sudden death in court was hardly unreasonable compared to achieving the purpose of the IMTFE. Next he appointed the American judge, Myron Cramer, who, being an army officer junior to MacArthur, did as he was ordered. Cramer had not played a significant role on the bench up until this point, and Northcroft was not particularly impressed with him. 'He never quite catches up with what is happening, tends to follow Patrick's lead in the frequent votings and relieves his confusion or exasperation by repeated mutterings of "Oh heck!"'[4]

Webb returned to Tokyo on 18 December 1947, but his authority over the bench, already weak, never recovered. Patrick, Northcroft and MacDougall had already taken matters into their own hands. In May 1947 Northcroft had summoned an expert in writing legal documents from New Zealand, Robert Quentin Quentin-Baxter. With his help, the three judges began writing their own judgement. Jaranilla joined them, then Mei and Zaryanov, creating a majority. In March 1948, they compelled Webb to accept that they, not he, would write the judgement of the IMTFE. The next month, the defence finished their case and the court adjourned. The final judgement was mostly a joint effort of British, Canadian and New Zealand drafters, with the latter perhaps playing the largest role. At the end of the trial, Northcroft was satisfied. He did not like the ad hoc nature of the tribunal and the judgement, but still felt the court had set a useful precedent.[5]

On 4 November 1948, the court resumed to hear the verdict. Webb, as president once more, read the majority judgement which he did not play any role in writing. On Count 1, the court found that all the defendants except Matsui and Shigemitsu had participated in a criminal conspiracy to establish militarism in Japan and wage aggressive war against other countries in the Asia-Pacific: 'The conspiracy existed for and its execution occupied a period of many years. Not all of the conspirators were parties to it at the beginning, and some of those who were parties to it had ceased to be active in its execution before the end. All of those who at any time were parties to the criminal conspiracy or who at any time with guilty knowledge played a part in its execution are guilty of the charge contained in Count I.'[6]

Joining all the defendants in a single conspiracy was probably the judgement's most controversial decision, and may have been based on a desire to draw a parallel with Germany. But as historian Richard Minear put it in his influential 1971 critique of the Tokyo Trial, 'Japan was not Germany; Tōjō was not Hitler; the Pacific War was not identical with the European War.'[7] Ironically, the IMT at Nuremberg had found that the Nazi leaders had engaged in 'separate plans rather than a single conspiracy', although they were all joined in common planning to wage aggressive war.[8]

When considering counts 27 to 36, on crimes against peace and aggressive war, the IMTFE directly followed the findings of the IMT. This made sense – for the two tribunals to come to a different decision on the legality of waging aggressive war would have left international law in chaos. The IMT held that the maxim *nullum crimen sine lege* (no crime without an established law) 'is not a limitation of sovereignty, but is in general a principle of justice . . . To assert that it is unjust to punish those who in defiance of treaties and assurances have attacked neighbouring States without warning is obviously untrue, for in such circumstances the attacker must know that he is doing wrong, and so far from it being unjust to punish him, it would be unjust if his wrong were allowed to go unpunished.'[9]

The IMT made a legal argument in support of this position, holding that the Kellogg–Briand Pact did make aggressive war illegal. 'The solemn renunciation of war as an instrument of national policy necessarily involves the proposition that such a war is illegal in International Law; and that those who plan and wage such a war, with its inevitable and terrible consequences, are committing a crime in so doing.'[10] Finally, the IMT held that enforcing this law would be impossible if individual men could not be held criminally responsible. In renouncing aggressive war, by default, the nations which ratified the Kellogg–Briand Pact had accepted the right of other nations to punish leaders who engaged in it regardless of their pronouncements at the time.

The IMTFE offered its 'unqualified approval' to these findings, and concluded, like the IMT, that its charter was 'not an arbitrary exercise of Power on the part of the victorious nations but is the expression of international law existing at the time of its creation'.[11]

On counts 54 and 55, conventional war crimes and crimes against humanity, the IMTFE found that these atrocities did occur and some of the defendants could reasonably be held responsible for them. In convicting Matsui for the Nanking Massacre, the majority held:

> He did nothing, or nothing effective to abate these horrors. He did issue orders before the capture of the City enjoining propriety of conduct upon his troops and later he issued further orders to the same purport. These orders were of no effect as is now known, and as he must have known. It was pleaded on his behalf that at this time he was ill. His illness was not sufficient to prevent his conducting the military operations of his command nor to prevent his visiting the City for days while these atrocities were occurring. He was in command of the Army responsible for these happenings. He knew of them. He had the power, as he had the duty, to control his troops and to protect the unfortunate citizens of Nanking. He must be held criminally responsible for his failure to discharge this duty.[12]

Controversially, the majority also found Hirota criminally responsible for the massacre. They held that once he became aware of the
atrocities he was under a duty to insist before cabinet that something
be done about them, and that 'his inaction amounted to criminal
negligence'.[13] Convicting a civilian politician for a war crime on the
basis of command responsibility was new, although the decision of
the IMTFE has been followed since – for example, in tribunals relating to the Rwandan genocide.[14] In contrast, Mutō was acquitted over
Nanking, although subsequently convicted of other crimes. While
the majority of the judges accepted that Mutō knew about the atrocities, they held that, due to his subordinate position to Matsui, he was
powerless to stop them.[15]

In addition to being convicted of waging a war of aggression,
Tōjō was also convicted of conventional war crimes in relation to the
treatment of prisoners of war and civilian internees. 'The barbarous
treatment of prisoners and internees was well known to Tōjō,' the
tribunal ruled. 'He took no adequate steps to punish offenders and
to prevent the commission of similar offences in the future.'[16] The
Burma Railway, where Tōjō authorised the use of prisoners as labourers without making arrangements to feed them or care for the sick,
was cited as an example. Nor did he undertake any investigation once
the poor condition of prisoner-of-war camps on the railway became
known. In their view, this made him criminally responsible for the
mistreatment and deaths of the prisoners.[17]

Former Foreign Minister Shigemitsu was also convicted on
count 55 (but not count 54) for the mistreatment of prisoners on the
same basis – he learned of the poor conditions in the prisoner-of-war
camps but did nothing.[18]

The judgement took eight days to read. All twenty-five defendants were found guilty of conspiracy, twenty-two were found guilty of
crimes against peace, and ten of conventional war crimes and crimes
against humanity. Unlike at Nuremberg, none were acquitted. The
defendants would learn their fate on 11 November. Tōjō knew he was

to be held chiefly responsible but he remained defiant. 'This is a trial by conquerors,' he announced to the press before hearing his conviction. 'The spirit of the Japanese people is certain to rise again. There are great difficulties ahead, and I pray the people will have courage to overcome them.'

He also expressed his satisfaction that the Emperor had been kept out of the trial.[19]

On 11 November, the defendants were called into the court one by one, in alphabetical order, to hear Webb read their sentences. Most took them without emotion, clearly resigned to their fate.[20] Tōjō was second last.

'Accused Hideki Tōjō, on the counts of the indictment of which you have been convicted, the International Military Tribunal for the Far East sentences you to death by hanging.' With those words, a judge of the High Court of Australia passed a death sentence on the wartime leader of one of the major Axis powers – unwillingly, as his own minority judgement would later show.

Tōjō had showed some signs of nervousness coming in, but he reacted to the sentence as if hearing it was a relief. He nodded, bowed deeply to the court, nodded again, and walked out. In the newsreels, it almost looks as if he had just been acquitted and told he could leave.

All up, seven defendants were sentenced to death – Generals Tōjō, Mutō, Kimura, Itagaki and Doihara for crimes against peace, war crimes and crimes against humanity; General Matsui for war crimes and crimes against humanity; and Foreign Minister Hirota for crimes against peace, war crimes, and crimes against humanity. Of the death sentences, the last two were the most controversial. Matsui's defenders maintained (and still do) that he had little control over the army at Nanking due to his illness, and that he took action to stop the massacre when he learned it was happening. Hirota was the only civilian to be given the death penalty, and his sentence was met with surprise both inside and outside Japan. Röling held that Hirota was certainly not guilty of a crime against peace, and while he had planned to make Japan a superpower in Asia, it was not through waging war. Röling accused his fellow judges of confusing Hirota's aims and methods.[21] Hirota's death sentence was for his failure to prevent the Nanking atrocities. As he was a civilian in Tokyo at the time, his defenders questioned how much he could have actually done. Indeed, it seems likely that Hirota was sentenced to death on a bare five–four majority.

Most of the remaining defendants were sentenced to life in prison, including Bason Hiranuma Kiichirō and former prime minister Koiso Kuniaki. In the judgement, Kido was held to have joined the conspiracy in 1937 and plotted with Prince Konoe to make Japan a totalitarian state, dominate China, and attack the Western powers. In particular, he was held to have misused his influence over the Emperor to advance the conspiracy. It is not recorded how he reacted to his life sentence, but as the journalists made no comment on him it is likely he took it impassively. Kido seems to have been lucky. The rumours were that he, Ōshima, Araki, and former navy minister Shimada Shigetarō escaped the death penalty by just a single vote.

Only Tōgō and Shigemitsu, both former foreign ministers, received lesser sentences. The court acknowledged that Tōgō had worked to prevent the war from breaking out, and had also taken to steps to compel Japan to adhere to the Geneva Conventions. But, the court held, once war broke out, Tōgō went along with it willingly. He was sentenced to twenty years' imprisonment. In sentencing Shigemitsu, the tribunal took into account the fact that he was in no way involved in the formulation of conspiracy, and by the time he became foreign minister in 1943 the country was effectively controlled by the military, and he had little influence over policy. These were all reasons why the Allies, except for the Soviet Union, did not want to prosecute him in the first place. Nonetheless, having prosecuted him, the court found him guilty and sentenced him to seven years' imprisonment. On hearing this, Shigemitsu put his elbows on the desk and buried his head in his hands. (A full list of the verdicts and sentences is given in Appendix A.)

With the last sentence read – Umezu, to life imprisonment – the IMTFE closed without ceremony.

In addition to the majority judgement, five judges – Webb, Jaranilla, Bernard, Röling and Pal – wrote separate opinions either concurring with or dissenting from the majority. These were not read in court.

Webb agreed with the majority on the law and the interpretation of the facts, but made some different findings of guilt regarding certain accused. His main point of difference, however, was on sentencing. At Nuremberg, he pointed out, defendants were not sentenced to death solely for waging aggressive war – the death penalty was reserved for those who also committed war crimes and crimes against humanity. Webb believed the IMTFE should have followed this principle, perhaps recognising that international law on crimes against peace was less well established than the law on conventional war crimes. 'It may well be that the punishment of imprisonment for life under sustained conditions of hardship in an isolated place or places outside Japan – the usual conditions in such cases [referring to the class-B and -C trials] – would be a greater deterrent to men like the accused than the speedy termination of existence on the scaffold or before a firing squad.'[22] Plus, he added, 'it may prove revolting to hang or shoot such old men.'[23]

Webb could not say that any sentence was manifestly inadequate or excessive, therefore he did not dissent. But he did throw petrol on a smouldering fire by calling for the immunity of the Emperor to be taken into account in sentencing the others. The Emperor's authority was required for the war, and if he did not want the war he should have withheld his authority. A British court, in cases where the leader of a criminal conspiracy is not available, would take that into account when sentencing his subordinates. Webb clarified his position: 'I do not suggest the Emperor should have been prosecuted. That is beyond my province. His immunity was, no doubt, decided upon in the best interests of all the Allied Powers. Justice requires me to take into consideration the Emperor's immunity when determining the punishment of the accused found guilty: that is all.'[24]

Even this measured comment caused outrage in Washington, with the State Department believing Webb had cast doubt on the legitimacy of his own tribunal. MacArthur was also furious, telling the US ambassador William Sebald that Webb was 'playing cheap politics' by appealing to anti-Hirohito sentiment in Australia.[25]

Jaranilla also issued a short concurring opinion. He agreed with the majority but felt that the court had dismissed too many counts from the indictment. Many more, he said, were consistent with the charter. Moreover, some of the penalties were 'too lenient, not exemplary and deterrent, and not commensurate with the gravity of the offense or offenses committed'.[26] He remained, to the end, the hardest of all the judges on the defendants.

Röling partially dissented from the majority. In a 250-page judgement, he maintained that the tribunal needed to consider whether the charter was consistent with international law. 'The victorious powers may form a tribunal and give it the power to punish acts or omissions, but it is for the tribunal to decide if those acts or omissions are crimes at international law,' he wrote.[27] He concluded that the law relating to crimes against peace was not yet developed to the extent that individuals could be held criminally responsible for waging aggressive war. It was, he said, a charge borrowed from the future. He also criticised the majority for taking too broad a view of command responsibility for conventional war crimes and crimes against humanity – he was particularly critical of Hirota's conviction over Nanking. His conclusion, though, was that while the judgement of the IMTFE was ex post facto law, it was not necessarily unjust. In an interview published in 1993, he compared the prosecution of the defendants at Tokyo with the prosecution of Dutch citizens who betrayed Jews to the Gestapo. What they did was legal, but punishing them for it was hardly unjust.[28] So in the end, he seemed to find the majority judgement legally weak but practically necessary.

Bernard dissented entirely from the majority, although he was critical of the judgement for different reasons than Röling was. He accepted the validity of the charges and that international law did allow for men to be prosecuted for crimes against peace, war crimes, and crimes against humanity. But in his view, the tribunal was so procedurally flawed the outcome could not be upheld. He cited the vagueness of the charges, the lack of clarity around individual responsibility, the lack of proof of a single conspiracy, and the holding men responsible through 'participation by omission'.[29] Essential principles of justice had not been respected, he claimed, and 'a verdict reached by a tribunal after a defective procedure cannot be a valid one'.[30] He also commented on the absence of the Emperor when there was evidence for him to be prosecuted – holding him to different standards was, he said, another flaw.[31]

Bernard's judgement, like Webb's, alarmed SCAP and the Emperor's defenders. The Emperor wrote to MacArthur to confirm that he had no intention of abdicating, and Keenan went back before the media to say again that there had been no grounds to prosecute him.[32]

These four separate opinions, though, were overshadowed by one: the mammoth and fiery dissent of Justice Pal. Running to 1,235 pages – only just short of the 1,444 pages of the majority – Pal's judgement was so long he had absented himself from the courtroom for most of the final months of the trial to write it.

Pal completely rejected the right of the victorious Allies to try Japan's leaders for waging aggressive war. To him, these charges could only be just if all nations in the international community, from an equal bargaining position, agreed to put aside their sovereignty and accept themselves legally bound to not attack each other. This had not happened, and furthermore, it could not happen while an unjust international system based on colonialism prevailed across Asia. Having won their empires in Asia by force, the Western powers could not now complain that the Japanese had used force against them. 'There can hardly be any justification for any direct and indirect attempt at maintaining, in the name of humanity and justice, the very status quo which might have been organized and hitherto maintained only by force by pure opportunist "Have and Holders",' he wrote.[33] Pal maintained that the trials would be inherently unjust unless the victors were tried alongside the defeated by the same standards.[34]

Pal rejected the charge of conspiracy; he, too, believed there was no basis for it in international law. Allowing it to stand would put a 'dangerous weapon in the hands of an unscrupulous victor', by giving them a catch-all charge to use when prosecuting the vanquished.[35]

Pal made two specific objections to the charges of aggressive war and crimes against peace. First, he considered them to be a violation of the principle of *nullum crimen sine lege* and therefore unenforceable. Second, even if there were laws prohibiting aggressive war, there was no evidence that Japan had breached them. In Pal's view, any war on reasonable grounds of self-defence was justifiable until the international community set more specific standards. Pal accepted that Japan's wars against China and the Western powers were justified by encirclement, threats to Japan and, above all, the menace of communism. To him, Japan's expansion into Asia was no different to the Monroe Doctrine, where the US opposed European colonialism in the Americas in the interests of its security. In particular, Pal talked a great deal about communism and the threat it posed. 'The whole world was preparing, and is, even now, preparing against the apprehended aggression of Communism and of the Communist state.'[36]

When it came to counts 54 and 55, the conventional war crimes and crimes against humanity, Pal accepted that Japanese armies had committed atrocities of a 'devilish and fiendish character'.[37] But he was cool on the evidence, citing exaggerated or fabricated accounts of atrocities from the First World War as examples of the distortion of facts for propaganda purposes. While he agreed that there had been 'horrible atrocities' in Nanking, he said it was 'difficult to read this evidence without feeling that there has been distortions and exaggerations'.[38]

Furthermore, he denied that the defendants could be held responsible for the atrocities even if they did happen. He rejected the idea they were co-ordinated from the highest levels of the military or government, and while acknowledging the atrocities were similar, wrote, 'I do not find any basis for inference there from that these were the result of a common plan or conspiracy of the persons charged with such a plan.'[39] He then insisted that mere dereliction of duty was not enough to prove responsibility, there had to be positive action. 'On this evidence I cannot ascribe any deliberate and reckless disregard of legal duty on the part of General Matsui in this respect,' he wrote.[40] Likewise with Hirota – Pal argued that members of a government are entitled to rely on its proper functioning.

He accepted there was overwhelming evidence of the mistreatment of prisoners of war, but said the perpetrators were not before the tribunal. They had already been dealt with by the Allies in the lesser class-B and -C trials held throughout the Pacific. And finally, as Japan had not ratified the Geneva Convention it was not obliged to follow it.

In what was probably his most inflammatory statement, Pal compared the atomic bombing of Hiroshima and Nagasaki to the Holocaust. 'If any indiscriminate destruction of civilian life and property is still illegitimate in warfare, then in the Pacific War, this decision to use the atom bomb is the only near approach to the directives of the German Emperor during the First World War and of the Nazi leaders during the Second World War,' he claimed. 'Nothing like this could be traced to the present accused.'[41] He wrote in conclusion: 'I would hold that each and every one of the accused must be found not guilty of each and every one of the charges in the indictment.'[42]

Pal's judgement was suppressed at the time, but after the end of the occupation it was taken up eagerly and re-published by Japanese nationalists and historical revisionists. Pal was feted by them on several postwar visits to Japan, and monuments to him have been built at both the Yasukuni Shrine in Tokyo and the Ryozen Gokoku Shrine in Kyoto.

And so the Tokyo Trial ended with disunity and disagreement.

There were a few public rallies for clemency for the condemned, and a nationalist organisation called the Greater Japan Youth Party published an advertisement in the press thanking the accused for shouldering Japan's guilt, and calling for their sentences to be commuted.[43] But most of the public was indifferent to the defendants' fate.

The defence unsuccessfully challenged the judgement in the US Supreme Court. They lobbied MacArthur to commute the death sentences, but despite his misgivings about the trial he confirmed both verdict and sentences on 24 November. In his final public statements, Tōjō repeated his satisfaction that the Emperor had escaped prosecution, confirmed his faith in the people of Japan, and called for world peace. He was now under the guidance of a Buddhist priest, Dr Hanayama Nobukatsu, who was pleased with the progress his pupil was making. 'Since he embraced the Buddhist faith six months ago, he has lost his belief in war,' Hanayama told the media in early December. 'A devout belief in Buddhism, together with the knowledge of the suffering the war has caused the world's peoples, has convinced him that there are other, better means of solving the world's problems.'[44]

On 21 December, Tōjō was told his sentence would be carried out the following night, shortly after midnight on 23 December. He bowed his head, and responded with, 'Okay, okay,' in English.[45] Asked if he had any last requests, he requested a Japanese meal and a cup of sake for himself and the other defendants, and for something to be done for the families of the convicted war criminals. He got neither. The next day, he was visited by Dr Hanayama, who took many notes of Tōjō's last thoughts and wishes. In the samurai tradition, Tōjō wrote a poem: 'This is goodbye/ But I shall be waiting beneath the moss/ Until the flowers in my beloved Japan/ Bloom once again.'[46]

Just before midnight on 22 December, Tōjō, Doihara, Matsui and Mutō were taken from their cells. Wearing US Army fatigues with a 'P' on the back and handcuffed to two guards each, they were taken to the Buddhist chapel where Dr Hanayama was waiting. Awkwardly, with their handcuffed hands, they each accepted a stick of incense. Eight minutes later, they were marched from the chapel and across the courtyard of the prison to the gallows. Itagaki, Kimura and Hirota, the lone civilian, would follow shortly after.

When the sun rose on 23 December, the process of justice at Tokyo was over. And the Allies were determined to put it behind them as quickly as possible.

# PART THREE

# SOLDIERS

The Australian class-B and -C trials of officers
and men of the Japanese Army and Navy

# X

# AUSTRALIA'S OWN TRIALS

Concurrently with the class-A trial at Tokyo, seven of the Allied powers represented on the bench – the United States, the United Kingdom, the Netherlands, Australia, Nationalist China, the Philippines and France – held class-B and -C trials throughout the Asia-Pacific (see Appendix B for more details). These trials began with the prosecution of General Yamashita by the United States in September 1945 and finished with the Australian trials at Manus Island in April 1951. Around 5,700 defendants were accused of conventional war crimes and crimes against humanity. At the same time, a similar program of trials was held in Europe directed against German war criminals and Axis collaborators.

The Soviet Union and Chinese communists did not participate in the class-A/B/C system in the Pacific, but held trials of their own. Following its investigations into Unit 731 of the Japanese Army and its chemical and biological warfare experiments, the Soviet Union held a secret trial of twelve defendants at Khabarovsk in December 1949. The Red Army may have also summarily executed as many as 3,000 actual or suspected Japanese war criminals. The Chinese communists detained around 1,000 Japanese soldiers for 're-education' and tried forty-five for war crimes in 1956. All were returned to Japan by 1964.[1]

Australia conducted 294 trials of 949 suspects, at Ambon, Morotai, Labuan, Wewak, Darwin, Rabaul, Singapore, Hong Kong and Manus Island (specifically, Los Negros) between November 1946 and April 1951. Of the defendants, 280 were acquitted and 644 were convicted; 138 were executed – 114 by hanging, 24 by shooting – and 498 given prison sentences of varying lengths (see Appendix C for more detail).[2] David Sissons notes that as some of the defendants were in more than one trial, the total number of persons tried was 814. Two condemned men died in custody, so the total number executed was 138.[3]

The Australian procedure for conducting class-B and -C trials was developed quickly between September and November 1945. In the weeks immediately after the end of the war, Australian forces captured a large number of suspects, while Justice Webb and his co-commissioners collected a significant amount of evidence relating to crimes. Evatt finally made the First Webb Report public on 11 September 1945 London time, shortly before Tōjō was arrested in Tokyo. Norman Makin, acting Minister for External Affairs in Evatt's absence, tabled the report in the House of Representatives. He confirmed the government's commitment to holding trials of Japanese suspected of class-A, -B and -C war crimes: '[I]t is our duty to future generations to ensure that all those responsible for those crimes against humanity shall be brought to justice. The investigations carried out over the last two years by Sir William Webb have proved that the atrocious behaviour which has marked the Japanese forces in all battle areas is a part of a policy of systematic terrorism, in which both the private soldier and the Japanese Army commanders have participated.'[4]

Unsurprisingly, the report caused a storm in the media, coming as it did on top of the first accounts of freed Australian prisoners of war. In an editorial entitled 'Japanese Savagery Must Be Punished', *The Age* newspaper argued:

> If there be any sentimentalist disposed to plead for a soft peace
> for Japan, he should ponder the revelations of innate Japanese

bestiality, cruelty and treachery . . . Every available proof of
Japanese savagery should be made known to the world at a moment
when far-reaching questions are about to arise as to what is to
be done with the Japanese people and their leaders guilty of the
abominations. Abhorrence must be translated into positive and
practical measures by the victorious Allies, to ensure that the world
be spared a repetition of such barbarities. The present indictment,
which amplifies and reinforces many other well-authenticated
records, makes it clear that beneath their veneer of western
civilisation the Japanese are a primitive people, still steeped in the
barbarisms that other countries abandoned centuries ago.[5]

There were demands in both parliament and the press for trials
to begin, particularly with the publicity surrounding the massacre of
Australian nurses at Bangka Island, an event which came to symbolise
Japanese brutality for many Australians.

Army Minister Frank Forde assured the House of Representatives
on 18 September 'that the policy supported by this Government is
that of arresting and trying, before a properly constituted tribunal, all
war criminals', but political pressure on the government continued to
mount.[6] In a letter to the editor in *The Argus*, a D. Carter reflected the
views of many when he or she wrote: 'The Australian public has given
freely of flesh and blood and money, and is entitled to demand that
the matter be given much quicker attention and more drastic action
than pertains in Germany, where, comparatively speaking, little has
been done to punish the criminals. It is galling to learn that known
Japanese criminals are at large and enjoying life.'[7]

On 21 September, Opposition Leader Robert Menzies made
a statement to *The Argus* that he was dissatisfied with the steps the
government had taken so far and wanted more and faster action.
But the process of deciding how to create courts to try the alleged
war criminals was not as simple as it seemed. The government was
proposing to try non-Australians for offences committed against

non-Australians in courts outside of Australia; for example, the murder of an Indonesian civilian by a Japanese soldier in the Netherlands East Indies. The British government had created a royal warrant to establish class-B and -C war crimes courts, but the Australian government felt that the novelty of the courts required new legislation. On 4 October 1945 a war crimes bill based closely on the British royal warrant was introduced simultaneously to both houses of parliament. After a brief debate it was passed, becoming the *War Crimes Act 1945* (Commonwealth) and the basis for Australia's class-B and -C trials.

Sections 7 and 12 of the Act empowered the Australian government to create courts to try 'violations of the laws and usages of war or war crimes against any person who was at any time resident in Australia, or against any British subject or citizen of an Allied Power'. Once the trials got underway, a few enterprising defence counsel challenged the jurisdiction of the courts based on the Act; for example, trials R5 and R6, concerning the mistreatment of German missionaries, who, being Axis civilians, were neither British subjects nor citizens of Allied powers. As they were living in the Australian territory of New Guinea, the court held they met the requirement of being 'at any time resident in Australia'. Other defence lawyers challenged prosecutions for murder, assault, and the use of forced labour on the basis that these acts were not 'violations of the laws and usages of war or war crimes' (for example, M9 and ML12). All were dismissed based on the terms of the Geneva and Hague conventions. In R172 and M20, a few extremely ambitious defence lawyers even tried to argue that the *War Crimes Act* itself was unconstitutional, as it went beyond the Commonwealth government's power to make laws with respect to defence or external affairs. These submissions were likewise dismissed.[8]

The courts were to be military courts, run along similar lines to a field general court martial.[9] In the British, and later the Australian, Army there had historically been different levels of courts martial, with the higher ones able to try more serious crimes and impose more serious sentences. A field general court martial was the highest, able to impose the death penalty.

Courts martial in the British system are adversarial, like common law courts, with a prosecution and defence. However, there is no judge or jury. Rather, the verdict and sentence are decided by a panel of officers by majority decision. The command of the armed forces was traditionally within the King's royal prerogative; the traditional protections of the common law, such as trial by jury, did not apply to courts martial. It is not necessary (nor, in many cases, practical) for the officers making up the bench to have any legal qualifications, and it is therefore common for a court martial to include a judge advocate – a lawyer to advise the court on matters of law. Sentences need to be confirmed by a superior officer, but there is traditionally no other right of appeal.

The Australian war crimes trials followed this procedure 'modified, adapted or added to by regulation' made under the *War Crimes Act*.[10] One significant – and controversial – modification was the relaxation of the rules of evidence. At common law, hearsay – someone reporting what someone else said to them – is not admissible in court unless an exception applies. Also, the author of any document admitted at court is usually required to appear for cross-examination on its content. Both the British royal warrant and the *War Crimes Act* (Section 9) dispensed with these two rules and allowed any statement or document to be admitted which appeared authentic, even if it would not be admissible in a field general court martial. The UNWCC had taken the view that this was necessary, as most war criminals could not be convicted without such evidence.

Judge Advocate General John Bowie Wilson criticised the Act in a report on Morotai trial M44 because 'none of the rules that have been considered necessary to protect accused persons apply . . . [M]uch of the evidence admitted in these proceedings even under the system of there being no rules of evidence, should not have been admitted as being relevant to the charge before the court.'[11] David Sissons was equally critical of this principle in his review. 'It seems to me that what they were saying was: "It is more important that an innocent man should go free than that a guilty man should hang; but this is true only where the innocent man is one of our own side. When he is an enemy national, it is not so important."'[12] As the trials went on and documentary evidence became more common, these questions would arise more frequently.

The Allies agreed among themselves that there would be no right of appeal from their courts, although all sentences would need to be confirmed by military authorities.[13] The *War Crimes Act* empowered courts to sentence offenders to death, a term of imprisonment, a fine, or an order to make restitution for stolen or destroyed property. The last two do not appear to have been used. On the death penalty, the Chifley government found itself caught between two strong competing forces. On the one hand, the Labor Party was moving against the death penalty in most states. The Queensland Labor government of Ted Theodore had abolished capital punishment in that state in 1922, and a moratorium on the death penalty had been maintained by Labor governments in Tasmania since 1934 (with one exception in 1946) and New South Wales since 1941.[14] Only in South Australia and Western Australia were Labor governments still carrying out hangings. On the other hand, most of the general public (including many Labor members) demanded the death penalty for Japanese war criminals.

Finally, the compromise was reached where a death sentence needed to be confirmed by the commander-in-chief of the army (from 1 December 1945, Lieutenant General Vernon Sturdee) on the advice of Judge Advocate General John Bowie Wilson. This was another modification to the procedure of Australian courts martial. Under the *Defence Act 1903*, a death sentence passed by an Australian court martial against an Australian soldier could only be confirmed by the Commonwealth cabinet directly. Like the relaxation of the rules of evidence, this came under criticism.

F.R. Sinclair, the Secretary for the Army, wrote to Army Minister Frank Forde: 'if one . . . takes a critical view of this procedure (and such a critical view will, I suggest, be taken in the years to come) it might be held that any departure from the normal methods of administration and justice cannot be justified, because the motives which underlie our activities in bringing our former enemies to trial cannot be said to be altogether disinterested or unbiased'.[15]

Forde sought advice from Webb, who replied: 'It would be wrong to assume that we must exercise the same meticulous care with sentences imposed on war criminals as we would with sentences imposed on our own people'.[16]

So the procedure stayed, and the Chifley government was able to avoid the uncomfortable task of confirming death sentences. Not sharing those qualms, the Menzies government did take it upon itself to review the death sentences passed on Manus Island in 1950 and 1951 at cabinet level.

Courts could sentence defendants to death by either hanging or shooting. The choice was often influenced by practical matters, such as whether there was a gallows at the location, or enough men to form a firing squad. There was also a perception that hanging was a less honourable death and therefore appropriate for the most serious crimes. 'I consider that shooting would be too easy a death for persons who have been guilty of the crimes that have been traced to the Japanese,' said Archie Cameron in a statement to the House of Representatives in a debate over the bill.[17] In practice, though, many firing squads failed to kill the condemned men in the first volley and hanging proved the more reliably fast method of execution.

Then there was the question of what to do with those sentenced to imprisonment.[18] Keeping them in Australia was unpopular, as it would be expensive and would probably grant a better standard of living than in war-ravaged Japan. But sending war criminals back home to serve their sentences was not popular either. The only other option was imprisoning them somewhere in Australia's external territories. Sturdee proposed putting them on a remote island where they could work on a plantation. However, no immediate decision was made, and as a result temporary 'war criminals compounds' were established wherever the suspects were first held. And there they stayed, until finally, on 15 March 1946, it was determined that all war criminals were to be kept in the compound in Rabaul in New Britain, and all those sentenced to prison were transferred there.

Having established a procedure for holding the trials, the government then needed to decide where they were to be held. In the House of Representatives on 21 September 1945, Norman Makin said the government was considering 'the holding of trials at a central point in the Pacific area, or at various places where atrocities have been committed'. The second option was in line with the Moscow Declaration, which said that German war criminals would be 'sent back to the countries in which their abominable deeds were done in order that they may be judged and punished according to the laws of these liberated countries'.[19]

With the passage of the *War Crimes Act*, the government was now waiting only on UNWCC approval to begin prosecuting the defendants. On 12 October 1945, Lord Wright of Durley advised Evatt that approval was needed only for class-A prosecutions and those requiring extradition. Australia could therefore proceed with trials for suspects already in its custody. On 24 October, the cabinet issued an order-in-council delegating the task of forming courts to division, corps and army commanders, and on 26 November the army ordered those commanders to form the courts as soon as possible. Trials commenced at Morotai on 29 November and at Wewak in Papua New Guinea on 30 November.[20]

The cases were tried by a bench of at least three officers, including the president. As the trials progressed, the courts tended to get larger and the officers more senior. The usual size was three at Morotai, Labuan, Singapore, Hong Kong and Wewak; four at Rabaul; and five at Manus Island. Up to half of the bench could be officers from the other Allies, and at different times British, American, Dutch, Indian and Chinese officers sat on Australian courts when their citizens were among the victims. Regulation 8 from the regulations made pursuant to the Act specified courts should consist of as many officers as possible of equal or superior rank to the accused, and at least one from the same service (army or navy). This requirement was difficult to meet in practice and was generally ignored.[21] Usually at least one member of the court had legal qualifications, although this does not seem to have been the case at one Rabaul and two Labuan trials. The president was usually a lieutenant colonel, although at times it was a major or a colonel. At the command responsibility trials at Rabaul the president was a major general, and at Manus Island, a brigadier. At the command responsibility trials at Rabaul a judge advocate was appointed as well.

The prosecution consisted of army officers with legal qualifications, and at the command responsibility trials at Rabaul and Manus, these were supplemented by a civilian barrister. The defence was usually a combination of Japanese lawyers and officers of the Australian Army Legal Corps (AALC). At first, the Japanese lawyers were simply found among the troops in the area at the time of surrender, but at later trials they were sent directly from Japan by the Japanese government. At Labuan the defence in some cases appears to have consisted of Japanese officers without legal qualifications. Translation was an even bigger problem than at Tokyo. Aside from the differences between English and Japanese, the courts also needed to deal with the problem of finding people with a high level of proficiency in both languages in either the Australian or Japanese armies throughout the South-West Pacific Area.

The Australian class-B and -C war crimes trials fell into three stages. The first ran from November 1945 to late 1946, where trials were established at Labaun, Wewak, Morotai, Ambon, Darwin and

Rabaul by local commands to try suspects for crimes committed in each area.[22] Rabaul was the most significant location and saw many trials for crimes against civilians throughout the Asia-Pacific, while the other locations saw fewer trials, almost all of which were concerned with crimes against Allied prisoners.

The second stage ran from 1946 to 1948, with trials in Rabaul, Singapore and Hong Kong. By this stage, the trials were coming under increasing criticism for taking too long, and there was pressure to wind them up. The Australian government intended to continue to hold trials in Hong Kong; however, in early 1948 the Hong Kong Administration needed its premises back. MacArthur would not allow the Australian government to hold trials in Japan, so the program stalled.

The Menzies government started the program again, and the final round took place at Manus Island (Los Negros Island) from 5 June 1950 to 9 April 1951. As it is not possible to cover all the trials in depth, I will focus on a number of interesting and illustrative cases in the following chapters.

# XI

# THE SANDAKAN
# DEATH MARCHES ON TRIAL

The first round of Australian class-B and -C trials began in November 1945 and tapered out over April to July 1946. Large numbers of soldiers, prisoners of war, internees and Japanese personnel were still being moved, and so transport by air and sea was limited. Many Australian troops were still overseas but lawyers and translators were in limited supply, and it was easier in some cases to hold mass trials. The trials often happened concurrently with the public revelation of Japanese atrocities and so became front-page news.

Most of the early trials concerned crimes against Allied prisoners. At Labuan, fifteen trials of 145 defendants were conducted from 3 December 1945 to 31 January 1946 for crimes committed against Australian and British prisoners of war in Borneo. And at Morotai in the Dutch Moluccas, twenty-five trials of 148 defendants (including ninety defendants transferred mid-trial from Ambon for M45, which was started there but never concluded) between 29 November 1945 and 28 February 1946 for crimes against Australian prisoners at Ambon or downed Allied airmen throughout the local area. And at Darwin, three trials of twenty-two defendants between 1 March and 29 April 1946 for crimes against Australian prisoners in Timor. The two trials of two defendants at Wewak,

Papua New Guinea, from 30 November to 11 December 1945 for mutilation of the dead and cannibalism.

In this chapter I will look at some examples from Labuan and Morotai relating to the Sandakan prisoner-of-war camp and the Sandakan–Ranau death marches.

Labuan is an island off the north coast of Borneo, formerly in British North Borneo, now part of Malaysia. Both the British and the Dutch established colonies on Borneo, which is rich in rubber and oil, and by the early twentieth century the island was divided into the smaller British north and the larger Dutch south. Borneo's resources, along with its central position in the East Indies, also made it attractive to Japan. The Japanese launched an invasion of the island from French Indochina almost immediately after the outbreak of the Pacific War, landing in the north on 16 December 1941, and the few Allied troops on the island had surrendered by April 1942.

Japanese occupation policy stated: 'In general, the Army has been charged with the administration of densely populated areas which demand complex administrative tasks, while sparsely populated primitive areas, which shall be retained in the future for the benefit of the Empire, have been assigned to the Navy.'[1] Accordingly, more developed North Borneo was assigned to the army and South Borneo to the navy.

Even by the standards of the Japanese Empire, the occupation of Borneo was harsh. An atmosphere of fear was enforced by the *Kempeitai* and *Tokkeitai*. Men were conscripted as *rōmusha* labourers, the women forced into military brothels. Attempts were made to forcibly 'Japanise' the population in South Borneo, and anti-Japanese plots, actual or suspected, were suppressed ruthlessly. The oppression of the Suluk ethnic group of North Borneo, including the burning of villages and the mass execution of men, was one of the war crimes prosecuted by the British Commonwealth at Tokyo.

This brutality extended to prisoners of war. Between mid-1942 and mid-1943, 2,000 Australian and 750 British soldiers captured in the

Fall of Singapore were transferred to North Borneo to work on an airfield at Sandakan. It seems they volunteered on the promise of better
food and an escape from the drudgery of imprisonment in Changi.
Of these 2,750 prisoners, only six survived the war. The others died at
Sandakan, or on two death marches between Sandakan and Ranau, or
were executed at Ranau at the end of the war.

Between May and July 1945, Borneo was recaptured for the Allies
by Australia's 6th, 7th and 9th divisions in a campaign that remains
controversial. Sacrificing the lives of Australian soldiers to recapture
territory in the Dutch East Indies once the Allies were preparing to
invade Japan itself was seen as a waste. Around 2,000 mostly British
prisoners of war and civilian internees were recovered at the Kuching
camp, liberated by the Australian 9th Division on 11 September 1945.
The death rate among British soldiers there had been two-thirds. Six
survivors of Sandakan were also found living in the jungle with the
native people, and from them was learned the fate of the others. Once
Japan surrendered, the men of the 9th Division moved quickly to
arrest suspects among them, and the Sandakan–Ranau death marches
became the main subject of the Labuan trials.

These were held under Australian control for simple convenience.
Britain did not have soldiers to spare from Malaya and Singapore
to send to Borneo, so the 9th Australian Division was left to manage
British North Borneo for the time being. The former civilian capi-
tal of Jesselton (modern Kota Kinabalu) had been destroyed in the
war, so the 9th Division chose Labuan as an alternative HQ. There
were not enough ships to transport the Japanese personnel still
on the island back to Japan for some months, so it made sense for
Australia to conduct the trials, and to conduct them in Labuan.
Those sentenced to imprisonment or death by hanging were sent to
Rabaul, where there was a semipermanent compound and a gallows.
Once the British resumed control in North Borneo, the Australians
left took their remaining suspects with them to continue trials
in Morotai.

The revelation of the fate of the prisoners left tensions running high, and David Sissons reported being disturbed at reports of the mistreatment of some suspects, but the conduct of the court proceedings themselves was cordial.[2] Captain Athol Moffitt, the Sydney barrister acting as lead Australian prosecutor, at one point went out of his way to explain the common law system to the Japanese Army defence lawyer. In return, the Japanese lawyer helped the translators with the exact meaning of certain Japanese phrases. In those early months, with the courts limited to the personnel they had on hand, they had to make do.

The two highest-profile trials at Labuan were those of Captains Takakuwa Takuo and Hoshijima Susumu (also Susumi), described in one newspaper article as Australia's public enemies #1 and #2 respectively.[3] Takakuwa had commanded the men on the Sandakan–Ranau death marches, while Hoshijima had been the commandant of Sandakan POW Camp. Between them they were held responsible for the worst war crimes ever inflicted on Australians, and for over 10 per cent of the Australian Army's deaths in the Pacific War. Both trials are interesting, but I will look at Hoshijima's in detail. He was brought to trial at Labuan (trial number ML28) on 8 January 1946, charged with the ill-treatment of POWs at Sandakan between September 1942 and May 1945.[4] The trial was high-profile enough that Army Minister Frank Forde came to visit the courtroom himself at one point, the only civilian to do so.

It is possible to take a charitable view of many Japanese commandants of prisoner-of-war camps. They were sent to remote locations with insufficient resources, given unachievable objectives, and left to control subordinates who had been indoctrinated to hate prisoners of war. But some commandants seemed to go out of their way to inflict as much suffering and death as they possibly could. Ikeuchi Masakiyo at Ambon was probably one. And Hoshijima, as far as we can tell from the evidence presented at his trial, was another.

The man charged with being directly responsible for the deaths of 1,100 Australian and British prisoners of war was born in 1908 in Okayama prefecture. He studied chemistry at Osaka Imperial University, where his academic career was distinguished. On graduating in 1934, he was employed as an engineer in the Dai Nippon Celluloid Company. In 1941, married with four children, he was drafted into the army. His youngest son was born only days before he left for the East Indies – he held him once before leaving. His engineering background and ability to speak workable English probably landed him the job at Sandakan.

Hoshijima made an immediate impression on the prisoners who arrived at his camp. Intimidating in appearance and haughty in demeanour, he gave a 'welcome speech': 'You will work until your bones rot under the tropical sun of Borneo. You will work for the Emperor. If any of you escapes, I will pick out three or four and shoot them. The war will last 100 years.'[5]

He made an immediate impression on the people in the courtroom as well. Almost all the journalists present wrote of the 'tall' and 'arrogant' Japanese captain.[6] Chief prosecutor Athol Moffit, having read the evidence, was curious to see Hoshijima in the flesh. He recorded his first sight of him:

> From the moment he was marched into the court by the Ghurka guards, it was apparent that he was an impressive man with a domineering personality. About six feet tall, a powerful athletic looking man, he towered above his diminutive guards and the Japanese defending officers. He clicked the heels of his well-polished boots, saluted with military precision and gazed intently, even defiantly, at those who were to try him. The corners of his mouth were slightly turned down to reveal the face of a determined and cruel man, characteristics to become apparent from the evidence presented to the court and from his demeanour before it in the many days of the trial.[7]

According to one journalist, he 'snarled' his plea of 'not guilty' to each of the four counts of the indictment.[8]

Moffitt had served as an artillery officer in the war before transferring to the Australian Army Legal Corps (AALC). Arriving in
Borneo seven weeks after the Japanese surrender, he moved into a
house vacated by a Japanese officer. It still had Japanese stationery
strewn over the floor and a poster of a geisha girl on the wall. In his
address to the court, Moffitt accused Hoshijima of having prisoners 'flogged like the galley slaves of twenty centuries ago' and sending
them to their deaths on the Sandakan–Ranau death marches.[9] The
commander of the marches, Captain Takakuwa, had already been
sentenced to death (trial ML17).

The main witness for the prosecution was Warrant Officer
William 'Bill' Sticpewich, one of the six survivors of the second
Sandakan–Ranau death march. Born in Newcastle in 1908, he had
made a name for himself as a speedway rider before enlisting in
Brisbane in 1940. He was assigned to the 8th Division and captured at
the Fall of Singapore in February 1942.[10] Moffitt wrote of him: 'He is
the typical Aussie – fairly rough, but hail fellow well met with a ton
of resource and personality in a rough way. He got on the right side
of the Japs and can speak a lot of Japanese . . . [B]eing very handy as a
carpenter and good at fixing machines, he made himself invaluable to
the Japs.'[11]

Sticpewich told a harrowing story of slow starvation. One of his
tasks as a carpenter at Sandakan was making coffins, but from June
1944 onwards, there were too many deaths and too few materials with
which to make them. There were food cuts in June and September,
and things became even worse with the beginning of Allied air attacks
in October. When work on the airfield ceased in January, the rice
ration was a mere 100 grams per man per day. It was further reduced
to 40. The prisoners were put to work cultivating vegetables but got
to eat little of what they grew. There was notionally a ration of meat
or fish, but these rarely appeared and were usually full of maggots
when they did. What little food there was could be withheld as a punishment, and entire working parties would go without food for the

The Japanese delegates board the USS *Missouri* during the surrender ceremony, 2 September 1945. Shigemitsu and Umezu are at the front, on the left and right respectively. (U.S. National Archives USA-C-2719)

Suzuki Kantarō, Prime Minister of Japan 1944–45.

H.V. Evatt, Australian Attorney-General and Minister for External Affairs, 1941–49. (Max Dupain, National Library of Australia PIC P2241/3 LOC Q33)

The infamous photo of Douglas MacArthur with Hirohito, 27 September 1945. Never before had the people of Japan seen the Emperor in such an unflattering light. (Harry S. Truman Library & Museum. Accession no. 98-2431)

Prince Konoe Fumimaro, Prime Minister of Japan 1937–39 and 1940–41. Despite his promise as a statesman, he was unable to prevent a militarist takeover of the Japanese government.

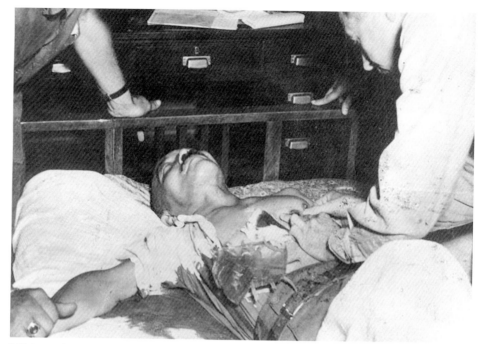

US Army doctors treat Tōjō after his attempted suicide. The sergeant who provided him with a life-saving blood transfusion was a veteran of the New Guinea campaign, and wanted to ensure his former adversary lived to face justice. (Harry S. Truman Library & Museum. Accession no. 98-2453)

The judges of the IMTFE. Top row, L to R: Radhabinod Pal (India), B.V.A. Röling (Netherlands), Edward Stuart McDougall (Canada), Henri Bernard (France), Harvey Northcroft (New Zealand), Delfín Jaranilla (Philippines). Bottom row, L to R: Lord Patrick (UK), Myron G. Cramer (US), Sir William Webb (Australia), Mei Ju-ao (China), I.M. Zaryanov (USSR). (U.S. National Archives III-SC-251115)

Chief Prosecutor at Tokyo, Joseph B. Keenan, whose erratic handling of the prosecution's case damaged the reptuation of the IMTFE.

The IMTFE Courtroom in session, 3 May 1946. The judges are on the left and the defendants on the right.

Kido Kōichi, Lord Keeper of the Privy Seal, in the witness box at the IMTFE.

A defiant Tōjō in the witness box at the IMTFE. (U.S. National Archives 238-FEC-48-138)

The bodies of Chinese civilians killed in the Nanking Massacre lie beside the Qinhuai River outside the city's West Gate. (Photograph by Moriyasu Murase)

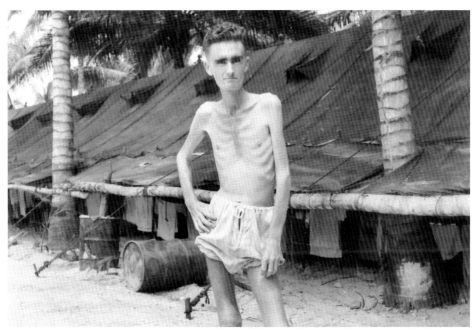

Private Leo Ayers on Ambon at the time of his liberation, August/September 1945. His condition shows the effects of two and a half years of Japanese captivity after being captured in the Fall of Singapore in February 1942. Many prisoners of war were in a similar state. (AWM 116271)

Japanese prisoners guarded by Australian military police outside the courtroom at Labuan, December 1945. The four prisoners – Lieutenant Ojima, Lieutenant Yamamoto, Captain Nakata and Captain Takino – were sentenced to death and shot. (AWM 123170)

Captain Hoshijima Susumu (centre) confers with his defence counsel at Labuan. Journalists consistently described him as 'tall' and 'arrogant'. (AWM 133913)

Three Australian escapees from Ranau. From L to R, Private Nelson Short, 2/18th Battalion; Warrant Officer Hector 'Bill' Sticpewich, Australian Army Service Corps; Private Keith Botterill, 2/19th Battalion. Sticpewich's testimony was critical to the prosecution at Labuan. (AWM OG3553)

The gallows at Rabaul, with a viewing platform for witnesses.

General Imamura Hitoshi, commander of the Eighth Area Army and defendant at Rabaul.
A quiet man with a fondness for gardening, he didn't match the profile of the ruthless and
fanatical Japanese commander.

Chint Singh identifying alleged war criminals at Mission Point, New Guinea, November 1945. Singh's evidence was critical in the trial of General Imamura Hitoshi. (AWM 098708)

Japanese defendants bow to the court at Darwin. This extremely deep bow is called *saikeirei*, and is used to show respect, humility or apology in Japanese culture. (AWM NWA1064)

The court at Darwin attracted the most media attention, as journalists were able to cover the trials without travelling to remote locations overseas. (AWM NWA1067)

Four Japanese prisoners on Morotai awaiting the outcome of their appeal. They had been sentenced to death for the execution of a downed Australian airman. (AWM OG3692)

Captain Iwasa Tokio listens as the court on Morotai finds him guilty of murdering an Australian POW. On the night before his execution, Iwasa played a lively tune on his shakuhachi, to which several women from the Australian Women's Army Service danced the jitterbug. (AWM OG3667)

Japanese soldiers face their accusers at Darwin, 1 March 1946, while an AIF soldier stands guard. (AWM NWA1040)

Prime Minister Robert Menzies' visit to Japan in 1957 marked a significant thawing in Australia–Japan relations, and shortly before it the remaining Japanese war criminals in Australian custody were quietly released. From L to R, Crown Prince Akihito, Pattie Menzies, Empress Kōjun, Emperor Hirohito, Robert Menzies. (Special Collections, Baillieu Library, The University of Melbourne, MENZ00196_0001)

Japanese Prime Minister Nobusuke Kishi (standing, at right) signs the Australia–Japan Commerce Agreement in 1957. A member of the Tōjō cabinet originally detained as a suspected class-A war criminal, Nobusuke was rehabilitated quickly and became a successful postwar politician. Australian Deputy Prime Minister and Country Party leader John McEwen (standing, at left) looks understandably enthusiastic at the prospect of Japanese markets being opened to Australian farmers. (Department of Foreign Affairs and Trade)

This monument to IMTFE judge Radhabinod Pal was added to Tokyo's Yasukuni Shrine in 2005.

infractions of one or two men. As in many camps late in the war, Hoshijima imposed a 'no work, no food' policy, meaning any men too sick or weak to work would starve.

These policies were often circumvented by the prisoners, who found ways of sharing what they did have. At his trial Hoshijima claimed that everything had run short by early 1945 and he distributed what he had, but Sticpewich maintained that the guards always had large quantities of rice, fish and vegetables. According to the prosecution, there were 80 or 90 tons of rice stored under Hoshijima's house even as men were dying of starvation.

Medicines also appear to have been withheld. Some medical supplies were received from the US Red Cross, and Hoshijima likewise maintained he had distributed them. Sticpewich denied this as well. The prosecution stated they'd found 160,000 quinine tablets at Sandakan, enough to save the lives of most of the men who had died of malaria. And it was not only the shortage of food and medicine which wore down the prisoners' health. When the boots they were captured in wore out, they were compelled to go barefoot. Many developed tropical ulcers on their legs and feet, which rotted, leaving gaping holes exposing raw flesh. The worst off were those who developed ulcers on the soles of their feet and could barely walk, and so couldn't work and were denied food. The use of human excrement in vegetable gardens resulted in deaths from dysentery, to add to those caused by beri-beri (in turn caused by a vitamin B1 deficiency), malaria and starvation. The death rate peaked in March 1945, with ten prisoners dying a night. Then, on 17 May, Hoshijima handed the surviving prisoners over to Captain Takakuwa for the march to Ranau. Of the 2,750 prisoners, 500 had already been sent to Ranau and around half of the remainder had died.

Life at Sandakan would have been hard enough, but Hoshijima made it worse with his many punishments for real or fanciful offences. Men were made to stand for an hour holding out weights and beaten if they dropped their arms. Beatings with sticks or rifle butts were a constant. Men were kicked in the testicles, or kicked in their ulcers to see if they were 'really sick', and some had their jaws broken. Cripples were beaten with their own crutches. According to Sticpewich, Hoshijima himself hit one man in the face with a stick so hard he lost an eye. As Sticpewich's testimony showed, hitting men in the face seemed to be something of a habit with the commandant.

The most striking stories of mistreatment concerned prisoners being confined for days or weeks at a time in a bamboo cage left out in the sun. This was not unique to Sandakan – it was done in various Japanese prison camps. Nor was it unique to prisoners of war – confinement in a cage for up to twenty days was a lawful punishment in the Japanese Army. Three cages of slightly different sizes were used at Sandakan, although the one the prosecution discussed most frequently was 4′6″ by 5′6″ at the base and about 4′6″ high (effectively one and a half metres each way). Caged prisoners were given no food for seven days and had no mosquito net; they were forced to sit at attention and were taken out and beaten if they relaxed. They were let out twice a day to use the latrine and receive additional beatings. Hoshijima always ordered the use of the cage as a punishment himself, and the sentence varied from seven to twenty-eight days. At one point, seven men were packed into the largest cage for four days. According to Sticpewich, many men upon release weighed less than 6 stone (38 kilograms), and fifteen died as a result of the confinement.

Sticpewich gave one specific example of three men, named Barber, Clements and Weeks, who were caught stealing from the prisoners' vegetable garden and put into the cage:

> Hoshijima addressed us and informed us that they had been caught going out of the camp thieving, and he took a very poor view of it and if there were any recurrences they would be shot on sight [one man, named John Orr, was later shot for the same offence]. He said they would be severely punished and he would also punish the camp, which he did by stopping our food ration for one day. At that

time the meal was cooked but we were not allowed to have it until the following morning . . . Clements returned to the camp very sick from the cage. He revived somewhat but about five weeks after he came out of the cage he died as a result of the treatment. Clements was a provost and a very big man. Weeks was taken out of the cage on a stretcher as he was too weak to walk. Within a week or a little more he also died and I consider the cage treatment caused his death. Weeks was suffering from paralysis and internal injuries.[12]

When Captain George Cook, the senior Australian officer in the camp, complained, Hoshijima hit him in the face.

Moffit concluded his opening address: 'There have been many PW camps in this war with grim records, but the name of Sandakan PW camp and the tragedy it represents will live long as a blot on the barbaric Japanese Army. The man responsible stands before the court.'[13]

In his statement to the court, Hoshijima brazenly brushed off the prosecution's allegations. 'As a result of the defeat of my country, I am now being tried here as a war criminal, something which I do not fully understand as I did my best for the PWs,' he said.[14] He insisted that he neither ordered nor permitted the ill-treatment of prisoners, and divided food and medicine equitably between the guards and prisoners. He was limited by circumstances, particularly the Allied air raids, which cut his supply lines, but did what he could. He was, he said, a cultured man who had had an exemplary career, had never been punished, and had consistently been given work normally allocated to someone of a higher rank. He claimed to have received many letters from prisoners thanking him for his kind treatment, but unfortunately he had burned them all (he did not say why). It was also unfortunate that none of the officers imprisoned at Sandakan were still alive, as he was certain they would have given him a good character reference. In particular, Captains Cook and Mills (the senior Australian and British officers respectively) were his good friends, although he admitted under cross-examination that he did hit them in the face once or twice.[15] Hoshijima complained of not receiving good translation, saying the Japanese-speaking Australians who had interviewed him could not even speak Japanese to primary school level. In short, he did his best in difficult circumstances and should be acquitted and allowed to return home to his family.

Hoshijima's counsel made several arguments in his defence, although between the impossibility of his position and the patchy translation of their remarks into English they sometimes come across as more tragicomic than persuasive. They argued that conditions at the camp had been good between August 1942 and September 1944, but had deteriorated following Allied air raids in October 1944. These had caused shortages of food and medicine, which had an adverse effect on guards and prisoners alike. He admitted some guards had mistreated the prisoners; however, Hoshijima could not be blamed for everything that went wrong in the camp. And while Hoshijima conceded that being put in the cage was 'not enjoyable', he denied it was fatal.[16] Those who died after being taken from the cage had died of 'sudden attacks of malaria'.[17] And as confinement to a cage was a lawful punishment in the Japanese Army, Hoshijima had not treated his prisoners any differently to his own men in this respect (although he doesn't appear to have ever caged his own men). In conclusion, Hoshijima had done everything he could for the prisoners of war, but unfortunately they had all died because of their 'physical unsuitableness as Europeans' to the tropics, and the mental and physical deterioration caused by the shock of being made a prisoner.[18]

In his cross-examination Moffitt pushed Hoshijima hard on this last point. If the deaths of the prisoners at Sandakan were caused by the disruption to supplies of food and medicine and the unsuitableness of people from temperate climates to the tropics, why did only one Japanese guard die? Hoshijima stuck to his position, maintaining that while he had issued equal quantities of medicines to both prisoners and guards, the Japanese were physically stronger and so didn't use theirs up as quickly. His counsel claimed that 'the white people are more vulnerable to a hot climate than are Formosans or Japanese'.[19] The court understandably rejected this unusual argument and convicted Hoshijima on all four counts.

'It is impossible to make any punishment fit this crime,' Moffitt told the court when it was considering sentencing. 'Even death by the ignominy of hanging, which I submit should be the penalty, is too good for this barbarian, ironically self-termed "cultured".'[20] In what was probably a foregone conclusion, the court sentenced Hoshijima to death by hanging on 20 January 1946. He bore his sentence impassively, saluting and then walking from the courtroom. The defence petitioned the verdict and sentence to the Australian military authorities using the same arguments they advanced in the trial, adding that Hoshijima had a young family in Japan and was a 'bright and broadminded man' whom it would be unjust to hang.[21] They provided a number of character references, including one from his Formosan servant.[22] Unsurprisingly, the petition was dismissed.

Australian authorities also pressed charges against many other guards at Sandakan, either for offences there or offences committed during the death marches. These cascaded down the Japanese military hierarchy to the bottom – the Formosans. The Japanese Empire won Formosa, as Taiwan was then known, from China as a spoil of victory in the First Sino-Japanese War of 1894–95. Holding it had initially been difficult and required a large army of occupation, but by the 1930s a significant number of Formosans had been assimilated into Japanese culture. The names of the Formosan defendants, for example, were all Japanese rather than the Formosan dialect of Chinese. The Japanese military began accepting Formosan volunteers in 1937 and then began conscripting Formosans in 1944.

All of the Formosans at Borneo appear to have been volunteers. The Imperial Army gave them a higher status than they would have had at home, although they still tended to find themselves in lower-status jobs, such as guarding prisoners of war. There remained language and cultural barriers between the Formosans and the Japanese, and while the Formosans were notionally educated in Japanese, not all had a great deal of schooling and so their ability in the language varied. I will now look at M18, the trial of twenty Formosan guards at Morotai from 7–9 January 1946 in relation to the second Sandakan–Ranau death march.[23]

In January 1945, as work on the airfield finished, the Japanese authorities in Borneo decided to move 500 prisoners from Sandakan to a new camp at Ranau, 163 miles (263 kilometres) away. They had to walk an extremely difficult track, built in haste by the Japanese Army, crossing swamps and mountains through the rugged interior of the island. It seems that the 500 prisoners on the first march were used as porters, and while it is not known how many died on the march itself, only five Australians and one British prisoner were still alive at Ranau when the men from the second march reached the camp in June.

On 29 May, the Sandakan camp was formally abandoned. The 536 prisoners fit enough to walk set off for Ranau on the second march, leaving 288 stretcher cases behind. Those men were never seen again, and soon after, the camp was burned by the retreating Japanese. After twenty-eight days, a further 183 prisoners reached Ranau – 142 Australian and forty-one British. The others had died on the way or been killed. Two escaped on the march.

On 4 July another four prisoners escaped from Ranau, one of whom died, and then on 28 July two more escaped. These were the last escapees from Ranau before the end of the war. One of these was Sticpewich, who had been tipped off by a friendly Formosan guard that Takakuwa was planning to kill the remaining prisoners. 'You go now. Go jungle. If you stay you will be mati. All men very short time mati mati,' the guard, Takahara, said to him.[24] The other was his friend, Private Herman Reither. Both were sheltered by local native people, who had apparently become pro-British and anti-Japanese by this stage of the war. Badly weakened from dysentery, Reither died on 8 August, two days before Sticpewich was rescued. When the two men made their escape, there were only thirty-two Australian and eight British prisoners still alive at Ranau. It seems certain they were all shot, possibly after the end of the war.

All of the twenty Formosans were accused of the murder of numerous unknown prisoners of war during the second Sandakan–Ranau death march, from 29 May to 25 June 1945. The chief witness for the prosecution was once again Warrant Officer Bill Sticpewich. A statement he gave to Justice Mansfield on 19 October 1945 as part of the Third Webb Inquiry was given as evidence, and he was flown to Morotai to testify in person.[25] Identifying individual guards could be difficult, as they were often known to the prisoners only by their nicknames. Private Nelson Short, who managed to escape from Ranau on 4 July, said he knew the guards by such names as 'The Indian', 'Euclid', 'Masturbation' and 'The Gold Toothed-Runt'.[26] (The court must have been curious about the origin of these unusual monikers, but it was not discussed.)

According to Sticpewich, Takakuwa ordered his men to begin breaking up the Sandakan camp at 9 am on 29 May. At 5 pm, all prisoners able to walk were told they would need to be ready to move within the hour. They were permitted to kill and cook some pigs. Some guards told the prisoners there would be more and better food at Ranau, others said they would all be killed there. Sticpewich thought they were simply boasting.

Shortly before 8 pm, they prepared to move. Takakuwa told the guards to move the prisoners in batches of fifty, with guards in front, behind and all around. There were to be no escapes. They set off as directed, stopping for the night after a few hours at the end of the sealed road.

The track after that was horrendous. There were ridges so steep the men had to struggle up them on all fours, then slide down the other side. In many places the mud was knee-deep. It would have been a struggle for fit, well-fed men, let alone those who had already endured a year at Sandakan on steadily dwindling rations. The prisoners started each day in their groups of fifty at between 6.30 and 7.30 am, and finished between 3 and 5 pm. The most distance covered in one day was 13 miles (21 kilometres), but the daily average was closer to 6 miles (9 kilometres). Many prisoners fell, and anyone who stopped to help was driven on with blows from rifle butts. Each man was given 4 pounds of rice (1.8 kilograms) per ten days, a meagre diet for an exhausting hike through jungle. To make things worse, the guards often demanded the food back some time later. Sticpewich quickly learned to distribute anything he was given among the men in his party, and when the guards later asked for it he claimed it had already been eaten.

The specific charge against the Formosans was that at various times they had been members of a party of soldiers led by Sergeant (or Sergeant Major) Tsuji which was responsible for following the marchers and killing the stragglers. Different men were assigned to Tsuji's party each day in order to spread the killing around, and the prosecution alleged that taking part in the killing was allowed or denied as reward or punishment respectively. All twenty Formosans pleaded not guilty, either denying they had killed any prisoners, or claiming they had only killed under the direct orders of their superiors, or when a prisoner asked to be shot and put out of his misery (a not implausible scenario in the circumstances). The prosecution claimed those who were in Tsuji's party without actually killing anyone were still guilty.

The defence made two main arguments: the difficulty of the track meant that deaths were inevitable, and those who killed prisoners on the direct orders of superiors should not be held responsible. The court rejected both, but still faced the challenge of allocating responsibility to each of the defendants individually. William Ballantyne Simpson, who replaced Wilson as Judge Advocate General on 31 March 1946, was critical of this and the other large trials held at Morotai for this reason.[27] When each of the guards gave his statement, Sticpewich made a short comment on what he knew of the guard's character and actions, which was recorded at the bottom. According to him, most of the guards beat the prisoners when ordered to but otherwise left them alone. Some were 'easy-going'.[28]

Sticpewich thought one of the worst guards was Fukushima Maso, known to the prisoners as 'Black Bastard' or 'Private Detective'. The latter name apparently came from his habit of reporting other guards to the officers if they failed to properly beat prisoners. He was twenty-one years old at the time of the trial, so he would have been around eighteen when he first arrived at the camp. In his own evidence, Fukushima denied killing any prisoners, although he did describe an execution he witnessed:

> About 1st August 45 remaining PWs in 110½ mile camp were killed. I was a member of S/M Tsuji's party and we took 10 PWs a short distance along the Tambunan Rd. The PWs rested and were given food and tobacco and then asked if there was anything they would like to say as they were about to be killed. They asked for tobacco and water and received them. One at a time we were ordered by Tsuji to bring a PW about 20 metres into the jungle. I took the first. This action was rendered necessary due to the lack of food and medicine. S/M Tsuji told me to kill the first PW but being a Formosan I refused to kill any. Tsuji then scolded me, and taking my rifle said 'this is the way' and shot the first PW (Cook). The PWs were killed by taking them one by one away from the group and shooting them.[29]

Fukushima listed the defendants responsible for the shooting, showing a willingness to report on his comrades that reflected his nickname. The court was not persuaded of his non-involvement, perhaps going on Sticpewich's character evidence, and he was convicted. He opted to say nothing to seek mitigation of his sentence and was sentenced to fifteen years' imprisonment.[30]

Another guard with a bad reputation was Yoshikawa Tatsuhito, known to the prisoners as 'Masturbation'. He was twenty-five years old, so would have been in his early twenties during the events at Sandakan. According to Sticpewich, 'when opportunity arose he was most cruel'.[31] Yoshikawa admitted he had been present at the execution of between fifteen and seventeen prisoners but, like Fukushima, denied taking part. He also named those who did and those who did not.[32] Under cross-examination, he said he had taken care of the prisoners as best he could and given them rice and bread when he had any to spare.[33] When asked by the prosecuting officer if he knew it was wrong to kill the prisoners he replied, 'Yes, I think so.' He was convicted, but requested a lenient sentence, telling the court his family needed him to support them: 'My father has tuberculosis, my mother rheumatism. I was fifth in the family. My brother above me had died and my second brother is not making much money. My third brother is a hunch back and he cannot walk at all. My fourth brother's whereabouts is unknown.'[34]

He was also sentenced to fifteen years' imprisonment.

At the other end of the scale was Yokota Kinzo. Sticpewich said, when Yokata was before him during interrogation, 'This man treated us fairly well, beat PWs under orders but was alright when on his own. He misappropriated foodstuffs and vegetables and gave them to the PWs.'[35]

Yokata was in Tsuji's party twice, and saw three or four prisoners killed each time. He admitted to killing a man on Takakuwa's direct order once. Later, at Ranau, he was sick with malaria and beri-beri and took no further part in events there. Based on his admission he was convicted. When being sentenced he told the court he was twenty-three years old and had enlisted to support his family. He was one of nine children of a farming couple, and his elder brother had a wife and three children but had gone missing. It fell to him to support his parents, siblings, sister-in-law, nieces and nephews, and he sent everything he earned as a guard home to them. 'I do not know what to say to my mother for what I have done,' he said.[36] He was sentenced to nine years' imprisonment, the shortest sentence at this trial.

Another in Sticpewich's good graces was Utsunomiya Seichi. He was in Tsuji's party three times, but denied ever killing prisoners or being present when they were killed.[37] 'This man is a good type,' Sticpewich said. 'He always took care of stores and misappropriated some to our favour.'[38] The court accepted Utsunomiya's evidence and acquitted him.

In total, two Formosans were acquitted and the remaining eighteen convicted and given sentences of nine to twenty years' imprisonment.

The defence submitted a petition against the length of the sentences written in broken English, suggesting it was drafted in Japanese and then translated by someone whose English was solid but not fluent. The petition pointed out that failing to follow orders in the Japanese Army resulted in the death penalty or a prison sentence, and under Japanese military law no subordinate would ever be held criminally responsible for following a clear order of his superior. Rather, he must carry out the order 'even if judged wrong by the common-sense [sic]'.[39] The defence again argued that the poor condition of the track meant deaths were inevitable, and it affected Japanese soldiers as well as prisoners. They claimed that a Japanese force of 500 had lost 300 men on the same track, and a force of 125 had lost 101.[40] There were so many dead bodies and skeletons along the track that the jungle was 'spooky' and scenery was 'miserable to look at'. The loss of 353 prisoners out of 560 was therefore not excessive.

In cross-examination, Sticpewich acknowledged that the road would have been hazardous even for fit men, but while he saw some graves with Japanese markers he denied seeing any Japanese actually die en route.[41] It was because Takakuwa knew of the difficulty of the road, the petition claimed, that he ordered a party to come behind, to help stragglers. Contrary to the prosecution's claim, it was not a killing party. Tsuji's men were assigned to 'try their best to bring such prisoners along following the main party and any of the strugglers [sic] who were too weak or sick to travel further on and seemed evidently to die soon when they were left behind in such lonely road in the thick jungle, might be disposed of as a means of last resources when it became impossible to bring them along by all means'.[42] If Takakuwa had wanted to kill all the prisoners, the defence said, he could have easily done so without going to all the effort of organising and managing the march.

In conclusion, read the petition, 'it may be considered too heartless to punish these poor Formosan employees with the imprisonments for such long years being charged with their faultless acts which they had been forced to do under such an irresistible circumstances as we had explained above'.[43]

Judge Advocate General Wilson reviewed the petition and recommended to Lieutenant General Sturdee that the sentences be reduced: 'I would suggest for your consideration that the sentences should be mitigated. It seems unnecessary and uneconomical that these men should be kept in Australian prisons for such a length of time under conditions which will probably be much better than the conditions in Japan, and I would suggest that the sentences might at least be reduced by half and that even at some later date consideration might be given to mitigating the remainder and returning the men to Japan and Formosa.'[44]

Sturdee declined to reduce the sentences. Sticpewich returned to Australia, but his lifetime supply of luck had run out in Borneo. Tragically, the man who survived Sandakan and the Sandakan–Ranau death march was hit by a car and killed in Melbourne a few years after the war ended.[45]

Hoshijima and Takakuwa both went to the gallows at Rabaul on 6 April 1946. It was not a particularly dignified affair, especially compared with the shootings on Morotai the previous month (as described in the prologue). It did not help that the authorities at Rabaul had been criticised for leniency in relation to their last executions, held on 20 March. Then, Sergeant Major Inagaki Masaru (R3) had been hanged for beheading a Chinese civilian, and naval worker Kikkawa Haruo (R4) for killing five New Britain natives with a hammer. According to *Sydney Morning Herald* reporter Colin Pura, the two men asked for drugs to steady their nerves and were given phenobarbital tablets. Inagaki, who had been anxiously smoking a cigarette, vomited up the tablets and so was given an injection of morphine.[46] This news was not received well, and the Housewives Progressive Association of Broken Hill wrote a letter of complaint to Prime Minister Ben Chifley about Japanese war criminals being let off too easily.[47]

Even had this not happened, it is unlikely Hoshijima and Takakuwa would have been given much sympathy. The night before their execution, their last requests, for beer, cigarettes and morphine, were all refused. Takakuwa asked for a clean set of clothes and was given an Australian Army-issue shirt and trousers. An officer seized them back, telling him, 'You won't swing in that uniform!' They were, however, permitted to write letters.[48]

Both men were summoned to the gallows at 7.45 am, having been closeted with a Buddhist priest. 'Takakuwa, heavy-featured and weighing more than 12 stone, looked insolent,' wrote the reporter for *The Sun*. 'Hoshijima, elegantly-dressed in a khaki jacket over a white silk shirt, grey riding breeches and polished leggings, gave a cheeky grin.'

Takakuwa muttered, 'I will pray for the Emperor,' as he was led to the scaffold. He was initially cocksure but looked less confident standing on the trap. As the hangman tied a green handkerchief over his eyes, he began shouting, *'Tenno Heika Banzai!'* The hangman hit him in the face with the rope to silence him and hanged him a few seconds later.

Hoshijima too began to shout, *'Tenno Heika Banzai!'* at the bottom of the steps to the scaffold. In a final touch of irony, given the commandant's preferred means of silencing protest at Sandakan, the provost hit him in the face, then hit him another three times after he kept shouting. On the final time, Hoshijima bit the provost's hand, drawing blood. The men dragged him onto the trap and bound him.

'This is for all the Aussies you murdered at Sandakan,' the hangman hissed at him as he pulled the lever.

'I wish he were a cat, we'd have hanged him nine times,' said an officer who was watching. The authorities had tried to keep the date of the execution secret, but hadn't been able to keep out gatecrashers entirely.

# RABAUL AND THE TRIALS FOR CRIMES AGAINST CIVILIANS

Rabaul was, until its destruction in a volcanic eruption in 1994, the administrative capital and main town of New Britain, a large island to the north-east of the island of New Guinea. Its main asset, from both a strategic and aesthetic perspective, was Simpson Harbour, an excellent natural anchorage ringed by mountains. It was built during German colonial rule (1884 to 1914), which ended when Rabaul was captured by the Australian Army and Navy at the start of the First World War. Under Australian administration, it became the capital of the territory of New Guinea.

Recognising the importance of the town and its harbour, Australia deployed the 2/22<sup>nd</sup> Infantry Battalion and supporting arms to the area in 1941. This 1,400-man contingent was called Lark Force. Rabaul came under Japanese air attack from early January 1942 onwards, and on the morning of 23 January an elite Japanese unit of between 3,000 and 4,000 men called the *Nankai Shitai*, or South Seas Force, began landing on the coral beaches. The Battle for Rabaul was over in a few hours, and the Japanese secured the town and harbour with only minimal losses.

The survivors of Lark Force retreated to the south, but without adequate supplies and water, many surrendered over the coming days. Some 140 surrendered Australian soldiers, including men from an ambulance unit, were massacred by the Japanese at the Tol and Waitavalo plantations on 4 February. Most of the massacres of surrendered troops were then unknown in Australia, but some survivors of New Britain escaped and returned to Australia by boat. Their accounts were published in the media.[1] In response, the Australian Army launched the Allen Inquiry into Japanese war crimes.

The Japanese decided to send almost all the remaining Western prisoners back to Japan rather than hold them on the island. They were transported on the *Montevideo Maru*, which was torpedoed and sunk by an American submarine near the Philippines on 1 July 1942. Around 800 Australian prisoners of war and 200 civilian internees perished, in the biggest loss of life in a maritime disaster in Australian history.

The Japanese turned Rabaul into a formidable fortress, the centre of their operations throughout Papua New Guinea and the Solomon Islands. In late 1942 it became the headquarters of the newly formed Eighth Area Army, and General Imamura Hitoshi was sent to command it.

Imamura, a tubby man with a fondness for gardening, did not look the part of a Japanese general. He had been born in Sendai, northern Honshu, in 1886. His father was a judge. Imamura graduated from the Imperial Japanese Army Academy in 1907 and was commissioned as a second lieutenant. Sent as a military attaché to the British Army during the First World War, he served on the Western Front with the East Lancashire Regiment. After the war, he rose steadily through the ranks to a staff officer and then commander of a division in China.

The Allies did not attempt to recapture Rabaul, but instead isolated and bypassed it. It was bombed heavily during the last two years of the war, and was often used for target practice by new Allied bomber crews. Cut off from the rest of the Japanese Empire, Imamura had his men cultivate land around the town to grow food, and dig tunnels into the volcanic rock to shelter from the bombs. He kept fit by working in his garden, three hours in the morning and two in the afternoon. He encouraged his soldiers to do the same, and despite their parlous situation the Japanese at Rabaul remained fairly healthy and in fairly good spirits to the end of the war.[2]

On 6 September 1945, Imamura surrendered to Sturdee aboard a British aircraft carrier, the *HMS Glory*. He held out his sword for Sturdee, who didn't take it, instead making him place it on the table. It was a snub. Imamura expected to have his sword returned, but Sturdee sent it to the War Museum in Canberra. In the following weeks, the Australian Army sent 2,700 men to re-occupy Rabaul. It was a gamble, as there were still 89,000 Japanese soldiers there. But Imamura proved co-operative.

'For three years and eight months Rabaul had been a place of mystery,' wrote reporter Eric Thornton. 'Unlike other Japanese held areas almost nothing was known of the fate of the prisoners of war.'[3] An immediate priority was to search for survivors of Lark Force, or any of the Australians captured in Papua New Guinea who might have been removed to New Britain. None were found, but there were large numbers of Chinese and Indian prisoners, along with twenty-eight mostly British POWs who had been captured in Malaya or Singapore and shipped to the island. They had been too sick to move before New Britain was cut off and so were left there.

'For the last 18 months they made me work in the jungle without boots, but what a change there was when their Emperor announced defeat,' one said. 'They crawled to us then, and treated us like millionaires. They gave us fish and their primest chickens; in fact anything we wanted; there were strange scenes when Tokyo surrendered. The Japanese cried bitterly and one cut his throat on parade.'[4]

Brisbane *Telegraph* war correspondent M.C. Warren noticed a similar attitude when he arrived. 'Thousands of bowing, saluting Japanese greeted us on a 50-mile tour of General Imamura's area,' he wrote. 'Japanese jumped off bicycles, slithered off trucks or raced to the side of the road to salaam our jeep convoy . . . some Japanese presented arms with shovels and sticks.'[5] They had moved out of their tunnels and were now living in huts. He described them as 'plump, well-conditioned' and 'very polite', but said it was hard to banish the picture of 'their starved, emaciated victims' from his mind. He noticed enormous stockpiles of arms and ammunition, which made him realise how much of a fight Imamura could have put up had he been attacked.

Major General Kenneth Eather, the commander of the 11th Division and the leader of the occupation force in Rabaul, followed Sturdee in taking a tough line with Imamura. When Imamura sent Eather a case of Japanese crab as a gift, Eather returned it with a terse note saying that when he wanted crab he would order him to produce it. When Imamura offered his slightly battered staff car to Eather, the Australian told him to find something better. Additionally, Eather also compelled Japanese officers to salute all Australian officers regardless of rank, so Imamura was compelled to salute Australian lieutenants.

Still, Eather found himself grudgingly admiring of how well Imamura had kept his force fed and their morale up. Even under constant air raids he had maintained 14,000 acres under cultivation, and the soldiers appeared to be cheerful. 'Imamura had prepared them to stay here forever, if necessary, and they accepted his edict without question,' Eather said. 'No Australian or American soldier would accept complete isolation and the probability of future annihilation so blandly.'[6]

The town, which had been destroyed by Allied bombing, needed to be rebuilt from the ground up. The Japanese soldiers were put to work clearing away rubble and jungle areas for parade grounds and building compounds. There were some 20,000 Japanese in hospital with malaria, but the others were working twelve-hour days.

'Major-General Eather . . . has wisely allowed the Japs to conduct their own administration, and is receiving the utmost co-operation from General Imamura, Jap commander,' wrote C.A. Burley, *Sun* correspondent, in November. 'All Jap slackers are handed over to their own officers for punishment, under a code which is notoriously harsher than ours.'[7]

One example of that was three men caught stealing food, who were sentenced to ten years' penal servitude. And whenever men were caught stealing, their officers were also punished. One major general, two colonels, five majors, four captains, one lieutenant, and a score of other ranks were sentenced to between two and twenty days' confinement for this reason. The force remained self-supporting with food.

Rabaul had a number of advantages as a trial location. It was on Australian territory, so Australia did not need to deal with any foreign government. And because the town had been destroyed, it was kept under army control and not immediately handed back to the civil authorities like the rest of New Britain. Its central location and excellent harbour and airstrip also made it fairly easy to assemble suspects, witnesses and resources. At the end of the war there were still 151,677 Japanese scattered throughout New Guinea, New Britain, the Solomon Islands and Nauru, most of them part of Imamura's command based in Rabaul.[8] And the convicted war criminals could be put to use rebuilding the town.

For these reasons, Rabaul quickly became the most important of the Australian war crimes trial locations, and two-thirds of the class-B and -C trials were held there, most in the first round, from 12 December 1945 to 31 July 1946. Many defendants convicted at other locations were also imprisoned or executed there. A gallows was built, which was handed over to the civilian authorities once the trials ended, and there were enough men to form firing squads. In total, eight squads were assembled at Rabaul, mostly for eleven death sentences handed down at Morotai and one at Darwin. These executions were conducted in May 1946, August 1946, and over three days between September and October 1947.[9]

The firing squads at Rabaul were plagued by problems. Prosecuting officer Kenneth Wybrow observed of the May 1946 execution that the 'drunkenness of the officers carrying out the executions could be explained by their nervousness at performing that unwelcome work, and their brutality to the Japanese by the drunkenness. Their conduct and bearing were a conspicuous contrast to the dignity and courage with which the Japanese met their end.'[10]

On one occasion, every man in the squad failed to hit his target, even though all had been approved as good marksmen. The condemned men then had to be shot in the head by the commanding officer with his pistol. It was, perhaps, issues like these which encouraged the courts to hand down death sentences by hanging rather than shooting.

In mid-February the Australian Army had quietly recruited Majors Thomas Upson and Ronald H. Hicks as hangmen. Both men had experience in the colonial administration of Papua New Guinea before the war, and both proved efficient and discreet. Although not all the hangings went smoothly, as the executions of the Sandakan officers showed.

Those awaiting trial at Rabaul, and those sentenced to imprisonment, were put in the war criminals compound, which was ready by December. Under Major Upson's command, the Japanese lived in timber and canvas huts roofed with iron, and were guarded by native police. At night, floodlights were used to watch for escapees.

By January 1946, 930 suspects were in the compound.[11] Most of the cases at Rabaul concerned war crimes against civilians or Chinese and Indian prisoners of war, and only a minority of the victims were Australian. This meant that the trials tended to attract less attention than those at Labuan, but they did demonstrate the Australian government's commitment to prosecuting war crimes regardless of the victims. I will now look in detail at two examples from the first round of Rabaul trials, from December 1945 to July 1946.

The first case tried at Rabaul (R1) concerned the rape of a Chinese woman, Betty Pang Woo, by a *Kempeitai* sergeant, Yaki Yoshio.[12] Woo was twenty-five at the time of the offence, and was described in the press as 'a pretty Chinese woman' and 'the wife of one of Rabaul's most respected Chinese citizens'.[13] The trial went from 12–13 December 1945, with the court closed for much of the proceedings, and there are only a few pages of transcripts. The case is worthy of attention because, while sexual violence against Asian women by Japanese soldiers was common, prosecutions for rape were rare. R1 is one of the few examples. A social stigma in many cultures pressured women not to talk about rape, but Woo was willing to speak out, and her mother-in-law was also willing to corroborate her account.

Woo had been employed by the Japanese in the kitchen at Massowa Plantation, about 30 miles (50 kilometres) from Rabaul. She testified that Yaki kept making unwelcome advances to her in pidgin English, which she always refused. In October 1944 he escalated his demands, saying her husband would be beheaded if she continued to refuse him. Then he tied her to a tree, put ants on her face, and left her there for three hours. Later he forced her to drink sake and dance, painted her face with powder and make-up, and raped her. Afterwards Woo avoided Yaki, and she told her mother-in-law about the rape a few days later.

Yaki was charged with two separate offences, rape and torture. In his defence, he did not deny a single sexual encounter with Woo, but insisted it was consensual; he also denied torturing her in any way. When asked why, having found a willing partner, he did not go back to her, he replied that he 'did not think it was [in the] military spirit'.[14]

The prosecution called two additional witnesses – Woo's mother-in-law, who confirmed that Woo had told her about the rape a few days after it happened, and Lieutenant Herbert Charles Gridley of the Royal Papuan Constabulary, who gave evidence as to Woo's good character. Gridley had been based at Rabaul from 1927 until the outbreak of the war, and knew Woo and her husband.

'I know the standards of the Chinese women better than any person at Rabaul,' he said, and stated she was 'an excellent character' and
'there is no doubt whatever as to her morality now'.[15]

He and his wife had invited Woo and her husband to afternoon
tea, which apparently was a significant endorsement of their place in
the Rabaul community.

In a common law court, the evidence from Woo's mother-in-law
would have been difficult to admit because of the rule against hearsay evidence (although there are, and were, exceptions). Providing
character evidence for an alleged victim, however, was in line with
contemporary standards for prosecuting rape – a woman of good
character would not consent to adultery. The defence warned of
the danger of accepting uncorroborated evidence, particularly
when the issue was one of consent, but the court accepted the prosecution's evidence and Yaki was convicted on both charges. He
was sentenced to death by hanging. As no reasons were given, we
do not know how they weighted the rape and torture conviction
when deciding on the sentence. At the time, the death penalty in
Australia was reserved for murder, piracy and treason; it was not
handed down for rape or torture, so Yaki's sentence was significantly
harsher than one an Australian civilian court would impose for the
same offence.

Yaki's sentence was confirmed by the First Army Headquarters
on 24 December 1945 and by Judge Advocate General Wilson on
5 March 1946. Unlike most of the condemned men, Yaki did not petition his conviction or sentence. According to the defence counsel,
General Imamura thought his crime so shameful that he forbade him
to do so.[16]

Yaki was the first prisoner to be sentenced to death at Rabaul, and
he went to the gallows on 18 April 1946. According to the reporter of
the *Townsville Daily Bulletin*, he died 'a cringing coward'. He had to
be assisted up the stairs of the gallows and showed great reluctance to
stand on the trap. He tried to shout '*Tennō Heika Banzai!*' but found

he had lost his voice, and his words 'drifted to a wheezing splutter' as the noose was pulled over his head.[17]

A number of trials at Rabaul dealt with crimes against Papua New Guineans and Pacific Islanders, referred to collectively as 'natives' in documents of the time. Five of them (R51, 52, 53, 68 and 70) related to the massacre of the civilian population of Ocean Island after the war, on 20 August 1945.

Ocean Island, modern Banaba Island in Kiribati, is a small coral atoll near the Gilbert Islands of Micronesia, about 6 square kilometres in size and rich in phosphate. The phosphate attracted the British, who colonised the Gilbert Islands in the nineteenth century. At the outbreak of the Second World War the nearby Marshall Islands were already a Japanese mandate, and Japanese forces from there occupied the Gilberts almost immediately. Ocean Island was occupied by the Japanese Navy from August 1942 onwards. Most of the prewar population of 2,500 was moved away, but 200 workers were retained and the island was garrisoned by 500 Navy personnel. The Americans captured the Gilbert and Marshall Islands in 1944, but bypassed Ocean Island and did not attack it. The garrison was therefore cut off.

The first trial, R51, was held over one day, on 26 April.[18] The president was a major, and there were three other officers and a judge advocate. Counsel for the prosecution and defence were both AALC officers. The principal witness for the prosecution was the only survivor of the massacre, a 28-year-old man from Nikunau Island named Kabunare. He gave testimony in Gilbertese through a translator.[19]

Before the war, Kabunare had signed up with the British Phosphate Commissioner to work on Ocean Island. During the Japanese occupation he remained on the Island and was employed by the Japanese as a fisherman. The terms of this 'employment' were unclear – the Japanese took all the fish the Islanders caught, only sometimes leaving some for them to eat, and slapped them in the face if they failed to catch any. The Islanders were forbidden to speak to the few European residents, none of whom were still alive at the end of the war. Kabunare believed they either died of malnutrition or were killed by the Japanese, but he didn't actually know this and was going on rumours.

One evening, one of the Japanese officers told the fishermen to come back early from fishing the next morning. At 9 am, about a hundred of them assembled in the billiard room at the base, where nine Japanese soldiers were present with fixed bayonets. Quickly and without explanation, one of the soldiers began tying the Islanders' hands behind their backs with string. They were then tied together in groups of about eight. Kabunare's group was led out of the room and along a narrow track beside the sea. The track climbed steadily and eventually led to a cliff dropping down to the breaking waves on one side. There they all stopped. The Islanders were blindfolded and directed to stand at the edge of the cliff. By this stage, they knew what was going to happen.

'Are you ready?' the man next to Kabunare asked him, an Islander named Falailiva.[20]

'Yes, I am ready to die,' Kabunare responded.

'Do you remember God?'

'Yes, I remember.'

As rifle shots rang out, they fell off the cliff into the water, and Kabunare felt Falailiva land on top of him. Kabunare found himself unharmed, although he was still tied up underneath Falailiva. He lay in the water, breathing each time a wave receded. He bit Falailiva's shoulder to see if he would respond – he was dead. Kabunare lay still for an hour, then struggled free and removed his blindfold. The Japanese were gone but the water around him was bloody. He cut his bindings on a sharp rock and went to each of the other Islanders in his group, but found them all dead. He then moved along the base of the cliff until he discovered a cave and hid there.

The next morning, he found two bodies washed into the mouth of his cave. They had swelled up under the tropical sun. Kabunare stayed in the cave for the day, while the Japanese came in canoes and towed the bodies away. That night, Kabunare left the cave and found a hiding place where he was able to forage for coconuts. He stayed in hiding for three months. When he saw the Union Jack flying over the police station, he thought it was a Japanese trick and did not come out. Finally, one day in December, he met some other Gilbert Islanders who told him the war was over and the Japanese had gone.

The first defendant was Lieutenant Commander Suzuki Naōmi, commander of Ocean Island. He did not deny that the Islanders had all been shot on his orders, but mounted a defence of military necessity. He argued that the Islanders were plotting against the Japanese and planning to rise in support of the Allies should they land on Ocean Island. He cited cases of weapons going missing and later being found in hidden caches, of men taking canoes and escaping, and one of his men being killed in mysterious circumstances. In July 1945, Suzuki noticed an increase in American air activity and feared the island was about to be attacked. He also saw some of the Islanders cheering the American planes and concluded that the garrison was in serious danger. 'I made up my mind to execute [the] natives for self-defence of the Japanese,' he told the court.[21]

Suzuki called together his four company commanders, told them he intended to kill the Islanders, and asked for their opinions. This was unusual, as the Imperial Japanese Navy was certainly no democracy and Suzuki, based on the testimony of his men, was not known for a consultative style of leadership. None of the company commanders wanted to kill the Islanders, who had been their employees for years, and they asked if there was another way to suppress the potential revolt. Suzuki deliberated further, but in the end concluded he had no choice. He felt 'very unpleasant and pityful [sic]' at the thought of killing the Islanders but could not forgive them for treason 'in spite of the last two years' pacification'.[22]

On the night of 19 August, he once again assembled his company commanders and ordered them to shoot the Islanders, keeping it as discreet as possible in case any of the men had reservations. He also ordered them to charge with disobedience anyone who failed to comply. In his defence, Suzuki referred to naval land regulations issued pursuant to the Emperor's order in August 1930, which told naval parties operating on land to be on guard against hostile inhabitants and to 'drive out and exterminate' any anti-Japanese riots.[23] He further claimed that when he had first taken over the post on Ocean Island, he was given orders by Rear Admiral Shibazake to kill the natives if they posed a threat. Suzuki denied the prosecution's allegation that the natives were killed because they knew about the killing of the island's European residents, and he also denied any knowledge of the fate of the Europeans.

In his testimony, he further denied knowing that the war had ended four days before the massacre. His only communication with the outside world was through an unreliable radio connection with his superior on Nauru. On 17 August Suzuki was told that the Japanese government was negotiating with the Allies, but he heard nothing further from Nauru until 22 or 23 August, when he was told about the surrender.[24]

The other defendant in R51 was Lieutenant Nara Yoshio, in charge of payment and food supply on Ocean Island. He was accused of murder for his part in gathering the Islanders together and dividing them up into parties for execution. He had received his orders with the others on the evening of 19 August. He claimed he had opposed them, due to 'humanitarian feeling', but felt he had no choice as he would be charged with disobedience otherwise.[25] The next morning, he assembled and divided up the Islanders as ordered, then went back to his office. Later, he heard the gunfire.

Under cross-examination, he maintained that he felt sorry for the Islanders but did not think the order was wrong or unlawful:

Q: Do you not think the mass killing of 200 natives would be a cruel and brutal act?

A: I did not think the act was brutal because we had been trusting
the natives but they had double-crossed us by making treason.
Q: Do you think it was justified?
A: Yes.[26]

Asked if he knew anything about international law, Nara said he
had studied it as part of his commerce degree at university.

Summing up their case, the defence counsel said the Islanders were
effectively in rebellion, having 'made all sorts of threats against the
Japanese, carried out acts of sabotage and committed war crimes'.[27]
Therefore the killing of them was in self-defence, and was also in
accordance with Suzuki's orders. In Nara's defence, he argued he was
not involved in the actual killing.

'The death of so many natives [is] necessarily abhorrent to members of the court,' the defence counsel concluded. 'The court must
disregard personal feelings in the matter and judge the accused according to the evidence and the appropriate rules of law.'[28]

The court was not persuaded, found both men guilty of murder,
and sentenced them to death by hanging. It was unusual to impose
a death sentence on a defendant not directly involved in killing,
but Nara's attitude had probably not counted in his favour. Both
men petitioned, and on 11 June 1946, Judge Advocate General
Simson upheld the verdict and Suzuki's sentence, but recommended
Nara's be commuted. Sturdee accordingly commuted his sentence
to twenty years' imprisonment. Suzuki was hanged at Rabaul on
23 July 1946.

In the subsequent trials relating to the massacre, the four company commanders (lieutenants) and three of the platoon commanders
(sub-lieutenants) were sentenced to death. Of the remaining platoon
commanders, seven received twenty years' imprisonment, three
received fifteen years, and one was acquitted. Two men of other ranks
(petty officers and warrant officers) were sentenced to seven years, and
one was acquitted. All pleaded the defence of superior orders.

One of the company commanders, Lieutenant Sakata Jiro (in trial R53), said he hated the idea of killing the natives and tried to talk Suzuki out of it, but Suzuki wielded 'absolute power' and once he gave the order 'my brain was no longer mine'. Sakata had called together his subordinates, drawn his sword to show his resolve, and ordered them to shoot the Islanders. The junior officers protested, but he insisted on the validity of the order, while 'keeping back my tears'. In order to ensure a fast and merciful death, Sakata had arranged for more than two soldiers to each Islander. After he had confirmed they were dead, he buried them at sea while praying for their souls.[29]

Under cross-examination, Sakata confirmed that he had told his subordinates that any who disobeyed would be shot.[30] In response to a question from one of the judges, he admitted he had studied the Geneva Convention 'but had forgotten the details'.[31] He was sentenced to death.

Further down the chain of command was Sub-Lieutenant Hanawa Eiji (R70), a platoon commander, who was sentenced to twenty years' imprisonment. He too maintained that he hadn't wanted to shoot the Islanders, but couldn't see that he had any choice: 'My parents were farmers and I only graduated from the primary school with difficulty, helping my family. I was appointed to be an officer in November 1944, about four years after I was called only for the reason officers' shortage, no replacement, so I was not regularly educated as an officer. And my duty was the same as when I was a P. O. [Petty Officer], though I became an officer, and I do not know about the international law and so on at all. Execution of the order was absolute as usual. Especially I was unwilling to shoot the natives to death, but obliged to do it.'[32]

Ocean Island provides an interesting example of how the courts in the early Australian trials dealt with a fairly large-scale war crime involving a hierarchy of defendants. The courts did not accept the defence of superior orders, but did not extend responsibility all the way down to the ordinary seamen who actually did the killing. This was different from the approach at Labuan, where the Formosan guards were held individually responsible for the killing of prisoners of war. There, Sticpewich, who had watched the events unfold over several months, was able to testify to the culpability of each defendant. Making a similar assessment for all 500 Japanese Navy personnel on Ocean Island would have been impossible.

In line with Nuremberg principles, the Rabaul court did consider the defence of superior orders in sentencing – the more senior officers received more severe sentences. Interestingly, it also probed the defendants on their knowledge of international law and appeared to deal more harshly with those who admitted familiarity with it.

# XIII

# COMMAND RESPONSIBILITY

The second round of trials, from 1946 to 1948, dealt with far fewer defendants than the first, but some of those defendants were much more important. The most significant of these were the command responsibility trials of senior officers at Rabaul (R172–R188) from 3 April to 6 August 1947. They were not accused of directly ordering or participating in war crimes, but rather of failing to prevent them. Their trials were the Australian equivalents of those conducted against Generals Yamashita and Homma by the US Army in the Philippines, and the Australian courts frequently referred to those cases. The command responsibility trials were larger and much more complex than the early trials, but drew heavily on the evidence and verdicts from them.

As the Second Australian Imperial Force was demobilised over late 1945 and early 1946 and the remaining Japanese personnel throughout the East Indies and South Pacific were repatriated, the various Australian courts closed. And in the long run, all the locations used for the first round of trials except Rabaul proved inadequate for various reasons. Ambon and Morotai were in the Netherlands East Indies and needed to be handed back to the Dutch. Labuan needed to be returned to the British, and the Australian Army had no desire to keep personnel at Wewak on a long-term basis – it was simply where the 6th Division had been when the Japanese surrendered. The trials at Darwin attracted a great deal of negative publicity, and the government decided not to hold any further trials in Australia afterwards.

By April 1946, only the court at Rabaul was still operating and the first round of trials there ended in July, even though there were still suspects in custody. Another small round was held from 7 December 1946 to 23 January 1947 (R168–R170), but in March 1947, the last Japanese at Rabaul, not being needed as suspects or witnesses, were repatriated.[1] In the meantime, other Australian courts were opened at more permanent premises in Singapore and Hong Kong. Along with the command responsibility trials these make up the second round of Australian trials.

In Singapore, the twenty-three trials of sixty-two defendants were held from 26 June 1946 to 11 June 1947. The Australian trials in Singapore were the result of political and budgetary considerations. Australian public opinion demanded those Japanese responsible for atrocities on the Burma Railway face justice. But Lord Louis Mountbatten, British commander in South-East Asia, had to balance these demands with the cases involving Asian civilians in Malaya and Singapore. The British Empire's prestige in Asia had taken a huge hit with the Fall of Singapore, and such trials could help restore its position. In December 1945, the Australian government therefore agreed to set up and fund a war crimes investigation unit in Singapore, called 1AWCS (First Australian War Crimes Section). Australia would conduct some of the trials involving the Burma Railway and crimes against both British and Australian POWs, freeing British resources for the trials involving crimes against civilians.

Of the twenty-three Australian trials at Singapore, eighteen concerned the Burma Railway, and a significant number involved Korean guards, who were in the same position as the Formosans in Borneo. The remaining cases concerned the execution of downed airmen, and the mistreatment of prisoners of war in the Netherlands East Indies and French Indochina. All death sentences were carried out by the British authorities, by hanging at Changi Prison. In total, 130 Japanese war criminals were hanged there, of whom eighteen had been convicted in Australian courts.

The trials were not quite finished when 1AWCS lost its accommodation in Singapore and was compelled to move to Hong Kong in November 1947. There, thirteen trials of forty-two defendants were held by the Australian authorities between 24 November 1947 and 25 November 1948. Originally there had been only one case scheduled for trial, involving the mistreatment of Australian POWs on Hainan Island. The other cases were added subsequently, covering a wide geographical area and a wide range of victims.

Of the thirteen trials, eight concerned prisoners of war and five concerned civilians. Ten defendants were sentenced to death but only five were actually executed. As at Singapore, the British authorities carried out all executions, by hanging at Stanley Prison. By 1948, both the British and Australian governments were uneasy about continuing to execute Japanese war criminals so long after the end of the war, hence the high rate of commutation. The trials at Hong Kong were also troubled by a lack of resources from both governments, and by pressure from MacArthur to conclude them. In November 1948, 1AWCS lost its premises in Hong Kong and the Australian trials there ended; 2AWCS, which had been raised in Tokyo in March 1946, continued the investigations. Originally created to work with SCAP for the American class-B and -C trials at Yokohama, 2AWCS now, on a limited budget, carried on in the hope that more trials would be held at some point.

At Rabaul, the command responsibility trials began in April 1947. The need to wait for the earlier trials to be resolved and the scaling back of the Australian Army's presence in New Britain caused the delay. Lieutenant Colonel Crofton Stephens, Chief Legal Officer from 1946 onwards, felt that the huts used in the earlier trials at Rabaul were not suitable for the trials of senior officers. They were also starting to deteriorate, but there was no money to rebuild them, and the court had to be stopped at those times when the rain on the tin roof made it impossible to hear what was going on.[2]

There were more people on the bench at the command responsibility trials and of a higher rank, reflecting their greater importance. There were seven officers, led by Major General John S. Whitelaw as president, as well as Judge Advocate Lieutenant Colonel John T. Brock. The prosecution was led not by an AALC officer, but a civilian barrister, Lennard C. Badham KC from the New South Wales bar. The Japanese government sent a defence team of fifteen lawyers and translators, led by senior legal officer Major General Yajima Masanori.

As a result, the legal submissions at the command responsibility trials were much longer than earlier ones, and the quality of the translation is far superior. The trials themselves also went for much longer, often a week or ten days, which could be an ordeal in the tropical heat. The court sat from 9.30 am to 12.30 pm, then from 2.30 to 4.30 pm, an onerous schedule for translators and stenographers. At one point, journalists reported the prosecutors playing noughts and crosses while submissions were being translated, while the president amused himself playing with a baby mouse. 'Unhappily the mouse died'.[3]

As an example of the command responsibility trials, I will look at that of Eighth Area Army general Imamura Hitoshi, overall leader of all Japanese forces in Rabaul and the surrounding area.

At the start of 1946, Imamura was living with thirty-seven other high-ranking Japanese Army and Navy officers at Talili Bay, about 12 miles (19 kilometres) from Rabaul. Living conditions there were not bad. In fact, they appeared to be exceptionally good: self-contained cottages with electricity and indoor plumbing, surrounded by lush gardens. An Australian journalist visited the compound in March and wrote a furious article, published in various newspapers around Australia as 'Japanese Officers Live High at Rabaul' (*The Age*), 'Jap Officers in Luxury, Australians Rough It' (*The Sun*), 'No Action Indicated on Japs' Luxurious Housing'

(*The Telegraph*) and '"Prison Paradise" For Japanese Officers' (the *Sydney Morning Herald*).[4] According to the journalist, Australians in Rabaul were 'disgusted beyond expression' that senior Japanese officers were living in comfort while Australian prisoners of war recovering in hospital had no eggs or fresh vegetables. 'This state of affairs demands a public inquiry,' he wrote, singling out Imamura in particular:

> General Hitoshi Imamura, who commanded the Eighth Army
> Group in the Java and Rabaul area, and who, I am informed,
> is wanted in Batavia for responsibility for the murder of about
> 500 natives in Java, is No. 1 man of the camp. Like all the other
> 37 senior officers, he lives in solitary splendour in a small house,
> extravagantly furnished, and elaborately equipped with new
> furniture. He has a separate bedroom, protected completely by
> flywire, and spotlessly clean sheets and hand-woven rugs so as
> not to soil his honourable feet. Imamura has an office of his own
> and several batmen. Bookshelves line the walls, and there are
> hand-painted vases containing small red flowers. I took all this in
> and wondered why he should want to return to Japan, when, in his
> own words, 'I never imagined I should be treated so well.'

In response, the Australian Army testily pointed out that the Japanese compound at Talili was entirely self-supporting, but it none-theless took away the poultry and goats.[5]

Imamura's good fortune did not last. In May, he and the other accused senior officers were moved to the war criminals compound. 'He has been deprived of the comfort of his well-appointed cottage, his sake, his whisky, his poultry, and his eggs,' wrote journalist Max Coleman. 'Now he has to rub shoulders with the lowliest Jap private.'[6] Coleman did acknowledge that Imamura bore the indignity of being searched by a native police 'boy' much better than another of the gen-erals did (as it turned out, Imamura was able to smuggle a bottle of poison into the compound, so it's questionable how thorough the search was). He would now need to take orders from native guards, attend two parades daily, and answer 'yes, sir' when the Australian corporal called the roll.

Imamura was hoping he would be put on trial quickly, to allow him to defend both himself and his subordinates. But the authorities in Rabaul pushed through the trials of the lower-ranking officers first, and so Imamura needed to endure the frustration of seeing his subordinates convicted and, in some cases, executed, while he was powerless to help them.

After a couple of months in the compound, he tried to kill himself. He bit on the small phial of poison he'd carried with him throughout the war (and smuggled into the compound) and then slashed at his throat with a razor blade. But the poison had lost its potency over the years and only made him sick, and the cut wasn't deep enough to kill him. He was found by a guard within a few minutes and rushed to hospital. Imamura recovered, telling his captors he'd tried to kill himself because he felt partly responsible for Japan's defeat. The guards kept a close eye on him from then on, although he promised not to attempt suicide again. The event was hushed up at the time but became public shortly before his trial.[7]

A significant number of charges against the officers in Imamura's command related to the mistreatment of Chinese, Indian and Indonesian POWs (the Indonesians served in the armed forces of the Dutch East Indies). Imamura's position, and that of the Japanese Army, was that these men were not legally prisoners of war.

Officially, Japanese policy distinguished between European prisoners, who were regarded as prisoners of war and put to work where their labour would be of use to the empire, and Asian prisoners, who were to be given the opportunity to join the Japanese in the creation of the Greater East Asia Co-Prosperity Sphere. Imamura maintained that all the Indians, Chinese and Indonesians under his command at the end of the war had been set free after capture and then volunteered to join the Japanese. The Indians, he argued, were *heiho*, or foreign servicemen in the Japanese Army or Navy. The Chinese and Indonesians were either *heiho* or had been willingly employed as labourers.

This interpretation was strenuously challenged by many of the Indians, Chinese and Indonesians themselves. When the Australian Army reoccupied Rabaul at the end of the war, they found a large number of these so-called volunteers, almost all in very poor shape. About 6,000 Indians were recovered in the South Pacific – they had been captured by the Japanese in Malaya or Singapore and sent to New Britain and the surrounding islands to work as labourers when they refused to join the pro-Japanese Indian National Army.

The British had learned from long and difficult experience that understanding religious difference was essential in governing India. The Japanese, though, tried to force the Hindus they captured to eat beef, the Sikhs to shave their beards and stop wearing turbans, and the Muslims to eat pork and pray towards the Imperial Palace in Tokyo rather than towards Mecca. When they refused they were beaten. They were forced to work seven days a week through the daylight hours, and were underfed and denied medical attention. One of the Indians found at Rabaul was the sole survivor of a labour company that had had 176 men when it was formed in February 1943.[8]

Ninety-nine of the earlier trials at Rabaul had dealt with the mistreatment of Indian prisoners of war, with Subedar Chint Singh serving as a witness in many of them. A Hindu soldier from the 2/12 Frontier Force Regiment captured in the Fall of Singapore, he was one of the forced labourers in New Britain.

There was also a sizeable number of Chinese in Japanese captivity in New Britain, either soldiers captured in China, civilians sent to Rabaul as labourers, or civilians living in the area before the war who were interned. All had suffered high death rates. Of the 1,500 soldiers sent to New Britain, 758 were alive at the end of the war; of 2,000 civilian labourers, 831 were alive; and of the 2,000 or so other civilians, 10 per cent had perished.[9] Forty-four of the Australian cases at Rabaul dealt with Chinese soldiers or civilians. While the Indians were British subjects and therefore more familiar with the common law and Australian Army practices, there was something of a cultural divide with the Chinese. For example, some did not understand why the Japanese accused of war crimes were not executed on the spot.[10] The slow repatriation of the Chinese to China also caused unrest, and at one point led to a small riot.

The final four cases at Rabaul dealt with Indonesians.

At first glance, the question of whether the Chinese, Indians and Indonesians volunteered or were coerced might seem irrelevant. However, the *War Crimes Act* only gave the Australian courts the power to try 'violations of the laws and usages of war or war crimes against any person who was at any time resident in Australia, or against any British subject or citizen of an Allied Power'. It gave no authority to try offences committed by the Japanese against members of their own armed forces, and the internal discipline of the Japanese Army and Navy was therefore outside the jurisdiction of the courts. If the Japanese Army flogged or shot its own workers as punishment for offences under Japanese military law, there was no war crime.

Imamura stuck to this line in a letter to Douglas MacArthur and the Australian government in April, in which he (unsuccessfully) sought a reprieve for some of his officers sentenced to death for shooting Indian labourers caught escaping.[11] Imamura, and the officers, claimed the Indians were being executed for desertion in accordance with Japanese military law. He had made the same argument when he appeared as a witness in the trial of Major General Hirota Akira, responsible for supply within his command. Hirota had been charged with the mistreatment and killing of Chinese prisoners of war and Papua New Guinea natives. Imamura claimed that the Chinese were volunteers recruited by the collaborationist government of Wang Jingwei. When asked in cross-examination why Chinese officers would consent to being sent as manual labourers to Rabaul, he said they had done so to escape starvation in China.[12]

In what a *Daily Advertiser* journalist described as a 'sensation' and a 'dramatic development', Imamura took responsibility for the offences Hirota had been charged with. 'I, not General Hirota, should be held responsible for these incidents if they occurred,' he informed the 'hushed courtroom'. 'I, as G.O.C. of the Eighth Army Group, assume responsibility for the military discipline affecting the 26th Supply Depot. Hirota's responsibility was supply only.'[13]

He was to get his opportunity, with his own trial (R175) beginning on 19 March. Imamura was charged with a violation of the laws and usages of war, in that he 'unlawfully disregarded and failed to discharge his duty' to prevent his subordinates committing brutal atrocities against the people of Australia and its allies.[14] The prosecution presented dozens of instances of the mistreatment or killing of Indian POWs, Chinese civilians and POWs, Indonesian civilians, Dutch civilians, and British POWs throughout Imamura's command, some of which had seen his subordinates convicted at earlier trials. He pleaded not guilty.

In his opening address, prosecutor Lennard Badham KC explained the concept of command responsibility: 'there is no allegation here that the Accused himself committed any of the things in respect of which complaint is made, but that he either expressly authorised them, or connived at them, or was so criminally negligent in respect of the duties devolving on him as commander, that he ought to have known of them, or did know of them and took no steps to prevent them or to see that they were not perpetrated.'[15]

The evidence against Imamura was mostly documentary, consisting of affidavits, extracts from the Third Webb Report, and material from earlier trials. As time passed, it became more common to have witnesses provide statements, rather than use the army's stretched resources to fly them to Rabaul. However, Indian soldier Chint Singh returned to testify in person.

Singh reported that after he was captured, he and his fellow Indians were pressured to join the Indian National Army, the military force of Subhas Chandra Bose's Provisional Government of Free India. According to Singh, about 20,000 joined it in September 1942 'after many tortures and punishments'.[16] Those who held out were beaten, called traitors to the cause of Asia and India, and told they would be sent to the Solomon Islands, then under heavy American air attack. Singh and the men of his unit were sent from Singapore to Wewak in Papua New Guinea in May 1943. Contrary to Imamura's claim, he insisted 'there was none among us who ever joined or intended to join an organisation of the Japanese'.[17]

The prosecution also presented affidavits by a number of Chinese officers telling a similar story. In conclusion, Badham argued, the Indians and Chinese were prisoners of war and therefore entitled to the protection of the Fourth Hague Convention of 1907 and the 1929 Geneva Convention. (The citing of specific treaties, and articles of those treaties, was a sign of the greater sophistication of the command responsibility trials.) The prosecution then went through all the individual instances of torture and murder, showing that these conventions had not been adhered to.

In his defence, Imamura stubbornly maintained that the Indians, Chinese and Indonesians were not prisoners of war. He called seven witnesses to his defence, but all were Japanese – clearly, the defence was not able to find an Indian, Indonesian or Chinese witness who would back up their claims. Under skilful cross-examination from Badham, Imamura found himself tied in knots trying to explain the status of the Indians.[18] If they were not prisoners of war, Badham asked, had they been released? Yes, Imamura replied. So they had the opportunity to leave and not serve the Japanese? Yes. Did any take it? Imamura was not aware; he denied there had been any coercion at Rabaul, but admitted he did not know what happened at Singapore. In the end, he could not explain how any of the Indians could have chosen anything other than service with the Japanese Army, making their volunteering look very much like a Hobson's choice.

In his closing address in Imamura's defence, Yajima held the same line. The ranks of the Indian National Army could not have been filled by force, he said, as such an army would be useless in battle. Indians were labourers in the Japanese Army, and it was 'natural' they would be executed if they tried to desert.[19] The treatment of the Indian prisoners of war was, therefore, outside the jurisdiction of the *War Crimes Act*.

Regarding the actual atrocities, Imamura maintained he knew nothing about them, and any officers who had tortured or executed civilians or prisoners had done so contrary to his orders. Cross-examined by Badham, though, he again found himself in difficulties. One exchange concerned the conviction and death sentence for Captain Ikeba Toma, who'd had a number of Indians shot for trying to escape in Bougainville.[20]

Q: First of all, did you issue, or were you concerned in issuing, an order that Indians who attempted to escape should be shot?

A: No.

Q: Did you issue an order that Indians who attempted to escape should be treated as enemies?

A: Yes, that is stated in the instruction which I referred to before.

Q: And do you know that Captain Ikeba interpreted it as meaning he could shoot the Indians without trial?

A: That is a mistake.

Q: What is a mistake?

A: When in the act of escaping they can be shot, but once caught they must be tried.

Q: Do you know that he said this in the course of his statement: 'I concluded that, acting on my own authority, I order to prevent any unexpected damage, such Indians should be shot.' Do you see that?

A: Yes.

Q: Was that a misinterpretation of your instructions?

A: Yes, it was a misinterpretation. Once they caught them they had
to try them.[21]

In Imamura's defence, Yajima submitted that the international law
relating to command responsibility was vague and unclear.[22] None
of the previous cases established a definite rule for holding a commander responsible for the actions of his men, particularly when they
were outside his direct supervision. Many of the individual atrocities
had taken place away from Rabaul, in Papua New Guinea or the East
Indies. Yajima argued that to hold Imamura responsible for them was
to form a connection that was simply too tenuous. In his lengthy concluding address, Yajima said it was not enough to prove that Imamura
had been the commander at Rabaul, and that his subordinates committed atrocities; the prosecution had to point to some unlawful act
or omission on Imamura's behalf. In Yajima's view, the prosecution
had not been able to do this.[23]

Badham, for his part, accused Imamura of 'seeking refuge in ignorance'.[24] It was 'preposterous' to argue that Imamura had not paid
attention to atrocities committed in his command. People had been
killed, Badham said, often brutally, and the dead called for justice.

After a lengthy concluding address by the judge advocate, the
court retired to consider its verdict. When they returned, Imamura
was convicted. Neither party made any submission on sentence. The
court adjourned for two minutes and then sentenced him to ten years'
imprisonment. A petition against his conviction and sentence was dismissed.

The sentences handed down at the command responsibility trials were relatively lighter than those at earlier trials. Part of this may
have been a cooling of the anti-Japanese feeling that had accompanied
the earlier trials; part of it may have been discomfort with the idea of
holding senior officers culpable for everything done under their command. Especially when the men of the court that sentenced Imamura
were senior officers themselves, commanders of battalions, brigades

or, in the case of the major general, divisions. And while the men under Imamura's command certainly committed heinous crimes, he was not in overall command of an atrocity on the scale of the Rape of Manila or the Bataan Death March. That probably counted in his favour.

So Imamura found himself returned to the war criminals compound. Still, his situation was not too bad. As the senior Japanese officer there, he was useful to the Australian authorities, and helped with the management of the other prisoners. When two men were caught stealing food, an Australian officer suggested they be sentenced to a week's hard labour. Imamura found the punishment too lenient, and they were given two.[25] Living in the 'General's Village' within the compound, Imamura had a great deal of freedom of movement, and was frequently seen out and about with Lieutenant Katayama Hideo.

Katayama was one of the most interesting characters at Rabaul. A devout Christian who spoke fluent English, he had been sentenced to death by shooting at Morotai in February 1946 (M43) for taking part in the execution of a downed Australian airman. His sentence was deferred, however, as he was needed at Rabaul as a witness in another trial. He arrived in May 1946 but it took a year for the trial to take place, so in the meantime he made himself useful around the compound as a translator. In his spare time he led church services and ministered the gospel to Australians and Japanese alike.

Katayama seems to have been an exceptionally personable man, and over time he became one of the most popular residents of the Rabaul compound. The Australian interpreters gave him tea, cigarettes and magazines, and even took him on a tour of Rabaul's Chinatown – a remarkable relaxation of security for a man on death row. He was touched that they began calling him 'Mr Katayama' – no Australians had ever so addressed him before.[26]

Not everyone liked him, though. One Australian officer, Lieutenant H.E. Smith, seems to have been his particular nemesis. One night a group of prisoners broke out of their cells to visit a man who was to be shot the next morning and keep him company. In fact, his sentence had been commuted, but one of the Australian officers had decided to let him spend the night thinking it was his last. Katayama let the escapees through his cell, and then tried to cover for them. The next day, Smith gathered a party of natives and beat him up. Imamura saw this and complained to Major Upson, the commander of the compound.[27]

The Japanese at Rabaul all seem to have had a high opinion of Upson. Imamura found him 'proper and fair'[28] while Katayama spoke of him as an 'Australian of high character who is respected by all the Japanese'. He 'instituted stern discipline', but 'possesses in his heart always a feeling of warm brotherly love'.[29] A number of prisoners wrote thankyou letters to Upson before their release, execution or suicide.

However, Katayama also recorded cases where guards, in defiance of Upson's orders, mistreated prisoners. His own beating at the hands of Smith and his posse was certainly one. Such incidents were more common in the early days, when there were a number of high-profile war criminals on death row, like Hoshijima and Takakuwa. Ikeuchi Masakiyo, the reviled commandant of the unusually lethal POW camp on Ambon, claimed in a letter smuggled out of the compound before his execution that he was repeatedly assaulted by the guards.

Allegations of assaults on prisoners continued into 1946 and 1947. Katayama wrote of the case of Corporal Mayama Kihachi, sentenced to six months for mistreatment of an Indian prisoner of war. Mayama was employed in the laundry and was caught peeking at the wife of an Australian NCO in the shower. He was confined to a cell, where it appears he was beaten up, and the next morning was found to have strangled himself. According to Katayama, all the Japanese questioned knew what had happened but stayed silent when questioned as they did not want Upson to lose face.[30]

Complaints about mistreatment at Rabaul did not go further than the compound, as letters were censored. Afterwards, a few were made public. Some repatriated war criminals claimed before a Japanese House of Representatives Committee in 1953 that their treatment in Rabaul had been 'cruelty itself', a claim the Australian government vehemently denied.[31] In late 1947 Katayama provided his list of incidents to Brigadier Edward Neylan, the new commander at Rabaul, but acknowledged that things had improved significantly since some of the problematic guards had left, and the compound was now a 'model prison'.[32]

Outside of these incidents, the prisoners at Rabaul do not seem to have been particularly ill-treated. They were put to work in the saw-mill, cutting wood for rebuilding the town, in road-building parties outside the compound, or growing vegetables and doing other tasks necessary to keep the compound running. Work hours were from 6.45 am to midday and from 1 pm to 4.30, six days per week. The men were relatively free within the compound, to the point where Chint Singh wanted a pistol to defend himself when he came to testify.[33]

Where possible, the previous professions of the war criminals were made use of. The most common was farm labourer – an interesting insight into the social background of the men who ended up convicted of war crimes. There were sixty other professions, including farmer, blacksmith, electrician, carpenter, mechanic, doctor and pharmacist. There was also a fountain pen dealer, who probably did not have the chance to use his professional skills while imprisoned. Some prisoners were also lent out under guard to civilian authorities, to work on the roads and the aerodrome, or, more alarmingly, bomb and mine disposals. Five were killed in industrial accidents on Rabaul, leading to petitions being signed by the others for dangerous work to be abolished and for the families of war criminals killed on the job to be compensated. These were not accepted.

When they weren't working, the prisoners were engaged in educational or religious activities, sport and recreation. They had access to a gramophone, a table tennis set and magazines, and a Buddhist and Christian priest held a service every Sunday.[34] But they could not receive luxuries from home. In early 1948 the Japanese government asked permission to ship some comfort items, including food, to the Japanese prisoners of war at Rabaul. The Department of the Army responded that there were no prisoners of war at Rabaul, only convicted war criminals who were not entitled to be issued with special comforts.[35]

But even with this policy, there were complaints in the Australian press that the war criminals were being treated too softly. On 19 December 1945 one press correspondent, on seeing the prisoners at Rabaul smoking Australian Army cigarettes, wrote: 'We do not want to "beat them up", because that would be sinking to their standards . . . But what I saw makes me feel that we have gone too far the other way.'[36] Another journalist who visited the compound in May 1948 reported 'fat and well fed' war criminals who 'never seem short of cigarettes' doing only 'light menial' tasks like digging the occasional drain in pumice-stone soil. In his impression, they were living a 'life of comparative comfort and ease' and were better off than many of the island's European residents. 'Returned servicemen and other people at Rabaul are disgusted with the lenient way in which the criminals are being treated,' he concluded.[37]

When the command responsibility trials at Rabaul ended in August 1947, operations there began to wind down. The final executions, both hangings and shootings, were held in October. The last firing squad was formed on 23 October for the executions of Lieutenants Takahashi and Katayama.

A lot of people had gone to a great deal of effort to save Katayama. Neylan had delayed his execution for as long as possible and asked the government to commute his sentence, and everyone in the compound had signed a petition in his favour. However, without any direction from Melbourne or Canberra to the contrary, Neylan was reluctantly forced to order the execution to go ahead. Facing the firing squad, Katayama sang a hymn, said the Lord's Prayer, and then prayed in English for good relations between Australia and Japan and for the health and happiness of everyone in the compound. 'It was an excruciating duty to shoot him,' wrote Georgina Fitzpatrick, not least because the firing squad was drawn from men in the compound who had lived with Katayama for nearly eighteen months.[38]

Takahashi and Katayama were the last people executed by firing squad under Australian law. The Rabaul court was closed in December 1947. The compound continued to operate as a prison, and the Australian government remained satisfied with it. Cyril Chambers, the acting Minister for External Territories, visited in January 1949 and found 'the grounds were in excellent condition, gardens and lawns having been laid out and all buildings inspected were spotlessly clean and tidy'.[39]

But once the town of Rabaul had been rebuilt and returned to the civilian authorities, there was less work for the war criminals to do and less political desire to keep them in New Britain. Over 1949 and 1950 they were transferred to Manus Island to work on rebuilding the Australian Navy base there, and the Rabaul compound was closed down. Rabaul's part in the trial and imprisonment of war criminals had come to an end.

# PART FOUR

# REACTIONS AND RESOLUTION

The end of the trials, reactions, and the release of the war criminals

# XIV

# RESPONSE AND CRITICISM

The trials in Tokyo and throughout the Pacific were intended for a number of audiences: the defendants themselves, the Japanese people, the citizens of Allied countries, and their current and former colonial subjects. There are few records of the reactions of the last group, but all the others left statements and documents indicating their thoughts.

The Allies may have been hoping for declarations from the Tokyo defendants like the one made by Rudolf Höss, the commandant at Auschwitz, while on death row: 'My conscience compels me to make the following declaration. In the solitude of my prison cell, I have come to the bitter recognition that I have sinned gravely against humanity. As Commandant of Auschwitz, I was responsible for carrying out part of the cruel plans of the "Third Reich" for human destruction. In so doing I have inflicted terrible wounds on humanity. I caused unspeakable suffering for the Polish people in particular. I am to pay for this with my life. May the Lord God forgive one day what I have done.'[1]

But if so, they were disappointed. When the Tokyo defendants did speak to the press or leave written statements, they generally maintained the same line they had taken in their defence: Japan's was a war of self-defence, the trials were victors' justice by the vengeful Allies, and their consciences were untroubled. Tōjō, newly converted to Buddhism, said he was happy about the trial, but this was because it had given him the 'opportunity to exonerate the Emperor'.[2] Indeed, those sentenced to death seemed to look forward to an opportunity to sacrifice their lives to protect the Emperor, as if their conviction and execution was a kind of Kamikaze mission.

What about the class-B and -C defendants? In addition to their personal letters and statements to the court, there are a few sources on their views. One is a collection of statements from those facing execution called *Seiki no Isho* (*Testament of the Century*). Published in 1953, following the end of the US occupation of Japan and its associated censorship, this was an effort by a committee of Sugamo prisoners to raise public awareness of the war criminals' situation. The other is a collection of questionnaires distributed to inmates at Sugamo in 1953, divided up by prosecuting power (such as 'BC-Class War Criminals Questionnaire: Australia'). These asked about the fairness of the trials and the sentences.

Overwhelmingly, the BC-class defendants had a negative view of the trials.[3] While most admitted these crimes took place, they generally denied their own involvement, or, if they admitted involvement, denied responsibility. They complained consistently that the trials were one-sided and unfair and that they had been ill-treated by the Allied authorities. Unless they had been in prison for some time (such as the defendants of the 1951 Manus Island trials) they generally did not reflect on the causes of the war crimes. A few 'regretted acts under orders contrary to the morals of humanity' but maintained they were only following orders and had no choice but to obey.[4] Many took the view that the trials were an inevitable consequence of defeat. *Kempeitai* Sergeant Shiraki Jin'ichi, who was executed by the Australians at Rabaul, wrote: 'I did what I believed to be right. I still believe that my actions were the right actions. I was subject to their trials because I was a citizen of a defeated country.'[5] Another convicted man wrote in the questionnaire that 'the war crimes trials were nothing more than something to gratify a retaliatory animosity of the victors against a defeated people'.[6]

'Whatever happens during a war, do not lose,' was the view of an army lieutenant convicted for his role in the Sandakan death marches.[7]

Some of these men were surprised by the outcome of their trial. Captain Haruo Watanabe described his as 'a mere sham' when he was prosecuted at Manus Island in 1950 for neglecting to give prisoners a fair trial at a court martial at Sandakan in March 1944. When he was acquitted, he was caught speechless and bowed low to the court.[8]

Some had more complex views. One of the navy senior petty officers tried at Rabaul for murdering Islanders wrote that he did not object to being put on trial, but thought the court should be run by a neutral country.[9] Others directed their anger not at the Allies, but at their own commanders and government. Quite a number expressed pacifist and anti-military views, believing war crimes were an inevitable result of war, and therefore war should be avoided at all costs. A former navy commander tried in Hong Kong for the murder of a detainee wrote that his trial was conducted fairly, and he was prepared to serve his sentence. But he said: 'War crimes and war are two sides of the same coin. War crimes flow on from war, so if you try to prevent war crimes from occurring, you must refuse war. Even though I will faithfully serve my time as a war criminal, for the reasons stated above, my sons will never become military men.'[10]

Criticism of the Japanese government was common. 'It cared nothing and did nothing for relatives of the men who died while in custody any more than it has cared anything or done anything for those since adjudged war criminals for obeying the military commands of those acting in the name of the Emperor,' wrote Navy Lieutenant Makota Sukarada, whose death sentence for the murder of Allied nationals at Koepang was commuted to life imprisonment.[11] His view – that those who served loyally were entitled to loyalty in return and had not received it – was widespread.

A few of the defendants did have positive views of the trials. Navy Captain Shirozu Wadami believed that the Australians who conducted his trial at Morotai had acted honourably in the service of their country, writing 'they held no hatred for us as individuals' and 'I hope that these trials will become a tie to bind good relations between Japan and Australia.'[12]

And finally, a number did come to accept they were personally responsible for war crimes. Warrant Officer Morimoto Kiyomitsu took responsibility for the execution of two downed pilots on Morotai, even though he was acting on superior orders: 'In the end, the responsibility was mine. I have absolutely no excuses for those who were executed.'[13]

The Allies were particularly concerned about the reactions of the Japanese public. And on the whole, it quietly accepted the trials. MacArthur wrote that he was pleasantly surprised by this, particularly given his own critical view of the trials themselves.[14]

Japanese commentary on the trials went through a series of different stages. When the first accounts of atrocities appeared in the press in September 1945, there was widespread shock and anger. The violence against Asian civilians in China and the Philippines was particularly troubling, given the government's claim that Japan was fighting a war to liberate Asia from European imperialism. A number of people turned to a traditional method of expressing grief, writing *waka* poems, and John W. Dower cites a number of examples published in magazines in the immediate postwar period. One read:

> *Vividly, the traces*
> *Of the Japanese Army's atrocities are shown*
> *Suddenly, a sharp gasp*
> *The crimes of Japanese soldiers*
> *Who committed unspeakable atrocities*
> *In Nanking and Manila*
> *Must be atoned for*
> *Seizing married women*
> *Raping mothers in front of their children*
> *This is the Imperial Army.*[15]

While the Japanese public readily accepted the Tokyo Trial narrative about being misled by their leaders, a number of writers nonetheless did accept that the Japanese had some collective responsibility for both the war and the atrocities. Critic Abe Shinnosuke wrote 'the majority of Japanese must bear responsibility for having been stupid'.[16] Or, as another writer put it, 'in every bit of food we ate, every piece of clothing we wore, a drop of the Chinese peoples' blood had seeped in'.[17]

In the circumstances, there was not much sympathy for the defendants at any level of trial. And if there had been, the Allied censorship of the Japanese media throughout the occupation would have prevented it from being published. Instead, the Japanese press carried articles praising peace and democracy. On 13 November 1948, the day of the Tokyo judgement, the *Asahi Shimbun* newspaper editorialised: 'The judgment of the Tokyo Trial has a special significance in the history of Japan and the world because it is a global expression of the determination for peace, which can be commonly held both by the victors and the vanquished, and is an oath of its practice among related countries.'[18]

Much of the early commentary in the Japanese press came from academics who had been censored and even imprisoned during the war. In *A Secret History of the War Defeat: A Note on War Responsibility* (*Haisen hishi senso sekinin oboegaki, Jiyu Shobo*) Cho Fumitsura accepted that Tōjō and the other leaders were chiefly responsible, but added: 'the people have a duty to pursue the cause of war responsibility by their own efforts, and I consider that if we do not do so we will not be able to establish a genuine democracy based on the principle of responsibility'.[19] Another writer, Ohama Shingen, went further:

> Each and every Japanese must resolve anew to keep watch on
> the proceedings of the trial from the standpoint of international
> justice, to scrutinize one by one the crimes which are under trial
> and the evidence brought forward, listen point by point to the

arguments of the prosecutors and the rebuttals of the defence lawyers, to reflect deeply about it, to renew our understanding and reaffirm our resolve . . . The Japanese people should regard this as a process which they must pass through in order to be reborn as internationalists and to be admitted to international society as it is reconstituted, and to that end it is far from excessive to say that the records of the International Military Tribunal should be compulsory reading for the Japanese people.[20]

Some took his advice. 'During the war we were forced to suffer a poor life; but we lost the war that Tōjō had said we would definitely win,' wrote one man. 'Now I came to learn through the Tokyo Trial and others that it was a reckless, aggressive war pursuing the interests of the privileged class and capitalists, and realised that we had been completely deceived.'[21] Curiously, he was a corporate executive.

However, as the Tokyo Trial dragged on, public interest had waned, and by the time the judgement came around, the attitude had shifted to apathy and passive acceptance.[22] As *Van* magazine editorialised in December 1947: 'When the war advocates now called "war criminals" first appeared on the stage we welcomed them with loud applause. When they fell, we followed along and spat on them. Now we have forgotten about them.'[23]

The Tokyo Trial took up most of the public's attention. Most ordinary Japanese people were only vaguely aware of the class-B and -C trials unless they knew the defendants. The only two books on the lesser trials were Munemiya Shinji's *The Ambon War Crimes Trials* (*Ambonto senpan saihanki*, Horitsu shinposha) in 1946, and Kadomatsu Shoichi's *Capital Punishment* (*Koshukei Jipusha*) in 1950. Otherwise there was little public comment.

The Australian public had mixed reactions. There were, of course, a handful of people who didn't see the need to bother with trials in the first place. 'The perpetrators of such frightful crimes against our nurses, soldiers, airmen, and probably sailors must be exterminated, and I fail to see why time should be wasted with trials and the hearing of appeals,' wrote one correspondent to the editor of the Adelaide *News*.[24] This position does not seem to have been seriously entertained in official circles.

Many people were obviously satisfied to see war criminals brought to justice. When a Quaker, Gilbert Foxcroft, wrote a letter to the *West Australian* criticising the execution of Japanese war criminals on Christian grounds, he drew a sharp response from George Gaunt, a former civilian internee of the Japanese. Far from being against Christian principles, Gaunt argued, the trial and execution of war criminals was necessary to protect Christian civilisation and the Christian concept of justice. 'When having defeated them, as we have done, we have every right to bring the culprits to justice in order to secure peace to the vast majority of humanity who so earnestly seek it,' he wrote.[25]

However, several persistent criticisms of the trials emerged: they were too lenient, they were progressing too slowly, or they failed to achieve their purpose. Complaints about the defendants being let off too easily cropped up at different times, but there was a barrage of them following the first Darwin trial (D1).[26] The three trials of twenty-two defendants held in Darwin between 1 March and 29 April 1946 were the only war crimes trials held in Australia. All related to crimes against Australian POWs during the Japanese invasion and occupation of Timor.

Nine of these defendants, members of the army and *Kempeitai*, were charged with various counts of mistreating prisoners from Australian infiltration parties captured from late 1943 to mid-1945. Three defendants were convicted of beating prisoners with a cane ('but not severely', the precis of the evidence noted)[27] and forcing them to kneel for long periods on a narrow log. This was referred to in the trial and the media reports as 'the log torture'.

The other six defendants were acquitted. Of the three convicted, one was sentenced to three months' imprisonment, the other two to a month each.

The defendants did not expect this outcome. According to *The Argus*, one of the acquitted men 'looked incredulously at the court when the verdict was translated, and then bowed in a dazed manner', while the man sentenced to three months went immediately 'to reassure himself from the interpreter that his sentence was three months – not years'.[28]

While the torture inflicted on the Australian captives in Timor should not be understated, it was obvious that the Japanese in Timor had a different attitude to those elsewhere – for example, in Borneo. However, in March 1946 the media was still carrying many accounts of atrocities throughout the Pacific, and the general public probably began to confuse them. Additionally, the 'log torture' was described in some articles as men's legs being 'crushed' by logs. As a result, there was an immediate impression that the defendants at Darwin had been effectively let off. Furthermore, as the trial was in Australia, it was covered closely by the media. The result was an explosion of criticism. In parliament, Army Minister Frank Forde was asked several times why the sentences had been so light.[29]

According to the *Sydney Morning Herald*, former prisoners of war 'declared that if the Government persisted in promulgating such ridiculous penalties they would not rest until the Darwin court was recalled and men competent to deal with Japanese barbarity had taken their place'.[30] Lieutenant General Gordon Bennett, former commander of the 8th Division, said 'he could not believe that any man who had been a prisoner in Malaya could be so lenient if he was a member of the court'.[31] Senior figures in the RSL likewise called for victims of Japanese atrocities to be made judges. The federal president of the Australian Legion of Ex-Servicemen, B.J. McDonald, said while it was not in the Australian make-up to seek vindictive revenge, 'a month's imprisonment was the usual punishment for a man convicted of cruelty to a dog'.[32] A direct protest was made to the prime minister by Sydney Smith, Secretary of the War Relatives Association.

In an angry letter to the editor of the *Sydney Morning Herald* the following day, 19 March, a former prisoner of war asked how the sentences could be so lenient when others had been sentenced to death for the torture of POWs at Ambon.[33] Another letter, by a Bob Beard of Adelaide, read:

> So the first comic opera war crimes trial ends at Darwin where justice was meted out on the 'Love thine enemies' basis, adorned with all the usual twaddle about British law and technical legal details which enabled six out of nine Japanese to be acquitted. The remaining three received much lighter sentences than an A.I.F. private who was A.W.L. [absent without leave] for a few days. But, of course, the Japanese were officers and therefore gentlemen. I have seen A.I.F. privates standing up for two hours awaiting the pleasure of an officer to try them for some trivial offence, with the certainty of heavy punishment hanging over their heads. There was no array of legal defence for these boys, no officer to say that they were honest products of a harsh system, as did the defence officer for the Japanese. The point is just how much longer Australians are going to suffer the waste of money and time on the so-called war trials, and put up with reading the nauseating details.[34]

As for complaints that the trials were taking too long, these first appeared in 1947 and became more forceful in 1948. Over the course of that year, attitudes towards Japan and the war crimes trials generally had shifted in Allied countries. MacArthur had no desire to occupy Japan indefinitely and he was increasingly in favour of negotiating an early peace treaty, ending the trials and removing Allied forces from the country. The Cold War was also taking more of the US government's attention. In June 1948, the Soviet Union began blockading West Berlin, and in October and November the Chinese communists won a series of decisive victories over the Nationalists in northern China, making a communist government increasingly likely.

In September 1948, MacArthur instructed the American authorities in Japan to refer all outstanding cases for trial by October, and to make every effort to complete the trials by the end of the year. This deadline was later extended to 30 April 1949, but the pressure to conclude the trials remained.[35] Australia, though, was slow to relinquish its wartime attitudes. There were anti-Japanese feelings on both sides of federal parliament, but they were particularly strong in Arthur Calwell. Minister for Immigration from 1945–49, Calwell was a defender of the White Australia policy and an opponent of rapprochement with Japan. He remained steadfastly opposed to Japanese war brides, sporting teams or businessmen coming to Australia: 'We don't want to see any Japanese on Australian shores in any circumstances or in any capacity . . . That goes for trade, as well as for sport. I think the feelings of those relatives of the men who were butchered fiendishly are more worthy of consideration by a Minister of State than profits to be made from trade and laurels to be won in sport.'[36]

Evatt also took a hard line: 'It would be wrong for Japan to be converted into an arsenal that would ultimately be turned in the direction of the South Pacific,' he said on 8 April 1948, adding that it would be an 'evil day for Australia if Japan is given capacity to rearm'. But later he took a moderate position, saying that 'while Japan must not be placed in a position to rearm or to re-create a dangerous war potential, restrictions on the Japanese economy should not go beyond what is necessary for military security and that Japan should have a workable economy'.[37]

Calwell's views were common in 1945, but by mid-1948 he was increasingly in the minority. On 8 May 1948, none other than General Thomas Blamey himself said that he agreed with those Americans who saw Japan as a 'buffer against the spread of Soviet imperialism'.[38] The leaders of the RSL were divided, with some supporting his comments and others criticising them.

Over 1948 the British Commonwealth Occupation Force was reduced as India and New Zealand withdrew their forces from Japan, and the UK and Australia scaled back their commitments. Increasingly, the US government took the view that its troops were in Japan to protect the country (and neighbouring South Korea) from communist aggression. The idea of Australians dying to defend the Japanese did not sit well with the Australian government or Australian public, but Australia fell into line with this position out of necessity.

In June 1948, the *Sydney Morning Herald* argued that it was time to bring the trials to a close: 'Certainly, the basic purposes for which they were initiated – to impress on the aggressor nations the measure of their guilt and to deter future potential aggressors – are no longer being served. "Justice," as [British Lord Chancellor] Lord Jowitt said, if spread over too long a period, begins to look like vengeance.'[39]

The Tokyo Trial came to a close in November 1948, and the US government freed the remaining class-A suspects on 26 December, finally abandoning plans to hold multiple class-A trials.[40] Over 1949, Australia held no trials even though suspects were still in custody – the government cited a lack of resources as the reason, and attracted increasing criticism for it.[41]

On 5 December 1949, with the US government threatening to release all remaining suspects which it held on Australia's behalf, the *Sydney Morning Herald* slammed the Australian government for 'bungling' the war crimes trials with 'inexcusable tardiness': 'The average ex-Serviceman feels that if they [the Japanese war criminals] were to get what was coming to them they should have got it quick, not least because that might have made some beneficial impression on Japanese public opinion. Now, when others have wiped the slate, our belated proceedings will be regarded as mere vindictiveness. It is not enough to do justice. We should also appear to do it.'[42]

The entire project of the class-B and -C war crimes trials was in fact gaining negative attention. Between May and July 1946, a US military tribunal at Dachau convicted seventy-three members of the Waffen-SS of the massacre of American POWs at Malmédy in 1944. The trial subsequently attracted scandal due to allegations that American interrogators had beaten confessions out of the suspects, starved them, or threatened to shoot them if they did not plead guilty. A media firestorm was followed by an investigation by a US Army commission, and finally, in 1949, an investigation by a US Senate sub-committee. While this played out, all the trials being conducted by the Allies in both the European and Pacific theatres came under more intense scrutiny. (The Third Geneva Convention, 1949, contained specific safeguards for prisoners of war being tried for war crimes, most likely in response to this attention.) All American-held suspects were released on 19 October 1949, and SCAP warned the Australian government that all suspects being held in Sugamo on Australia's behalf would be released on 1 November unless the Australian gov-ernment could provide a good reason to keep them. A request for an extension was refused: '. . . G.H.Q. [headquarters] is unable to discover adequate grounds on which to justify their detention for a further indefinite period. More than 4 years after the termination of hostilities and after from 1 to 2 years after the original apprehension of the majority of the suspects their continued incarceration without specific charges and without even a certain prospect of eventual trial can scarcely be reconciled with fundamental concepts of justice . . .'[43]

But with Australia then entering an election campaign, MacArthur held off the release. Additionally, as the Cold War came to domi-nate international relations, the idea of enforcing peace and justice through international agreements waned. Whereas the First World War had ended with the foundation of the League of Nations and the concept of international co-operation, the Second had ended with a world divided between the two superpowers. Many Westerners thought it unlikely a new international order could be established by co-operating with Stalin's totalitarian regime in the Soviet Union. On 30 June 1949 Evatt presented a bill ratifying the United Nations con-vention against genocide to the House of Representatives. Pointing out that the Australian government was unlikely to commit genocide, Liberal MP Jo Gullett went on to say, 'Genocide is being practised now in Hungary, Poland and Czechoslovakia against the leaders of racial and religious groups. They are being persecuted and put to death, but there is no condemnation of such crimes because it might affect a powerful nation. We wait in vain for condemnation of these crimes to come from the United Nations. I say frankly that I regard this bill as nothing more nor less than a piece of pious humbug.'[44]

Country Party MP Joe Abbott went further, describing the bill as 'one of those pious pieces of humbug which the Minister for External Affairs [Evatt] so often brings back to this country when he returns from one of his many excursions overseas'. Country Party MP Archie Cameron pointed out that slavery was ended by force and not an international agreement, and he was not persuaded that the convention would work. In the mindset of the Cold War, the military strength of the West was seen as a better safeguard of peace and freedom than international agreements, which included totalitarian communist states.

Finally, there was the criticism that the trials were not achieving their purpose of exposing the dangers of militarism to the Japanese. One such critic was George Caiger, Australian intelligence officer on MacArthur's staff and former English lecturer in Japan. In May 1946 he wrote:

> Most of those on trial as war criminals will proudly accept martyrdom. Seen against this background the trials of war criminals will not scotch, still less kill, the Japanese will to power. The trials may play a part in laying a necessary foundation for re-education, but they cannot in themselves change Japanese ways of thinking . . . [L]et us be clear on two points: – (1) Only the Japanese can solve this dilemma (and they may fail); (2) our present task is to prevent future aggression (and we must not fail). I submit that the only sure and safe way to prevent aggression is to continue what has been

begun, complete disarmament . . . then, if they have not solved
their dilemma of pre-Christian ideas upsetting the 20th century, it
will not matter.[45]

   Caiger also argued that because the Japanese public did not understand the idea of holding individuals responsible for war crimes, the
purpose of the trials was therefore questionable:

> At Morotai, Rear-Admiral Hamanaka is said to have shouted:
> 'This is a conspiracy against myself and Japan,' when sentenced to
> death. These two hints of the defendants' attitude indicate that
> they are entirely ignorant of the Anglo-American ideals of justice.
> This is to be expected, but even if the defendants are baffled by
> the proceedings, it is vitally important that the Japanese public
> should be made to understand what it is all about . . . The
> Rear-Admiral, being more intelligent than many of his countrymen,
> realises that the trials are directed against the whole system for
> which he stands, and is naturally shocked at this challenge to the
> divine order of things. But it is not enough for one Rear-Admiral
> to glimpse a half-truth. The Japanese people must be taught that
> these trials are evidence of rising standards of world morality in
> the attempt to pillory aggression, to brand those who start wars as
> guilty of a crime against humanity . . . Rear-Admiral Hamanaka
> was also appalled at the thought that the trials were a conspiracy
> against 'myself'! This reveals how the minds of those conducting
> the trials and the minds of the defendants are moving along
> parallel lines, with only infinitesimal chances of meeting. We
> are prosecuting an individual because of our ideas of personal
> responsibility. The Japanese think only in terms of official
> responsibility. The Rear-Admiral's exclamation shows something
> of the difficulty of erecting a democratic edifice on non-democratic
> foundations, as well as the gulf between Occidental and Japanese
> ideas of justice.[46]

This idea that the trials had failed to bridge the gap between Western and Japanese concepts of justice remained widespread. In a parliamentary debate in 1950, Labor MP Tom Burke of Perth claimed that the trials had achieved little or nothing for this reason. They had, he said, brought Australia down to the level of its enemies, and had not made war or war crimes less likely in the future. Burke wanted to know 'by what standards should we try the Japanese who are now awaiting trial? They were born, not in a British community, but in a foreign land the ethics and laws of conduct of which are very different from our own . . . In present circumstances it is impossible to ensure that British justice or any other type of justice shall be upheld in these war trials . . . we have not done a thing that this country, and the world, will laud us for in future, and that we have done nothing to achieve the high purposes to which we set ourselves.'[47]

On 25 June 1950 North Korea invaded South Korea, and the threat of a war against communism in Asia, which had been hanging over the occupation of Japan and the war crimes trials since 1948, was now a reality. The United Nations Security Council condemned the invasion and passed a resolution encouraging member states to provide military aid to South Korea. Shortly afterwards, the United States and Australia began transferring their occupation forces from Japan to South Korea. Australia had already been planning to withdraw its forces, which consisted of 2,356 Australian personnel, including an infantry battalion and an RAAF squadron, and from mid-1950 onwards, BCOF really only continued to exist to support Commonwealth military operations in Korea.[48] The war that had been fought against Japan was looking less and less relevant to the modern world.

# XV

# ALLIED WAR CRIMES: A DOUBLE STANDARD?

One persistent criticism of the entire Allied program of war crimes trials in all theatres is that the prosecuting countries held a double standard by ignoring their own war crimes. Allied war crimes were raised throughout the process of planning for the trials, through the trials themselves by the defendants, in the media, and by critics of the trials up to the present day.

First, and perhaps most reasonably, critics of the trials pointed out that the Soviet Union had committed most of the same war crimes as Germany and Japan. Josef Stalin's regime was one of the most repressive and lethal ever to have existed. Taking into account deaths from forced resettlement, imprisonment in labour camps and outright execution, Stalin's regime killed at least 4 or 5 million people and probably many times more. And before that, the Soviet Union had conspired with Germany through the Nazi–Soviet Pact of 1939 to invade Poland and divide it up. It had invaded and conquered the Baltic States without provocation. And, perhaps most relevantly to Tokyo, it had declared war on Japan on 8 August 1945 in violation of a non-aggression pact. Furthermore, if conspiracies to wage aggressive war are taken into account, it had done so on the urging of the Western Allies.

Advancing into Germany in the winter and spring of 1945, the Soviet Red Army carried out a systematic campaign of summary execution, plunder and mass rape, vividly described by dissident Aleksandr Solzhenitsyn in his poem 'Prussian Nights'.[1] Then, after the war, the Soviet government expelled some 2 million ethnic Germans from Eastern Europe, annexed Polish and German territory, forcibly re-incorporated the Baltic States into the Soviet Union, and established authoritarian puppet states in regions conquered by the Red Army.

The mindset which led to these atrocities carried over into the trials. Over April and May 1940, the Soviets massacred 22,000 captive Polish army and police officers and university professors at Katyn. Then, at Nuremberg, they brazenly tried to pin the crime on the Nazis. The judges and prosecutors sent by Moscow to Nuremberg and Tokyo had generally been active participants in Stalinist repression. The principal Soviet judge at Nuremberg, Iona Timofeevich Nikitchenko, had presided over a number of Stalin's show trials in the 1930s.

Unsurprisingly, the conduct of the Soviet government and armies was repeatedly thrown into the faces of the Allies. Hans Frank, Nazi Governor-General of Poland, said in his final statement to the court at Nuremberg after being sentenced to death for war crimes and crimes against humanity: 'Every possible guilt incurred by our nation has already been completely wiped out today, not only by the conduct of our war-time enemies towards our nation and its soldiers, which has been carefully kept out of this Trial, but also by the tremendous mass crimes of the most frightful sort which – as I have now learned – have been and still are being committed against Germans by Russians, Poles, and Czechs, especially in East Prussia, Silesia, Pomerania, and Sudetenland. Who shall ever judge these crimes against the German people?'[2]

The Soviet Union was only involved in the Pacific War for a week, from 8–15 August 1945. In that time the Red Army overran Manchuria, and it continued to advance after the surrender, driving into Korea down to the 38th parallel. Some 600,000 soldiers of the Kwantung Army were captured by the Soviets and sent to forced labour camps in Siberia. And kept there, over the winter of 1945–46, as thousands died from starvation and disease. Like political prisoners in the Soviet Union, many were repeatedly interrogated or subjected to communist 're-education' programs. The process of repatriating them only began in late 1946, while Japan's leaders were being tried for, among other things, using prisoners of war as slave labour. The last of the Kwantung Army soldiers were not released until 1956, by which time anywhere from 38,000 (the number conceded by the Soviet government in 1991) to 100,000 had died.[3] It is possible that more Japanese prisoners died in Soviet captivity than did Western prisoners in Japanese captivity.

Second, there was the intentional strategic bombing of German and Japanese cities by the Allies, which killed up to a million civilians in both countries. In its definition of war crimes, the Nuremberg Charter included the 'wanton destruction of cities, towns, or villages, or devastation *not justified by military necessity*' (emphasis added). The Allies maintained their bombing had been justified. In a speech on 9 August 1945, President Harry Truman said of the use of the atomic bomb on Hiroshima (which he had described as 'an important Japanese Army base'): 'Having found the bomb we have used it. We have used it against those who attacked us without warning at Pearl Harbor, against those who have starved and beaten and executed American prisoners of war, against those who have abandoned all pretense of obeying international laws of warfare. We have used it in order to shorten the agony of war, in order to save the lives of thousands and thousands of young Americans.'[4]

Truman's argument was compelling, but in the end, it appeared he had fallen back to justifying the mass killing of enemy civilians by military necessity. In other words, killing Japanese civilians was justified to save the lives of American soldiers. As Justice Radhabinod

Pal wrote in his dissent: 'I do not perceive much difference between what the German Emperor is alleged to have announced during the First World War in justification of the atrocious methods directed by him in the conduct of that war and what is being proclaimed after the Second World War in justification of these inhuman blasts.'[5]

The defendants at trials in both theatres raised the strategic bombing of their cities. Sentenced to death at Nuremberg, German General Alfred Jodl said: 'In a war such as this, in which hundreds of thousands of women and children were annihilated by layers of bombs or killed by low-flying aircraft, and in which partisans used every – yes, every single means of violence which seemed expedient, harsh measures, even though they may appear questionable from the standpoint of international law, are not a crime in morality or in conscience.'[6]

Placed on trial at Yokohama for executing downed American airmen, Lieutenant General Okada Tasuku maintained he had held a lawful court martial where the men were convicted of bombing civilians in violation of the (unratified) 1923 Hague Convention. His defence failed, and he was convicted and hanged.

Was the bombing of cities illegal? The law on this point was unclear. Germany and Japan both bombed enemy cities during the war, and the Allies were careful never to prosecute their leaders for it, or to in any way imply it might have been illegal. There was no specific convention prohibiting strategic bombing, such as the Hague Conventions that specifically forbade the mistreatment of prisoners of war and attacks on hospitals and hospital ships.[7] Then again, at the time of the Hague Conferences in 1899 and 1907, there was no such thing as strategic bombing, so while the delegates did consider the dropping of bombs from balloons they gave no attention to the bombing of cities by aircraft. The 1923 Hague Conference, coming in the wake of strategic bombing by both sides in the First World War, proposed the resolution (Article XXII): 'Aerial bombardment for the purpose of terrorizing the civilian population, of destroying or damaging private property not of a military character, or of injuring non-combatants is prohibited.' But this resolution was never formally adopted.

Nonetheless, the consensus of international opinion ran against the bombing of civilians. In 1937, both the bombing of Shanghai by the Japanese and the bombing of Guernica by the German air force in the Spanish Civil War drew widespread condemnation. On 30 September 1938 the League of Nations passed a resolution declaring 'the intentional bombing of civilian populations is illegal'.[8] On 1 September 1939, US President Franklin Roosevelt spoke in even stronger terms: 'The ruthless bombing from the air of civilians in unfortified centers of population during the course of the hostilities which have raged in various quarters of the earth during the past few years, which has resulted in the maiming and in the death of thousands of defenseless men, women, and children, has sickened the hearts of every civilized man and woman, and has profoundly shocked the conscience of humanity.'[9]

Yet only two years later, Roosevelt gave his endorsement to the bombing of German cities.

The British, too, came around to the view that mass bombing was necessary. The first strategic air raid on a German city by the RAF was directed at Mannheim in December 1940, and the bombing escalated from there. A UK Air Staff paper on 23 September 1941 put the position simply: 'The ultimate aim of the attack on a town area is to break the morale of the population which occupies it. To ensure this we must achieve two things: first, we must make the town physically uninhabitable and, secondly, we must make the people conscious of constant personal danger. The immediate aim, is therefore, twofold, namely, to produce (i) destruction, and (ii) the fear of death.'[10]

The United States took the same view when it entered the war, and the bombing increased up to the devastating fire-bombing raids on Dresden and Tokyo and the atomic bombing of Hiroshima and Nagasaki.

Class-B and -C war criminals also justified their actions with reference to the bombs. In an interview with a *Sydney Morning Herald* journalist in a 1953, Navy Sub-Lieutenant Tsuruoka Ikuzo, whose death sentence for the murder of Allied prisoners at Koepang was commuted to fifteen years' imprisonment, asked: 'Surely those responsible for dropping the atomic bombs on Hiroshima and Nagasaki are war criminals? In view of this, although I am labelled as a war criminal, my conscience is untroubled. I did no more than to carry out orders.'[11]

The bombing of cities may have been legal under existing laws, although it is a fair point that existing law was stretched at Nuremberg and Tokyo. Of course, it was stretched there in favour of the Allies. But even if the bombing of cities had been legal, it cast a moral cloud over the war crimes trials. As Sandra Wilson, Robert Cribb, Beatrice Trefalt and Dean Aszkielowicz concluded: 'The firebombing of Tokyo in 1945 and the atomic-bombing of Hiroshima and Nagasaki cast doubt on the legitimacy of virtually all war crimes charges against Japanese military personnel, because they suggested that truly extreme actions could be justified by military necessity.'[12]

Thirdly, the Allies were also accused of committing war crimes in the conduct of their armies in battle. As Paul Ham wrote of the Kokoda Campaign: 'Neither side took prisoners if they could avoid it. The Australians took a tiny number on the Kokoda Track; the Japanese took a handful. Both sides killed surrendering as well as captive troops.'[13] More seriously, the killing of wounded or surrendered Japanese soldiers in violation of the laws of war was sometimes endorsed by officers. Dennis Warner, an Australian historian, described his own experience in Bougainville:

> 'But sir, they are wounded and want to surrender' a colonel
> protested to [a major general] at the edge of a cleared perimeter
> after a massive and unsuccessful Japanese attack.

'You heard me, Colonel' replied [the major general], who was only yards away from the upstretched Japanese hands. 'I want no prisoners. Shoot them all.'

They were all shot.[14]

Such conduct, common throughout Allied armies in the Pacific, had several causes. One was the fanaticism and brutality of Japanese soldiers, and their unwillingness to surrender or take prisoners themselves. Another was practical caution, as the Japanese would commonly booby-trap the wounded or dead, or pretend to surrender to lead Allied soldiers into a trap. Then, too, there was the sight of mutilated Allied soldiers or captured civilians. And finally, the greater acceptability of racist attitudes at that time.

A merciless approach to the Japanese was often sanctioned at the highest levels. General Blamey told Australian troops in Papua New Guinea in 1942 that 'beneath the thin veneer of a few generations of civilisation he is a subhuman beast who has brought warfare back to the primeval, who fights by the jungle rule of tooth and claw, who must be beaten by the jungle rule of tooth and claw'.[15] The next year, in a similar situation, he described the Japanese as 'a curious race, a cross between the human being and the ape', and added, 'we must go on to the end if civilisation is to survive . . . we must exterminate the Japanese'.[16]

Ultimately, the Japanese were viewed as a unique enemy, worse than the Germans or Italians and less deserving of mercy. One Australian soldier who fought in Africa and Greece before the Pacific wrote: 'my regard for Tony [the Italian] was always impersonal, and for the Fritz [German] . . . tinged with admiration, but none of us knew anything but vindictive hatred for the Jap'.[17]

But once safely in Australian custody, Japanese prisoners were generally safe. At the end of the war there were 5,500 of them in Australia,[18] and all up, around 35,000 Japanese POWs were taken by the Western Allies and the Nationalist Chinese.[19] There were rumours of Japanese prisoners being thrown from planes when airlifted from Port Moresby, and the guards reporting they had 'committed hara-kiri'. It is not impossible, of course, that they did actually jump to escape the shame of surrender.[20]

The allegations against Allied troops did not end with the war. Accusations of murder, looting and rape were made during the occupation of Japan. Historian Takemae Eiji wrote: 'U.S. troops comported themselves like conquerors, especially in the early weeks and months of occupation . . . In Yokohama, Chiba and elsewhere, soldiers and sailors broke the law with impunity, and incidents of robbery, rape and occasionally murder were widely reported in the press.'[21] Eight hundred crimes, including 303 cases of rape, were reported against BCOF troops in Hiroshima in 1946.[22] Two cases in particular have attracted recent media attention in Australia: 'A former prostitute recalled that as soon as Australian troops arrived in Kure in early 1946, they "dragged young women into their jeeps, took them to the mountain, and then raped them. I heard them screaming for help nearly every night". Such behaviour was commonplace, but news of criminal activity by the occupation forces was quickly suppressed.'[23]

And the other, by Allen Clifton, an Australian officer:

> I stood beside a bed in hospital. On it lay a girl, unconscious, her long, black hair in wild tumult on the pillow. A doctor and two nurses were working to revive her. An hour before she had been raped by 20 soldiers. We found her where they had left her, on a piece of waste land. The hospital was in Hiroshima. The girl was Japanese. The soldiers were Australians. The moaning and wailing had ceased and she was quiet now. The tortured tension on her face had slipped away, and the soft brown skin was smooth and unwrinkled, stained with tears like the face of a child that has cried herself to sleep.[24]

It is impossible to know how widespread this sort of behaviour was, as it was certainly under-reported. The Australian Army, and the Allies generally, cannot be held legally or morally responsible for all of the crimes committed by their soldiers. But they can be criticised if their official response was inadequate.

Australian troops, and BCOF troops generally, were discouraged from fraternisation with the Japanese. When they arrived in Japan, Lieutenant General Northcott issued this order: 'In dealing with the Japanese [you are] dealing with a conquered enemy who has by making war against us caused deep suffering and loss to many thousands of homes throughout the British Empire. Your relations with this defeated enemy must be guided largely by your own individual good judgment and your sense of discipline. You must be formal and correct. You must not enter their homes or take part in their family life. Your unofficial dealings with the Japanese must be kept to a minimum.'[25]

While military personnel could be court-martialled for rape, theft and murder, these crimes were under-prosecuted, as well as under-reported, and sentences imposed were often slight. One rape by an Australian soldier that was reported to the police resulted in a court martial, a conviction, and a sentence of ten years' penal servitude. But the conviction was overturned due to lack of evidence.[26]

It is fair to say that Australian military courts dealt more harshly with Japanese soldiers accused of crimes against civilians than with Australian soldiers, and they promoted reports of the former while suppressing reports of the latter. But it is not clear what effect this had, either morally or legally, on the Allied war crimes trials. I will return to this question in the conclusion.

# XVI

# THE FINAL ROUND: MANUS ISLAND

Manus Island is the largest of the Admiralty Islands, which lie about 300 kilometres north of Papua New Guinea and about two degrees south of the equator. Manus is of volcanic origin, mostly covered in tropical rainforest, and has a range of low mountains running along its spine. Its principal settlement is Lorengau in the far east of the island, from where a causeway runs to nearby Los Negros Island. Between Manus and Los Negros is Seeadler Harbour, one of the finest anchorages in the region – in the Second World War the US Navy was able to securely anchor a thousand ships there.

The Admiralty Islands were part of German New Guinea when they were captured by the Australians in 1914. They were then captured by the Japanese in April 1942, and recaptured by the Americans in February 1944. The Americans left in 1948 and the islands came back under Australian control.

The Chifley government decided to rebuild the Australian Navy's base at Seeadler Harbor using Japanese war criminals serving prison terms as labour. Starting in February 1948, the government began transferring prisoners from Rabaul to a new compound at Manus near Lombrum, a process completed by early 1950.[1] In the federal election of 10 December 1949 the Chifley Labor government was defeated and

Robert Menzies led the Liberal–Country Party coalition into office. At its first cabinet meeting, the new government dealt with a long message from MacArthur demanding the Australian trials be completed by 31 December 1949. At the time, 191 suspects were still being held on Australia's behalf.[2]

The Menzies government was suspicious of Japan, but not to the extent the previous government had been. A rebuilt Japan was a potential threat, but also a potential trading partner and ally against communism. And Menzies and his ministers were fiercely critical of holding men without trial. 'The previous Prime Minister very properly said that it is inexcusable to hold men year after year without bringing them to trial,' Country Party MP Larry Anthony told the House of Representatives in March 1950. 'Whether they be Japanese or German, they are entitled to a fair and speedy trial in accordance with the tenets of British justice.'[3]

MacArthur had granted the new government a short extension to decide what to do, and on 11 January 1950 it announced that trials would commence on Manus Island with all possible speed.[4]

On 23 February 1950 Menzies made a statement to the House of Representatives explaining his government's policy towards the remaining suspects in Australian detention. 'As the war was a crucial struggle against aggression and injustice,' he told the House, 'so our conduct in victory should be marked by an adherence to those great principles of clear allegation, prompt trial, and unswerving execution of judgment which have characterized the whole development of what we call, in simple but proud terms, British justice.'[5]

He announced that the government would bring to trial those cases 'involving charges of murder or other revolting crimes or charges in relation to which, on conviction of the accused persons involved, the sentence of death might be appropriate'. Menzies justified the decision to hold the trials on Manus Island on the odd basis that it was the closest Australian territory to Japan. The government was unwilling to hold more trials in Australia itself after the adverse publicity of the Darwin trials. The authorities in Hong Kong would not allow any further Australian trials to be held there, and nor would MacArthur allow them in Japan, as they were not, in his view, directly connected with the occupation. It's likely that Manus was selected because the convicted war criminals already in prison were being assembled there to work on an Australian naval base and it was distant enough from Australia to prevent the trials becoming a media show.

Menzies further announced that those defendants accused of lesser crimes, and those who were unlikely to be convicted due to insufficient evidence, would be released.

This last point did not sit well with some MPs. Eddie Ward, Labor MP for East Sydney, rhetorically asked the House, 'I am wondering whether this is an act of appeasement towards the Japanese nation. There appear to be elements in the world who are now endeavouring to strengthen Japan because they consider that it could be a possible buffer against the Soviet [Union] in the event of any future hostilities with that nation. No doubt this is another act of appeasement of enemy countries on the part of the Government.'[6]

A heated exchange between Ward and new Minister for External Affairs Percy Spender followed, with Ward repeatedly asking Spender how many suspects had been released, and Spender reluctant to give a straight answer. Finally, he gave the number of seventy-one.

Liberal MP Bill Graham supported Menzies but also called for reconciliation with Japan, saying: 'If we, as British people, are to maintain our standards of justice, we are forced to mete out to the Japanese, Germans and Italians – our three foes in the last war – the same measure of justice. Germany again trades with Australia, and an Italian grand opera company visited this country last year, yet we are still looking at the Japanese with suspicion. I admit that there are many people who will always have feelings of rancour and hatred for the Japanese, but, from a national viewpoint, if we are to maintain our standards for posterity, we must put aside those feelings.'[7]

And so the Manus Island trials came under criticism before they began.


The Japanese were accommodated in five huts made of galvanised iron with cement bases, and there was also a mess hut, a recreation hut and a hospital hut. At night the men were locked in the dormitories, which were lined with neat plank bunks. The Australian Navy took command of the facility in March 1950, and it became formally known as RAN War Criminal Compound Manus Island. On 16 January 1951 the government released the War Crimes (Imprisonment) Regulations, setting out various matters for the prisoners – a work schedule (nine hours per day, six days a week), discipline, medical care, the right to send one letter home every six weeks (censored for political matters), and the right to make a complaint. A schedule to the regulations laid out the daily food ration, including (with unusual exactness) two-sevenths of an ounce of tea, 7 ounces of biscuits or 8 ounces of bread, half an ounce of flour, 10 and two-sevenths ounces of rice, 8 ounces of potatoes, 2 ounces of onions, 6 ounces of tinned vegetables, 3 and three-sevenths ounces of herrings or pilchards, 3 and three-sevenths ounces of tinned meat and vegetables, and various other items, down to soap and tooth powder. The prisoners were then put to work rebuilding the naval base.

The Australian government also built a facility to hold the trials at Nutt Point on Los Negros, 3 miles (4.8 kilometres) from the compound: the trials are still referred to as the Manus Island trials even though they were held on Los Negros. A series of quonset huts – prefabricated corrugated iron structures with a semi-circular cross-section – were laid out: a large one for the trials themselves, open on either side to allow sea breezes through and with a room for the judges to retire in at the back, and a series of smaller ones for living quarters. The huts accommodating the prisoners were surrounded with barbed wire.

Finding people to run the trials was harder, as enough time had elapsed since the end of the war for prosecuting Japanese war criminals to have lost much of its urgency and the Menzies government, sensitive to criticism of the trials, wanted only the best lawyers and interpreters. It made a sound choice to head the court with Justice Kenneth Townley of the Queensland Supreme Court, brigadier in the army and former judge advocate at Morotai. Gerard Brenann, future chief justice of the High Court of Australia, was his associate, and his speeches, interviews and writings are a fruitful source on the trials.[8] Lieutenant Colonel Norman Quinton, section commander at Manus, also sat on the court, and had responsibility for the executions.

Unlike in the other trials, there was no geographical connection between the crimes and Manus Island. The events prosecuted had happened across the Pacific theatre, from Burma to Bougainville, but the cases had not been ready for trial at Morotai, Labuan, Rabaul or Singapore. The Australian war crimes investigations units, 1AWCS in Hong Kong and 2AWCS in Tokyo, had been busily gathering evidence over 1948 and 1949, although they were hampered by lack of resourcing. Investigation had also been held up by the civil war in the Netherlands East Indies. Some of the defendants were in custody at Sugamo or the Australian compound, with some already serving sentences, but some were living freely in Japan and needed to be arrested by occupying authorities.

In all cases but two, the trials were for the murder of Australian prisoners of war, and there was some criticism of this Australian focus. The exceptions were the killing of seventeen Javanese civilians by injecting them with an experimental anti-tetanus vaccine (LN25) and mutilating a dead Australian prisoner (LN22). One member of 2AWCS in Tokyo was so enraged that the suspect in a case he was investigating had walked free – a Japanese soldier wanted for the brutal rape of an eleven-year-old Papua New Guinean girl – that he refused to join the prosecution at Manus.[9]

The chief prosecutor was Charles Rooney, whom Brennan described as 'a colourful Irish expatriate, who wore a monocle which would drop from his eye as he affected surprise at any answer which did not appeal to him'.[10] He had to be evacuated in September 1950 after a bad asthmatic reaction to the tropical climate, leaving the prosecution to his three AALC juniors. The defence consisted of Japanese lawyers led by Nakayama Chōji, an elderly member of the Tokyo bar who had been in the defence team at Hong Kong. He was familiar with Australia, having lived in Sydney before the war, and even placed a bet on the November 1950 Melbourne Cup. As the Japanese lawyers were often not familiar with Anglo-Australian law, Major George Dickinson, a Sydney barrister, was engaged to help the defence.

All up, 113 defendants were indicted to stand in nineteen separate trials, which ran from 5 June 1950 to 9 April 1951. The prisoners were guarded by native 'boys' who got bored, fell asleep and dropped their rifles to the floor with a clatter. Service personnel and civilians came to watch the trials at first, but the crowd of spectators diminished over time. Most of the evidence was documentary, and there were few witnesses. The most noteworthy was General Imamura Hitoshi, former commander of the Eighth Area Army, who was serving a ten-year sentence following his conviction at Rabaul. He appeared for the defence in full uniform, complete with four rows of medal ribbons, including a British Military Cross awarded during the First World War.[11] When asked by a defence counsel if a Japanese soldier had a right to disobey an order that was contrary to the principles of humanity, he said that 'an order given by a superior officer could not be a violation of humanity and would have to be obeyed'.[12]

In the isolated location Brennan struggled with the lack of legal resources. Others struggled in different ways. Major Clarke, a Japanese linguist, had to be medically evacuated after suffering hallucinations that may have been connected with his partiality to the 'Singapore Cocktail', a drink of his own invention consisting of a mixture of liqueurs topped with a dash of ginger ale and a slice of lemon.

The facilities were likewise limited, and the judges, prosecution and Dickinson all shared the same mess. Brennan thought this irregular, particularly as the Japanese defence lawyers were excluded.[13]

I will now look at two of the trials in detail – those of Lieutenant General Nishimura Takuma in June 1950 and Navy Lieutenant Tsuaki Takahiko in March 1951.[14]

Nishimura was then sixty-two years old and was already serving a life sentence in Hong Kong for other crimes. He had entered the Imperial Japanese Army Academy in 1903 and been commissioned as an officer in 1910. During the rapid Japanese advance through Malaya from December 1941 to February 1942 he was the commander of the Konoe Division, serving under General Yamashita. Nishimura and his aide, Nonaka Shoichi, were indicted for the massacre of around a hundred Australian and forty Indian POWs at Parit Sulong in Malaya on 22 January 1942.[15]

There was one survivor of the massacre, Lieutenant B.C. Hackney of the 2/29th Battalion, who gave evidence through a written statement. Wounded by shrapnel, he and the other prisoners, many also wounded, were held by the Japanese in a wooden building. According to Hackney, Nishimura arrived at the site by car, inspected the prisoners, gave some orders to his subordinates, and left. That evening, the prisoners had their hands tied behind their backs, and they were led (or dragged) from the building, driven with kicks, rifle butts and bayonets to a clearing in the forest. There they were killed en masse with rifles and machine guns in a 'most violent and wicked' massacre.[16] Hackney was pulled down when the men around him fell and was overlooked by the Japanese in the dusk. The bodies of the other men were dragged into the centre of the clearing, piled up, doused with petrol and set alight. Many were still alive, and Hackney reported them 'screaming and yelling terribly' as they burned.[17]

The prosecution tendered statements by three Japanese witnesses claiming Nishimura, upon inspecting the prisoners, gave the order to a subordinate to 'instruct the officer in charge of the prisoners of war

STERN JUSTICE

to execute all the prisoners of war by firing squad and then cremate all their dead bodies'.[18]

In his defence, Nishimura acknowledged he had visited the place where the prisoners were held but he claimed his orders were to deal with (or dispose of) the prisoners by taking them to the rear. He said he knew nothing of the massacre until he was charged with it.

The case came down to one question: whether Nishimura had used the word *shobun* (dispose of or deal with) or *shokei* (execute) in his orders. Nishimura claimed he had said *shobun*, but the witnesses and Nishimura's co-defendant Nonaka insisted on *shokei*. Based on the evidence of the witnesses, the court convicted both Nishimura and Nonaka. On 22 June 1950, Nishimura was sentenced to death and Nonaka to imprisonment for six months. Nishimura was the first defendant to be given a death sentence at Manus.

Both men petitioned. Nishimura insisted he had never given an order to kill the prisoners, and furthermore, no divisional commander would ever give such a detailed order as 'execute the prisoners by firing squad'.[19] Nonaka said he was merely 'like a speaking tube' and should not be held responsible for the order he relayed.[20] Nakamura, the defence counsel, further argued that Nishimura posed no further danger in a demilitarised Japan, public opinion in Australia was turning against executions of war criminals, and hanging Nishimura could damage the global anti-communist cause by creating resentment between Australia and Japan.[21] Nonetheless, the conviction and sentences were both upheld by the commander on Manus Island on 7 July 1950 and by Judge Advocate General Simpson on 7 August 1950.

Following this, however, a new controversy arose. The three Japanese witnesses had used almost identical wording when quoting Nishimura's order. Given they were recalling a conversation that happened eight years previously, this was unusual; it suggested that the person who took the statements, Captain James G. Godwin of 2AWCS in Tokyo, may have put the words into the witnesses' mouths. Georgina Fitzpatrick and her co-authors concluded that this would have been difficult, as Godwin could speak only rudimentary Japanese and depended on an interpreter and stenographer, and that it is difficult to see how he could have had the opportunity to coerce the witnesses.[22] But this still showed a fundamental flaw in the trial process in not having the witnesses made available for cross-examination.

While there is no guarantee that Nishimura ordered the prisoners killed, he certainly had a case to answer. If he did order his subordinates to 'deal with' the prisoners and then left and gave them no further attention, he must at least bear some responsibility for the massacre. He himself obliquely acknowledged this from the dock. 'I am deeply sorry that, due to my carelessness, such an incident happened,' he said upon hearing his death sentence. 'I wish to give prayers with sorrow to those who were killed.'[23] Whether the death penalty was appropriate in his case, however, remains controversial to this day.

Tsuaki Takahiko probably thought he had left the war well and truly behind him when he was arrested by the occupation authorities on 20 February 1950 in his village of Tonomi, Yamaguchi prefecture, in the far west of Honshu. He was then in his mid-thirties. He had been drafted into the navy for six months in 1937, had left and worked as a merchant seaman and for a railway company, and gotten married in 1939. He was redrafted in 1941 and commissioned as a second lieutenant.

Returning to Tonomi after the war, Tsuaki found his previously comfortable situation turned upside down. His family once owned 12 and a half acres (5 hectares), but 12 and a quarter of them had been taken by the government in the land reforms. He and his wife persevered, farming the remaining quarter-acre as best as they could and winning the respect of the community. When Tonomi decided to introduce democracy at the local level in 1947 in line with the national reforms, Tsuaki was elected village headman. He worked hard, his constituents approved of his efforts, and he concentrated on farming, the affairs of the village, and raising his young son. Then he was arrested in connection with the Laha Massacres at Ambon.

Ambon is a small island in the centre of the archipelago formerly known as the Moluccas, now the Maluku Islands. The city also called Ambon was the capital of the Dutch Moluccas and the site of a large military base, including an important airfield at Laha. Shortly after the Japanese offensive began in early December 1941, the Australian government decided to reinforce the Dutch and Dutch colonial troops stationed there with the 2/22$^{nd}$ Battalion and supporting arms. The combined Dutch–Australian force still proved inadequate to hold Ambon, and the Japanese swiftly conquered it between 30 January and 3 February 1942. Following the Allied surrender, over 300 Dutch and Australian troops were summarily executed by the Japanese Army and Navy in four separate incidents known as the Laha Massacres. The survivors were either sent to a prison camp at Hainan in Indochina or left on Ambon, which quickly became one of the worst Japanese prisons under the sadistic commander Ikeuchi Masakiyo. Of the 528 men of the 2/22$^{nd}$ Battalion left on Ambon, only 119 survived captivity. The massacres and the appalling prison conditions on the island were the subject of the Australian war crimes trials held at Ambon.

Tsuaki was charged with murder along with two others, Warrant Officer Kanamoto Keigo and Seaman First Class Nakamura Shikao, and their trial began at Los Negros on 9 March 1951.[24] All pleaded not guilty.

Tsuaki had been serving on a minesweeper as part of the Ambon invasion force. On 2 February 1942, it struck a mine and sank; twenty were killed and seven injured. The remaining men, between seventy and eighty, were organised into a naval platoon on Ambon under Tsuaki's command. They were not issued with rifles or ammunition, but were instead put to work inspecting billets. A day or two later Tsuaki was told by the special duty lieutenant that he was to proceed to Laha to take part in the execution of prisoners of war.

Tsuaki and the special duty lieutenant do not seem to have got along particularly well. Several times in his evidence, Tsuaki said he felt he was being belittled for being only a reserve officer. He said he was 'embarrassed and upset' by the order to take part in an execution, and his unease may have showed.[25] He did not get more information from the special duty lieutenant except the fact that the executions would not be by shooting because of the noise. Returning to his men, he found they now had rifles, bayonets and ammunition.

At 1 pm, Tsuaki and thirty of his men were taken in a launch from their quarters to Laha airfield. The men knew nothing of the mission. At the airfield, the special duty lieutenant briefed them and put them to work digging graves. When these were finished, he told Tsuaki (according to Tsuaki's testimony): 'You, a commanding officer, must take the initiative in this execution. The first prisoners of war will now be sent to the execution place, so make the necessary preparations.'[26] Tsuaki had lost his own sword in the sinking of the minesweeper but he had been lent a new one. He felt he was being pressed into joining the execution because of his earlier reservations.

When Tsuaki returned to the gravesites, only six or seven of his men were there. At 5 pm the first two prisoners were brought over – their hands were bound but they were not blindfolded. Tsuaki beckoned the first one forward and asked him his name and age in English. At his trial he could not remember the prisoner's name, but recalled his age being somewhere between nineteen and twenty-one. Tsuaki was surprised, thinking he looked much older. Tsuaki did not know his nationality, but as he answered in English he was probably Australian rather than Dutch. 'I could not help but admire his bravery,'[27] Tsuaki recalled, saying that the prisoner had stepped forward confidently even though his fate was obvious. Tsuaki described what happened next: 'I desired to set a good example to others who were present, including my subordinates, but I had not had previous experience [executing prisoners] and therefore did not feel very confident. Observing all the rules of Japanese swordsmanship, I beheaded the prisoner with one stroke . . . [B]ecause of my success in decapitating the prisoner I felt I had fulfilled my duty and moved away from the grave.'[28]

Tsuaki said he left soon afterwards and did not see the rest of the executions.

Warrant Officer Kanamoto's evidence painted a bleak picture of what happened next. An officer told the men that 'anyone who wants to can have a go', inviting them to come forward and behead or bayonet the prisoners. As they killed the prisoners, each Japanese sailor shouted, 'This is in revenge for ~,' naming a comrade who had been killed when the minesweeper sank. As in many other cases, it seems that the Japanese made no effort to check if the prisoners were actually dead before burying them, and Kanamoto spoke of the wounded moaning in the pits as they were buried alive. He denied killing anyone himself but admitted he lent his sword to another sailor. To his annoyance, it came back notched and dented – clearly the mass-produced swords issued to junior officers were not designed to cut through bone. These lurid reports were naturally picked up by the Australia media. For example, an article in the *Courier-Mail* was entitled 'Frenzy of Revenge at Ambon – Crazed Japs Butchered 200 Diggers'.[29]

In Tsuaki's defence, Nakayama argued both military necessity and command responsibility. He admitted that large numbers of prisoners were executed in violation of international law, but claimed they had been unruly and threatening to revolt. The execution could therefore be seen as 'a means of self-defence and [an] emergency measure',[30] and as there was no legal officer at Laha, the defendants had no means of knowing the order was unlawful. Nakayama further argued that the defendants had played only a minor part, and consideration should be given to the fact that Tsuaki did not kill the man out of revenge. Instead, he was setting an example for his subordinates of the most humane way to kill with a sword in accordance with the warrior code of *bushidō*.[31] Nakayama's examination of Tsuaki included the following exchange:

Q: Did you think that the commanding officer's order was a legal one?

A: I had no doubt about the commanding officer's order at all. I thought it would be just for us to follow the commanding officer's order.

Q: How did you feel when you cut the victim?

A: I thought I had to have courtesy to the victim and had to cut him well. I thought cutting him well would not cause him much pain.[32]

In response to a question from the prosecution, Tsuaki said he had no idea how prisoners of war were to be treated. Asked if he knew of the humane treatment of Russian prisoners in the Russo-Japanese War, he said he had 'heard such a story' but did not recall it at the time.[33]

The court was not entirely convinced by Nakayama, and convicted Tsuaki and Kanamoto but acquitted Nakamura. On 19 March 1950, Tsuaki was sentenced to death and Kanamoto to life imprisonment.[34]

In a petition against the verdict and sentence, Tsuaki pointed out that he had no knowledge of military law and no experience of commanding men on land, he was scolded when he showed hesitation regarding the executions, and he felt his sentence was harsh compared with others convicted for the Laha Massacres at different tribunals.[35] Tsuaki seems to have been a popular and well-respected man, and the Australian government received dozens of pages of petitions from his wife, his classmates, and residents of his village, all attesting to his good character. Tsuaki's wife wrote of their three-year-old son constantly asking when his father would come home so they could go fishing together.[36] The Tonomi villagers described Tsuaki as a 'democratic and self-sacrificing man' and 'a man of high character who is thought to have had a strong animosity against the inhuman acts taken place during the War'.[37] They praised his work in dismantling feudalism in the village, improving infrastructure and education, coaching the

Tonomi Middle School baseball team, and taking the lead in educating young people on the ways of a new and peaceful Japan.

It was all to no avail. Tsuaki's sentence was confirmed by the commanding officer at Manus on 17 April 1951 and upheld by Judge Advocate General Simpson on 27 April 1951. Finding that the sentence was legal, Simpson did not look at the character references.


The Manus Island trials, and the Australian class-B and -C trials generally, ended on 9 April 1951 with the acquittal of Seaman First Class Miyazaki Jyosuke on a charge of murdering an Australian prisoner of war at Koepang in 1942. Defence counsel Nakayama pronounced himself satisfied with the 'extremely fair' process: 'Even accused war criminals told me they had been struck by the fairness of their trials. At the beginning of the trials we Japanese lawyers were handicapped because of our ignorance of British law – in Japan the law is modelled on the German system – however, the court was patient and gave us every possible assistance. Every help was given us to allow the other side of the picture to be presented.'[38]

The barrister George Dickinson was less satisfied, being fiercely critical of the *War Crimes Act*, the inability of the defendants to object to either the jurisdiction of the court or the admission of evidence, and the reliance on documentary evidence. However, he did approve of the way in which Townley handled the trials.[39]

At the time the trials ended, no executions had yet been carried out, even though Nishimura had been sentenced to death ten months previously. The Australian Army had not carried out an execution since October 1947 at Rabaul, as all men condemned by Australian courts at Singapore and Hong Kong were hanged by the British authorities there. The government, searching for a hangman before the trials started, approached Major Thomas Upson, who had supervised the executions at Rabaul. He was on Manus, having been commander of the compound there, and even though he had been discharged from the army following a serious car crash on 14 February 1950 he was still willing to give his expertise. He promised to donate the £30 fee for each execution to a fund for the education of children whose fathers had died in Japanese captivity.

This proposal was inexplicably announced to the press and then slammed by the opposition in parliament as an act of prejudgement. Kim Beazley Sr pointed out that Upson's promise to donate the fee to charity would provide an incentive to sentence more men to death.[40]

The government, hypersensitive as ever to criticism of the trials, cancelled Upson's appointment and began to look elsewhere. There were many volunteers. Lieutenant Colonel Quinton interviewed eight men from the Department of Works and Housing (DWH) who were then based at Manus to assess their motives for volunteering. The results were not satisfactory. According to the DWH official present at the interviews, 'it was patently obvious that seven of them just wanted to kill someone'.[41] The eighth, a veteran of the 7th Division, said he wanted to do his duty as a good Australian. He was selected and proved diligent, attending practice sessions in his own time. The 1946 instructions on hanging were updated and sent to him at Manus.

The government wanted the gallows prepared in secret to avoid further accusations of prejudgement, but this was difficult as parts had to be sent from Australia. In the end, an official flew from Sydney to Manus Island with 20 pounds of excess luggage. Construction began in the forest near the compound once the first death sentence was pronounced. Twenty condemned cells were also built.

Unlike its predecessor, the Menzies government involved itself actively in the trials and considered each death sentence at cabinet level. It sought advice broadly, particularly given the controversy over Nishimura, finally making its decision on 25 May 1951. On the counsel of Judge Advocate General W.B. Simpson, it commuted eight sentences but upheld five, including Nishamura's and Tsuaki's. Nishimura had been held in solitary confinement for nearly a year by this point, attracting more controversy.

The defendants in the Manus trials had a lot of time to reflect on their wartime experiences, and Japan had been rebuilt and democratised in the meantime. Their final writings on the trials therefore tended to be longer, more complex and less critical than those who were sentenced in 1945 and 1946. A *Kempeitai* lieutenant, for example, wrote of the value of 'the exposure of the so-called discipline, command, esprit de corps, and above all human character of the senior officers of Japan's former military units'.[42] Tsuaki, in his reflection, was critical of the Japanese military rather than the trials process:

> It was pointed out that we committed acts in violation of
> international treaties during war. But most people would be
> unaware that these acts are violations. Even if they were aware they
> were violations, they could not have objected because that was
> not permitted in relation to military orders at the time. In short,
> I believe this came about because of the irresponsible arrogance,
> the disregard for human rights and laws, and the fanatical ideas of
> those who were responsible for issuing orders . . . Even if the trials
> were not undertaken with a sense of retaliation, the different way
> of thinking between Japanese and Westerners, and the difference in
> culture and the military command system at the time, etc, surely led
> to our disadvantage.[43]

At 6 pm on 10 June 1951, Quinton informed the prisoners that they would be hanged early the following morning. They were given a meal of 'fine Japanese food' and left with a Buddhist priest overnight.[44] Tsuaki waved the priest away and slept soundly.

In the morning the men were hooded, taken from their cells and driven in a black van to the gallows. The other war criminals in the compound were left in their huts and not sent to work, for fear they would revolt or otherwise try to stop the executions.

A group of journalists clustered uncomfortably around the railing in the confined shed as each man was led in. Tsuaki was hanged first, at 5 am. The *Queensland Times* journalist noted that he was apparently unconcerned.[45] The other four followed at thirty-minute intervals, as a heavy rainstorm passed over the island. Warrant officer Ipachi Miyamoto told the assembled journalists, 'I hope Japan and Australia can become friends and remain friends.' Nishimura was hanged at 6 am, giving three shouts of *Banzai!* before the trapdoor was sprung. The last to the gallows was Navy Lieutenant Suzuki Yutaka, hanged at 7 am for the murder of a member of the RAAF at Kokas, New Guinea, in or about December 1944. His was the last execution of a war criminal by the Australian government, and the last ever execution carried out by the Australian federal government. It was also the last carried out anywhere as part of the class-B and -C war crimes trials in the Pacific. After it was over, the executioner went to the mess boasting he'd 'just killed five Japs'.[46] Major Upson would have been a much better and more discreet choice.

Like the army at Rabaul, the navy on Manus Island maintained the prisoners were 'not entitled to the privileges afforded to prisoners of war' and their treatment must be 'humane but not lenient'.[47] They were put to work building the naval base, working in the sawmill, and growing vegetables. The isolation had the advantage of security. No Japanese war criminals were known to escape from Australian custody at either Rabaul or Manus, although one did escape from a Tokyo hospital after he was returned to Japan for medical treatment.[48]

Still, life in the Manus Island compound was not excessively austere.[49] There was a recreation hut with a library, playing cards, board games and musical instruments, and also facilities for football, tennis and table tennis. This last seems to have been the most popular; from August to December 1951 alone, 252 table tennis balls were ordered. A monthly movie night was initiated in 1950, but the hundred or so films on the island were all prewar, and with constant use in the hot and humid climate they wore out. The war criminals had more luck with fishing trips, which were both popular and useful for bringing variety to the food supply, and parties of the prisoners went fishing at various beaches and bridges every Sunday.

In spite of the no-gifts policy, the International Red Cross was permitted to supply clothing, books, musical instruments and beer. Other organisations also sent packages, for example, the Japanese YMCA sent Christmas hampers in 1951 containing Japanese tea and other goods. Even the Australian Red Cross supplied items at times. While the prisoners continued to write letters of complaint, these seemed to focus more on isolation and boredom than actual mistreatment. On 18 July 1950, General Imamura Hitoshi wrote to the International Red Cross Society of his 'monotonous life' on the 'isolated island'.[50]

As at Rabaul, some in the Australian press complained that the war criminals at Manus had it too good. Journalist and RAAF veteran Alan Underwood visited the island in November and wrote a series of articles published around Australia under headlines like 'Less Work, More Luxury for Jap War Criminals' (the *Sydney Morning Herald*), 'War Criminals Get the "Soft" Treatment' (the *Courier-Mail*), and 'Japanese War Criminals "Taking It Easy"' (*The Advertiser*).[51] According to Underwood, the prisoners at Manus had originally been 'servile and industrious' but since the 1951 Peace Treaty had become 'arrogant and lazy'. He found their hours of work had shortened – they began work at 8.15, took fifteen minutes off for morning and afternoon tea, and an hour and a half for lunch, and finished at 4.15. They were fed special Oriental dishes, read whatever books they wanted to regardless of censorship, had their own equipment for playing baseball and volleyball, and got taken fishing every Sunday. 'Riding in an official's car at Los Negros last week, I noticed a Jap criminal leaning against a shed,' he wrote. 'Immediately he saw our car he seized a pick and held it above his head. When the car had passed, he threw the pick down again.'

Underwood concluded that the prisoners were suffering only from 'tropical boredom' and separation from their families, and wondered if the authorities were taking it easy on them to discourage them from rebelling or trying to escape. But it was 'softer treatment than Australian ex-servicemen would like to see dealt out to them'. Nonetheless, Underwood was impressed by General Imamura. Describing him as the 'Best Jap' at Los Negros, he praised him for helping with the smooth administration of the compound and for his success in horticulture: 'To raise a garden in the sterile coral and clay of Manus and Los Negros is an achievement. General Imamura's little patch is an oasis of tomatoes, eggplant, and beans. I watched this wrinkled, slightly-built soldier staking up his tomatoes. He ignored my interest. In his ginger pink prison uniform and raghat, he seemed like any retired Australian – wearing his oldest clothes for pottering about the garden.'[52]

In July 1953, the compound was closed and the remaining war criminals were returned to Japan on the merchant ship *Hakuryu Maru*; 147 were to serve out the remainder of their sentences in Sugamo Prison, while eighteen had finished their sentences and were now free. As they were leaving, a special correspondent for the *Sydney Morning Herald* interviewed them.[53] According to him, two facts stood out – all were unrepentantly denying responsibility for war crimes, but 'strangely willing and diligent, [they] had almost an essential role in Australia's slow, difficult rebuilding of the Manus base as a naval and air outpost'.

'The war criminals were among the most useful members of the Manus Island community, and the perplexing problem up there now is how they are going to be replaced as a skilled work force,' he wrote. But he was unsure if the trials and sentences had the desired effect. 'I could not find one who showed any repentance,' he observed. 'Without exception, those I spoke to declared that they had been unjustly convicted and that anything they had done was in obedience to orders of their superiors.'

Some of the prisoners he interviewed raised the atomic bombs, the defence of following orders, the responsibility of the entire Japanese

nation, or specific criticisms of the Japanese government. Lieutenant
Colonel Kiyoshi Miyakawa, sentenced to life imprisonment for the
murder of Australian and other Allied prisoners of war at Bougainville
in 1943, said: 'The trials were neither legitimate nor consistent. I will
not cease to challenge them. Some I know to be guilty have been
found not guilty, and some I know to be guiltless have been found
guilty, even executed. The fact that some Allied countries are releasing
war criminals from serving the balance of their sentences is a further
inconsistency which is unfair to us.'

Navy Lieutenant Nara Yoshio, sentenced to twenty years for taking
part in the murder of the Ocean Islanders, maintained he had merely
handed the natives over to an execution party on his superior's orders.
'The whole Japanese nation should accept the responsibility,' he
said. 'We should not be the scapegoats.' Surgeon-Captain Nakamura
Hirosuto, convicted of carrying out fatal medical experiments on
Javanese civilians, said he did not think people from a temperate climate should have been kept working for so long in the tropics, but
he nonetheless admitted that the Australian Navy's treatment of the
prisoners had been good. And last of all, there was General Imamura.
Then sixty-seven, he said working in his garden had kept him fit and
he had no critical comment to make. 'As I am one of those who must
accept responsibility for Japan's defeat, I will go into retirement when
I am released,' he said. True to his word, he lived in quiet retirement
after his release from Sugamo in 1954 until his death in 1968.

Once they were in Sugamo, the prisoners would not enjoy
freedom of movement, and there would be no more fishing and swim-
ming on tropical beaches. But they would be near their families again.
As the *Hakuryu Maru* pulled away from Manus Island, the Australian
government's responsibility for keeping war criminals ended. But it
retained the right to determine whether they were paroled or released
early, and at the time, it was not inclined to allow them to walk free
before their sentences ended.

# XVII

# RECONCILIATION AND REHABILITATION

On 8 September 1951 the war against Japan was finally brought to its conclusion with the Treaty of San Francisco. All the countries that had fought Japan signed the treaty except for the Soviet Union and China. The Chinese communists had defeated the Nationalist government and driven it to Taiwan and other outlying islands, establishing the People's Republic of China (PRC). As the Allies could not decide which government to invite to the conference they invited neither. The Soviet Union attended the conference preceding the treaty, but protested against the actual terms on the basis that China was not invited and Japan was apparently being drawn into a specifically anti-Soviet military alliance with the United States. The Nationalist Chinese government subsequently entered into the Treaty of Taipei with Japan on 28 April 1952, and the People's Republic of China came to an accord with Japan on 29 September 1972.

In December 1951 former US senator and prominent Republican John Foster Dulles gave a speech in Tokyo where he said that Japan had not only a right to rearm, but a duty to do so in order to meet the threat of communism. This got a cool reaction in the Australian parliament and press, where suspicion of Japan was still high.[1] When the bill ratifying the Treaty of San Francisco came up for debate in the

Australian House of Representatives, it was criticised not only by the opposition, but also MPs on the government benches.[2] Liberal MP Alexander Downer Sr expressed the concerns that many felt:

> It is common knowledge that the genesis of this treaty was in Washington, rather than in London or Canberra. No government of this country would ever originate such proposals . . . They were presented by the United States of America to the powers assembled in San Francisco last year, more as a fait accompli than as a tentative approach to an intricate problem. The United States of America declared beforehand that the provisions now embodied in this bill were to be its terms. By virtue of America's position since the war as the principal world power – certainly in the Pacific – the opinions of smaller nations availed little.

Downer did not believe the treaty addressed the causes of Japanese belligerence, so he could not support it. Like many others, he predicted that Japan would once again become the dominant power in East Asia. 'Despite their evil attributes, the Japanese possess higher qualities of character than do other Asian peoples,' he concluded.

Fred Daly, Labor MP for the Sydney seat of Grayndler and known for his lively expression, quoted a British article with approval:

> General Macarthur [sic], surely one of the greatest missionaries of all time has, almost single-handed, reformed the Japs. The brains that engineered Pearl Harbour [sic], the hands that turned, beat, flayed and stabbed the white man in the islands of the Pacific, in Malaya, in Siam and in Hong Kong are now clean, guiltless innocent hands. The deceitful grin of Tokyo has become an honest friendly smile and the Americans have agreed to defend the democratic Japanese while the Japanese have agreed to defend the generous Americans. It is a very, very beautiful friendship.

Daly went on to explain:

> That article exemplifies the sceptical attitude towards the peace
> treaty of most people in Australia and elsewhere in the democratic
> world. It is too soon for us to forgive the Japanese and enter into
> an alliance with them. Their guilt is still fresh. They should not
> be accorded equal rights with other peoples until they have paid
> some penalty and have atoned in some measure for the unspeakable
> atrocities that they committed against humanity . . . The Labor
> party believes that Japan has not been able to expiate its crimes in
> six short years. This Government wishes to re-admit Japan to the
> society of nations too early, and it is being too generous.

He then talked at length about the perceived Japanese threat to
Australian industry, a significant concern on the Labor side of politics.
Daly's fellow Labor MP Tom Andrews agreed. While he acknowledged that the Japanese had many good qualities, 'nevertheless it is
part of their nature to glorify power and to act ruthlessly in the pursu-
ance of power'. He concluded that the threat of communism was not
grave enough to justify the threat of a rearmed Japan.

These concerns were mirrored in the press. 'Don't trust the
Japanese,' former commander of Australia's 8th Division, Lieutenant
General Gordon Bennett, told *The Argus*. 'They are cheeky now and
I have no doubt they will soon be building up for the next war to
regain the face they have lost.'[3] The Australian public shared these
anxieties. In an August–September 1951 poll, 63 per cent of respondents opposed a peace treaty with Japan, and 60 per cent believed that
within twenty years Japan would once again be a threat to Australia.[4]

The Treaty of San Francisco also brought to an end the Allied
occupation of Japan, and full sovereignty was returned to the Japanese
government. The BCOF was disbanded on 28 April 1952.[5] But Japan
could not turn loose the convicted war criminals. Under Article 11
of the treaty, Japan had accepted the judgements of the IMTFE and

other war crimes courts and agreed to carry out the sentences imposed. It also agreed that it would not grant clemency, nor reduce sentences or grant parole except on the decision of the government that had imposed the sentence. For those prisoners sentenced by the IMTFE, this would require the recommendation of a majority of countries on the tribunal.

All of the surviving class-A war criminals and a majority of the Class-B and -C were then in Sugamo, a fairly new prison in Tokyo that had been used to hold political prisoners during the war. It was handed over to the American Eighth Army in October 1945, and the first Japanese war criminals arrived on 16 November. A total of 4,726 people were believed to have been held at Sugamo postwar, with a peak population of 1,862 in January 1950.[6] Despite occasional complaints from the inmates, it seems conditions were generally good. Once some renovations on the prison was finished, there was no hard labour. In the early years, those inside were often better fed than those outside, and there were games and movies, and so many prisoners enrolled in educational courses the prison became known jokingly as 'Sugamo University'. The Americans introduced a parole system in 1950, and following the end of the occupation the prison received a steady stream of visitors, including entertainers, journalists and politicians.

At the time the treaty was negotiated, Article 11 was of relatively little concern, for either the Japanese government or public. But during the 1950s, a movement to bring the class-B and -C criminals back to Japan and release them grew in numbers and popularity. The campaigners argued that these men were as much the victims of their superiors as they were perpetrators of crimes. A national petition for their release was launched in June 1952, called the Campaign of Love (*ai no undō*), and a support association for the Sugamo prisoners was also formed.

A number of significant publications besides *Seiki no isho* were produced in Sugamo in support of the campaign. The Sugamo Legal Affairs Committee produced an 852-page volume called *The Truth*

*About War Crimes Trials* (*Senpan saiban no jisso*), which focused on the unfairness of the trials and the mistreatment of the prisoners by their Allied captors. Shorter versions were also made available. The Japanese government also began collecting documentation relating to the class-B and -C trials, then all held overseas.

Lieutenant Katō Tetsutarō provides an interesting case of a politically active class-B and -C war criminal.[7] Katō was an economics graduate from a prominent Christian family and was working for the North China Development Corporation when he was conscripted into the army as an officer in the Sino-Japanese War. He was subsequently returned to Japan and placed in command of a prisoner-of-war camp at Niigata in 1944, perhaps because of his knowledge of foreign languages. The prisoners in the camp, who were mostly Americans, reported that Katō had a fiery temper but made genuine efforts to improve conditions, including by securing food and medicine. But Katō was troubled by one man, named Frank Spears, who repeatedly escaped. After one escape, Katō went out with a party of soldiers and recaptured him. This time, Katō demanded that Spears promise to stop escaping. When Spears refused, Katō then either bayoneted him to death personally or ordered another man to do so: different accounts were given at Katō's two trials, but in terms of his guilt or innocence this was irrelevant.

After the war, Katō was wanted by the Americans as a suspected war criminal but managed to evade capture until 1948. He travelled the country disguised as a monk, and at one point even worked as a translator for the US Army. Eventually captured, he was brought to trial, convicted and sentenced to death. In February 1949, his sentence went to MacArthur for review. Katō was fortunate to have high-profile friends and relatives lobbying on his behalf. They argued that mitigating evidence of Katō's good treatment of the prisoners had not been presented, and so he had not had a fair trial.

As it turned out, Katō's cunning in hiding himself for three years almost certainly saved his life. Had he been tried in 1946 or 1947, he would have surely been hanged. Now, however, his file hit MacArthur's desk during the critical time when the American class-B and -C trials at Yokohama were winding down and American policy towards Japan had shifted towards rapprochement. MacArthur quashed Katō's conviction and sent him for a new trial, where substantially more evidence of Katō's good qualities as camp commander was presented to the court. In June 1949, in one of the last ever US trials in Japan, he was convicted again but given a life sentence. MacArthur immediately commuted it to thirty years.

So Katō found himself in Sugamo Prison just as the campaign for the release of prisoners was getting underway. He participated in the campaign by writing, publishing an article in the magazine *Sekai* under a pseudonym in October 1952. The prison authorities failed to identify him as the author, although they may have had their suspicions.

Then, in 1953, two significant anthologies of the writings of Sugamo inmates were published: *Are kara shichinen: gakuto senpan no gokuchū kara no tegami (Seven Years After the End of the War: Prison Letters from Drafted Student War Criminals*, commonly referred to as *Seven Years Later*) and *Kabe atsuki heya: BC-kyū senpan no jinseiki (The Thick-Walled Room: Life Stories of BC-class War Criminals*). While both collections encouraged sympathy with the class-B and -C war criminals, they were not works of nationalist propaganda. Some prisoners admitted their crimes, others criticised the government for its militaristic policies before and during the war. Both books showed the influence of the developing peace group within Sugamo. *Seven Years Later* was edited by Katō's father, and Katō submitted two essays, once again under pseudonyms.[8]

In one of these essays in *Seven Years Later*, Katō reproduces a letter he claims was written by a 'Sergeant Akagi' shortly before his execution. Katō makes it clear at the start of the essay that he will blend fact and fiction to make his point, and it is implied Katō has invented Akagi to present views he either holds or is sympathetic with.

Akagi writes that he has been sentenced to death for withholding medicine from American prisoners of war, even though there was no medicine available. The shortage was the fault of war profiteers, but they had escaped prosecution, leaving him to take the blame. His senior officers paid bribes and escaped; there were no good men among them. He criticises the court in which he was convicted, saying he was a victim of poor translation and errors in procedure. He also claims he was not fed enough in prison and was mistreated by his American captors. Finally, he complains, he is going to be executed when war crimes committed by the Allies have gone unpunished.

For a long time, Akagi writes, he hoped the Emperor would save him. Now he has been forced to recognise that the Emperor will leave him to die to appease the Americans (the fact that the essay contains direct criticism of the Emperor may be why Katō decided to use the literary device of posing as a dead man). Akagi rages against the Emperor, pointing out that he served him faithfully and was ready to die for him. All he got in return were seven or eight cigarettes when he was fighting in China and some cakes when he was in a field hospital – the little luxuries that the Imperial Palace would occasionally send to troops overseas. The Emperor had approved the decision to invade China, which in Akagi's view made war crimes inevitable. Or, to go even further, war itself is a crime.

If he is to be reincarnated, Akagi concludes, he would not want to be Japanese. He would not even want to be human. Nor would he want to be a cow or horse, as they are forced to work for humans. Instead, he would want to be a shellfish, clinging to a rock in the deep ocean. The shellfish has no worries because it knows nothing, it is not concerned about its family and children, and it is not forced to go to war for the Emperor. It is left alone. As Sandra Wilson summarised: 'The general tenor of Katō's writings was that war criminals were victims: of their own superior officers, of their own government, and of the Americans. Katō was alarmed at Japan's rearmament in the early 1950s, critical of the conservative government of Yoshida Shigeru, and even critical of the public campaign for the release of war criminals, on the grounds that former senior military officers were using the campaign to further their own political careers.'[9]

The advocates for the imprisoned war criminals then took their campaign from the page to the screen. TV was rare in Japan in the 1950s, but film became very big, with the average Japanese person making ten trips to the cinema per year in that decade.[10] Both foreign and Japanese films were popular and drew large audiences. American movies set in the Second World War gave the Japanese public their first view of the war from the other side. Indeed, for many, it was their first view of the war at all unless they had actually served in it. Films about Japanese history also filled theatres, and Kurosawa Akira's big samurai-era pictures such as *Rashomon* (1950) and *Seven Samurai* (1954) also gained attention in the West.

Films about the war and the war criminals were also made, often showing similar themes to *The Thick-Walled Room* and *Seven Years Later*. In the 1952 movie *Sugamo no haha* ('Mother of Sugamo') a widowed woman who has lost three of her four sons in the war waits at the dock for the return of the fourth, who was a prison-camp guard overseas. When he arrives he is arrested and placed on trial as a war criminal by the Americans. Convicted of slapping POWs, he is given a thirty-year sentence. The film promoted the idea that some of the offences for which the class-B and -C war criminals were convicted were trivial.

A film version of *The Thick-Walled Room* was made in 1953 by Kobayashi Masaki, but was not released until 1956. It has more depth than some others, and actually forces viewers to confront the reality of Japanese war crimes. Some Sugamo prisoners are portrayed as still believing in Japan's imperial destiny, and reciting nationalist propaganda; others express pacifist views, and one has become a communist. The question posed for the audience is: who is responsible for the crimes committed by the prisoners? Them, their officers, the government, or Japan itself?

The biggest and longest lasting drama was probably *Watashi wa Kai ni Naritai* (*I Want to Be a Shellfish*), a 1958 TV series adapted into a 1959 film.[11] The title came from the writings of Katō Tetsutarō, although the plot was drawn from different sources than the Sergeant Akagi letter. A barber from Shikoku is conscripted into the army and ordered by his commanding officer to bayonet a captured American airman. He is convicted and sentenced to death by an American tribunal (in reality, no privates were sentenced to death for killing prisoners on the direct orders of their superiors, so the scenario is entirely fictitious). As he is led to the gallows, the unfortunate barber gives a shorter version of Akagi's shellfish monologue.

With support building for the campaign to release the B- and C-class war criminals, politicians, entertainers and journalists began to visit Sugamo in increasing numbers. A group of members of the Liberal Democratic Party formed an association in their support. On 9 June 1952 both houses of the Diet resolved that the government should lobby for all the class-B and -C war criminals being held overseas to be returned to Japan and subsequently released. The motion was opposed by Iwama Masao on behalf of the Communist Party, who claimed the resolution showed a lack of remorse for Japan's wartime actions. The other members jeered him.[12]

This was the first significant foreign policy project of the Japanese government following the restoration of its powers, and in some cases involved difficult, three-party negotiations between Japan, another newly independent Asian country, and its former colonial power. The war criminals convicted at the Tokyo Trial and the American trials in Japan were already in Sugamo, so the government turned to the repatriation of those being held overseas. This process was uneven, and like the trials themselves was heavily influenced by political considerations.

The first prisoners to be returned were those held by the two Allies in the weakest position, Nationalist China and the Netherlands. When, by 1949, it was clear that Nationalist China was losing the war against the communists it sent all the class-B and -C war criminals it was holding to Sugamo.[13] Excluded from the Treaty of San Francisco, Nationalist China then agreed to release all of them under a general amnesty in April 1952.[14] This was the first unconditional release of B- and C-class criminals by an Allied power, and was further prompted by the government's desire to have Formosans being held by the other Allies returned to Taiwan.

Under a peace treaty that came into effect on 27 December 1949, the Netherlands recognised the independence of the new Republic of Indonesia, ending Dutch colonial influence in the Far East. The Republic inherited the government of the Netherlands East Indies along with responsibility for the war criminals. Some of the Indonesian republican leaders had been backed by the Japanese during the war, and the Dutch, fearing the government might release the prisoners, transferred them from Cipinang prison to Sugamo in December 1949.[15] Indonesia, with many bigger issues to be concerned with, did not object to them being released.

The French followed, with the release of prisoners in their overseas territories in 1950, and the UK in 1951. The expense of keeping the men in captivity was a problem, and holding them was unpopular in the countries of South-East Asia now moving towards independence. The French- and British-held prisoners were also subsequently paroled and then unconditionally released.

By 1953, the only countries still holding class-B and -C war criminals outside Japan were the Philippines and Australia. They were also the last countries to execute them – in 1951.[16] The Japanese government found both difficult to persuade. The Filipino government maintained, not without justification, that no country except China had been more devastated by Japan than the Philippines. There were fresh memories of the Sack of Manila, the death marches of captured Filipino troops, and the destruction of monasteries. Japanese Navy orders issued between December 1944 and February 1945 quoted in the IMTFE judgement were seen as typical of Japanese attitudes in the archipelago: 'When killing Filipinos, assemble them together in one place as far as possible thereby saving ammunition and labour.'[17]

So even as attitudes towards Japanese war criminals began to soften in other countries, they remained hard in the Philippines. This was typified by the hanging of fourteen Japanese war criminals in New Bilibid Prison in Muntinlupa, on the night of 19 January 1951. It was the first execution of Japanese war criminals anywhere since 1948 and a stern message to Tokyo.[18]

The Japanese government nonetheless began to petition Filipino President Elpidio Quirino for the return and eventual release of the remaining class-B and -C criminals. A popular 1952 song by Watanabe Hamako, 'Ah, Montenrupa no yo wa fukete' ('It's getting dark in Muntinlupa') raised awareness of the Japanese still held at Muntinlupa. But the government's overtures received a negative reaction in Filipino newspapers. One letter to the editor of the *Philippines Free Press* pointed out that a fair trial was more than the Japanese gave the Filipino civilians they summarily executed.[19]

But the Philippines was a poor, newly independent country in need of economic opportunities and allies in its region, and Japan, having rebuilt its own economy, was eventually in a position to offer both. As a result, on 27 June 1953, President Quirino announced that all Japanese war criminals would be returned to Sugamo. They arrived in Yokohama in December, and were pardoned by President Quirino in what he announced was an act of Christian forgiveness.[20] In 1956, an agreement was concluded whereby Japan pledged $800 million in reparations to the Philippines, and in 1960 the two countries concluded a significant treaty of amity and co-operation.

At the time of the 1951 Peace Treaty, Australia was still holding Japanese war criminals on Manus Island and in prisons shared with

British authorities in Hong Kong and Singapore. The last prisoners held in Rabaul had been transferred to Manus in March 1949. In
August 1951, the remaining Japanese war criminals in Hong Kong
and Singapore were sent to Sugamo. That same year, the Australian
government enacted Statutory Rule No 11, which authorised remis-
sions of sentences in cases of good conduct. Those prisoners serving
sentences of between five and twenty-five years were eligible to have
them shortened by a quarter, and those serving life terms were eligible
for release after thirty years. The first to have their sentences remitted
were those sentenced at Labuan on 9 January 1946, who were released
on 8 January 1955.

From August 1952 on, Australia began to receive persistent requests
for the repatriation and release of its class-B and -C war criminals. At
this point, there were still roughly 180 at Manus Island, and fifty being
held on Australia's behalf in Sugamo.[21] The Australian government
was also under pressure to bring its approach to the war criminals
into conformity with the other Allies, particularly the United States.
The Menzies government was considering Japan as a market for
Australian wool and wheat, and Japan, in turn, recognised the importance of Australia to its economic development and security in the
Asia-Pacific. In December 1952, a Japanese ambassador was appointed
to Canberra.

The prisoners on Manus Island themselves were also active on
their own behalf. On 10 September 1951 they wrote a petition asking
to be returned to Japan, pointing out they were the only war criminals still held within the British Commonwealth.[22] And in June 1953,
the Japanese House of Representatives petitioned Queen Elizabeth
on the occasion of her coronation to send them back to Japan.[23] These
efforts were successful, and the Manus Island compound was closed
in July 1953. By the end of that year, all the war criminals convicted
by the Allied tribunals under the class A, B and C system were back
in Japan.[24] The Japanese government then set about securing their
release. A number of the class-A criminals convicted at Tokyo, such

as former Foreign Minister Shigemitsu Mamoru, had already been paroled or released on MacArthur's orders. Due to ill health, Kido was also released that year. In 1951 he had again written to the Emperor advising him to abdicate; the Emperor again refused. Kido kept a low profile for the rest of his life, dying in 1977 in the Imperial Palace Hospital.

The Japanese government found Australia still wary of consenting to release its war criminals, and various requests made between 1952 and 1955 were refused. In one such request, on 3 August 1955, the Japanese proposed a general release of all war criminals to commemorate the tenth anniversary of the end of the war. The Australian government did not accept the proposal.[25]

But there were cracks appearing. In May 1954, the US government urged Australia to go easier on Japan. The Australian Cabinet resolved on 17 August 1954 that '. . . Australia should give special attention to the need to prevent the formation of a close alliance between Japan and communist China; and that Australia should be guided by the principle of allowing Japan, through co-operation with non-communist nations, to have reasonable facilities for taking part in its own defence, and for meeting her economic difficulties by expanding her export trade, and for developing her political and economic life and institutions in a way that will strengthen Japan's association with the west.'[26]

Under American control, Sugamo prisoners received a monthly rating on their behaviour ranging from 'unsatisfactory' to 'very excellent'. The Japanese authorities continued with this system when they resumed control of the prison in April 1952, although they regularly reported prisoners' behaviour as 'excellent' or 'very excellent'. The exception seems to have been the small group of politically active prisoners, including Katō.[27] In April 1955, in line with its allies, the Australian government introduced a system whereby war criminals held on behalf of Australia became eligible for release on parole after completing the major part of their sentences. In July 1956 the system was expanded so war criminals were eligible for release after completing a minimum of a third of their sentence or a maximum of ten years.[28] This added to the remission of sentences for good conduct, and saw more of the war criminals released.


Over 1956 and 1957, the Australia–Japan relationship continued to improve. In October 1956, the Japanese flag was raised at the Melbourne Olympic Games by an Australian Second World War veteran, in a show of reconciliation.[29] That same year saw a significant relaxation of the White Australia policy begin. In January 1957, the Japanese embassy in Canberra reported to Tokyo that there was a 'developing genuine friendship' between the two countries.[30] Plans were rapidly being made for Robert Menzies to visit Japan, and for the new Japanese Prime Minister Kishi Nobusuke to visit Australia. In March 1957, with Menzies' visit approaching, the Australian government quietly approved the release of all remaining war criminals.[31] The final war criminal under Australian control was released from Sugamo on 28 June 1957,[32] and that year, Australia and Japan signed a historic trade agreement.

On 5 September 1957, Eddie Ward, the Labor member for East Sydney, who had closely followed the trials, accused Billy McMahon, then Minister for Primary Industry, of breaking his assurance that the war criminals would not be released if they were returned to Japan.[33] McMahon denied giving any such assurance, but insisted that the prisoners at Manus Island had needed to be returned on humanitarian grounds. He told the House of Representatives: 'On at least two occasions I had visited Manus Island, and during my visits there I had inspected the war criminals at the Manus compound. I came to the conclusion that the conditions under which they were living were totally unsatisfactory and should not be continued. The climate up there is rigorous. It is a climate in which ordinary human beings cannot live for very long periods.'[34]

His answer did not satisfy Ward. 'What about their crimes against Australian servicemen?' he asked. Clyde Cameron, Labor MP for Hindmarsh in South Australia, was also not persuaded:

> McMahon: I want to make it perfectly clear that I was not willing to continue to persecute these people and to compel them to be separated from their families, because connexion with their families does mean a lot to these people. I was not prepared to compel them to live in a most —
> Cameron: A lot of criminals in the Adelaide gaol are going mental, too.
> McMahon: Oh, shut up!
> Speaker: Order!
> McMahon: Mr. Speaker, these people on the other side of the House giggle their heads off. One minute they pretend that they care and the next minute they ridicule their own suggestions, showing what hypocrites they are . . .[35]

The issue was, nonetheless, resolved, and by May 1958, Sugamo was empty. Katō Tetsutarō was released on 31 March 1958, one of the last of the class-B and -C to be paroled.[36] By December 1958, all prisoners on parole were made unconditionally free.[37] Katō was freed on 29 December 1958, a week after the screening of the second part of the TV series *I Want to Be a Shellfish*.[38]

Japan also succeeded in recovering its remaining prisoners from the Soviet Union and communist China. The Soviets continued to hold Japanese POWs after 1950, claiming they were guilty of war crimes (although it is not clear what, if any, process of trial they were subject to). But by December 1956, all known survivors had been repatriated save for those who had married and started families and so elected to stay. The People's Republic of China released its prisoners over 1956 and 1957. Controversially, it also published an anthology called *The Three Alls: Japanese Confessions of War Crimes in China*. Unfortunately for the accuracy of the historical record it had a communist slant and was dismissed by Japanese nationalists as propaganda when it was published in Japan in 1957.

In the European theatre, there was also a steady release of convicted German and other European Axis war criminals. The Soviet Union released its convicted German war criminals in 1955, and the Western Allies agreed to the release of those held in prisons in Germany over the late 1950s. By the end of the 1950s, the only war criminals from the Second World War still behind bars were Albert Speer, Baldur von Schirach and Rudolf Hess, three class-A criminals convicted at Nuremberg and held in Spandau Prison in Berlin. Releasing them before the expiry of their sentences required the agreement of the four prosecuting powers at Nuremberg, and the Soviet Union vetoed any such proposal. Speer and von Schirach were released in 1966 when their twenty-year sentences ended, and Hess died in prison in 1987.

By 1967, Australia and Japan were enjoying a close and profitable relationship. Japan was Australia's largest trading partner, providing a ready market for its beef, wool and wheat. In return, Australians bought Japanese cars, electronics, and other manufactured goods. And so the sword-wielding soldier shouting 'Banzai!' was replaced by the Toyota Corolla, the Fujifilm camera, and the Sony radio. Japan had presented a new image to the world.

# CONCLUSION

# JUSTICE OR REVENGE?

David Sissons, translator at Morotai, devoted much of his life to researching the Australian war crimes trials. In 1985 he wrote an article published in the *Sydney Morning Herald* recounting a story involving a visiting Japanese author. The author had showed him a picture of a monument built on Mount Sagane to commemorate the Japanese men sentenced to death in the Australian war crimes trials. It bore the inscription: 'These trials were nothing more than vengeance, the proud victors exercising arbitrary judgment over the vanquished.' The author asked Sissons if he agreed with the inscription. 'The question called for a "yes" or "no" answer. I'm afraid my reply must be more complex,' was Sissons' response.[1]

There are many such questions about the trials, and even seventy years later, not all can be answered. Not least, the question of whether they should have been held at all. George Kennan, Director of Policy Planning at the US State Department, accepted the moral right of the Allies to punish Japan's leaders but said the punishment should not be 'surrounded with the hocus-pocus of a judicial procedure which belies its real nature'.[2] Others were even more blunt: Bert Röling, the Dutch judge at the IMTFE, used to play tennis with MacArthur's Chief of Intelligence, General Charles Willoughby. Willoughby was an unlikely friend for the liberal Dutch academic, being an ultra-conservative career soldier with limited faith in Japanese democracy, but they got along well. MacArthur called him 'my pet fascist' in reference to his right-wing political views and sycophantic attitude. Shortly after the Tokyo Trial concluded, Willoughby remarked to Röling that it 'was the worst hypocrisy in recorded history'.[3]

Ultimately, though, it's hard to see if any of the alternatives would have been any better. At the end of the Second World War the Allies had three options: release the Axis leaders; summarily execute or otherwise punish them, along with others responsible for atrocities; or put them on trial. It is unlikely the first two would have set a better precedent than the third, or painted the Allies in a better light. Nor do the war crimes committed by the Allies change this argument. What the Allies can be criticised for is not referring the major trials to an entirely neutral court, or for failing to prosecute war criminals of their own, but these failures hardly mean the Axis war criminals were treated unfairly, or that summarily executing or releasing them would have been a better option.

Having decided to hold war crimes trials, the Allies then had to grapple with the problem of deciding who to prosecute and how to prosecute them. The question of who to prosecute was problematic in Germany as well as in Japan, but particularly so in the latter. At one end of the scale, the Emperor was shielded; at the other, junior officers and men found themselves on trial for their lives for following the orders of their superiors. Today, the 'Nuremberg defence' ('I was only following orders') is viewed with contempt, and pleading it is seen as a sign of cowardice and moral weakness. But the Japanese in the 1940s had a very different view of obedience, and this culture clash is readily apparent in the Australian class-B and -C trials.

Japan had adopted a German-style legal system as part of its modernisation. But it was built on centuries of Confucianism, a philosophy that prizes social harmony, and lays out a means of achieving it through mutual obligations.[4] Leaders and those in positions of power and authority are responsible for making morally correct decisions, and their subordinates are responsible for obeying them. Obedience is a virtue in and of itself. Superiors, in turn, are responsible for their subordinates' actions. See, for example, the punishment of officers in the Japanese Army and Navy for the misdeeds of their men, a form of collective punishment hardly compatible with Western ideas of justice.

Even today, legacies of this system can be seen in Japan, where solving problems through litigation is regarded as contrary to social harmony and therefore discouraged. As a result, Japan has far fewer lawyers per person than do English-speaking countries, and it is still not uncommon for Japanese parents to issue public apologies when their children are convicted of crimes, or even accused of crimes.[5] To the Japanese soldiers raised in such a society, being tried in a court of law for following the orders of their lawful superiors was inherently contradictory – the criminal justice system exists to punish those who threaten the social order, not those who uphold it.

Of course, the natural destination of this train of thought is the prosecution of the Emperor, the man ultimately responsible for the morality of society as a whole. And some Japanese people certainly were shocked at Hirohito's failure to take responsibility for the crimes of his subordinates, as a leader was expected to. One such man was Watanabe Kiyoshi, who reflected on his changing relationship with the Emperor in his 1983 memoir *Kudakareta Kami* (*Shattered God*).[6]

Watanabe joined the navy as a fifteen-year-old, a devoted Emperor-worshipper who accepted the propaganda of the militarists without question. When his battleship, the *Musashi*, was sunk at the Battle of Leyte Gulf, he watched an officer jump into the sea holding a heavy, gilt-framed portrait of the Emperor as a weight to drown himself. Returning to Japan after the war, Watanabe assumed the Emperor would abdicate or commit suicide, or at the very least, make a sign of contrition. But Hirohito's behaviour shocked him. When the Emperor met a veteran on one of his tours, the Emperor exhorted the veteran to work as hard for peace as he had for war. Could not the

Emperor make an apology? Watanabe fantasised about taking him to the bottom of the sea to show him the skeletons of those who died shouting his name, or tying him up by the feet and beating him with a stick to knock some sense of shame into him (this was a punishment in the Japanese Navy).

The photo of MacArthur and the Emperor also shocked Watanabe, as did the Emperor's calm co-operation with SCAP. When Watanabe saw an American GI walking down the street arm in arm with a Japanese woman, he got into a fight with the GI and was arrested. The police then lectured him for causing trouble. In April 1946, learning that anyone could now write to the Emperor, he sat down and composed a letter. He said he wished to end their relationship and enclosed a cheque for 4,282 yen – everything he was paid when he was in the navy. 'Now I owe you nothing,' he said, addressing the sovereign with the informal word for 'you' (*anata*) normally used only when addressing social equals or inferiors.

Should the Emperor have been prosecuted? For more than four decades after the Second World War, Hirohito was the leader of a peaceful, democratic Japan. He pursued his interest in marine biology and published a number of scientific papers. In all that time, he stayed true to the Tokyo Trial version of events, where he was cast as the helpless victim of the militarists. He never admitted any personal responsibility for the millions of deaths in a war fought in his name, or for the atrocities carried out by the armies who fought it. He was, according to biographer Herbert Bix, 'the prime symbol of his people's repression of their wartime past'.[7]

Over time, his international reputation was rehabilitated. In 1975 he made his first and only visit to the United States, patting a koala at San Diego Zoo and visiting Disneyland. On his return, a Japanese journalist asked him, 'Your Majesty, at your White House banquet you said "I deeply deplore the unfortunate war". Does Your Majesty feel any responsibility for the war itself, including the opening of hostilities? Also, what does Your Majesty think of so-called war responsibility?'[8]

It was not a question the Emperor particularly wanted to answer, as his body language and demeanour showed. 'I can't answer that kind of question because I haven't thoroughly studied the literature in this field, and so don't really appreciate the nuances of your words,' he responded stiffly. It was a strange response from someone who had been at the centre of the events he was talking about.

Asked about the dropping of the atomic bombs, he responded with: 'It's very regrettable that nuclear bombs were dropped, and I feel sorry for the citizens of Hiroshima. But it couldn't be helped because it happened in wartime.' It was not a popular remark.

The Shōwa Era finally came to an end on 7 January 1989. At 7.55 am Grand Steward Fujimori Shōichi emerged from the inner recesses of Fukiage Palace and announced the Emperor's death to Japan and the world. World leaders were invited to the funeral; reactions were mixed.[9] US President George H.W. Bush, a veteran of the US Navy in the Pacific War, committed to attending, saying, 'I feel you look ahead, don't always look back.' The governments of Japan's other former enemies, including Australia, also took Bush's position. But not everyone was willing to overlook Hirohito's central role in the war. In South Korea, newspapers demanded an apology from the Japanese government as a precondition to representatives attending the funeral, and student protestors threw fire bombs at the Japanese cultural centre in Seoul. In the UK, Harold Payne, president of the Federation of Far Eastern Prisoners of War Association, criticised the decision by the Thatcher government to send Prince Philip and Foreign Secretary Geoffrey Howe. 'With all these high dignitaries going, the Japanese will assume they are being exonerated for all the dreadful things they did in the war,' he said.

Bob Tizard, New Zealand's Defence Minister, who had served in the RNZAF during the war, said Hirohito should have been hanged or shot as a war criminal. He was echoing the view taken by many in Wellington in 1945, but in 1989 the government was quick to confirm that Tizard was speaking only on his own behalf. In Australia,

Bruce Ruxton, Victorian RSL president, said that attending the funeral would be an 'obscene act': 'Hirohito was the biggest war criminal on Earth, he would have made Adolf Hitler look like a Sunday school teacher. He condoned the slaughter of as many as 40 million Chinese in the years leading up to World War II. Going to Hirohito's funeral would be like going to the funeral of the devil. If our trade dollar demands that we send representatives then it is a sad state of affairs for this country.' His view was rejected by other RSL leaders, including Queensland RSL president Sir Albert Abbott.

But Victorian trade union leader John Halfpenny agreed with him: 'The emperor's death should be noted as the passing of a notorious but unrepentant war criminal.' He said it would be inappropriate for the federal government to pay tribute to 'a person who bore a substantial amount of the responsibility for the atrocities carried out by Japanese military forces against Australians and Pacific Islanders during World War II'.

In defending his decision to send Governor-General Bill Hayden and Trade Minister Michael Duffy, Prime Minister Bob Hawke said 'the level of representation at the funeral reflects the importance which the government attaches to Australia's relationship with Japan . . . While it is appropriate to remember times of war, it is more appropriate to realize Japan is our major trading partner.' Nonetheless, Hawke did not go himself.

At the funeral, Japanese Prime Minister Takeshita Noboru delivered a short eulogy, describing the late Emperor as a pacifist and a constitutional monarch who prayed throughout his reign for world peace. 'Regarding the great war, which had broken out contrary to his wishes, when he could no longer bear to watch the nation suffering its evils, he made the heroic decision and, disregarding his own welfare, ended it.'[10] So the Japanese government maintained its position.

Not everyone in Japan took the same line. In December 1988, as the Emperor lay dying and crowds held vigils outside the palace, a member of the Communist Party asked Liberal Democratic Party Mayor of Nagasaki, Motoshima Hitoshi, what he thought about Hirohito's responsibility for the war. Motoshima, who had been drafted into the Imperial Army, said, 'If I look at the descriptions in Japanese and foreign histories, and reflect on my experiences in the military in the education training of soldiers, in that regard I think the Emperor has war responsibility. But based on the will of a majority of Japanese and Allied countries, the Emperor escaped and became a symbol in the new Constitution, and we have to act under that understanding.'[11]

It was an extremely mild comment, but enough to cause a furious political debate, both within the LDP, which took a traditionally conservative position on the monarchy, and outside it. And the controversy went beyond debate. On 18 January 1990, eleven days after the end of the official mourning period following the Emperor's death, Motoshima was shot in the chest outside the Nagasaki city hall. He survived, and the police arrested the would-be assassin, forty-year-old Tajiri Kazumi. It emerged that he was a member of an extreme right-wing group called the Spiritual Justice School.

When Hirohito's son, Akihito, was enthroned, he took the name *Heisei* ('achieved peace'). Certainly, Japan had achieved peace. While it is easy to find things to criticise about MacArthur, his occupation of Japan was ultimately a success. In light of later attempts to reform societies through military occupation, it was a remarkable achievement and vindicates the decisions he made. Japan has now been a peaceful democracy for seventy years, and while there were many reasons why militarism in Japan was extinguished, the co-operation of the Emperor was almost certainly one. Not prosecuting Hirohito may have been a legal travesty but a practical necessity.

There were many others, though, who escaped prosecution on less-defensible grounds. Ishii Shirō, the leader of the chemical and biological warfare centre Unit 731, was given immunity from prosecution by SCAP in exchange for his research, which had been carried out on Chinese prisoners of war and civilians. Another who went unprosecuted was Colonel Tsuji Masanobu, a *Tōseiha* fanatic who hated the

West and had pushed hard for war. As a senior officer in Malaya, the Philippines and New Guinea, he left a trail of atrocities in his wake. He was, perhaps, the individual most responsible for the brutality of the Bataan Death March, and may have ordered and committed the crimes for which his commander, Lieutenant General Homma, was shot. He was long pursued after the war by British authorities who intended to bring him to trial for the summary execution of Chinese Singaporeans suspected of being pro-British, but he evaded capture. Returning to Japan, he made the successful transition to a pro-Western, anti-communist politician under General Willoughby's protection.[12] In 1952, he was elected to the Diet.

Perhaps the most extreme example of a likely war criminal who went free is Kishi Nobusuke. An ardent nationalist and militarist, Kishi was effectively in charge of the economic development (or exploitation) of the puppet state of Manchukuo from 1936 to 1939. While there, he imposed a command economy on the province, made free use of forced labour, and was implicated in conscripting Chinese and Manchurians as comfort women for the Imperial Army. He then moved into national politics, serving as Tōjō's Minister for Commerce and Industry in the cabinet that approved the attack on Pearl Harbor. Arrested as a class-A war crimes suspect, he was locked up in Sugamo. Fortunately for him, a small but influential group of Americans identified him as a possible future leader of Japan, and he was eventually released without being charged in 1948.

From there, his career recovered rapidly, aided by American money. He was elected to the Diet as a Liberal in 1953, and following the merger of the Liberal and Democratic Parties into the Liberal Democratic Party (LDP), became Prime Minister in 1957. He was feted as a Cold War ally on visits to the Australia and the United States – in the latter he addressed both houses of Congress, threw the first pitch at a New York Yankees baseball game, and played golf with President Eisenhower in a racially segregated country club that made a special dispensation to admit him. Yet he remained, to the

end, unrepentant in his nationalist views, pushing for the release of
convicted war criminals, the rolling back of constitutional restrictions
on the Emperor's involvement in politics, and Japanese rearmament.
While it is not reasonable to expect the Allies to have prosecuted every
war criminal, there were clearly political considerations as well as legal
ones in the choices.

Even some of the convicted class-A war criminals returned to public life. Foreign Minister Shigemitsu Mamoru, sentenced to seven
years' imprisonment, was elected to the Diet in 1952 and became deputy prime minister. There had been significant doubt over whether he
should have been prosecuted or convicted in the first place, but his
example probably emboldened others more culpable than he. Kaya
Okinori, Tōjō's Finance Minister, who was sentenced to twenty years'
imprisonment, was also elected to the Diet and became Minister for
Justice. Hoshino Naoki, sentenced to life imprisonment for crimes in
Manchukuo, was released and became a senior corporate executive.

But not everyone fared so well. The class-B and -C war criminals
often faced stigma in society and difficulty finding jobs. Attempts
by supporters to rehabilitate them were not entirely successful. One
former soldier wrote: 'I was redrafted, but as a result I became a war
criminal. Subsequently, I wanted to receive compensation from the
government even though it was good I received the minimum term
of imprisonment. We became war criminals and spent ten gruelling
years overseas. How does the Japanese government deal with that? We
are ignored, as an annual stipend of 10,000 yen could not guarantee
even subsistence after we returned to Japan. If they have money for
corruption, then the government must pay us, who are struggling to
survive, some compensation for our time in prison as war criminals.'[13]

In other words, those who had loyally followed orders were entitled to be compensated by the government for the consequences of
following those orders. It was a common view.

As for the question of how to prosecute the suspects, having a
neutral power conduct the trials would certainly have removed all

suggestions of victors' justice. At the end of the First World War, the German government proposed a compromise with the Allies whereby those of its officers suspected of war crimes would be tried by a court of neutral powers. This suggestion was made again at the end of the Second World War for all levels of trials. A senior petty officer with the Japanese Navy who was tried at Rabaul for the Ocean Island massacre wrote: 'I am not opposed to war crimes trials per se. But I object strongly to the so-called retaliatory trials of the victor over the vanquished. If they were impartial trials moderated by the conditions of a neutral third country (meaning having the same command relations as those in Japan), then it is possible to think that even war crimes trials could prevent future troubles.'[14]

This would have probably been harder to achieve in practice than principle, as one or more neutral powers would have needed to have been found willing to commit to the laborious and resource-intensive process. And by the end of the Second World War, with most of the world having joined the Allies in some way or another, the burden would have fallen on a handful of countries like Ireland, Sweden and Switzerland. This would have made the trials scattered through the Pacific particularly impractical. Waiting, for example, for a Swiss court to be established at Labuan in Borneo would have taken years. An Australian military court using troops already there, even if less impartial, was much faster. It is probably a fair criticism to make of the Allies, though, that they did not consider this idea in depth, particularly for the class-A trials.

But they should certainly be given credit for the expansive bench at the Tokyo Trial, which included judges from Asia, and for the openness of the proceedings, although they can fairly be criticised for giving the defence too little time to prepare. MacArthur's choice of Webb for president was, in retrospect, not the best, but it's difficult to see how he could have foreseen that. The real problems with Tokyo lie in the specific charges and the findings of guilt against individual defendants, and these can be traced back to problems with the prosecution.

Firstly, the IMTFE did produce a well-researched and complete record of Japan's plunge into the abyss. Many thousands of pages have been written on the rise of Nazism in Germany and the demise of the Weimar Republic, but the rise of militarism in Japan and the demise of the Taishō Democracy has attracted less attention. The IMTFE transcript represents a good starting point for researchers to draw on. However, attempting to use this narrative to tie the defendants together in a conspiracy was overreach. The prosecution argued for a conspiracy for its own convenience, and the court should have not accepted their argument.

On the charge of crimes against peace, Tokyo was always going to follow Nuremberg. From a legal perspective, Nuremberg was the only precedent. And from a political perspective, for Tokyo to find that Nuremberg was wrong would have retrospectively vindicated not only Japan's wartime leaders, but Germany's as well.

But the charges remained controversial. George Finch, in a review of a 1947 book about Nuremberg, claimed the charge of crimes against peace was based on 'treaties which are refuted by the acts of the signatories in practice . . . unratified protocols or public and private resolutions of no legal effect'.[15] Others, including Justice Pal, made the same claim. While Nuremberg and Tokyo were the high-water mark of the idea of crimes against peace, the precedent they set ultimately had more moral than legal force. The United Nations was not able to agree on a definition of aggression in international law until Resolution 3314 of 1974, and while this definition was carried over into the Charter of the International Criminal Court (ICC) in 1998, it does not yet have jurisdiction to prosecute individuals for these crimes. The obvious paradox is that states do not generally initiate force without real prospect of success, but that initiation of force can only be put to trial if its perpetrators are defeated.

Finally, there were the charges of conventional war crimes and crimes against humanity, at both Tokyo and the class-B and -C trials. Establishing that the Holocaust was a crime was the great innovation at Nuremberg, but the trials in the Pacific closely followed existing law. All of the crimes against civilians and prisoners took place in countries Japan had conquered, and so could all be considered conventional war crimes under existing international law. This put the Allies on firm legal ground in all their courts in the Pacific.

From Tokyo, we can move to the Australian trials – were they fair? Narrelle Morris and Tim McCormack identified the following factors as demonstrating fairness in the Australian trials: the application of established legal principles, the consistency of procedure, the dedication of the officers involved, and the high number of acquittals and successful petitions.[16] I agree with this list, and I would also add the willingness of the Australian courts to prosecute crimes against non-Australian victims, which showed a desire to enforce international law consistently and not simply take revenge on those responsible for atrocities against Australians.

On the flipside, Morris and McCormack identified the following consistent problems with the trials: trials of many defendants (most famously M41, with ninety-one accused), conflict of interest among the court members (as at R55, where Chinese officers who had been prisoners of the Japanese sat on an Australian court trying Japanese and Formosan guards for murdering Chinese POWs in the same camp), difficulties in translation, and inconsistencies in sentencing.[17] To this list I would add the time taken to prosecute the defendants in the later trials, the length of time some defendants were held without trial, and, in some cases, an over-reliance on documentary evidence. Morris and McCormack felt, however, that these problems tended to be confined to specific trials, and there were no systemic abuses throughout them. I share this conclusion.

Once the trials finished, neither the prosecutors nor the prosecuted had much interest in talking about them. In an August 1955 Japanese poll, 66 per cent of respondents accepted the prosecution and punishment of wartime leaders by the victors as 'inevitable', but 63 per cent also said that the victors' war trials went too far. Overall, the attitude was still apathy and passive acceptance.[18] The Japanese viewed the Tokyo Trial almost as a force of nature, like the earthquakes that periodically trouble their islands. It made little appearance in public discourse over the next few decades, with only sixteen articles referring to the Tokyo Trial appearing in the *Asahi Shimbun* in 1960s and only sixteen in the 1970s.[19] Discussion was kept alive in a small group of critics, initially started by some of the defence lawyers and then including nationalist historians. The class-B and -C trials were largely ignored. And once Japan was rebuilt and presenting its new face to the world, there was little reason to dwell on shameful memories.

The Allies, too, did not like to draw attention to the Tokyo Trial. The proceedings of the Nuremberg Trials were proudly published in both English and French, but it was many years before the proceedings at Tokyo were published in full in English and Japanese. When the Japanese government approached the Australian government throughout the 1950s and 1960s for copies of the records of class-B and -C trials, Australia repeatedly refused until assured they were for historical research only. The quiet release of the war criminals was met with little interest, and the court records were only made available to the Australian public via the National Archives in 1975.

What debate there was during this time on the Allied program of trials in the Pacific was dominated by their critics. The most influential of these in the English-speaking world was probably American writer Richard Minear, with his 1971 *Victor's Justice: The Tokyo War Crimes Trial*. Minear admitted that his book was overtly political, something obvious from the dedication on the first page: 'Dedicated to the many Americans whose opposition to the war in Indochina has made them exiles, criminals or aliens in their own land.'[20] Minear set out to demolish the credibility of the Tokyo Trial and its verdict and to demonstrate Tōjō's innocence, even though he acknowledged Japanese war crimes are 'as repugnant to me as current American acts in Indochina'.[21] Minear went through the problems with the trial, from its legal basis to its procedure, and concluded those problems rendered it invalid. His book was significant in establishing the IMTFE's negative reputation. While Nuremberg is now seen as a triumph in spite of its issues, Tokyo has not been favoured by history's verdict.[22]

Over the 1980s and 1990s, the trial returned to public attention in Japan. First there was a TV documentary in 1983, then the debate over war responsibility following Hirohito's death in 1989. In the Murayama Statement of 1995, the Japanese government formally took responsibility for waging a war of aggression in Asia and committing war crimes, essentially vindicating the IMTFE's findings without necessarily endorsing all of them. Opinion polls at the time showed that the majority of Japanese agreed with this view. But nationalists have continued to criticise the 'masochistic view of history' or the 'Tokyo view of history', and the debate in the country remains heated even today. For example, the Yūshūkan museum, attached to the Yasukuni Shrine, presents a view of the Pacific War essentially identical to the one Tōjō presented to the IMTFE. According to its displays, the Kwantung Army was compelled to use force against China due to 'anti-Japanese harassment and terrorism', and the Second Sino-Japanese War spread beyond the Marco Polo Bridge Incident due to 'the prevailing anti-Japanese atmosphere in China'.[23] The evidence unearthed by the Allied war crimes trials, particularly the statements by men and women who actually witnessed the crimes, are perhaps the best resource available to those both within and outside Japan who would challenge this narrative.

Ultimately, the war crimes trials following the Second World War are known for the notoriety of the defendants and the scale of their crimes. This makes Nuremberg far more famous than Tokyo, and leaves the class-B and -C trials in the Pacific less famous still. Language barriers, the unavailability of records is one reason, and a lack of interest by popular historians or writers of fiction is another.

'Posterity cannot condemn us if we deal with our enemies in the strictly legal way recognised by International Law, to which, after all, our enemies should have professed their adherence,' Webb wrote in June 1945.[24] Can posterity condemn the Australian trials? They would certainly be judged deficient by the standards of a modern war crimes court. However, as international law scholar William Schabas described it, criticising them on these grounds is like 'modern-day architects criticizing the Parthenon because it doesn't have ramps for the disabled and proper emergency exits'.[25] The few modern scholars who have looked at the Australian trials in depth have acknowledged their problems but generally approved of them as an effort to enforce international law. As Emmi Okada wrote of them, 'in many respects [they] fell short of the international law standards of justice that we have evolved today. Yet, at least in a great majority of cases, there was nevertheless a notable exercise of legalistic restraint and an effort to achieve procedural integrity (despite the shortcomings of the [War Crimes Act]), which belies a simplistic view that the Australian trials were nothing more than vengeance disguised as law.'[26]

In 1945, giving in to anti-Japanese hysteria and taking revenge would have been easy. It is to the great credit of the AALC officers, civilian lawyers, and other Australian military personnel and civilians involved in the trials that this, in most cases, did not happen. It is perhaps fitting to give the last words to the Japanese defence team on Morotai, the men responsible for defending Okada Tomiyoshi, whose trial I described in the prologue. In a letter to prosecuting officer Captain John Myles Williams, written shortly before they left the island in March 1946, they wrote: 'We have sent letters of thanks to a few Australian officers, mostly legal officers who have done greatly for the benefit of the Japanese accused, but of course it was you who introduced us to all these excellent defending officers. You, therefore, favoured us not only with direct kindness but with a great deal of indirect kindness. When we reconsider the things by changing mutual positions, we are not quite certain whether we could favour the defeated with such kindness.'[27]

In doing what they could to ensure the accused Japanese a fair trial, the men behind the Australian war crimes trials gave moral vindication to the sacrifices made by their comrades to defeat them.

# APPENDIX A:
# IMTFE VERDICTS
# AND SENTENCES

The counts of the indictment on which the tribunal made findings were as follows. Counts 1 to 36 dealt with class-A war crimes, and counts 54 and 55 class-B and -C war crimes.

- Count 1: Participating as leaders, organisers, instigators, or accomplices in the formulation or execution of a common plan or conspiracy to wage wars of aggression and wars in violation of international law
- Count 27: Waging aggressive war against China
- Count 29: Waging aggressive war against the United States of America (including the Philippines)
- Count 31: Waging aggressive war against the British Commonwealth
- Count 32: Waging aggressive war against the Netherlands (the invasion of the Dutch East Indies)
- Count 33: Waging aggressive war against France (the occupation of French Indochina)
- Counts 35 and 36: Waging aggressive war against the Soviet Union
- Count 54: Ordering, authorising, and permitting inhumane treatment of prisoners of war and others
- Count 55: Deliberately and recklessly disregarding their duty to take adequate steps to prevent atrocities

| Defendant | Counts indicted for | Counts convicted on | Sentence | Fate |
|---|---|---|---|---|
| General Araki Sadao | 1, 27, 29, 31, 32, 33, 35, 36, 54 and 55 | 1 and 27 | Life imprisonment | Paroled 1955, died 1966 |
| General Kenji Doihara | 1, 27, 29, 31, 32, 33, 35, 36, 54 and 55 | 1, 27, 29, 31, 32, 35, 36 and 54 | Death | Hanged 23 December 1948 |
| Colonel Hashimoto Kingoro | 1, 27, 29, 31, 32, 54 and 55 | 1 and 27 | Life imprisonment | Paroled 1954, died 1957 |
| Field Marshal Hata Shunroku | 1, 27, 29, 31, 32, 35, 36, 54, and 55 | 1, 27, 29, 31, 32 and 55 | Life imprisonment | Paroled 1954, died 1962 |
| Baron Hiranuma Kiichirō | 1, 27, 29, 31, 32, 33, 35, 36, 54 and 55 | 1, 27, 29, 31, 32 and 36 | Life imprisonment | Paroled and died 1952 |
| Hirota Kōki, Foreign Minister | 1, 27, 29, 31, 32, 33, 35, 54, and 55 | 1, 27 and 55 | Death | Hanged 23 December 1948 |
| Hoshino Naoki, Chief Cabinet Secretary | 1, 27, 29, 31, 32, 33, 35, 54 and 55 | 1, 27, 29, 31 and 32 | Life imprisonment | Paroled 1958, died 1978 |
| General Itagaki Seishirō | 1, 27, 29, 31, 32, 33, 35, 36, 54 and 55 | 1, 27, 29, 31, 32, 35, 36 and 54 | Death | Hanged 23 December 1948 |
| Kaya Okinori, Finance Minister | 1, 27, 29, 31, 32, 54 and 55 | 1, 27, 29, 31 and 32 | Life imprisonment | Paroled 1955, served as Minister for Justice 1963–64, died 1977 |
| Marquis Kido Kōichi, Lord Keeper of the Privy Seal | 1, 27, 29, 31, 32, 33, 35, 36, 54 and 55 | 1, 27, 29, 31 and 32 | Life imprisonment | Paroled 1953, died 1977 |
| General Kimura Heitarō | 1, 27, 29, 31, 32, 54 and 55 | 1, 27, 29, 31, 32, 54 and 55 | Death | Hanged 23 December 1948 |
| General Koiso Kuniaki, Prime Minister 1944–45 | 1, 27, 29, 31, 32, 36, 54, and 55 | 1, 27, 29, 31, 32 and 55 | Life imprisonment | Died in prison 1950 |
| General Matsui Iwane | 1, 27, 29, 31, 32, 35, 36, 54 and 55 | 55 | Death | Hanged 23 December 1948 |
| General Minami Jirō | 1, 27, 29, 31, 12, 54 and 55 | 1 and 27 | Life imprisonment | Paroled 1954, died 1955 |
| Lieutenant General Mutō Akira | 1, 27, 29, 31, 32, 33, 36, 54 and 55 | 1, 27, 29, 31, 32, 54 and 55 | Death | Hanged 23 December 1948 |

| Defendant | Counts indicted for | Counts convicted on | Sentence | Fate |
|---|---|---|---|---|
| Admiral Oka Takasumi | 1, 27, 29, 31, 32, 54, and 55 | 1, 27, 29, 31 and 32 | Life imprisonment | Paroled 1954, died 1973 |
| Lieutenant General Ōshima Hiroshi, Ambassador to Germany | 1, 27, 29, 31, 32, 54 and 55 | 1 | Life imprisonment | Paroled 1955, died 1975 |
| General Satō Kenryō | 1, 27, 29, 31, 32, 54 and 55 | 1, 27, 29, 31, and 32 | Life imprisonment | Paroled 1956, died 1975 |
| Shigemitsu Mamoru, Foreign Minister | 1, 27, 29, 31, 32, 33, 35, 54, and 55 | 27, 29, 31, 32, 33 and 55 | Seven years' imprisonment | Paroled 1950, served as Foreign Minister 1954–56, died 1957 |
| Admiral Shimada Shigetarō | 1, 27, 29, 31, 32, 54 and 55 | 1, 27, 29, 31 and 32 | Life imprisonment | Paroled 1955, died 1976 |
| Shiratori Toshio, Ambassador to Italy | 1, 27, 29, 31 and 32 | 1, 27, 29, 31 and 32 | Life imprisonment | Died in prison 1949 |
| Lieutenant General Suzuki Teiichi | 1, 27, 29, 31, 32, 35, 36, 54 and 55 | 1, 27, 29, 31, and 32 | Life imprisonment | Paroled 1955, died 1989 |
| Tōgō Shigenori, Foreign Minister | 1, 27, 29, 31, 32, 36, 54 and 55 | 1, 27, 29, 31, and 32 | Twenty years' imprisonment | Died in prison 1955 |
| General Tōjō Hideki, Prime Minister 1941–44 | 1, 27, 29, 31, 32, 33, 36, 54 and 55 | 1, 27, 29, 31, 32, 33 and 54 | Death | Hanged 23 December 1948 |
| General Umezu Yoshijirō | 1, 27, 29, 31, 32, 36, 54 and 55 | 1, 27, 29, 31, and 32 | Life imprisonment | Died in prison 1949 |

# APPENDIX B: THE PACIFIC CLASS-B AND -C TRIALS

The exact figures for the number of class-B and -C trials in the Pacific, as well as the number of defendants and their sentences, are difficult to identify with certainty. Yuma Totani gives the following breakdown, based on Japanese government figures:[1]

- The United States – 456 trials against 1,453 suspects at Guam, Kwajalein, Manila, Shanghai and Yokohama. Philip R. Piccigallo, writing in 1979, gave the numbers as 474 trials of 1,409 defendants with 1,229 convictions and 163 death sentences. Of the trials, 319 were held at Yokohama (996 defendants, 854 convictions, 51 death sentences), 11 in Shanghai (75 defendants, 67 convictions, 10 death sentences), 97 in the Philippines (215 defendants, 195 convictions, 92 death sentences), and 47 in the Pacific Islands (123 defendants, 113 convictions, 10 death sentences).[2] The trials commenced with the prosecution of General Yamashita in Manila in September 1945 and continued until the last trials at Yokohama in October 1949. Both the US Army and Navy conducted trials, following slightly different procedures. The army conducted the trials in the Philippines (prior to independence on 4 July 1946), Shanghai and Yokohama, while the navy conducted the trials on the American Pacific Islands such as Guam.
- The Netherlands – 448 trials against 1,038 suspects at Ambon, Balikpapan, Banjarmasin, Batavia (modern Jakarta), Hollandia (Jayapura), Kupang, Makassar, Manado, Medan, Morotai, Pontianak and Tanjung Pinang.

Robert Cribb also gives the numbers of 1,038 suspects and 448 separate trials, and states that there were 236 death sentences, 747 prison terms, and 55 acquittals.[3] The most significant Dutch court was the *Temporaire Krijgsraad* (temporary courts-martial) in Batavia, which tried a third of the Dutch cases. Those sentenced to prison terms were held at Cipinang prison in Batavia (Jakarta), those sentenced to death executed by firing squad.[4] The Dutch trials were naturally overshadowed by the civil war in the Netherlands East Indies between the colonial authorities and the Indonesian Republic under Sukarno, which the Indonesian Republic was steadily winning. The Dutch trials were later criticised (including by a former judge at Batavia) for focusing too much on European victims, suppressing evidence, and taking too little trouble to confirm the accuracy of the evidence it did allow.[5]

- The United Kingdom – 330 trials against 978 suspects at Alor Setar, Hong Kong, Jesselton (Kota Kinabalu), Johore Baru, Kuala Lumpur, Labuan, Penang, Rangoon (Yangon), Singapore and Taiping. Philip R. Piccigallo gives the numbers as 306 trials of 920 defendants, with 811 convictions, 279 death sentences handed down, and 265 death sentences carried out.[6] The British trials began in Singapore on 21 January 1946 and continued into late 1948.

- Australia – 294 trials against 949 suspects, at Ambon, Morotai, Labuan, Wewak, Darwin, Rabaul, Singapore, Hong Kong, and Manus Island (specifically, Los Negros) between November 1946 and April 1951. Of the defendants, 280 were acquitted and 644 were convicted; 138 were executed – 114 by hanging, 24 by shooting – and 498 given prison sentences of varying lengths.[7] David Sissons notes that as some of the defendants were in more than one trial, the total number of persons tried was 814. For this and the additional reason that 2 condemned men died in custody, the total number executed was 138.[8]

- Nationalist China – 605 trials against 883 suspects at Beijing, Nanking (Nanjing), Guandong, Hankou, Jinan, Shanghai, Shenyang, Taipei, Taiyuan and Xuzhou. Philip R. Piccigallo gives the numbers as 605 trials, 883 accused, 504 convictions, and 350 death sentences. The Chinese trials proceeded from October 1946 to February 1949, shortly before the Nationalist Chinese Government was defeated by the Chinese Communists.[9]

- The Philippines – 72 trials against 169 suspects at Manila. Beatrice Trefalt gives the numbers as 151 defendants, 73 trials, 137 guilty verdicts, and 79 death sentences.[10] The Philippines took over the class-B and -C trials process from the US on 1 January 1947, and most of the defendants were prosecuted for crimes against civilians. The prison terms were served at New Bilibid Prison in Muntinlupa, Manila, and the executions carried out there by hanging.

- France – 39 trials against 230 suspects at the Permanent Military Tribunal in Saigon between 1945 and 1950. Philip R. Piccigallo gives the same numbers, as well as 198 convictions, 63 death sentences passed, and 26 death sentences carried out.[11] Some death sentences were handed down in absentia. The French trials, like the Dutch, were hampered by a war of independence in the colony. In the French case, the trials of Japanese war criminals became entangled with the trials of alleged collaborators, many of whom were members of the Viet Minh communist insurgency.[12]

The exact number of defendants will probably never be known, as some were tried by two countries. An example is Lieutenant General Nishimura Takuma, tried by both the United Kingdom and Australia for different war crimes in Malaya. Australian researchers have, at different times, given the total number of defendants at 5,677[13] or 5,706[14] rather than 5,700. Other sources put the total number of death sentences at 1,041[15] or 984,[16] although all agree that not all the death sentences were carried out; some prisoners escaped, committed suicide, or died in custody from natural causes. The total number executed may have been around 920. Sandra Wilson states that 475 defendants were sentenced to life imprisonment and 2,944 to other prison terms.[17]

Other Allies participated in the process but did not conduct any trials. Canada actively supported Britain's trials in Hong Kong, where Canadian troops had been taken prisoner, but conducted no trials of its own in the Far East. Nor did New Zealand, which accepted British, American and Australian control of the class-B and -C trials.

# APPENDIX C:
# THE AUSTRALIAN
# CLASS-B AND -C TRIALS

Figures from David Sisson's *The Australian War Crimes Trials and Investigations*. The key for 'Type of victims' is as follows – note this is the type of victims per trial, not the total number of victims overall:

- N: Natives (used to mean Melanesian and Polynesian people)
- C: Chinese civilians
- W: Western civilians
- APW: Australian prisoners of war and captured members of infiltration parties
- BPW: British prisoners of war
- IPW: Indian prisoners of war
- CPW: Chinese prisoners of war
- NPW: Indonesian prisoners of war
- AC: Crashed aircrew
- D: Mutilation of the dead and cannibalism

| Location | Dates | Number of trials | Type of victims | Number accused | Number convicted | Sentence | | | |
|---|---|---|---|---|---|---|---|---|---|
| | | | | | | Hanging | Shooting | Prison (life) | Prison (other) |
| Labaun | 3/12/45–3/1/46 | 15 | APW: 15 | 145 | 128 | 2 | 5 | 5 | 116 |
| Wewak | 30/11/45–11/12/45 | 2 | N: 1 D: 1 | 2 | 1 | - | - | - | 1 |
| Morotai (inc. Ambon) | 29/11/45–28/2/46 | 25 | APW: 7 AC: 18 | 148 | 81 | - | 25 | - | 56 |

| Location | Dates | Number of trials | Type of victims | Number accused | Number convicted | Sentence | | | |
|---|---|---|---|---|---|---|---|---|---|
| | | | | | | Hanging | Shooting | Prison (life) | Prison (other) |
| Rabaul | 12/12/45–6/8/47 | 188 | N: 25<br>C: 17<br>W: 4<br>APW: 11<br>BPW: 2<br>IPW: 100<br>CPW: 22<br>NPW: 2<br>AC: 3<br>D: 2 | 390 | 266 | 84 | 3 | 8 | 169 |
| Darwin | 1/3/46–29/4/46 | 3 | APW: 3 | 22 | 10 | - | 1 | - | 9 |
| Singapore | 26/6/46–11/6/47 | 23 | APW: 22<br>AC: 1 | 62 | 51 | 18 | - | 6 | 27 |
| Hong Kong | 24/11/47–25/11/48 | 13 | N: 3<br>W: 2<br>APW: 4<br>BPW: 1<br>AC: 3 | 42 | 38 | 5 | - | 4 | 29 |
| Manus Island | 5/6/50–9/4/51 | 26 | N: 1<br>APW: 21<br>AC: 3<br>D: 1 | 113 | 69 | 5 | - | 16 | 48 |
| TOTAL | | 295 | N: 30<br>C: 17<br>W: 6<br>APW: 83<br>BPW: 3<br>IPW: 100<br>CPW: 22<br>NPW: 2<br>AC: 28<br>D: 4 | 924 | 644 | 114 | 34 | 39 | 455 |

# ACKNOWLEDGEMENTS

The Australian class-B and -C war crimes trials have attracted little attention outside of academic circles. However, I have benefited tremendously from the work of others who have gone before me, particularly Georgina Fitzpatrick, Tim McCormack, Narelle Morris, Dean Aszkielowicz, Sandra Wilson, Robert Cribb, Utsumi Aiko, Kōta Udagawa, Steven Bullard, Emmi Okada, and the late David Sissons. I am also indebted to Kirsten Sellars and Yuma Totani for their commentary on the Tokyo Trial, and John Dower and Herbert Bix for their books on Shōwa-era Japan. Not being able to read Japanese, I am particularly grateful to Japanese-speaking writers and academics who have been able to make Japanese sources available in English. I am pleased to have been able to continue my relationship with the same agent and the same publisher I worked with on *The Last Fifty Miles*, and I would like to thank Lyn Tranter of Australian Literary Management and Ben Ball, formerly of Penguin, for their ongoing support. I have once again found the staff at Penguin very professional and easy to work with, including lead editor Meredith Rose, who co-ordinated the entire project on a tight time frame. I would also like to thank Sam Dipnall at the Law Institute of Victoria for helping me network in the field of international human rights law. And finally, I would like to thank Brian Hurlock for reading and commenting on the first draft of the manuscript, and for consistently backing me through the difficult times as well as the triumphant ones.

# NOTES

*References to web pages for DFAT (Department of Foreign Affairs and Trade) have been confined to the main page only.*

## PROLOGUE

1   Okada's trial was Morotai M27. The transcript and other documents are in the National Archives of Australia at NAA A471 80722 – series number A471, control symbol 80772, barcode 822577.

2   'Japanese N.C.O. to Die', *The Advertiser*, 4 February 1946, p 1, at http://nla.gov.au/nla.news-article48689612

3   National Archives, op. cit., p 88. Minor errors in the transcripts of trials have been corrected throughout.

4   ibid., p 89.

5   ibid., pp 92–95.

6   ibid., pp 7–8.

7   Bullard, Stephen, 'The Emperor's Army: Military Operations and Ideology in the War Against Australia', *Australia's War Crimes Trials, 1945–51*, ed. Fitzpatrick, Georgina; McCormack, Tim; Morris, Narrelle, Brill Nijhoff, Netherlands, 2016, p 53; Aszkielowicz, Dean, 'Repatriation and the Limits of Resolve: Japanese War Criminals in Australian Custody', *Japanese Studies*, vol. 31, no. 2, September 2011, p 213.

8   Fitzpatrick, Georgina, 'Death Sentences, War Criminals and the Australian Military', Fitzpatrick; McCormack et al., op. cit. pp 322–323.

9   'Soldiers Want Guilty Japs to Die', *Daily Telegraph*, 22 February 1946, cited in Okada, Emmi, 'The Australian Trials of Class B and C Japanese

War Crime Suspects, 1945–51', *Australian International Law Journal*, vol. 4, 2009, pp 47–80, available at http://www.austlii.edu.au/au/journals/AUIntLawJl/2009/4.pdf, p 50.

10   Jakobs, Giselle, 'British Procedure for Military Executions by Firing Squad (1950)', 3 September 2014, at http://www.josefjakobs.info/2014/09/british-procedure-for-military.html. The 1950 procedure was little changed from that used in the first half of the twentieth century.

11   Aiko, Utsumi & Udagawa, Kōta, transl. Bullard, Steven, 'The "Post-War" of the BC-Class War Criminals: How Did War Criminals React to the Australian Trials?', Fitzpatrick, McCormack, et al., op. cit., p 762. Yamamoto's trial was ML36; his account is in the 1953 edition of *Testament of the Century*, pp 491–492.

12   ibid., p 763. Yabe's trial was M12; his account is on p 505.

13   Fitzpatrick in Fitzpatrick, McCormack, et al., op. cit., p 338.

14   ibid., p 326.

15   ibid., p 339.

16   'Executions at Morotai', *Sydney Morning Herald*, 8 March 1946, p 3.

17   ibid.

18   Fitzpatrick in Fitzpatrick, McCormack, et al., op. cit., p 339.

19   'Japs Pay Penalty', *Courier-Mail*, 8 March 1946, p 1.

## INTRODUCTION

1   Wilson, Sandra; Cribb, Robert; Trefalt, Beatrice; Aszkielowicz, Dean, *Japanese War Criminals: The Politics of Justice After the Second World War*, Columbia University Press, United States, 2017, p 274; Crowe, D., *War Crimes, Genocide, and Justice: A Global History*, Palgrave Macmillan, United States, 2014.

2   'Former Auschwitz guard Reinhold Hanning convicted in German trial', ABC News, 18 June 2016, at http://www.abc.net.au/news/2016-06-17/former-auschwitz-guard-convicted-in-german-trial/7522334

3   Piccigallo, Philip R., *The Japanese on Trial: Allied War Crimes Operations in the East, 1945–1951*, University of Texas Press, United States, 1979,

p 264; Wilson, Sandra, 'After the Trials: Class B and C Japanese War Criminals and the Post-War World', *Japanese Studies*, vol. 31, no. 2, September 2011, pp 141–151.

4    See p 348 (note 2 under Part Three, Chapter 1) for more on the numbers.

5    Cribb, Robert, 'Avoiding Clemency: The Trial and Transfer of Japanese War Criminals in Indonesia, 1946–1949', *Japanese Studies*, vol. 31, no. 2, September 2011, p 161.

6    'Australia Demands Justice', *Sydney Morning Herald*, 11 September 1945, p 1.

7    'Blain Urges: Treat Japs Like Bad Children', *Tweed Daily*, 1 October 1945, p 1.

8    Dower, John W., *War Without Mercy: Race and Power in the Pacific War*, Faber & Faber, United States, 1986, p 33.

9    ibid., p 527.

10   Johnston, Mark, *Fighting the Enemy: Australian Soldiers and their Adversaries in World War II*, Cambridge University Press, United Kingdom, 2000, p 79.

11   ibid., p 88.

12   See for example, Wyzanski, Charles E., 'Nuremberg: A Fair Trial? A Dangerous Precedent', *The Atlantic*, April 1946, at https://www. theatlantic.com/magazine/archive/1946/04/nuremberg-a-fair-trial-a-dangerous-precedent/306492/

13   Arbour, Louise, 'The Rule of Law and the Reach of Accountability', *The Rule of Law*, ed. Le Roy, Katherine & Saunders, Cheryl, The Federation Press, Australia, 2003, p 104.

14   Sellars, Kirsten, 'Imperfect Justice at Nuremberg and Tokyo', *European Journal of International Law*, vol. 21, no. 4, 2010, pp 1085–1102.

15   Wilson, 'After the Trials', op. cit., p 146.

16   Aiko & Udagawa, op. cit., p 761. Gōto's trial was R48; his statement is in *Testament of the Century*, p 484.

17   ibid.

18   Wilson, 'After the Trials', op. cit., p 141.

## CHAPTER I

1    Hoyt, Edwin P., *Warlord: Tojo Against the World* (2001 ed.), Cooper
     Square Press, United States, 1993, p 6.

2    Cited from the Harry S. Truman Library at https://www.trumanlibrary.
     org/publicpapers/index.php?pid=100

3    Cited from the Japanese government website at http://www.ndl.go.jp/
     constitution/e/etc/c06.html

4    Bix, Herbert P., *Hirohito and the Making of Modern Japan*, Harper
     Perennial, United States, 2016 (2nd ed.), p 515.

5    Dower, John W., *Embracing Defeat: Japan in the Aftermath of World
     War II*, Penguin, United Kingdom, 2000, p 91.

6    Bix, op. cit., p 491.

7    Cited from the Japanese government website at http://www.ndl.go.jp/
     constitution/e/etc/c02.html

8    Bix, op. cit., p 15.

9    Brendon, Piers, *The Dark Valley: A Panorama of the 1930s*, Vintage Books,
     United States, 2002, p 451.

10   Also referred to as the Minister for War, but the Ministry was
     responsible only for the Army.

11   Bix, op. cit., p 513.

12   Frank, Richard, *Downfall: The End of the Imperial Japanese Empire*,
     Penguin, United States, 1999, pp 296–297.

13   ibid.

14   ibid.

15   Bix, op. cit., p 517.

16   Foreign Relations of the United States, Historical Documents,
     740.00119 PW/8–1045, at https://history.state.gov/historicaldocuments/
     frus1945v06/d406

17   Truman, Harry S., *Year of Decisions*, Hodder & Stoughton, United
     Kingdom, 1995, p 360–362.

18   Totani, Yuma, *The Tokyo War Crimes Trial: The Pursuit of Justice in the
     Wake of World War II*, Harvard University Press, United States, 2008,
     p 46.

19   DFAT Record 177, Addison to Commonwealth Government,
     Cablegram D1415 LONDON, 11 August 1945, 2.47 a.m, AA : A1066,
     P45/10/1/3, ii, at http://dfat.gov.au/

20   Wood, James, 'The Australian Military Contribution to the Occupation
     of Japan, 1945–1952', Australian War Memorial, 2014, available at
     https://www.awm.gov.au/sites/default/files/BCOF_history.pdf, p 3.

21   Carrel, Michael, 'Australia's Prosecution of Japanese War Criminals:
     Stimuli and Constraints', *The Legacy of Nuremberg: Civilising
     Influence Or Institutionalised Vengeance?*, ed. Blumenthal, David A. &
     McCormack, Timothy L.H., Koninklije Brill, BV, Netherlands, pp 239,
     240.

22   DFAT Record 164, Evatt to Oldham for Addison, Cablegram 222
     CANBERRA, 9 August 1945, AA : A3196, 1945, FOLDER,
     OUTWARDS MOST SECRET, 0.20804/825, at http://dfat.gov.au/

23   DFAT Record 169, Smuts to Evatt, Cablegram 69, 9 August 1945,
     2.51 p.m, AA : A3195, 1945, at http://dfat.gov.au/

24   Murphy, John, *Evatt: A Life*, New South Press, Australia, 2016, p 1.

25   Bolton, G.C., 'Evatt, Herbert Vere (Bert) (1894–1965)', *Australian
     Dictionary of Biography*, National Centre of Biography, Australian
     National University, 1996 at http://adb.anu.edu.au/biography/evatt-
     herbert-vere-bert-10131/text17885

26   DFAT Record 178, Commonwealth Government to Addison,
     Cablegram 230 CANBERRA, 12 August 1945, AA : A1066, P45/10/3, ii,
     at http://dfat.gov.au/

27   DFAT Record 181, Attlee to Chifley, Cablegram 289 LONDON,
     12 August 1945, 12.12 a.m., AA : A1066, P45/10/1/3, ii, at http://dfat.
     gov.au/

28   DFAT Record 208, Addison to Commonwealth Government, AA :
     A1066, P45/10/1/2, at http://dfat.gov.au

29   Truman, op. cit., p 363.

30   DFAT Record 179, Addison to Commonwealth Government, Cablegram
     D1429 LONDON, 11 August 1945, 10.34 p.m, AA : A1066, P45/10/1/3, ii,
     at http://dfat.gov.au/

## CHAPTER II

1   Frank, op. cit., p 297.

2   Meiji Japan had reformed its aristocracy along British lines. Konoe's
    title of *kōshaku* was actually closer to duke in the European system, but
    'prince' is the official English translation. He was not a member of the
    Imperial family.

3   Bix, op. cit., p 492.

4   Frank, op. cit., p 298.

5   Bix, op. cit., p 519.

6   Frank, op. cit., p 311.

7   Bix, op. cit., 519.

8   Frank, op. cit., p 315.

9   Kodera, Atsushi, 'Master recording of Hirohito's war-end speech
    released in digital form', *The Japan Times*, 15 August 2015, at http://www.
    japantimes.co.jp/news/2015/08/01/national/history/master-recording-
    hirohitos-war-end-speech-released-digital-form/

10  Dower, *Embracing Defeat*, op. cit.

11  Aihara Yū, letter to *Asahi Shimbun* newspaper, 16 May 1995, quoted in
    Dower, *Embracing Defeat*, op. cit., pp 33–34.

12  *Emperor Hirohito*, 2005 BBC Discovery Channel Co-Production.

13  Australian War Memorial at https://www.awm.gov.au/articles/
    encyclopedia/pow/ww2/civilian_internees

14  British military records at https://www.forces-war-records.co.uk/
    prisoners-of-war-of-the-japanese-1939-1945

15  Australian War Memorial at https://www.awm.gov.au/articles/
    encyclopedia/pow/general_info

16  Wigmore, Lionel, *Australia in the War of 1939–1945, Series 1 – Army,
    Volume IV – The Japanese Thrust*, Australian War Memorial, 1957,
    p 635.

17  ibid., p 637.

18  MacArthur, Douglas, *Reminiscences*, McGraw-Hill, United States, 1964,
    p 265.

19  ibid., p 101.

20  Herman, Arthur, *Douglas MacArthur: American Warrior*, Random House, United States, 2009, p xi.

21  Fairbank, John K., 'Digging Out Doug', *New York Review of Books*, 12 October 1978.

22  Herman, op. cit., p 499.

23  '500,000 Watch Victory March in City', *Sydney Morning Herald*, 17 August 1945, p. 5; 'Peace Celebrations in the City', *The Age*, 15 August 1945, p 5.

24  'The Hour of Victory', *Sydney Morning Herald*, 16 August 1945, p 2.

25  'Canberra in State of Suspense', *The Argus*, 15 August 1945, p 3.

26  'Japanese War Criminals', *The Age*, 17 August 1945, p 2.

27  'Hirohito as War Criminal', *Sydney Morning Herald*, 20 August 1945, p 3.

## CHAPTER III

1   Dower, *Embracing Defeat*, op. cit., p 59.

2   'Japs Try Own Officers', *Sydney Morning Herald*, 29 June 1946, p 3.

3   Dower, *Embracing Defeat*, op. cit., 125–126.

4   Wood, op. cit., p 25.

5   Wigmore, op. cit., p 358.

6   Weld, H.A., 'Webb, Sir William Flood (1887–1972)', *Australian Dictionary of Biography*, National Centre of Biography, Australian National University, 2002, at http://adb.anu.edu.au/biography/webb-sir-william-flood-11991/text21499

7   Sissons, David, 'The Australian War Crimes Trials and Investigations', p 5, at https://www.ocf.berkeley.edu/~changmin/documents/Sissons%20Final%20War%20Crimes%20Text%2018-3-06.pdf

8   Ham, Paul, *Kokoda*, HarperCollins, Australia, 2004, p 192.

9   House of Representatives Hansard, 30 November 1944.

10  Senate Hansard, 4 October 1945 (Senator Ashley); Sissons, op. cit., p 7.

11  Wilson, Sandra, 'Prisoners in Sugamo and Their Campaign for Release, 1952–1953', *Japanese Studies*, vol. 31, no. 2, September 2011, p 174.

12  McCormack, Tim & Morris, Narrelle, 'The Australian War Crimes Trials, 1945–1951', Fitzpatrick, McCormack, et. al., op. cit., p 18.

13 Dower, *Embracing Defeat*, op. cit., p 290.

14 ibid., p 287.

15 ibid.

16 Herman, op. cit., p 654.

17 Kase's account is quoted in MacArthur, op. cit., pp 272–277.

18 ibid., p 272.

19 ibid.

20 Long, Gavin, *Australia in the War of 1939–1945, Series 1 – Army, Volume VII – The Final Campaigns*, 1963, Australian War Memorial, p 553.

21 'Tojo Attempts Suicide', *The Age*, 12 September 1945, p 1.

22 Dower, *Embracing Defeat*, op. cit., p 492.

23 'Yamashita for Trial at Once', *Sydney Morning Herald*, 4 October 1945, p 1.

24 Sissons, op. cit., p 7.

25 Royal Warrant – Regulations for the Trial of War Criminals, 18 June 1945, A.O. 81/1945, available at http://avalon.law.yale.edu/imt/imtroyal. asp

26 Sides, Hampton, 'The Trial of General Homma', *American Heritage*, February/March 2007, vol. 58, issue 1, at http://www.americanheritage. com/content/trial-general-homma

27 ibid.

28 Law Reports of Trials of War Criminals, vol. IV, United Nations War Crimes Commission, 1947, at https://www.loc.gov/rr/frd/Military_Law/ pdf/Law-Reports_Vol-4.pdf, p 12.

29 MacArthur, op. cit., pp 295–296.

30 ibid., p 296–298.

31 ibid.

## CHAPTER IV

1 'No Immunity for Japan's Emperor', *The Argus*, 14 August 1945, p 2.

2 Rix, Alan, *The Australia–Japan Political Alignment: 1952 to the Present* Routledge, United States, p 97.

3 Sissons, op. cit., p 11.

4    Trotter, Ann, 'New Zealanders and the International Military Tribunal for the Far East', *New Zealand Journal of History*, vol. 23, no. 2, 1989, pp 142–156, at http://www.nzjh.auckland.ac.nz/docs/1989/NZJH_23_2_03.pdf

5    Sissons, op. cit., p 11.

6    ibid.

7    Totani, op. cit., p 53.

8    Dower, *Embracing Defeat*, op. cit., p 288.

9    ibid.

10    ibid., p 293.

11    ibid., p 285.

12    MacArthur, op. cit., p 288.

13    ibid.

14    Dower, *Embracing Defeat*, op. cit., pp 285–287.

15    Japanese government website: http://www.ndl.go.jp/constitution/e/etc/glossary.html

16    Dower, *Embracing Defeat*, op. cit., p 229.

17    Wood, op. cit., p 10.

18    ibid., p 10–11.

19    Sissons, op. cit., p 12.

20    ibid., p 13.

21    ibid.

22    'Round-Up in Japan', *The Advertiser*, 20 November 1945, p 1.

23    Dower, *Embracing Defeat*, op. cit., p 476.

24    ibid., p 326.

25    'Konoye's Arrest Ordered', *The Argus*, 7 December 1945, p 1.

26    'Sought Solace in Oscar Wilde's Books', *The Argus*, 18 December 1945, p 16.

27    Caiger, George, 'The Japanese Misunderstand War Guilt Trials', *Sydney Morning Herald*, 5 February 1946, p 2.

28    ibid.

29    'Justice Criticises Jap Trials Appointment', *The Argus*, 22 March 1946, p 24.

30    'Webb Appointment "Misapprehension"', *Sydney Morning Herald*, 23 March 1946, p 5.

31   Dower, *Embracing Defeat*, op. cit., p 314.

32   Totani, op. cit., p 57.

33   'New Concept in British Relations: Australia Acts For Empire', *The Argus*, 14 March 1946, p 2.

34   Dower, *Embracing Defeat*, op. cit., p 9.

35   Bix, op. cit., pp 2–3.

36   Dower, *Embracing Defeat*, op. cit., p 323.

37   'Naming of Hirohito as War Criminal', *The Argus*, 18 January 1946, p 20.

38   Totani, op. cit., p 55.

39   Sissons, op. cit., p 14.

40   ibid.

41   ibid.

42   Totani, op. cit., p 55.

43   ibid.

44   MacArthur, op. cit., p 288.

45   Dower, *Embracing Defeat*, op. cit., p 467.

### CHAPTER V

1    'War Crimes Road Show', *Time* magazine, 20 May 1946.

2    Röling, Bert V.A. & Cassese, Antonio, *The Tokyo Trial and Beyond*, Polity Press & Blackwell Publishers, United Kingdom, 1993, p 20.

3    'Sir W. Webb in Star Role at War Trial', *Courier-Mail*, 26 August 1946, p 3.

4    ibid.

5    Sang, Mickaël Ho Foui, 'Justice Bernard: France', *Beyond Victor's Justice: The Tokyo War Crimes Trial Reconsidered*, ed. Tanaka, Yuki; McCormack, Tim; Simpson, Gerry, Martins Nijhoff Publishers, 2011, Netherlands.

6    Röling & Cassese, op. cit., 1993, p 28.

7    ibid.

8    'Tojo Splendid in Incident at War Trial', *Courier-Mail*, 4 May 1946, p 1; IMTFE transcript, ed. Pritchard, R. John & Zaide, Sonia, Garland Publishing, 1981, vol. 1, pp 20–22.

9    Trotter, op. cit., p 147.

10   Chang, Iris, *The Rape of Nanking: The Forgotten Holocaust of World War II*, Basic Books, United States, 1997, p 27.

11   'Tojo Splendid In Incident At War Trial', *Courier-Mail*, 4 May 1946, p 1.

12   Röling, for example, was convinced Ōkawa was feigning madness. Röling & Cassese, op. cit., p 35.

13   'War Crimes Road Show', *Time* magazine, 20 May 1946.

14   Cited from http://www.armenian-genocide.org/Affirmation.160/current_category.7/affirmation_detail.html

15   Bryant, Michael, *A World History of War Crimes: From Antiquity to the Present Day*, Bloomsbury, United Kingdom, 2015, p 137.

16   http://avalon.law.yale.edu/wwii/moscow.asp

17   http://avalon.law.yale.edu/wwii/cairo.asp

18   Wilson, Cribb, et al., op. cit., p 17.

19   London Agreement (http://avalon.law.yale.edu/imt/imtchart.asp), and Nuremberg Charter (http://avalon.law.yale.edu/imt/imtconst.asp)

20   Sellars, Kirsten, *Crimes Against Peace and International Law*, Cambridge University Press, United Kingdom, 2013, p 178.

21   IMTFE vol. 112, Conference in Chambers, 24 June 1947, cited in Sellars, *Crimes Against Peace ~*, op. cit., p 188.

22   IMTFE, vol. 20, pp 49, 772.

23   Keenan, Joseph, 'Trial of Far Eastern War Criminals', *Department of State Bulletin 14* (1946) 847, cited in Sellars, *Crimes Against Peace ~*, op. cit., p 201.

24   Röling & Cassese, op. cit., p 38.

25   ibid., p 52.

26   Ramseyer, J. Mark & Rasmusen, Eric, B. *Why is the Japanese conviction rate so high?* 12 July 2000, at http://www.rasmusen.org/published/Rasmusen-01.JLS.jpncon.pdf

27   Trotter, Ann, 'Justice Northcroft: New Zealand' in Tanaka, McCormack, et. al. p 82.

28   Sellars, *Crimes Against Peace ~*, op. cit., p 236.

29   Patrick to Normand, *c.* January 1947, 3: LCO 2/2992, 2 TNA;
     Northcroft to O'Leary, 18 March 1947, 3: Box 1, AAOM 7130 W4676,
     NANZ, cited in Sellars, *Crimes Against Peace ~*, op. cit., p 236.

30   Röling & Cassese, op. cit., p 65.

31   Sellars, *Crimes Against Peace ~*, op. cit., p 235.

32   Röling & Cassese, op. cit., p 30.

33   Totani, op. cit., p 34.

34   Röling & Cassese, op. cit., p 31.

35   Totani, op. cit., p 34.

36   J. Keenan to C. Keenan, 4 November 1947, 4: Doc 752, Box 2,
     Keenan papers, HLS, cited in Sellars, *Crimes Against Peace ~*, op. cit.,
     p 187.

## CHAPTER VI

1    IMTFE, vol. 1, p 28.

2    Comyns Carr to Shawcross, 19 March 1946, FO 371/57427, TNA, cited
     in Sellars, *Crimes Against Peace ~*, op. cit., p 191.

3    IMTFE, vol. 17, pp 42, 394.

4    IMTFE, vol. 17, pp 42, 391–92.

5    Keenan, Joseph B. & Brown, Brendan F., *Crimes Against International
     Law*, Public Affairs Press, United States, 1951, p 157.

6    Wilson, Cribb, et al., op. cit., p 12.

7    Benesch, Oleg, *Inventing the Way of the Samurai: Nationalism,
     Internationalism and Bushidō*, Oxford University Press, United
     Kingdom, 2014.

8    Durschmied, Erik, *Blood of Revolution: From the Reign of Terror to the
     Rise of Khomeini*, Arcade Publishing, United States, 2002, p 254.

9    Kawakami, Kiyoshi Kari, *Japan and World Peace*, The Macmillan
     Company, United States, 1919, pp 45–62, cited from http://www.shsu.
     edu/~his_ncp/Kawa1.html

10   Brendon, op. cit., pp 202–203.

11   ibid., p 202.

12   Benesch, op. cit., p 177.

13    ibid., p 196.

14    Brendon, op. cit., p 218.

15    'General Apathy at Tokyo Trial', *The Argus*, 29 June 1946, p 7.

16    Totani, op. cit., pp 37–38.

17    IMTFE, vol. 13, pp 31, 331.

18    'Tojo Accepts Blame For Japan's Actions During War', *Sydney Morning Herald*, 27 December 1947, p 1.

19    Statement by Tōjō Hideki, p 201.

20    IMTFE, vol. 15, pp 36, 251.

21    Totani, op. cit., p 39.

22    Röling & Cassese, op. cit., p 37.

23    Totani, op. cit., p 39.

24    ibid.

## CHAPTER VII

1     Quilliam to Prime Minister, 'Report on the Proceedings...', 29 January 1948, 50: EA2 1948/36B 106/3/22 Part 7, NANZ, cited in Sellars, *Crimes Against Peace ~*, op. cit., p 189.

2     Brendon, op. cit., p 212.

3     ibid., p 636.

4     ibid., p 635.

5     ibid., p 660.

6     Wyzanski, op. cit.

7     IMTFE, vol. 10, p 21,075; p 23,751.

8     IMTFE, vol. 9, p 20,479.

9     IMTFE vol. 9, pp 20,480–20,481.

10    IMTFE, vol. 9, p 20,081.

11    IMTFE, vol. 17, p 43,161.

12    IMTFE, vol. 17, p 43,051.

13    Quilliam to Prime Minister, 'Report on the proceedings...', 29 January 1948, EA2 1948/36B 106/3/22 Part 7: 29/1/48, NANZ, cited in Sellars *Crimes Against Peace ~*, op. cit., p 221.

14    ibid., p 222.

## CHAPTER VIII

1    Wyzanski, op. cit.

2    Bryant, op. cit., p 2.

3    ibid., pp 2–4.

4    Wyzanski, op. cit.

5    Wilson, 'After the Trials', op. cit., p 142.

6    Chang, op. cit., pp 56–57.

7    *Emperor Hirohito*, 2005 BBC Discovery Channel Co-Production.

8    Chang, op. cit., pp 100–101.

9    Cited from https://thenankingmassacre.org/2015/07/04/reference-the-
     new-york-times-article-9-january-1938/

10   Chang, op. cit., p 51.

11   Brendon, op. cit., 462.

12   IMTFE, vol. 20, pp 48, 668.

13   Chang, op. cit., p 150.

14   IMTFE Doc 1735, available at http://uvallsc.s3.amazonaws.com/imtfe/
     s3fs-public/29835.jpg

15   IMTFE, vol. 2, 2595, available at http://imtfe.law.virginia.edu/
     collections/sutton/7/27/statement-hsu-chuan-ying-nanking

16   Totani, op. cit., p 130.

17   ibid.

18   IMTFE, vol. 16, pp 40, 111.

19   IMTFE, vol. 7, pp 16, 132.

20   Gilfedder, Deirdre, 'Decolonisation in South-East Asia', *British
     Decolonisation 1918–1984*, ed. Davis, Richard, Cambridge Scholars
     Publishing, United Kingdom, 2013, p 67.

21   Lone, Stewart, *Japan's First Modern War: Army and Society in the
     Conflict with China, 1894–1895*, Macmillan, United Kingdom, 1994,
     p 145.

22   Senatore, Holly E., 'Bushido: The Valor of Deceit', paper delivered at
     Convention of the International Society for Military Ethics, 1 January
     2010. Senatore gives the number of prisoners as 1,795.

23   Lone, op. cit., p 143.

24  Sibley, N.W. & Smith, F.E., *International Law as Interpreted During the Russo-Japanese War*, T. Fisher Unwin & William Blackwood and Sons, United Kingdom, 1905.

25  Towle, Philip A., 'Japanese Treatment of Prisoners in 1904–1905 – Foreign Officers' Reports', *Military Affairs*, vol. 39, no. 3, October 1975, pp 115–118; Hickman, John, 'Explaining the Interbellum Rupture in Japanese Treatment of Prisoners of War', *Journal of Military and Strategic Studies*, vol. 12, issue 1, Fall 2009, pp 1–20.

26  Kowner, Rotem, 'Remaking Japan's Military Image During the Russo-Japanese War, 1904–1905', *The Historian*, vol. 64, issue 1, September 2001, p 31.

27  ibid., p 34.

28  Benesch, op. cit., pp 107–109.

29  Strauss, Ulrich, *The Anguish of Surrender: Japanese POWs of World War II*, 2003, University of Washington Press, United States, p 20.

30  Dower, *War Without Mercy*, op. cit., p 22.

31  Dower, *Embracing Defeat*, op. cit., p 277.

32  Strauss, op. cit., pp 38–39.

33  ibid.

34  Williamette University, http://www.willamette.edu/~rloftus/ H381WaySubjects.html

35  Dower, *War Without Mercy*, op. cit., p 205.

36  Totani, Yuma, *Justice in the Asia-Pacific Region 1945–1952: Allied War Crimes Prosecutions*, Cambridge University Press, United States, 2015, p 67.

37  Bix, op. cit., p 466.

38  Bullard, op. cit., p 56.

39  Totani, *Justice in the Asia-Pacific ~*, op. cit., p 69.

40  ibid., pp 142–143.

## CHAPTER IX

1  Sang, op. cit., p 96.

2  Röling & Cassese, op. cit., p 30.

3    Gascoigne to FO, 11 November 1947, FO 371/63820, TNA, cited in
     Sellars, *Crimes Against Peace ~*, op. cit., p 242.

4    Northcroft to O'Leary (second letter), 10 November 1947, Box 1,
     AAOM 7130 W4676, NANZ.

5    Trotter, 'Justice Northcroft', op. cit., pp 90–91.

6    IMTFE, vol. 20, pp 49, 669, 770.

7    Minear, Richard H., *Victor's Justice: The Tokyo War Crimes Trial*,
     Princeton University Press, United States, 1971, p 135.

8    http://avalon.law.yale.edu/imt/judlawco.asp

9    Transcript of the IMT, p 444.

10   ibid., p 445.

11   IMTFE, vol. 20, pp 48, 439.

12   IMTFE, vol. 20, pp 49, 826.

13   IMTFE, vol. 20, pp 49, 821.

14   Prosecutor v Jean-Paul Akayesu, case number ICTR 96-4, 2 September
     1998.

15   IMTFE, vol. 20, pp 49, 820.

16   IMTFE, vol. 20, pp 49, 845.

17   IMTFE, vol. 20, pp 49, 846.

18   IMTFE, vol. 20, pp 49, 831.

19   'How The Japanese Took Sentences', *The Argus,* 13 November 1948, p 5.

20   ibid.

21   Röling & Cassese, op. cit., p 45.

22   Concurring judgement of Justice Webb, p 17.

23   ibid., p 18.

24   ibid., pp 19–20.

25   Sellars, *Crimes Against Peace ~*, op. cit., p 255.

26   Concurring judgement of Justice Jaranilla, p 34.

27   Dissenting judgement of Justice Röling, p 8.

28   Röling & Cassese, op. cit., p 67–70.

29   Dissenting judgement of Justice Bernard, p 15.

30   ibid., p 18.

31   ibid., p 19.

32    Dower, *Embracing Defeat*, op. cit., p 460.

33    Dissentient judgement of Justice Pal, Kokusho-Kankokai Inc, 1999, pp 116–117.

34    ibid., p 10.

35    ibid., p 572.

36    ibid., p 461.

37    ibid., p 620.

38    ibid., p 607.

39    ibid., p 595.

40    ibid., p 634.

41    ibid., at p 621.

42    ibid., p 697.

43    'Tojo: Last words', *Courier-Mail*, 20 November 1948, p 1.

44    'Tojo's Plea For Peace', *Sydney Morning Herald*, 3 December 1948, p 3.

45    Hoyt, op. cit., p 1.

46    ibid., p 2.

## CHAPTER X

1    Dower, *Embracing Defeat*, op. cit., p 449.

2    There remains uncertainty on the exact numbers – these are from David Sissons in 'Sources on Australian Investigations into Japanese War Crimes in the Pacific', *Journal of the Australian War Memorial*, Issue 30, April 1997, available at https://www.awm.gov.au/journal/j30/sissons.asp. The original data gives 296 trials of 924 defendants. However, Sissons notes that one trial at Labuan was entered twice in error and some defendants were tried in more than one trial. In a speech to the House of Representatives on 5 September 1957, Prime Minister Robert Menzies gave the following numbers: 644 convicted, 148 executed, and 496 sentenced to imprisonment. In my view, Sissons' numbers are more likely to be accurate. See also Okada, Emmi, 'The Australian Trials of Class B and C Japanese War Crime Suspects, 1945–51', *Australian International Law Journal*, 2009, vol. 4, pp 47–80, available at http://www.austlii.edu.au/au/journals/AUIntLawJl/2009/4.pdf, p 50, at footnote 13.

3    Sissons, op. cit., p 20.

4    House of Representatives Hansard, 12 September 1945 (Norman Makin).

5    'Japanese Savagery Must Be Punished', *The Age*, 11 September 1945, p 2.

6    House of Representatives Hansard, 18 September 1945.

7    'Justice on War Criminals', *The Argus*, 15 September 1945, p 9.

8    For a full discussion on jurisdictional issues, refer McCormack, Tim,
     'Jurisdiction of the Australian Military Courts 1945–51', Fitzpatrick,
     McCormack, et al., pp 61–102.

9    Senate Hansard, 4 October 1945.

10   ibid.

11   Sissons, op. cit., p 16.

12   ibid.

13   Cribb, Robert, 'Avoiding Clemency: The Trial and Transfer of Japanese
     War Criminals in Indonesia, 1946–1949', *Japanese Studies*, vol. 31, no. 2,
     September 2011, p 161.

14   Lennan, Jo & Williams, George, 'The Death Penalty in Australian Law',
     *Sydney Law Review*, vol. 34, no. 2, 2012, pp 659–694.

15   Sissons, op. cit., p 16.

16   ibid.

17   House of Representatives Hansard, 4 October 1945.

18   Morris, Narrelle, 'The Australian War Criminals Compounds at Rabaul
     and on Manus Island, 1945–53', Fitzpatrick, McCormack, et al., op. cit.,
     pp 695–697.

19   House of Representatives Hansard, 21 September 1945.

20   Sissons, op. cit., p 17.

21   ibid., p 22.

22   ibid., p 19.

## CHAPTER XI

1    Ooi, Keat Gin, *The Japanese Occupation of Borneo, 1941–45*, 2010, Taylor
     & Francis, United States, p 39.

2    Fitzpatrick, Georgina, 'The Trials at Labuan', Fitzpatrick, McCormack,
     et al., op. cit., p 439.

3   'Jap Criminals Hanged for Borneo Horror', *The Newcastle Sun*, 6 April 1946, p 1.

4   Trial ML28, A471 80777 parts 1 and 2.

5   Moffitt, Athol, *Project Kingfisher*, ABC Books, Australia, 1995, p 55.

6   'Arrogant Jap Charged With Mass Slaughter', *Daily Mercury*, 11 January 1946, p 2; 'Arrogant Jap Captain on Trial', *Morning Bulletin*, 11 January 1946, p 1.

7   Moffitt, op. cit., p 73.

8   ibid. He was charged with: 1. He permitted POWs to be closely confined and beaten, leading to at least one dying, 2. He authorised and permitted POWs to be tortured and beaten by soldiers under his command, 3. He failed to provide food and medical care, 4. He forced sick POWs to undertake manual labour.

9   Transcript, part 1, p 88.

10   'Freed from Borneo Prison Camp', *Newcastle Morning Herald and Miners' Advocate*, 31 August 1945, p 5.

11   Moffitt, op. cit., p 72.

12   Transcript, part 1, p 101, minor errors corrected.

13   Part 1, p 93.

14   ibid., p 25.

15   ibid., pp 125–126.

16   ibid., p 18.

17   ibid., p 19.

18   ibid., p 23.

19   ibid., p 158.

20   Part 2, p 56.

21   Part 1, p 14.

22   ibid., p 18.

23   M18 transcript, A471 80772.

24   Moffitt, op. cit., p 1.

25   His statements can be read at pp 94–97 of transcript of M18.

26   Transcript of Hoshijima's trial, ML28, part 2, p 68.

27   Morris, Narrelle & McCormack, Tim, 'Were the Australian Trials Fair?',
     Fitzpatrick, McCormack, et al., op. cit., p 796.

28   Transcript of M18, p 110.

29   ibid., p 117.

30   ibid., p 90.

31   ibid., p 115.

32   ibid.

33   ibid., p 69.

34   ibid., p 89.

35   ibid., p 130.

36   ibid., p 91.

37   ibid., p 129.

38   ibid.

39   ibid., p 10.

40   ibid., p 13.

41   ibid., p 89.

42   ibid., p 9.

43   ibid., p 21.

44   ibid., p 6.

45   Moffitt, op. cit., p 13.

46   'Japanese Needed Drugs On Scaffold Steps', *Sydney Morning Herald*,
     21 March 1946, p 3.

47   Fitzpatrick, 'Death Sentences, War Criminals ~' op. cit., p 345.

48   'Jap Criminals Hanged for Borneo Horror', *Newcastle Sun*, 6 April
     1946, p 1; 'Japs Hanged for Borneo Horror', *The Sun*, 6 April 1946, p 1;
     'Executed for Death March', *The Age*, 8 April 1946, p 3.

## CHAPTER XII

1   'Massacre by Japanese', *Sydney Morning Herald*, 10 April 1942, p 7.

2   'How Imamura Kept Fit', *The Examiner*, 10 October 1945, p 1.

3   'Prisoners' Hell at Rabaul', *Cairns Post*, 10 September 1945, p 1.

4   ibid.

5   'Rabaul Japs Run to Bow & Scrape', *The Telegraph*, 21 September 1945, p 3.

6   'Aussies Were Toughest in Dealing With Japs', *Truth*, 11 November 1945, p 8; 'AIF Tougher Than Yanks When Dealing With Japs', *Evening Advocate*, 12 November 1945, p 4.

7   'Japs Work 12-Hour Day Building Compounds' in *The Sun*, 13 November 1945, p 7.

8   Fitzpatrick, Georgina, 'The Trials at Rabaul', Fitzpatrick, McCormack, et al., p 513.

9   Fitzpatrick, 'Death Sentences, War Criminals ~', op. cit., p 341.

10  ibid.

11  Fitzpatrick, 'The Trials at Rabaul', op. cit., p 513.

12  R1 transcript, NAA A471 80747.

13  'Jap Hanged For Raping Chinese', *Courier-Mail*, 20 April 1946, p 5.

14  R1 transcript, p 16.

15  ibid., p 18.

16  Sissons, op. cit., p 44.

17  'Jap Dies a Cringing Coward', *Townsville Daily Bulletin*, 20 April 1946, p 1.

18  R51 transcript, NAA A471 80796.

19  The testimony starts in the R51 transcript at p 32 and is repeated in the others.

20  ibid., p 33.

21  ibid., p 50.

22  ibid., p 51.

23  ibid.

24  ibid., p 25.

25  ibid., p 52.

26  ibid., p 28.

27  ibid., p 29.

28  ibid.

29  R53 transcript, NAA A471 80798, p 64.

30  ibid., p 24.

31  ibid., p 25.

32  R70 transcript, NAA A471 80983, p 72.

## CHAPTER XIII

1   Fitzpatrick, 'The Trials at Rabaul', op. cit., p 562.

2   ibid., p 550.

3   ibid., p 552.

4   'Japanese Officers Live High at Rabaul', *The Age*, 23 March 1946, p 1;
    'Jap Officers in Luxury, Australians Rough It', *The Sun*, 22 March 1946,
    p 3; 'No Action Indicated on Japs' Luxurious Housing', *The Telegraph*,
    23 March 1946, p 3; "Prison Paradise' For Japanese Officers', *Sydney
    Morning Herald*, 23 March 1946, p 1.

5   'Jap Generals to Lose Fowls, Goats – Army Acts', *The Sun*, 24 March
    1946, p 2.

6   'Luxury at End for Jap General', *The Mail*, 4 May 1946, p 5.

7   'Jap general tried to suicide', *The Sun*, 30 March 1947, p 10.

8   Fitzpatrick, 'The Trials at Rabaul', op. cit., p 525.

9   ibid., p 528.

10  ibid., p 529.

11  'Jap General's Plea for Men', *Courier-Mail*, 11 April 1946, p 4.

12  'Japanese General Accepts Blame in Trial of Colleague', *Daily Advertiser*,
    29 March 1947, p 5.

13  ibid.

14  R175 transcript, NAA A471 81635 PART A–E.

15  ibid., p 37.

16  ibid., p 40.

17  ibid., p 41.

18  ibid., pp 75–76

19  ibid., p 125.

20  This was R90. Ikeba was also convicted in R86 and R87, and hanged
    pursuant to a warrant issued for R87.

21  ibid., p 86.

22  ibid., p 71.

23  ibid., p 116.

24  ibid., p 114.

25  Fitzpatrick, 'The Trials at Rabaul', op. cit., p 555.

26   ibid.

27   ibid.

28   General Imamura to HRH the Duke of Gloucester, Governor-General, 23 July 1946, NAA: MP742/1, 336/1/1205, cited in Fitzpatrick, 'The Trials at Rabaul', op. cit., p 554.

29   Morris, 'The Australian War Criminals Compounds ~', p 720.

30   Fitzpatrick, 'The Trials at Rabaul', op. cit., p 557.

31   Morris, 'The Australian War Criminals Compounds ~', op. cit., p 720.

32   ibid.

33   'Indian Officer in Fear of Jap Prisoners', *Examiner*, 25 March 1947, p 1.

34   Morris, op. cit., p 720.

35   ibid., p 721.

36   ibid., pp 722–723

37   'Jap Criminals Have Easy Time at Rabaul', *The Argus*, 8 June 1948, p 4.

38   Fitzpatrick, 'Death Sentences, War Criminals ~', op. cit., pp 352–353.

39   Pages 98–99 of 'Report on Visit to Papua New Guinea by Acting Minister for External Territories (The Honourable Cyril Chambers), 11–22 January 1949', NAA: A518, C16/2/6.

## CHAPTER XIV

1    Tennenbaum, Joseph, 'Auschwitz in Retrospect: The Self-Portrait of Rudolf Hoess', *Jewish Social Studies*, vol. 15, nos. 3–4, 1953, p 235.

2    'Tojo: Last words', *Courier-Mail*, 20 November 1948, p 1.

3    Aiko & Udagawa, op. cit., pp 766, 776.

4    ibid., p 767.

5    ibid., p 762. Shiraki's trial was R36; his statement is in the 1953 edition of *Testament of the Century*, p 493.

6    ibid., p 767.

7    ibid., p 768. Originally from the questionnaire for Australia.

8    'Japanese Bowed When Acquitted', *The Age*, 17 November 1950, p 9.

9    Aiko & Udagawa, op. cit., p 769.

10   Aiko & Udagawa, op. cit., p 773.

11    The Japanese Who Have Left Manus Are Still Unrepentant War
      Criminals', *Sunday Herald*, 2 August 1953, p 9.

12    Aiko & Udagawa, op. cit., p 763. Shirozu's trial was M41; his statement
      is in *Testament of the Century*, p 506.

13    Aiko & Udagawa, Kōta, op. cit., p 762. Morimoto's trial was M32; his
      statement is in *Testament of the Century*, pp 489–490.

14    Herman, op. cit., pp 701–702.

15    Dower, *War Without Mercy*, op. cit., pp 505–506.

16    ibid., p 505.

17    ibid., p 507.

18    Futamura, Madoka, 'Japanese Societal Attitudes Towards the Tokyo
      Trial: A Contemporary Perspective', in *The Asia-Pacific Journal:
      Japan Focus*, vol. 9, issue 29, no. 5, 19 July 2011, at http://apjjf.
      org/2011/9/29/Madoka-Futamura/3569/article.html

19    Aiko, Utsumi, *Journal of the Australian War Memorial*, issue 30, April
      1997, at https://www.awm.gov.au/articles/journal/j30/utsumi, citing
      *Kyokuto kokusai gunji saiban kenkyu*, vol. 1, Heiwa Shobo, 1947,
      pp 4–5.

20    ibid.

21    ibid.

22    Futamura, op. cit.

23    Dower, *Embracing Defeat*, op. cit., p 508.

24    'Letters to the Editor', *News*, 5 February 1946, p 2.

25    'War Criminals', *West Australian*, 15 May 1946, p 12.

26    D1, NAA A471 80708.

27    Transcript, p 1.

28    'Japs Dazed by Court's Verdict: Six Acquittals at Darwin Trial', *The
      Argus*, 16 March 1946, p 4.

29    House of Representatives Hansard, 20 March 1946.

30    'Demands for Sterner Darwin Trials', *Sydney Morning Herald*, 18 March
      1946, p 3.

31    ibid.

32    ibid.

33   'The Darwin Sentences', *Sydney Morning Herald*, 19 March 1946,
     p 2.

34   'Letters to the Editor', *News*, 18 March 1942, p 2.

35   Wilson, Sandra, 'War Criminals in the Post-war World: The Case of
     Katō Tetsutarō', *War in History*, vol. 22, no. 1, 2015, p 103.

36   Rix, op. cit., p 18.

37   Wood, op. cit., p 51.

38   ibid.

39   'Time to Close War Crimes Accounts', *Sydney Morning Herald*, 16 June
     1948, p 2.

40   'Japanese Leaders Freed; No Trial', *Sydney Morning Herald*, 27 December
     1948, p 3.

41   Aszkielowicz, op. cit., p 216.

42   'Australian Bungling of War Trials', *Sydney Morning Herald*, 5 December
     1949, p 2.

43   Sissons, op. cit., p 21.

44   House of Representatives Hansard, 30 June 1949.

45   Caiger, George, 'Behind The Japanese Plea of "Self-defence"', *Sydney
     Morning Herald*, 21 May 1946, p 2.

46   Caiger, 'The Japanese Misunderstand War Guilt Trials', op. cit., p 2.
     For a press account of Rear Admiral Hamanaka's trial, refer to 'Jap
     Rear-Admiral Sentenced to Death', *Canberra Times*, 16 January 1946,
     p 1.

47   House of Representatives Hansard, 16 March 1950.

48   Wood, op. cit., p 65.

## CHAPTER XV

1    Duffy, Christopher, *Red Storm on the Reich: The Soviet March on
     Germany, 1945*, Atheneum, Maxwell Macmillan International, United
     States, 1991; Kershaw, Ian, *The End: Germany 1944–1945*, Penguin,
     United Kingdom, 2011.

2    Nuremberg Trial Proceedings vol. 22, 31 August 1946, morning session,
     at http://avalon.law.yale.edu/imt/08-31-46.asp

3      Dower, *Embracing Defeat*, op. cit., pp 51–52; Dähler, Richard, 'The Japanese Prisoners of War in Siberia 1945–1956', *Internationales Asienforum*, vol. 34, no. 3–4, 2003, pp 285–302; Ito, Masami, 'Surviving the Postwar Soviet Detention Camps', *Japan Times*, 22 August 2015, at http://www.japantimes.co.jp/news/2015/08/22/national/history/surviving-postwar-soviet-detention-camps/#.WWmKOelLfIU

4      From the Harry S. Truman Library at https://www.trumanlibrary.org/publicpapers/?pid=104

5      Dissenting judgement of Justice Pal, op. cit., pp 66–67.

6      Nuremberg Trial Proceedings, op. cit.

7      Gómez, Javier Guisández ,'The Law of Air Warfare', *International Review of the Red Cross* no. 323, 30 June 1998, at https://www.icrc.org/eng/resources/documents/article/other/57jpcl.htm

8      Danen, Gene, *International Law on the Bombing of Civilians,* at http://www.dannen.com/decision/int-law.html

9      ibid.

10     http://www.nationalarchives.gov.uk/education/heroesvillains/transcript/g1cs3s2t.htm

11     'The Japanese Who Have Left Manus Are Still Unrepentant War Criminals', *Sunday Herald*, 2 August 1953, p 9.

12     Wilson, Cribb, et al., op. cit., p 273.

13     Ham, op. cit., p 529.

14     Dower, John W., *War Without Mercy*, op. cit., p 63.

15     ibid., p 33.

16     ibid., p 71.

17     Ham, op. cit., p 526.

18     Wood, op. cit., p 65.

19     Strauss, Ulrich, *The Anguish of Surrender: Japanese POWs of World War II*, 2003, University of Washington Press, United States, ix.

20     Ham, op. cit., p 529.

21     Svoboda, Terese, 'U.S. Courts-Martial in Occupation Japan: Rape, Race, and Censorship', *The Asia-Pacific Journal*, vol. 7, issue 21, no. 1, 23 May, 2009.

22  Tanaka, Yuki & Tanaka, Toshiyuki, *Japan's Comfort Women: Sexual Slavery and Prostitution During World War II*, 2003, Routledge, p 126.

23  Gerster, Robin, *Travels in Atomic Sunshine: Australia and the Occupation of Japan*, Scribe, Australia, 2008, pp 112–118.

24  Tanaka & Tanaka, op. cit., pp 126–127.

25  Wood, op. cit., pp 30–31.

26  Tanaka & Tanaka, op. cit., p 127.

## CHAPTER XVI

1   Morris, op. cit., p 709.

2   House of Representatives Hansard, 23 February 1950 (Robert Menzies).

3   ibid., 16 March 1950 (Larry Anthony).

4   'War Trials to be Speeded Up', *The Age*, 12 January 1950, p 1.

5   House of Representatives Hansard, 23 February 1950.

6   ibid., 16 March 1950.

7   ibid.

8   See for example AWM S03304 for the interview; his speech at the launch of *Australia's War Crimes Trials 1945–51*, 29 November 2016, at https://www.awm.gov.au/commemoration/speeches/australias-war-crimes-trials

9   Fitzpatrick, Georgina, 'The Trials on Manus Island', Fitzpatrick, McCormack, et al., pp 668, 678.

10  ibid., p 675.

11  'In All His Splendour', *Sydney Morning Herald*, 15 June 1950, p 3.

12  'General's Evidence', *The Age*, 16 June 1950, p 4.

13  ibid., p 671.

14  For Nishimura, NAA A471, 81942, Manus Island Trial LN2; for Tsuaki, NAA A471, 81967, Manus Island Trial LN24.

15  Different sources give different numbers; these are approximate figures.

16  Hackney's evidence is also summarised in 'Brutal Treatment', *The Age*, 20 June 1950, p 4.

17  Transcript NAA A471, 81942, p 6.

18    ibid., pp 6–7.

19    ibid., p 10.

20    ibid., pp 9, 15.

21    ibid., pp 17–18.

22    Nishimura's conviction has remained controversial for other reasons. In *Snaring the Other Tiger*, Ian Ward suggests Nishimura was convicted wrongly, but on further analysis it seems likely that the document he relied on was fabricated. Refer to Fitzpatrick, 'The Trials on Manus Island', in Fitzpatrick, McCormack, op. cit., p 682.

23    'General to Hang', *Sydney Morning Herald*, 23 June 1950, p 3.

24    NAA A471, 81967, Manus Island Trial LN24.

25    Transcript, p 474.

26    ibid., p 475.

27    ibid., p 476.

28    ibid.

29    '"Frenzy of revenge" at Ambon', *Courier-Mail*, 10 March 1950, p 1.

30    Transcript, p 541.

31    ibid., p 544.

32    ibid., p 282.

33    ibid., p 290.

34    'Ambon Massacre: Jap. Sentenced to Death; Another to Life in Gaol', *Warwick Daily News*, 20 March 1951, p 1.

35    Transcript, pp 5–8.

36    ibid., p 24.

37    ibid., pp 31, 36.

38    'Trials Conclude at Los Negros', *Sydney Morning Herald*, 10 April 1951, p 3; Australian War Court Winds Up – Japanese Extol our Fairness in War Trials', *The Argus*, 10 April 1951, p 5.

39    Fitzpatrick, 'The Trials on Manus Island', op. cit., p 671.

40    House of Representatives Hansard, 6 June 1950, Kim Beazley Sr.

41    Fitzpatrick, 'Death Sentences, War Criminals –', op. cit., p 362.

42    Aiko & Udagawa, op. cit., p 769.

43    ibid., p 769, quoting *Testament of the Century*, p 515.

44 'Manus Hangings To-day', *Sydney Morning Herald*, 11 June 1951, p 1.

45 'Five Japanese War Criminals Executed', *Queensland Times,* 12 June 1951, p 1.

46 Fitzpatrick, 'Death Sentences, War Criminals ~' op. cit., p 362.

47 Morris, 'The Australian War Criminals Compounds ~' op. cit., p 721.

48 ibid., p 731.

49 ibid., pp 721–729.

50 NAA: MP375/13, quoted in Morris, 'The Australian War Criminals Compounds ~', op. cit., p 720.

51 'Less Work, More Luxury for Jap War Criminals', *Sydney Morning Herald*, 20 November 1951, p 2; Underwood, Alan, 'War Criminals Get the "Soft" Treatment', *Courier-Mail*, 20 November 1951, p 2; Underwood, Alan, 'Japanese War Criminals "Taking It Easy"' *The Advertiser* (Adelaide) 20 November 1951, p 2.

52 ibid.

53 The Japanese Who Have Left Manus Are Still Unrepentant War Criminals', *Sunday Herald*, 2 August 1953, p 9.

## CHAPTER XVII

1 'Japan "Has Duty To Rearm"', *Sydney Morning Herald*, 14 December 1951, p 3.

2 House of Representatives Hansard, 22 February 1952.

3 'Gen. Gordon Bennett lands', *The Argus*, 22 February 1952, p 5.

4 Rix, op. cit., p 97.

5 Wood, op. cit., p 67.

6 Wilson, 'Prisoners in Sugamo ~', op. cit., pp 171–174.

7 Wilson, 'War Criminals in the Post-war World ~', op. cit., pp 87–110.

8 For an analysis of Katō's writing, refer to Wilson, Sandra, 'War, Soldier and Nation in 1950s Japan', *International Journal of Asian Studies*, vol. 5, no. 2, 2008, pp 187–218, at pp 198–200.

9 Wilson, 'War Criminals in the Post-war World ~' op. cit., p 107.

10 Wilson, 'War, Soldier and Nation ~', op. cit., p 204.

11    Schilling, Mark, '"Watashi wa Kai ni Naritai": Making a case for a "war criminal"', *Japan Times*, 21 November 2008.

12    Trefalt, Beatrice 'Hostages to International Relations? The Repatriation of Japanese War Criminals from the Philippines', Japanese Studies, Volume 31, Number 2, September 2011, pp 191–211, p 203.

13    Wilson, 'After the Trials ~', op. cit., p 144.

14    Wilson, 'Prisoners in Sugamo ~', op. cit., p 172.

15    Cribb, op. cit., pp 165–169.

16    Wilson, 'After the Trials ~' op. cit., p 144.

17    IMTFE, vol. 20, pp 49, 643.

18    Trefalt, op. cit., p 191.

19    ibid., p 200.

20    ibid., p 205.

21    Aszkielowicz, op. cit., p 219.

22    Morris, 'The Australian War Criminals Compounds ~' op. cit., p 729.

23    ibid., p 730.

24    Wilson, 'After the Trials ~', op. cit., p 141.

25    Senate Hansard, September 1955 (Senator Spicer).

26    Rix, op. cit., pp 11–12.

27    Wilson, 'War Criminals in the Post-war World ~', op. cit., p 107.

28    House of Representatives Hansard, 5 September 1957 (Prime Minister).

29    'Digger Raises Japanese Olympic Flag', *Canberra Times*, 31 October 1956, p 16.

30    Rix, op. cit., p 14.

31    ibid., p 13.

32    Aszkielowicz, op. cit., p 226.

33    House of Representatives Hansard, 5 September 1957 (Prime Minister).

34    ibid., 11 September 1957.

35    ibid.

36    Wilson, 'War Criminals in the Post-war World ~', op. cit., p 108.

37    Aszkielowicz, op. cit., p 226.

38    Wilson, 'War Criminals in the Post-war World ~' op. cit., p 108.

## CONCLUSION

1     Sissons, David, 'The Trials: Were They Justice or Vengeance?', *Sydney Morning Herald*, 26 August 1985, p 9.

2     Sellars, *Crimes Against Peace ~*, op. cit., p 257.

3     Röling & Cassese, op. cit., p 88.

4     For example, Hahn, Elliott J., 'An Overview of the Japanese Legal System', *New Journal of International Law and Business*, no. 5, 1984, pp 517–539; Luney, Percy J. Jr, 'Traditions and Foreign Influences: Systems of Law in China and Japan', *Law and Contemporary Problems*, vol. 52, no. 2, 1989, pp 129–150.

5     'The Japanese Parents who Apologise for their Children', *BBC*, 31 December 2016, http://www.bbc.com/news/world-asia-37480934

6     Dower, op. cit., p 345.

7     Bix, op. cit., p 17.

8     ibid., p 676.

9     Power, Julie & Sutton, Candace, 'Hirohito: Fury Over Funeral', *Sun-Herald*, 8 January 1989, p 1; Chira, Susan, 'Tokyo Funeral Forces Choice By Old Foes', *New York Times*, 13 January 1989; Slavin, Stewart, 'Attending Hirohito Funeral a Touchy Issue', *UPI News Feature*, 20 February 1989.

10    Bix, op. cit., p 685.

11    Sanger, David E., 'Mayor who Faulted Hirohito is Shot', *New York Times*, 19 January 1990.

12    Dower, op. cit., p 512.

13    Aiko & Udagawa, op. cit., p 775.

14    ibid., p 769.

15    Sellars, 'Imperfect Justice at Nuremberg and Tokyo', op. cit., p 1089.

16    Morris & McCormack, 'Were the Australian Trials Fair?' op. cit., pp 789–790.

17    ibid., pp 795–805.

18    Futamura, op. cit.

19    ibid.

20    Minear, op. cit.

21 ibid., p ix.

22 Sellars, 'Imperfect Justice at Nuremberg and Tokyo', op. cit., p 1093.

23 Blatt, Michael, 'Yushukan Museum Whitewashes Wartime Atrocities', *Shanghai Daily*, 16 January 2014.

24 Letter from Sir William Webb to Mr JDL Hood, 26 June 1945, NAA, A:1066, H45/580/6/2, cited in Morris & McCormack, 'Were the Australian Trials Fair?' op. cit., p 783.

25 Schabas, William, *Unimaginable Atrocities: Justice, Politics and Rights and the War Crimes Tribunals,* Oxford University Press, UK, 2012.

26 Sissons, 'The Trials: Were They Justice or Vengeance?' op. cit., cited in Okada, Emmi, 'The Australian Trials of Class B and C Japanese War Crime Suspects, 1945–51', *Australian International Law Journal*, vol. 4, 2009, pp 47–80, at http://www.austlii.edu.au/au/journals/AUIntLawJl/2009/4.pdf

27 Letter from Kobayashi Akira, S. Tamura, K. Kagiyama, F. Suzuki, M. Kudoh & Y. Kanehiro to J.M. Williams, Morotai, 1 March 1946, held in John Myles Williams Papers, box 3, folder 3, Mitchell Library, State Library of NSW, cited in Morris & McCormack, 'Were the Australian Trials Fair?' op. cit., p 783.

### APPENDIX B

1 Totani, *Justice in Asia and the Pacific ~*, op. cit., p 9.

2 Piccigallo, op. cit., p 95.

3 Cribb, op. cit., p 161.

4 ibid., p 164.

5 ibid., pp 160–161.

6 Piccigallo, op. cit., p 120.

7 See note 334 for details on the debate on the numbers.

8 Sissons, 'The Australian War Crimes Trials and Investigations', op. cit., p 20.

9 Piccigallo, op. cit., p 120.

10 Trefalt, op. cit., p 193.

11    Piccigallo, op. cit. p 208; Schoepfel, Ann Sophie, 'Justice and Decolonisation: War Crimes on Trial in Saigon', *War Crimes Trials in the Wake of Decolonization and Cold War in Asia, 1945–1956*, ed. Kerstin von Lingen, Palgrave Macmillan, Switzerland, 2016.

12    Cribb, op. cit., p 168.

13    Wilson, 'After the Trials ~', op. cit., pp 141–151.

14    Wilson, Cribb, et al., op cit.

15    ibid.

16    Wilson, 'War, Soldier and Nation ~', op. cit., pp 187–218.

17    ibid.

# BIBLIOGRAPHY

## BOOKS AND ARTICLES

Aiko, Utsumi and Kōta Udagawa, translated by Steven Bullard. 'The "Post-War" of the BC-Class War Criminals: How Did War Criminals React to the Australian Trials?' In *Australia's War Crimes Trials, 1945–51,* edited by Georgina Fitzpatrick, Tim McCormack and Narrelle Morris. Netherlands: Brill Nijhoff, 2016, pp 755–780.

Arbour, Louise. 'The Rule of Law and the Reach of Accountability'. In *The Rule of Law*, edited by Katherine Le Roy and Cheryl Saunders. Australia: The Federation Press, 2003, pp 104–135.

Aszkielowicz, Dean. 'Repatriation and the Limits of Resolve: Japanese War Criminals in Australian Custody'. In *Japanese Studies*, Volume 31, Number 2, September 2011, pp 211–229.

Bassiouni, M. Cherif. 'Perspectives on International Criminal Justice'. In *Virginia Journal of International Law*, Volume 50, Issue 2, 2010, pp 269–317.

Beasley, W.G. *The Meiji Restoration*. United States: Stanford University Press, 1973.

Benesch, Oleg. *Inventing the Way of the Samurai: Nationalism, Internationalism and Bushidō*. United Kingdom: Oxford University Press, 2014.

Bix, Herbert P. *Hirohito and the Making of Modern Japan*. United States: Harper Perennial, 2016 (first published 2000).

Bolton, G.C. 'Evatt, Herbert Vere (Bert) (1894–1965)'. In the *Australian Dictionary of Biography*, National Centre of Biography, Australian National University, 1996. Available at http://adb.anu.edu.au/biography/evatt-herbert-vere-bert-10131/text17885

Brendon, Piers. *The Dark Valley: A Panorama of the 1930s*. United States: Vintage Books, 2002.

Bryant, Michael. *A World History of War Crimes: From Antiquity to the Present Day*. United Kingdom: Bloomsbury, 2015.

Bullard, Stephen. 'The Emperor's Army: Military Operations and Ideology in the War Against Australia'. In *Australia's War Crimes Trials, 1945–51*, edited by Georgina Fitzpatrick, Tim McCormack and Narrelle Morris. Netherlands: Brill Nijhoff, 2016.

Chang, Iris. *The Rape of Nanking: The Forgotten Holocaust of World War II*. United States: Basic Books, 1997.

Cribb, Robert. 'Avoiding Clemency: The Trial and Transfer of Japanese War Criminals in Indonesia, 1946–1949'. In *Japanese Studies*, Volume 31, Number 2, September 2011, pp 151–171.

Carrel, Michael. 'Australia's Prosecution of Japanese War Criminals: Stimuli and Constraints'. In *The Legacy of Nuremberg: Civilising Influence Or Institutionalised Vengeance?*, edited by David A. Blumenthal and Timothy L. H. McCormack. Netherlands: Koninklije Brill, 2007, p 239–257.

Crowe, D. *War Crimes, Genocide, and Justice: A Global History*. United States: Palgrave Macmillan, 2014.

Dähler, Richard. 'The Japanese Prisoners of War in Siberia 1945–1956'. In *Internationales Asienforum*, Volume 34, Numbers 3–4, 2003, pp 285–302.

Danen, Gene. *International Law on the Bombing of Civilians*. Available at http://www.dannen.com/decision/int-law.html

Dower, John W. *War Without Mercy: Race and Power in the Pacific War*. United States: Faber & Faber, 1986.

—— *Embracing Defeat: Japan in the Aftermath of World War II*. United Kingdom: Penguin, 2000 (first published 1999).

Duffy, Christopher. *Red Storm on the Reich: The Soviet March on Germany, 1945*. United States: Atheneum, Maxwell Macmillan International, 1991.

Durschmied, Erik. *Blood of Revolution: From the Reign of Terror to the Rise of Khomeini*. United States: Arcade Publishing, 2002.

Fairbank, John K. 'Digging Out Doug'. In *The New York Review of Books*, 12 October 1978.

Fitzpatrick, Georgina. 'War Crimes Trials, "Victor's Justice" and Australian Military Justice in the Aftermath of the Second World War'. In *The Hidden Histories of War Crimes Trials*, edited by Kevin Jon Heller and Gerry Simpson. Oxford University Press, 2013, pp 327–247.

——'Death Sentences, War Criminals and the Australian Military'. In *Australia's War Crimes Trials, 1945–51*, edited by Georgina Fitzpatrick, Tim McCormack, and Narrelle Morris. Netherlands: Brill Nijhoff, 2016, pp 326–370.

——'The Trials at Rabaul'. In *Australia's War Crimes Trials, 1945–51*, edited by Georgina Fitzpatrick, Tim McCormack, and Narrelle Morris. Netherlands: Brill Nijhoff, 2016, pp 507–567.

Frank, Richard. *Downfall: The End of the Imperial Japanese Empire*. United States: Penguin, 1999.

Futamura, Madoka. 'Japanese Societal Attitudes Towards the Tokyo Trial: A Contemporary Perspective'. In *The Asia-Pacific Journal: Japan Focus*, Volume 9, Issue 29, Number 5, July 2011. Available at http://apjjf. org/2011/9/29/Madoka-Futamura/3569/article.html

Gamble, Bruce. *Invasion Rabaul: The Epic Story of Lark Force, the Forgotten Garrison, January–July 1942*. United States: Zenith Press, 2014.

Gerster, Robin. *Travels in Atomic Sunshine: Australia and the Occupation of Japan*. Australia: Scribe, 2008, pp 112–118.

Gilfedder, Deirdre. 'Decolonisation in South-East Asia'. In *British Decolonisation 1918–1984*, edited by Richard Davis. United Kingdom: Cambridge Scholars Publishing, 2013, pp 61–78.

Gómez, Javier Guisández. 'The Law of Air Warfare'. In *International Review of the Red Cross*, Number 323, June 1998, pp 347–363.

Grotius, Hugo. *Hugo Grotius on the Law of War and Peace, Student Edition*, edited by Stephen C. Neff. United Kingdom: Cambridge University Press, 2012.

Hahn, Elliott J. 'An Overview of the Japanese Legal System'. In *New Journal of International Law and Business*, Number 5, 1984, pp 517–539.

Ham, Paul. *Kokoda*. Australia: HarperCollins, 2004.

Herman, Arthur. *Douglas MacArthur: American Warrior*. United States: Random House, 2009.

Hickman, John. 'Explaining the Interbellum Rupture in Japanese Treatment of Prisoners of War'. In *Journal of Military and Strategic Studies*, Volume 12, Issue 1, Fall 2009, pp 1–20.

Ito, Masami. 'Surviving the postwar Soviet detention camps'. In *Japan Times*, 22 August 2015. Available at https://www.japantimes.co.jp/news/2015/08/22/national/history/surviving-postwar-soviet-detention-camps#.WzVqANIzZaQ

Johnston, Mark. *Fighting the Enemy: Australian Soldiers and their Adversaries in World War II*. United Kingdom: Cambridge University Press, 2000.

Hoyt, Edwin P. *Warlord: Tojo Against the World*. United States: Cooper Square Press, 2001 (first published 1993).

Lennan, Jo and George Williams. 'The Death Penalty in Australian Law'. In *Sydney Law Review*, Volume 34, Number 2, 2012, pp 659–694.

Luney, Percy J. Jr. 'Traditions and Foreign Influences: Systems of Law in China and Japan'. In *Law and Contemporary Problems*, Volume 52, Number 2, 1989, pp 129–150.

Kawakami, Kiyoshi Kari. *Japan and World Peace*. United States: The Macmillan Company, 1919.

Kershaw, Ian. *The End: Germany 1944–1945*. United Kingdom: Penguin, 2011.

Kodera, Atsushi. 'Master recording of Hirohito's war-end speech released in digital form'. In *The Japan Times*, 15 August 2015. Available at http://www.japantimes.co.jp/news/2015/08/01/national/history/master-recording-hirohitos-war-end-speech-released-digital-form/

Kowner, Rotem. 'Remaking Japan's Military Image During the Russo-Japanese War, 1904–1905'. In *The Historian*, Volume 64, Issue 1, September 2001, pp 19–38.

Kushner, Barak. *The Thought War: Japanese Imperial Propaganda*. United States: University of Hawai'i Press, 2006.

Lone, Stewart. *Japan's First Modern War: Army and Society in the Conflict with China, 1894–1895*. United Kingdom: Macmillan, 1994.

Long, Gavin. *Australia in the War of 1939–1945, Series 1 – Army, Volume VII – The Final Campaigns*. Australia: Australian War Memorial, 1963.

MacArthur, Douglas. *Reminiscences*. United States: McGraw-Hill, 1964.

McCormack, Tim and Narrelle Morris. 'The Australian War Crimes Trials, 1945–1951'. In *Australia's War Crimes Trials, 1945–51*, edited by Georgina Fitzpatrick, Tim McCormack and Narrelle Morris. Netherlands: Brill Nijhoff, 2016, pp 1–26.

McCormack, Tim. 'Jurisdiction of the Australian Military Courts 1945–51' in *Australia's War Crimes Trials, 1945–51*. In *Australia's War Crimes Trials, 1945–51*, edited by Georgina Fitzpatrick, Tim McCormack and Narrelle Morris. Netherlands: Brill Nijhoff, 2016, pp 59–102.

Moffitt, Athol. *Project Kingfisher*. Australia: ABC Books, 1995.

Morris, Narrelle and Tim McCormack. 'Were the Australian Trials Fair?' In *Australia's War Crimes Trials, 1945–51*, edited by Georgina Fitzpatrick, Tim McCormack and Narrelle Morris. Netherlands: Brill Nijhoff, 2016, pp 781–809.

Minear, Richard H. *Victor's Justice: The Tokyo War Crimes Trial*. United States: Princeton University Press, 1971.

Murphy, John. *Evatt: A Life*. Australia: New South, 2016.

Naimark, Norman M. *The Russians in Germany: A History of the Soviet Zone of Occupation, 1945–1949*. United States: Belknap Press of Harvard University Press, 1995.

Okada, Emmi. 'The Australian Trials of Class B and C Japanese War Crime Suspects, 1945–51'. In *Australian International Law Journal*, Volume 4, 2009, pp 47–80. Available at http://www.austlii.edu.au/au/journals/AUIntLawJl/2009/4.pdf

Ooi, Keat Gin. *The Japanese Occupation of Borneo, 1941–45*. United States: Taylor & Francis, 2010.

Paine, S. C. M. *The Sino-Japanese War of 1894–1895: Perceptions, Power, and Primacy*. United Kingdom: Cambridge University Press, 2005.

Piccigallo, Philip R. *The Japanese on Trial: Allied War Crimes Operations in the East, 1945–1951*. United States: University of Texas Press, 1979.

Ramseyer, J. Mark and Eric B. Rasmusen. *Why is the Japanese conviction rate so high?* 12 July 2000, available at http://www.rasmusen.org/published/Rasmusen-01.JLS.jpncon.pdf

Rix, Alan. *The Australia-Japan Political Alignment: 1952 to the Present.* United States: Routledge, 1988.

Röling, Bert V. A. and Antonio Cassese. *The Tokyo Trial and Beyond.* United Kingdom: Polity Press & Blackwell Publishers, 1993.

Sang, Mickaël Ho Foui. 'Justice Bernard: France'. In *Beyond Victor's Justice: The Tokyo War Crimes Trial Reconsidered,* edited by Yuki Tanaka, Tim McCormack and Gerry Simpson. Netherlands: Martins Nijhoff Publishers, 2011, pp 93–102.

Schabas, William. *Unimaginable Atrocities: Justice, Politics and Rights and the War Crimes Tribunals.* United Kingdom: Oxford University Press, 2012.

Schilling, Mark. '"Watashi wa Kai ni Naritai": Making a case for a "war criminal"'. In *Japan Times,* 21 November 2008.

Schoepfel, Ann Sophie. 'Justice and Decolonisation: War Crimes on Trial in Saigon'. In *War Crimes Trials in the Wake of Decolonization and Cold War in Asia, 1945–1956.* Edited by Kerstin von Lingen. Switzerland: Palgrave MacMillan, 2016, pp 167–194.

Sellars, Kirsten. 'Imperfect Justice at Nuremberg and Tokyo'. In *European Journal of International Law,* Volume 21, Number 4, 2010, pp 1085–1102.

—— *Crimes Against Peace and International Law,* 2013. United Kingdom: Cambridge University Press, 2013.

Senatore, Holly E. 'Bushido: The Valor of Deceit'. Paper delivered at the Convention of the International Society for Military Ethics, 1 January 2010.

Sibley, N.W. and F.E. Smith. *International Law as Interpreted During the Russo-Japanese War.* United Kingdom: T. Fisher Unwin & William Blackwood and Sons, 1905.

Sides, Hampton. 'The Trial of General Homma'. In *American Heritage,* Volume 58, Issue 1, February/March 2007. Available at http://www. americanheritage.com/content/trial-general-homma

Sissons, David. 'Sources on Australian Investigations into Japanese War Crimes in the Pacific'. In *Journal of the Australian War Memorial,* Issue 30, April 1997. Available at https://www.awm.gov.au/journal/j30/sissons.asp

—— 'The Australian War Crimes Trials and Investigations', 2006. Available at https://www.ocf.berkeley.edu/~changmin/documents/Sissons%20Final%20War%20Crimes%20Text%2018-3-06.pdf

Strauss, Ulrich. *The Anguish of Surrender: Japanese POWs of World War II.* United States: University of Washington Press, 2003.

Svoboda, Terese. 'U.S. Courts-Martial in Occupation Japan: Rape, Race, and Censorship'. In *The Asia-Pacific Journal,* Volume 7, Issue 21, Number 1, May 2009.

Tanaka, Yuki and Toshiyuki Tanaka. *Japan's Comfort Women: Sexual Slavery and Prostitution During World War II.* United States: Routledge, 2003.

Trefalt, Beatrice. 'Hostages to International Relations? The Repatriation of Japanese War Criminals from the Philippines', *Japanese Studies,* Volume 31, Number 2, September 2011, pp 191–211.

Tennenbaum, Joseph. 'Auschwitz in Retrospect; the Self-Portrait of Rudolf Hoess'. In *Jewish Social Studies,* Volume 15, Numbers 3–4, 1953, pp 203–236.

Totani, Yuma. *The Tokyo War Crimes Trial: The Pursuit of Justice in the Wake of World War II.* United States: Harvard University Press, 2008.

—— *Justice in Asia and the Pacific Region, 1945–1952: Allied War Crimes Prosecutions.* United States: Cambridge University Press, 2015.

Towle, Philip A. 'Japanese Treatment of Prisoners in 1904–1905 – Foreign Officers' Reports'. In *Military Affairs,* Volume 39, Number 3, 1975, pp 115–118.

Trotter, Ann. 'New Zealanders and the International Military Tribunal for the Far East'. In the *New Zealand Journal of History,* 1989, Volume 23, Number 2, pp 142–156. Available at http://www.nzjh.auckland.ac.nz/docs/1989/NZJH_23_2_03.pdf

Truman, Harry S. *Year of Decisions.* United Kingdom: Hodder & Stoughton, 1955.

Turnbull, Stephen. *The Samurai: A Military History.* United Kingdom: Osprey Publishing, 1977.

Weld, H.A. 'Webb, Sir William Flood (1887–1972)'. In the *Australian Dictionary of Biography,* National Centre of Biography, Australian National University, 2002. Available at http://adb.anu.edu.au/biography/webb-sir-william-flood-11991/text21499

Wilson, Sandra. 'War, Soldier and Nation in 1950s Japan'. In
*International Journal of Asian Studies*, Volume 5, Number 2, 2008,
pp 187–218.

—— 'After the Trials: Class B and C Japanese War Criminals and the Post-
War World'. In *Japanese Studies*, Volume 31, Number 2, September 2011,
pp 141–151.

—— 'Prisoners in Sugamo and Their Campaign for Release, 1952–1953'.
In *Japanese Studies*, Volume 31, Number 2, September 2011, pp 171–191.

—— 'War Criminals in the Post-war World: The Case of Katō Tetsutarō'.
In *War in History*, Volume 22, Number 1, 2015, pp 87–110.

Wilson, Sandra, Robert Cribb, Beatrice Trefalt and Dean Aszkielowicz.
*Japanese War Criminals: The Politics of Justice After the Second World War.*
United States: Columbia University Press, 2017.

## PRIMARY SOURCES

First Webb Report, 'A Report on Japanese Atrocities and Breaches of the Rules
of Warfare'. 15 March 1944, AWM226, 5

Second Webb Report, 'A Report on War Crimes against Australians
Committed by Individual Members of the Armed Forces of the Enemy'.
31 October 1944, AWM226, 7

Third Webb Report, 'A Report on War Crimes Committed by Enemy Subjects
Against Australians and Others'. 31 January 1946, AWM226, 8

M27 transcript, NAA A471 80722

LN2 transcript, NAA A471 81942

LN24 transcript, NAA A471 81967

M18 transcript, A471 80772

ML28 transcript, A471 80777 part 1 and part 2

R1 transcript, NAA A471 80747

R51 transcript, NAA A471 80796

R53 transcript, NAA A471 80798

R70 transcript, NAA A471 80983

R175 transcript NAA A471 81635 parts A–E

## CONTEMPORARY ARTICLES

'Massacre by Japanese' in the *Sydney Morning Herald*, 10 April 1942, p 7.
    Available at http://nla.gov.au/nla.news-article17804888

Editorial in the *Riverine Herald*, 4 April 1945, p 4. Available at http://nla.gov.
    au/nla.news-article116612136

'No Immunity for Japan's Emperor' in *The Argus*, 14 August 1945, p 2.
    Available at http://nla.gov.au/nla.news-article965391

'Canberra in State of Suspense' in *The Argus*, 15 August 1945, p 3. Available at
    http://nla.gov.au/nla.news-article980983

'Peace Celebrations in the City' in *The Age*, 15 August 1945, p 5. Available at
    http://nla.gov.au/nla.news-article204021008

'The Hour of Victory' in the *Sydney Morning Herald*, 16 August 1945, p 2.
    Available at http://nla.gov.au/nla.news-article17950190

'500,000 Watch Victory March in City' in the *Sydney Morning Herald*,
    17 August 1945, p 5. Available at http://nla.gov.au/nla.news-
    article17950407

'Japanese War Criminals' in *The Age*, 17 August 1945, p 2. Available at
    http://nla.gov.au/nla.news-article204015929

'Hirohito as War Criminal' in the *Sydney Morning Herald*, 20 August 1945,
    p 3. Available at http://nla.gov.au/nla.news-article27920479

'Freed from Borneo Prison Camp' in the *Newcastle Morning Herald and
    Miners' Advocate*, 31 August 1945, p 5. Available at http://nla.gov.au/nla.
    news-article134371052

'Prisoners' Hell at Rabaul' in the *Cairns Post*, 10 September 1945, p 1. Available
    at http://nla.gov.au/nla.news-article42461131

'Australia Demands Justice' in the *Sydney Morning Herald*, 11 September 1945,
    p 1. Available at http://nla.gov.au/nla.news-article17952744

'Japanese Savagery Must Be Punished' in *The Age* 11 September 1945, p 2.
    Available at http://nla.gov.au/nla.news-article205654242

'Tojo Attempts Suicide' in *The Age* 12 September 1945, p 1. Available at
    http://nla.gov.au/nla.news-article205648064

'Justice on War Criminals' in *The Argus* 15 September 1945, p 9. Available at
    http://nla.gov.au/nla.news-article971433

'Rabaul Japs Run to Bow & Scrape' in *The Telegraph*, 21 September 1945, p 3. Available at http://nla.gov.au/nla.news-article188766310

'Bringing War Criminals To Justice' in *The Argus* 21 September 1945, p 3. Available at http://nla.gov.au/nla.news-article967676

'Blain Urges: Treat Japs Like Bad Children' in the *Tweed Daily*, 1 October 1945, p 1. Available at http://nla.gov.au/nla.news-article194386179

'Yamashita for Trial at Once' in the *Sydney Morning Herald*, 4 October 1945, p 1. Available at http://nla.gov.au/nla.news-article17955046

'How Imamura Kept Fit' in the *Examiner*, 10 October 1945, p 1. Available at http://nla.gov.au/nla.news-article91950372

'Aussies Were Toughest in Dealing With Japs' in *Truth*, 11 November 1945, p 8. Available at http://nla.gov.au/nla.news-article203118032

'AIF Tougher Than Yanks When Dealing With Japs' in the *Evening Advocate*, 12 November 1945, p 4. Available at http://nla.gov.au/nla.news-article212282473

'Japs Work 12-Hour Day Building Compounds' in *The Sun*, 13 November 1945, p 7. Available at http://nla.gov.au/nla.news-article229019043

'Round-Up in Japan' in *The Advertiser*, 20 November 1945, p 1. Available at http://nla.gov.au/nla.news-article48678154

'Konoye's Arrest Ordered' in *The Argus*, 7 December 1945, p 1. Available at http://nla.gov.au/nla.news-article12157202

'Sought Solace in Oscar Wilde's Books' in *The Argus* 18 December 1945, p 16. Available at http://nla.gov.au/nla.news-article12159157

'Arrogant Jap Charged With Mass Slaughter' in the *Daily Mercury*, 11 January 1946, p 2. Available at http://nla.gov.au/nla.news-article171130593

'Arrogant Jap Captain on Trial' in the *Morning Bulletin*, 11 January 1946, p 1. Available at http://nla.gov.au/nla.news-article56430860

'Naming of Hirohito as War Criminal' in *The Argus*, 18 January 1946, p 20. Available at http://nla.gov.au/nla.news-article22222779

'Japanese N.C.O. To Die' in *The Advertiser*, 4 February 1946, p 1. Available at http://nla.gov.au/nla.news-article48689612

'Letters to the Editor' in *News*, 5 February 1946, p 2. Available at http://nla.gov.au/nla.news-article128345344

Caiger, George. 'The Japanese Misunderstand War Guilt Trials' in the *Sydney Morning Herald*, 5 February 1946, p 2. Available at http://nla.gov.au/nla.news-article27916866

'Will They Hang?' in the *Courier-Mail*, 21 February 1946, p 2. Available at http://nla.gov.au/nla.news-article50276363

'Japs Pay Penalty' in the *Courier-Mail* 8 March 1946, p 1. Available at http://nla.gov.au/nla.news-article50289350

'Executions at Morotai' in the *Sydney Morning Herald*, 8 March 1946, p 3. Available at http://nla.gov.au/nla.news-article27918492

'New Concept In British Relations: Australia Acts For Empire' in *The Argus*, 14 March 1946, p 2. Available at http://nla.gov.au/nla.news-article22233980

'Japs Dazed by Court's Verdict: Six Acquittals at Darwin Trial' in *The Argus*, 16 March 1946, p 4. Available at http://nla.gov.au/nla.news-article22234712

'Demands for Sterner Darwin Trials' in the *Sydney Morning Herald*, 18 March 1946, p 3. Retrieved September 26, 2017, from http://nla.gov.au/nla.news-article17972706

'Letters to the Editor' in *News*, 18 March 1942, p 2. Available at http://nla.gov.au/nla.news-article128347422

'The Darwin Sentences' in the *Sydney Morning Herald*, 19 March 1946, p 2. Available at http://nla.gov.au/nla.news-article27919165

'Japanese Needed Drugs On Scaffold Steps' in the *Sydney Morning Herald*, 21 March 1946, p 3. Available at http://nla.gov.au/nla.news-article17973037

'Jap Officers in Luxury, Australians Rough It' in *The Sun*, 22 March 1946, p 3. Available at http://nla.gov.au/nla.news-article228795673

'Justice Criticises Jap Trials Appointment' in *The Argus*, 22 March 1946, p 24. Available at http://nla.gov.au/nla.news-article22235834

'Webb Appointment "Misapprehension"' in the *Sydney Morning Herald*, 23 March 1946, p 5. Available at http://nla.gov.au/nla.news-article17973389

'Japanese Officers Live High at Rabaul' in *The Age*, 23 March 1946, p 1. Available at http://nla.gov.au/nla.news-article206796477

'No Action Indicated on Japs' Luxurious Housing' in *The Telegraph*, p 3, 23 March 1946. Available at http://nla.gov.au/nla.news-article188433560

'"Prison Paradise" For Japanese Officers' in the *Sydney Morning Herald*, 23 March 1946, p 1. Available at http://nla.gov.au/nla.news-article17973291

'Jap Generals to Lose Fowls, Goats--Army Acts' in *The Sun*, 24 March 1946, p 2. Available at http://nla.gov.au/nla.news-article228790495

'Jap general tried to suicide' in *The Sun*, 30 March 1947, p 10. Available at http://nla.gov.au/nla.news-article228988592

Wyzanski, Charles E. 'Nuremberg: A Fair Trial? A Dangerous Precedent' in *The Atlantic*, April 1946. Available at https://www.theatlantic. com/magazine/archive/1946/04/nuremberg-a-fair-trial-a-dangerous-precedent/306492/

'Jap Criminals Hanged for Borneo Horror' in the *Newcastle Sun*, 6 April 1946, p 1. Available at http://nla.gov.au/nla.news-article158281150

'Japs Hanged for Borneo Horror' in *The Sun*, 6 April 1946, p 1. Available at http://nla.gov.au/nla.news-article229456169

'Executed for Death March' in *The Age*, 8 April 1946, p 3. Available at http://nla.gov.au/nla.news-article206106450

'Jap General's Plea for Men' in the *Courier-Mail*, 11 April 1946, p 4. Available at http://nla.gov.au/nla.news-article50260694

'Jap Hanged For Raping Chinese' in the *Courier-Mail*, 20 April 1946, p 5. Available at http://nla.gov.au/nla.news-article50254252

'Jap Dies a Cringing Coward' in the *Townsville Daily Bulletin*, 20 April 1946, p 1. Available at http://nla.gov.au/nla.news-article62878101

'Tojo Splendid in Incident At War Trial' at the *Courier-Mail*, 4 May 1946, p 1. Available at http://nla.gov.au/nla.news-article50267278

'Luxury at End for Jap General' in *The Mail*, 4 May 1946, p 5. Available at http://nla.gov.au/nla.news-article55937548

'War Criminals' in the *West Australian*, 15 May 1946, p 12. Available at http://nla.gov.au/nla.news-article50341011

Caiger, George. 'Behind The Japanese Plea of "Self-defence"' in the *Sydney Morning Herald*, 21 May 1946, p 2. Available at http://nla.gov.au/nla.news-article17987676

'General Apathy at Tokyo Trial' in *The Argus*, 29 June 1946, p 7. Available at http://nla.gov.au/nla.news-article22254790

'Japs Try Own Officers' in the *Sydney Morning Herald*, 29 June 1946, p 3.
    Available at http://nla.gov.au/nla.news-article29766658

'Sir W. Webb in Star Role at War Trial' in the *Courier-Mail*, 26 August 1946,
    p 3. Available at http://nla.gov.au/nla.news-article49343548

'Indian Officer in Fear of Jap Prisoners' *Examiner*, 25 March 1947. Available at
    http://nla.gov.au/nla.news-article61005685

'Japanese General Accepts Blame in Trial of Colleague' in *Daily Advertiser*,
    29 March 1947, p 5. Available at http://nla.gov.au/nla.news-
    article145149025

'Jap Criminals Have Easy Time at Rabaul' *The Argus*, 8 June 1948, p 4.
    Available at http://nla.gov.au/nla.news-article22548607

'Time to Close War Crimes Accounts' in the *Sydney Morning Herald*, 16 June
    1948, p 2. Available at http://nla.gov.au/nla.news-article18074602

'Japanese Trials' in the *Sydney Morning Herald*, 2 August 1948, p 1. Available at
    http://nla.gov.au/nla.news-article18079863

'How The Japanese Took Sentences' in *The Argus,* 13 November 1948, p 5.
    Available at http://nla.gov.au/nla.news-article22697526

'Tojo: Last words' in the *Courier-Mail*, 20 November 1948, p 1. Available at
    http://nla.gov.au/nla.news-article49924726

'Tojo's Plea For Peace' in the *Sydney Morning Herald*, 3 December 1948, p 3.
    Available at http://nla.gov.au/nla.news-article18100079

'Japanese Leaders Freed; No Trial' in the *Sydney Morning Herald*, 27 December
    1948, p 3. Available at http://nla.gov.au/nla.news-article18091978

'Australian Bungling of War Trials' in the *Sydney Morning Herald*, 5 December
    1949, p 2. Available at http://nla.gov.au/nla.news-article18147916

'War Trials to be Speeded Up' in *The Age*, 12 January 1950, p 1. Available at
    http://nla.gov.au/nla.news-article187351500

'In All His Splendour' in the *Sydney Morning Herald*, 15 June 1950, p 3.
    Available at http://nla.gov.au/nla.news-article18166892

'General's Evidence' in *The Age*, 16 June 1950, p 4. Available at http://nla.gov.
    au/nla.news-article206235382

'Brutal Treatment' in *The Age*, 20 June 1950, p 4. Available at http://nla.gov.au/
    nla.news-article206234137

'Japanese General's Defence' in *The Age*, 21 June 1950, p 6. Available at
    http://nla.gov.au/nla.news-article206233104

'General to Hang' in the *Sydney Morning Herald*, 23 June 1950, p 3. Available
    at http://nla.gov.au/nla.news-article18169988

'Japanese Bowed When Acquitted' in *The Age*, 17 November 1950, p 9.
    Available at http://nla.gov.au/nla.news-article206409804

'"Frenzy of revenge" at Ambon' in the *Courier-Mail*, 10 March 1951, p 1.
    Available at http://nla.gov.au/nla.news-article50101712

'Ambon Massacre: Jap. Sentenced to Death; Another to Life in Gaol' in the
    *Warwick Daily News*, 20 March 1951, p 1. Available at http://nla.gov.au/nla.
    news-article190775006

'Trials Conclude at Los Negros' in the *Sydney Morning Herald*, 10 April 1951,
    p 3. Available at http://nla.gov.au/nla.news-article18207736

'Australian War Court winds up – Japanese extol our fairness in war trials'
    in *The Argus*, 10 April 1951, p 5. Available at http://nla.gov.au/nla.news-
    article23035835

'Manus Hangings To-day' in the *Sydney Morning Herald*, 11 June 1951, p 1.
    Available at http://nla.gov.au/nla.news-article18212805

'Five Japanese War Criminals Executed' in the *Queensland Times*, 12 June 1951,
    p 1. Available at http://nla.gov.au/nla.news-article124620071

Underwood, Alan (article credits an unnamed correspondent but is identical
    to Underwood's other articles). 'Less Work, More Luxury for Jap War
    Criminals' in the *Sydney Morning Herald*, 20 November 1951, p 2.
    Available at http://nla.gov.au/nla.news-article18240217

Underwood, Alan. 'War Criminals Get the "Soft" Treatment' in the *Courier-
    Mail*, 20 November 1951, p 2. Available at http://nla.gov.au/nla.news-
    article50227384

Underwood, Alan. 'Japanese War Criminals "Taking It Easy"' in the Adelaide
    *Advertiser*, 20 November 1951, p 2.

'Japan "Has Duty To Rearm"' in the *Sydney Morning Herald*, 14 December
    1951, p 3. Available at http://nla.gov.au/nla.news-article18244274

'Gen. Gordon Bennett lands' in *The Argus*, 22 February 1952, p 5. Available at
    http://nla.gov.au/nla.news-article23164514

'Digger Raises Japanese Olympic Flag' in the *Canberra Times*, 31 October 1951, p 16. Available at http://nla.gov.au/nla.news-article91226412

Power, Julie and Candace Sutton. 'Hirohito: Fury Over Funeral' in the *Sun-Herald*, 8 January 1989, p 1.

Chira, Susan. 'Tokyo Funeral Forces Choice By Old Foes' in the *New York Times*, 13 January 1989. Available at http://www.nytimes.com/1989/01/13/world/tokyo-funeral-forces-choice-by-old-foes.html

Slavin, Stewart. 'Attending Hirohito funeral a touchy issue', *UPI News Feature*, 20 February 1989

Sanger, David E. 'Mayor who Faulted Hirohito is Shot' in the *New York Times*, 19 January 1990. Available at http://www.nytimes.com/1990/01/19/world/mayor-who-faulted-hirohito-is-shot.html

# INDEX